William G. Horder

The hymn lover:

An account of the rise and growth of English hymnody. Third Edition

William G. Horder

The hymn lover:
An account of the rise and growth of English hymnody. Third Edition

ISBN/EAN: 9783337872496

Printed in Europe, USA, Canada, Australia, Japan

Cover: Foto ©Thomas Meinert / pixelio.de

THE HYMN LOVER.

THE HYMN LOVER.

AN ACCOUNT OF THE RISE AND GROWTH OF ENGLISH HYMNODY.

BY

W. GARRETT HORDER,

Editor of "The Treasury of American Sacred Song," &c.

THIRD EDITION, REVISED.

LONDON:

J. CURWEN & SONS LTD., 24 BERNERS STREET, W.

J CURWEN & SONS LTD
PRINTERS
24 BERNERS ST
OXFORD ST W

PREFACE.

This book has been written at the request of the Publishers, who, in common with myself, discerned the need for a work which should put within the reach of the ever increasing number of persons interested in the subject, an account of the rise and growth of Hymnody in England. The large number of enquiries I have received, especially from persons desiring to illustrate the subject in Lectures or Sermons, shows how widespread is the interest in regard to hymns; whilst the difficulty I have felt in naming any one book as likely to meet such need forced on my own mind the conviction that some such work as the present was required. When such enquiries have reached me I have been compelled to give the titles of a considerable number of works which treat of the subject, some of which are out of print, and others difficult to obtain save at considerable cost.

Moreover, all existing books with which I am acquainted, either deal with a portion only of the subject, or if they deal with the whole, do so more after the manner of works for reference than for continuous reading. I am not acquainted with a single book which even attempts to give a connected view of the whole subject, in such a way as to serve as an introduction to the study of Hymnody. This is the task, which in these pages I have set before myself; with what success must be left to the judgment of my readers. I have, indeed, attempted to provide such a book as I myself desired, but failed to discover, when many years ago I turned my attention to the subject, and I am not without hope that the book thus written will furnish to many an outline which further reading and research may enable them to fill in. I have appended a list of the principal works on the subject for the benefit of those who may desire to pursue the study still further.

Beyond this I have, in accordance, not only with the wishes of the Publishers, but my own judgment, treated the subject with such critical faculty as I possess, in the hope that it may do at least a little to elevate the public taste in relation to hymns. Doubtless some will differ from certain of my estimates; all I can claim is that they have been carefully and honestly formed, and whether sound or not, they may at least lead to a more careful consideration of the words sung in worship than has hitherto been usual.

It is strange that Hymns, which now form so large a part of public worship, should not have been made one of the subjects of study included in the course prescribed for theological students, as is the

Prayer Book in that of Colleges connected with the Episcopal Church. Such a study would prove both an interesting and useful addition to the present course, and would probably be pursued with avidity by a considerable proportion of candidates for the ministry.

Critical readers of these pages may perhaps discern a want of proportion in the space given to various writers. This has not been accidental but of set purpose. Of Hymn-writers concerning whom much has been previously written, such as Isaac Watts or Charles Wesley, I have said comparatively little; only sufficient to indicate their special characteristics, and the influence they exerted. Of others, concerning whom little, if anything, has been written such as T. H. Gill, and T. T. Lynch, I have said more, in the hope that their writings might thus be made more widely known. My references to hymns have proceeded on the principle that where they were well known it was necessary to quote merely the first line; where they were little known to quote more fully—in some cases, the whole, in others, the finest verses.

Many attempts have been made to give a definition of what a good hymn should be. Definitions are proverbially difficult, and in the case of hymns especially so. Lord Selborne in the preface to "The Book of Praise," says: "A good hymn should have simplicity, freshness, and reality of feeling; a consistent elevation of tone, and a rhythm easy and harmonious, but not jingling or trivial. Its language may be homely, but should not be slovenly or mean. Affectation or visible artifice is worse than excess of homeliness: A hymn is easily spoilt by a single falsetto note. Nor will the most exemplary soundness of doctrine atone for doggerel, or redeem from failure a prosaic, didactic style." This is good, as far as it goes, but it does not go far enough. It does not discriminate between sacred poetry and what is properly a hymn. It does not lay sufficient stress on the poetic element as a vital necessity to a hymn. Nor does it insist on poetic unity, and the avoidance of mixed or incongruous imagery as vital to hymns of the noblest kind; whilst it says nothing of the need that hymns should, in some one part at least, be addressed to the Divine Being. It seems to me that hymns of the noblest type should be compositions addressed either in the way of praise, prayer, confession, or communion to the great Object of all worship. This is the real point of difference between Hymns and Sacred Poetry—a hymn is a piece of sacred poetry, but a piece of sacred poetry is not of necessity a hymn; it cannot rightly be described as such unless at least the last of the characteristics I have named be found in it. Exceptions to this may be permitted in Hymnals, in the case of verses calculated to kindle devotional feeling; but they must ever be regarded as exceptions. Even when they are allowed, there is always, to the sensitive mind, a kind of incongruity in the singing of verses addressed by the worshippers to one another, or to a particular portion of the congregation supposed to need the exhortations they contain, as in such hymns as "Stand up, stand up for Jesus," or "Go labour on, spend and be spent." Still worse is it when a congregation sings a whole hymn to the preacher as in "Tell me the old, old story." Such hymns cannot rightly be prefaced by the old formula which *should* be applicable—"Let us sing to the praise and glory of God." I am not prepared to say that such hymns should be excluded from our collections for public worship; on the principle that the object of worship is to arouse devotional feeling, they may be included, but they cannot rightly be regarded as hymns, and their use should be the exception and not the rule. The cardinal test of a hymn should be that it is in some one, if not the whole of its parts, addressed to God. The bulk of it may consist of description of the soul's condition, or of the state it desires to reach, or of the glory of nature or the tenderness of providence; but to make it a *real hymn* it must at least conclude with words of confession or prayer or thankfulness addressed to "Him in whom we live and move and have our being," that to all going before may be given a Godward direction.

Of the subject matter of hymns, it may be said that though the doctrine of the writer may, and indeed must underlie, it should not be presented in a doctrinal, much less a dogmatic form. In this respect the Psalms are a model, for, in them, the doctrinal conceptions of the writers are transfigured by the depth and fervency of their religious feeling. A hymn is not versified dogma. The dogma may be there, but it must take on poetic and therefore undogmatic forms. Many a noble hymn is sadly marred by the introduction in some of its parts of theologic phrases, such as "God in three persons, blessed Trinity," in Heber's otherwise splendid hymn, "Holy, Holy, Lord God almighty." Not a line analogous to that can be found in the whole range of the Psalter. In this line, the good Bishop ceases to be a poet and becomes a theologian. Doctrine should be spoken from the pulpit, not sung from the pew. The essence of poetry is that it pierces to the heart of a subject—the true poet is a *Seer* whose eye reaches through the letter to the spirit. The true hymnist is in his measure also a seer, and so first discerns and then reveals in his verse, the hidden verities which lie underneath the phrases in which doctrine is commonly expressed. He, of all men should realise that "the flesh profiteth nothing" but only the inner spirit of which the flesh is but the outward expression. Thus the visible and external is transfigured by that which is unseen and eternal.

It is only another way of stating the same fact to say that the poetic element must be present to render rhymed lines a hymn. Rhyme is not poetry, but only jingling prose. There must be that undefinable element which we call poetic—that happiness and compactness of phrase which catches the ear, lingers in the memory, and kindles the imagination; not in the larger and freer sense in which it is used in poetry of a secular kind; but within narrower limits and of a more sober type, the poetic element must be present, or the verses remain prose and cannot rightly be called a Hymn. The hymn belongs to Lyric rather than Didactic or Epic Poetry, and should have such aptness and melody of expression that the words when *said*, as well as when *sung*, shall be musical, shall, as the name 'Lyric' implies, have the ring of the harp through them. Given this and almost any metre may be allowed. In recent years congregations have grown accustomed to a vast variety of metres which have been skilfully utilised by hymnists in their verse. This has given to composers a wider musical field in which to work and has been one great factor in rendering hymns so popular an element in our modern worship.

Perhaps the limits which are desirable, as to variety in metre, have now been reached Future hymn-writers should find quite sufficient scope for the exercise of their gifts within the very great variety of metres in which their predecessors have worked. If it should be extended much farther, the number of tunes necessary for congregations to learn in order to sing the hymns included in their collections, will exceed the capacity of all but select and exceptionally musical ones, and perhaps of only a certain number, even in such congregations. It is not desirable that Psalmody should be thus restricted; it should rather be within the capacity of all worshippers to bear a part therein.

As a general rule, it is well that each hymn should be associated with a particular tune—not of necessity the same one in every congregation, since taste and capacity greatly differ—but this principle should not be made too rigid, since a congregation tires more quickly of a tune than a hymn, and a change of tune will often give a new lease of life to, and keep in use, a well-loved hymn, of which, if it were always sung to the same tune, the people would tire.

Those who are responsible for the conduct of Psalmody in the Church should be as familiar with the Hymn-book as the Tune-book, so that, where they possess liberty to set hymns to any tunes they desire, their selection of tunes may be determined by the substance and spirit of the hymns, and even where the fixed-tune system is in vogue, they may render the tune in a style in full sympathy with the sentiment of each verse of the hymn.

The pleasant duty remains of acknowledging the valuable aid I have received from Mr. W. T. Brooke, who has read the proof sheets of this volume as they were passing through the press, and to whose wide knowledge of Hymnody I am indebted, both for valuable suggestions and correction of the proofs. I am also indebted to my friend the Rev. Robert Ricards, who has felt the deepest interest in my task, and helped me greatly to make my story more clear to its readers. For information embodied in the chapter on the Hymns of other religions, I am indebted to kind communications from Sir Wm. Muir, Professors Max Muller and Dr. James Legge, of Oxford, Professor Owen, C. Whitehouse, M.A., of Cheshunt College, the Rev. G. O. Newport, of India, and the late Mr. Paul Isaac Hershon. I have to thank my friend, Mr. Arthur Boutwood, for preparing the Indices.

Some small portions of this book had previously made their appearance in the pages of *The Sunday Magazine*, *The Christian World*, and the *Theological Monthly*. I am indebted to the proprietors of these periodicals for permission to include such portions in this work.

I trust that these pages will lead many to take a more intelligent interest in the hymns they so often sing—and serve to introduce hitherto unknown hymns to their notice, and even do some little to elevate the public taste which often has not been any too discriminating. I shall be abundantly repaid for the labour expended on this book if it should bear a part, however small, in enabling any to comply with the injunction of the Psalmist, "Sing ye praises with understanding."

PREFACE TO NEW EDITION.

In the present edition I have endeavoured to bring the work up to date, so far as this could be done without entirely recasting it. I trust that in its revised form it may continue to help forward the movement toward a more thoughtful use of hymns.

CONTENTS.

Poetry! thou sweet'st content
That e'er Heaven to mortals lent!

GEORGE WITHER.

I do but sing because I must,
And pipe but as the linnets sing.

ALFRED TENNYSON.

The first true worship of the world's great King
From private and selected hearts did spring.

HENRY VAUGHAN.

The gift, whose office is the Giver's praise,
To trace Him in His word, His works, His ways!
Then spread the rich discovery, and invite
Mankind to share in the divine delight.

WILLIAM COWPER.

God sent His singers upon earth
With songs of sadness and of mirth,
That they might touch the hearts of men,
And bring them back to heaven again.

HENRY WADSWORTH LONGFELLOW.

There are in this loud stunning tide
Of human care and crime,
With whom the melodies abide
Of the everlasting chime;
Who carry music in the heart,
Through dusky lane and wrangling mart,
Plying their lowly task with busier feet
Because their secret souls a holy strain repeat.

JOHN KEBLE.

Yet, when I remember the tears I shed at the Psalmody of Thy Church, in the beginning of my recovered faith; and how at this time I am moved, not with the singing, but with the things sung, when they are sung with a clear voice and modulation most suitable, I acknowledge the great use of this institution. Thus I fluctuate between peril of pleasure and approved wholesomeness, inclined the rather (though not as pronouncing an irrevocable opinion) to approve of the use of singing in the Church; that so by the delight of the ears, the weaker minds may rise to the feeling of devotion. Yet when it befalls me to be more moved with the voice than the words sung, I confess to have sinned penally, and then had rather not hear music.—AUGUSTINE ("Confessions").

Worship is transcendent wonder—wonder for which there is no limit or measure; that is worship.—THOMAS CARLYLE.

Make the Church full of praise, and it will be full of God. God and His praise cannot be apart. "O Thou that inhabitest the praises of Israel." —JOHN PULSFORD.

A good hymn is a more valuable contribution to Christian literature than vast tomes of theology: for it will sing to the ages after the tomes are mouldering on the shelves.—E. H. SEARS.

THE HYMN LOVER.

CHAPTER I.

HYMNS OF OTHER RELIGIONS.

Hymns are to be found in the literature of nearly every religion, but so far as we are able to judge, save in the Hebrew and Christian, they have rarely been used as a constant and integral part of worship.

That hymns formed no part of the worship of the Greeks is clear from the fact that their temples were not constructed as places of religious assembly or for public devotion, but as a shelter for the image of the god, and a habitation for the deity supposed to be attached to his image. They were generally confined localities, and half-dark within on account of the absence of all window-light. Bright light was not required, as, in fact, no religious observances ordinarily took place in the temple.* "Greece never had a sacred book, she never had any symbols, any sacerdotal caste, organised for the preservation of dogmas. Her poets and her artists were her true theologians."† Some small place was assigned to hymns in the worship of Rome.

* Döllinger, "Gentile and Jew," I, 239.
† Renan, "Studies in Religious History."

"Many prayers and hymns were taken up with the praise of the gods and salutations to them. Arnobius speaks of morning serenades sung with an accompaniment of fifes as a kind of *reveille* to the sleeping gods, and of an evening salutation in which leave was taken of the deity, with the wishing him a good night's rest."*

Professor Max Muller has referred me to his History of Sanskrit Literature for information on this point, and the conclusion I draw therefrom is that although the Hindus had much of poetry both Epic and Hymnic, yet that the hymns were chiefly used for meditation or recital. "Women were not allowed to learn the Sacred songs of the Vedas, the knowledge of which constituted one of the principal requirements for a Brahman before he was admitted to the performance of the sacrifices. As it was necessary, however, for a husband to perform sacrifices together with his lawful wife, and as passages of the hymns speak clearly of man and wife as performing sacrifices in common, it was laid down in the Sûtras that the husband or the priest should at the sacrificing itself, make his wife *recite* those hymns which were necessary for the ceremony."

The Sametri who had to slay the sacrificial animals learnt the hymns appointed by heart, and were allowed on account of the difficulty of mastering the euphonic rules for recitation, to mutter them, so that no one at a distance could hear or understand them. Some part of the sacrifice had to be accompanied by songs, and hence another class of priests arose whose particular office it was to act as the chorus, which was more than

* Döllinger, "Gentile and Jew," II, 77.

a mere chanting. A third class called the Hotres recited certain hymns during the sacrifice in praise of the deities to whom any particular act of the sacrificer was addressed. Their recitation was loud and distinct, and required the most accurate knowledge of the rules of euphony.

The Rev. G. O. Newport, who for nearly a quarter of a century has laboured as a missionary in India, has been good enough to send me the following note:—

"In Hindu worship, so far as I have seen it in South India—and I think it is much the same in this respect throughout the whole country—there is no periodic gathering of the people into the temples for united religious service. There is no fixed hour for assembling, nor is there any regular priestly observance or ceremony at any stated part of the twenty-four hours. Individuals who are eligible for admission to any particular temple, may go in and prostrate themselves, and repeat their prayers, &c., whenever they please. United gatherings at stated hours and seasons for religious service, as in our Christian worship, are unknown. There cannot, therefore, be any congregational singing or musical performance in the Western sense in these temples. And yet singing in connection with the worship is not altogether absent. On anniversary festival days and in processions there are always songs sung in honour of the gods. Some of these songs are so obscene in their nature that even respectable votaries of the Hindu religion are taking active steps to put down the public singing of them. The female attendants on the idol, called *Dhasis* in the south, who are, in fact, temple prostitutes, are all professional singers of these religious songs. The priests also join in, and the masses of the people too, according to their knowledge and musical ability. There must also be certain times when the priests and the Dhasis practise together these songs within the temple limits; and perhaps this may be done as in some way an act of worship, but not as part of a public service in which ordinary worshippers participate. I write thus, because on one occasion when travelling late at night I heard a sound of singing in a temple, and went to the very wall within the outer gate without being discovered. The villagers were asleep, the temple was almost in darkness, only a dim lamp here and there flickering in the gloom; there was evidently no religious observance going on, and yet there was the singing of Hindu songs by various voices manifestly accustomed thereto. It was perhaps a kind of rehearsal in anticipation of a forthcoming festival. I believe I am strictly accurate when I say there is nothing corresponding to our choir or congregational singing at the ordinary every-day religious observances in Hindu temples. What is done on festival occasions would correspond largely to the singing of songs by the choir when marching at the head of a Sunday school procession, and would have about as much of religious worship in it.

"As to the subject matter of the songs thus used, so far as my knowledge goes, it consists of the names, titles, epithets, &c., of the gods in general, and of that god in particular in whose honour the festival is being held. And when it is remembered that the various names of one single god in the Hindu Pantheon amount to a thousand, it will be seen that a great deal of song may be expended in this one direction only. But not the names only, the traditional acts and behaviour, the life-scenes of the gods, are sung at length. It is in the very realistic description of some of these unmentionable incidents that the obscenity, above referred to, consists. Even when deeds and events of an innocent and pure character are thus sung, there is nothing more of spiritual worship in it than in the recitation of an epic poem. The singer confesses no need, asks no blessing, reveals no yearning, expects no response. There is no communion of thought and feeling, no aspiration for purity, no laying hold of moral strength. In this lies the great difference between the religious songs of Hindu worship and the hymnody of Christian worship."*

Buddhism was to Brahmanism what Puritanism was to Anglicanism. Like Puritanism it laid stress chiefly on the individual, but went far beyond it since it abolished the idea of church and worship. Its hymns, some of which are of exceeding beauty (in their English dress the thoughts but not the form are exhibited), were used only for private recitation and edification. Indeed, they have neither churches nor services in which they could be sung.

"Judged by its primitive texts," says Rénan, "Buddhism appears like a simple doctrine, without mythology, *devoid of worship*, giving scope to unlimited freedom of thought." To offer prayers to the *devas* is sheer puerility.

Dr. Legge of Oxford has been good enough to write

* *cf.* Also Dean Church's lectures on "The Sacred Poetry of Early Religions."

me the following interesting letter, which shows the place occupied by hymns in the Confucian system.

"The vast field of Chinese literature is remarkable for the absence of works on theology. There is no dogmatic teaching of religion in the Confucian system; and it is a consequence of this that we find in it no compositions which we can properly designate as hymns, having a place and application of their own, sung or chanted with or without instrumental accompaniment, in religious services.

"Yet the prayers used in the worship of God by the sovereigns of China, and by them and others in the services of the ancestral temple, have very much of the character of hymns. We have the Book of Poetry, containing in all 305 pieces, which Confucius is said to have selected from ten times as many current in his time, and 'which he sang over to his lute.' Forty of them are called Praise-songs, or songs of the Temple and Altar, and were employed in the royal worship of ancestors. A favourable specimen of them is the following hymn (so I will call it), addressed to Hâu-chî, the Father of Agriculture:—

O thou accomplished, great, Hâu-chî,
To thee alone 'twas given
To be by what we owe to thee,
The Correlate of Heaven.

On all who dwell within our land,
Grain-food did'st thou bestow;
'Tis to thy wonder-working hand
This gracious boon we owe.

God had the wheat and barley meant
To nourish all mankind;
None would have fathomed His intent,
But for thy guiding mind.

Man's social duties thou did'st show
To every tribe and state,
From Thee the polished manners flow
That stamp our land 'The Great.'

You will observe that in this hymn, while it is addressed to Hâu-chî, he is not confounded with God, but celebrated as His servant. And this is a characteristic of the religion of China. From first to last in the history of the empire, extending over about 5,000 years, God—now named Heaven, now Ti or Ruler, and now *Shang-Ti* or Supreme Ruler—stands forth single and supreme, 'Without equal or second.'

"The old Confucian Book of Poetry unfortunately does not contain any of the hymnic prayers addressed at the great royal or imperial services to God. But many such are to be found all along the stream of history in accounts of the imperial sacrifices since the beginning of our Christian era. The most remarkable group of them, which I have met with, was used on a special occasion in the year 1538. It consists of eleven addresses to the Spirit of God, in which the devotions of the worshippers rose to a high pitch of adoring reverence. They are all rhymed, and in measure somewhat irregular. You will find them all translated in the first of my lectures on 'The Religions of China,' published by Hodder and Stoughton in 1881."

Sir Wm. Muir says that "the services of the Mussulmans are confined (apart from the sermon or address) to recitations from the Coran and corresponding invocations. They do not, so far as my knowledge extends, use hymns in their worship. Many parts of the Coran are (like the Psalms) nothing but hymns. They are not, however, sung, but only repeated like the other portions. The Persian Soofias have many hymns; but whether they use them in divine service or not, I cannot say."

My friend Prof. Owen C. Whitehouse (see the Addenda to his translation of Schrader's "Cuneiform Inscriptions and the Old Testament," vol. II), says:—

"But, though the ancient Hebrews did not possess highly-developed metrical systems like the Greeks, it is by no means improbable that they did possess syllabic metre of a certain kind. Dr. Gustav Bickell has, in fact, made the bold, and it appears to me not unsuccessful attempt to show that they did, in his *Carmina veteris Testamenti metrice.* His ingenious theory involves certain textual alterations—some of which are quite admissible, and go far to improve the sense. Canon Cheyne of Oxford seems disposed to accept not only Dr. Bickell's views, but in some cases the textual emendations which arise out of them. On the other hand, the veteran scholar of Leipzig, Franz Delitzsch, in the preface to his latest edition of the Psalms, maintains a sceptical attitude towards Bickell's discoveries.

"Putting aside, however, debateable matter of this kind it may be said broadly that the ancient Semitic poetry consisted in a *rhythm or assonance of similar or contrasted ideas.* This is usually designated parallelism.

"The ancient Babylono-Assyrian hymns are in many instances translations from older non-Semitic Sumero-Akkadian lays. Many of these hymns are merely formulæ of incantation of which numerous examples may be found in Lenormant's Chaldean Magic. But there are some remarkable songs which are of a more exalted character, and though containing mythological elements, nevertheless express spiritual and devout thought. Most of these belong to a class called 'Penitential Psalms,' of which an interesting collection has recently been edited by Zimmern. Here is a specimen :—

"Exalted mistress, whose command prevails,
The prayer will I utter: What is good to thee do to me,
My Lady, from the days of my youth I have been fastened to the yoke of sin
Food have I not eaten, weeping was my refreshment.

[Water have I not drunk], tears were my drink;
[My heart was no longer merry], my disposition no longer bright.

. . . . .

O my Lady, teach me to know my doings, forgiveness (or peace), assure unto me.

"Another example I will cite in Prof. Sayce's rendering :—

"My Lord, in the anger of His heart, has punished me;
God in the strength of His heart has taken me;
Istar, my mother, has seized upon me and put me to grief.
God, who knoweth that I knew not, has afflicted me;
Istar, my mother, who knoweth that I knew not has caused darkness.

I prayed, and none takes my hand:
I wept, and none held my palm;
I cry aloud, but there is none that will hear me;
I am in darkness and hiding, and dare not look up."

Here we observe not only that *parallelismus membrorum* which characterizes Hebrew poetry but also a *strophic arrangement* as clearly marked as in the Psalter.

"On the subject of musical instruments we learn from Prof. Sayce that the ancient Babylonians had *seven* or *eight* different kinds, including the harp, the lyre, and the tambourine. The lyre was employed in feasts and the harp in sacred music.

"The harp comes down from very ancient times. On a fragment of a bas-relief, perhaps as old as 3,000 B.C., which I find figured in Fritz Hommel's History of Babylonia and Assyria, there is a representation of a harp with *twelve* strings, and a musician standing by with outstretched hand fingering the middle string.

"The following citation from Mr. Pinches' Babylonian Texts shows that music accompanied the sacrifices (Sayce's Hibbert Lectures, 1887, appendix iv., p. 514):—

> 'In the month of life and the festivals of sacrifices may glad music be sounded.
> Let the four zones behold his countenance.
> To those that bring (?) his nourishers may he grant life and goodness of heart!' "

Among the Greeks and Romans, the people were, as a rule, exhorted to be silent when the sacrificial rite—the slaying of the victim—was in actual process of accomplishment. *Euphēmeite*, or *favete linguis* was the formula addressed to the crowd upon such solemn occasions; the people waited in prayerful awe and silence, that no ill-starred utterance might mar the sacrificial omens. There may have been on special occasions the chanting of a solemn litany. Great public festivals were celebrated with song—the Dithyrambic lays were sung at the festival in honour of Dionysos. There were also the songs of the Priests of Mars, and of the Fratres Arvales, of which Mommsen gives examples in his "History of Rome." Horace's "Carmen Sæculare" furnishes another illustration of the compositions which were probably used among the Romans.

But so far as the material before us enables us to form an opinion, it is that hymns, as an essential of worship, have been mostly characteristic of the Christian, and in less degree, of its progenitor, the Hebrew religion. Nor is this much to be wondered at, since it is the only religion calculated to draw out at once the two elements necessary to such a form of worship—awe and love—awe which lies at the heart of worship, and love which kindles it into adoring song. For this, Brahmanism is too metaphysical, Buddhism too much opposed to the utterance of its emotion, if indeed it has any, Confucianism too much of a morality—too little of a religion, Mohammedanism too fatalistic in its conception of God. For it must never be forgotten that the character of worship is determined by the worshipper's conception of the Being to whom it is offered. Where the conception does not waken emotion there is little song in its worship, for song is the child not of philosophy but of feeling. None of these religions have aroused feelings which could only find adequate expression as the worshippers exclaimed, "O come let us sing unto the Lord, let us make a joyful noise to the rock of our salvation."

But it is to the Hebrew race that we must turn to find the noblest conception of God, and as a consequence the truest conception of worship—a conception in which awe before His greatness and emotion before His goodness are combined. In that, rather than in any other race, we discover the true origin of hymnody. There the religious nature of man more fully asserts itself—there the inner thought of his heart gets earliest and best expression. It is not strange, therefore, that this race so richly endowed with the religious element should have been chosen for the grand mission of giving to the world the noblest conception of worship. Their fitness for this mission sprang naturally from that conception of God as a person, which the more firmly it is grasped, the more real the worship becomes; whilst we cannot fail to observe that their hymnody becomes more tender as this idea of the personality of God is enlarged by the recognition of his gracious and lovable attributes. And as this people undoubtedly possessed a nature disposed to musical expression, it is not surprising that we find among them so spontaneous and early a development of worship-song. It is in this Hebrew race we find the true rise and onward flow of the river of song.

CHAPTER II.

HYMNS OF THE OLD TESTAMENT.

The hymns of the Old Testament were not originated by Divine command, but were, as we have indicated, the spontaneous outflow of the religious nature. No form of worship requiring song was instituted by Moses. No order of singers is included among the officers of the Tabernacle. Indeed, the earliest history of the chosen race is practically without song. As it has been said, "we read of altar and prayers and accepted intercessions, and we feel sure that those who walked in the light like Enoch or Abraham, must have had their hearts kindled with music; but from the green earth rising out of the flood—from the shadow of the great rock at Mamre, from the fountains and valleys and upland pastures of the Promised Land, where the tents of the Patriarchs rose amidst their flocks—from the prisons and palaces of Egypt we catch no sound of sacred song." But then this is a subject with which history did not concern itself—and we must not infer from this silence the utter absence of song—for scattered over the earlier history there are traces of its presence. The first examples, as we should expect, are of a very informal character—the product of some crisis in the life of the individual or the nation. Improvised songs born of great occasions, though to our colder western temperament almost impossible, are yet comparatively common among Eastern people like the Hebrews, even to this day. It is a common gift among the Italians.* The first of such songs is that of Miriam in celebration of the delivery of Israel from their Egyptian pursuers—"Sing ye to Jehovah, for He hath triumphed gloriously, the horse and his rider hath He thrown into the sea," but although this is the first recorded, it is almost certain that it was preceded by others; since before this we read of instruments of music. For since the two greatest fountains of song have ever been love and religion, we may feel sure that those who had reached to the use of musical instruments, however rude, would employ them to accompany the words of passion or devotion, which in exalted moments would spring to their lips. In Gen. iv. 21, we are told that "Jubal was the father of all such as handle the harp and the pipe," that is, of all string and wind instruments. Whilst in verses 23, 24 we have Lamech's song to his wives—the first example of a song, though not a sacred one, in the pages of Scripture, yet possessing many of the features of later Semitic poetry. Later on we read in the account of

* Professor Dowden records a striking instance of this in his life of Shelley, when the poet and his wife in Pisa listened to the improvisation of Signor Sgricci, an Italian of about 23 years of age. Members of the audience inscribed subjects for poetry on slips of paper which were thrown into a vase from which a boy drew one paper at a time at random, and the subject was announced, on which the Italian poured forth his unpremeditated verse. "It seemed," says Mary Shelley, "not the work of a human mind, but as if he were the instrument played upon by the superhuman inspiration of God." And is it not true that the highest poetry comes, in the first instance, as an improvisation? Is there not a very close connection between inspiration and improvisation?

Laban's interview with Jacob of "songs with tabret and with harp" (Gen. xxxi. 7). It is not at all likely that such a song as that of Miriam could have been uttered, if she had not previously been accustomed to lyric improvisation. So grand an outburst and so equal to its grand occasion, although doubtless touched and enlarged by the Editor of the book which records it, implies not only aptitude but exercise. Whilst the fact that she led a procession of women who chanted a chorus to her song, shows that songs had before this, in the time of their Egyptian captivity, been wedded to music. Somewhat later in the history we find that when Moses returned from the mount, he heard the people, who had made a calf for worship, joining aloud in a song to their newly fashioned God. It is all but certain that the Lawgiver himself was the author of the 90th Psalm which has aptly been called "The swan song of Moses." This may have been the first contribution—the nucleus, of that wonderful collection we call "The Book of Psalms," into which were gathered the noblest lyric utterances of widely severed times. We catch here and there in the sacred history glimpses of the widening and deepening river of song to which those we have mentioned were the first tributary streams. In the Book of Numbers, xxi. 17, we have the song which Israel sang "Spring up, O well." In the Book of Judges we meet with the song of Deborah and Barak, which was cast in a distinctly metrical form, and sung with a musical accompaniment—another improvisation by a Prophetess, that is one in a measure trained to music and song. But as the religious life of the nation grew deeper this kind of improvised song led the way to a school for the cultivation of music and sacred utterance. This was a chief function of the schools of the prophets which came into such prominence in the time of Samuel. Dean Stanley says "Whatever be the precise meaning of the peculiar word, which now came first into use as the designation of these companies, it is evident that their immediate mission consisted in uttering religious hymns or songs, accompanied by musical instruments, psaltery, tabret, pipe, and harp, and cymbals. In them, as in the few solitary instances of their predecessors, the characteristic element was that the silent seer of visions found an articulate voice, gushing forth in a rhythmical flow, which at once riveted the attention of the hearer. These, or such as these, were the gifts which under Samuel were now organised, if one may so say, into a system. From Ramah, the double height of the watchmen, they might be seen descending, in a long line or chain, which gave its name to their company, with psaltery, harp, tabret, pipe, and cymbals." From this school under Samuel the Prophet, David, the sweet singer of Israel, probably caught the inspiration which afterwards found expression in the Psalms, which form so important a part of the Psalter, that the book as a whole has been known as "The Psalms of David." It is impossible to say with certainty what portions of the Psalter we owe to his pen, probably they are fewer than is commonly supposed; but the impetus he gave to sacred song is indicated by the fact, that though some portions of the book belong to an age earlier than his; and that the larger portion came into being long after he had passed away, yet that the whole book goes under his name. The Book of Psalms was doubtless thus ascribed just as the Book of Proverbs was to his son Solomon, because, as Professor Cheyne says, "Solomon had become the symbol of plain ethical 'wisdom,' just as David had become the representative of religious lyric poetry."* But then a reputation like this does not grow out of nothing. David not only contributed to the songs of the people, but through him the service of song was added to the ordinary worship of the sanctuary, and made a fixed and integral part of the daily offering to Jehovah. Before his time, if ever connected with the Tabernacle at all, it had been fitful and occasional, depending to a large extent on individual enthusiasm. "For so mighty an innovation no less than a David was needed. The exquisite richness of verse and music so dear to him—'the calves of the lips'—took the place of the costly offerings of animals. His harp or guitar was to him what the wonder-working staff was to Moses, the spear to Joshua, or the sword to Gideon."

Thus sacred song found its way into the regular services of the Temple, and the Psalms became the liturgical hymn-book of the Jewish church. How completely the union of song and sacrifice (in the national worship) had been effected and how certainly it met the divine approval was made manifest at the dedication of the Temple. In the account contained in 2 Chron. v. 12, we read "Also the Levites which were the singers, all of them, even Asaph, Heman, Jeduthun, and their sons, and their brethren, arrayed in fine linen with cymbals and

* "Job and Solomon," p. 132.

psalteries and harps, stood at the east end of the altar, and with them an hundred and twenty priests sounding their trumpets: it came even to pass when the trumpeters and singers were as one, to make one sound to be heard in praising and thanking the Lord; and when they lifted up their voice with the trumpets and cymbals, and instruments of music, and praised the Lord, saying, For he is good, for his mercy endureth for ever: that then the house was filled with a cloud, even the house of the Lord; so that the priests could not stand to minister by reason of the cloud; for the glory of the Lord filled the house of God." Whilst in the 7th chapter of the same book we find that when Solomon had made an end of praying, that all the children of Israel bowed themselves with their faces to the ground upon the pavement, and worshipped, and gave thanks unto the Lord, *saying*, "For he is good; for his mercy endureth for ever." Thus, prayer and praise—the two most vital elements of a true worship, are found as integral parts of the service. It is somewhat difficult to say with certainty what place was afterwards held by sacred song in the regular services of the Temple. Certain Psalms have been identified as having been used at particular seasons. But it is generally admitted that from this time onward, save when interrupted by the calamities which befell the nation, song, no less than sacrifice, held its ground as part of the Jewish worship.

Mr. Paul Isaac Hershon, a distinguished Rabbinical scholar, has been good enough to furnish me with the following note as to the use of the Psalms:—

"On all ritual occasions the position of the Levites

in the Temple was on a raised platform technically called '*Duchan.*'* This seems to have been in the front of, and considerably lower in height than the Duchan occupied by the Priests, on the east of the altar, from whence they could see both the Levites and the Israelites when they blessed the whole congregation present." (See Numb. vi. 24-26.)†

"The Levites, without the accompaniment of any of their usual musical instruments, used to *sing* in the Temple on each day of the week a different Psalm. On the first day of the week they sung Ps. xxiv.; on the second day of the week, Ps. xlviii; on the third, Ps. lxxxii.; on the fourth, Ps. xciv.; on the fifth, Ps. lxxxi.; on the sixth, Ps. xciii.; and on the holy Sabbath-day, Ps. xcii."‡

"On other occasions various other Psalms were *sung*, and sung so loud that their voice could be heard as far as Jericho,§ a distance of about 12 miles. On such occasions the youngsters of the Levites were permitted to enter the Hall of the Sanctuary in order to spice with their fine 'thin voices' the rougher voices of the elder Levites."||

"The same Psalms that were sung in the Temple are now merely repeated by every orthodox Jew in his daily morning-prayer. Having no Temple, the priest does not sacrifice and the Levite does not sing!

'I-chabod! the glory is departed!'
'How shall we sing the Lord's song in a strange land!'"

---

* "Yoma," fol. 20*b*.

† Dr. Levy's "Rab. Lex.," p. 382, c. 1.

‡ "Rosh-hashanah," fol. 31*a*, and also in Anglo Jewish Liturgy.

§ "Tamid," fol. 30*b*.

|| "Erchin," fol. 13*b*.

"The Song of Moses, Ex. xv., and also Psalms cxlv.-cl., are repeated at Morning-Prayer every day all the year round. The cxlv. is repeated *thrice* daily, and he who never fails to do so may be sure to inherit eternal life" ("Berachoth," fol. 4*b*).

"The voice of a woman is an obscenity" ("Kiddushin," fol. 70*a*); "hence when men sing assisted by women, it is impudence; and when women sing assisted by men, it is as fire applied to tow" ("Sotah," fol. 48*a*).

Tradition has much to say about musical instruments, but now only one or two quotations must suffice. "No man could hear the voice of his neighbour in the Temple at Jerusalem when the Magreypha (organ) played" ("Tamid," fol. 33*a*).

"A ram has but one voice when alive but seven after he is dead. How so? His horns make two trumpets, his hip-bones two pipes, his skin makes a drum, his larger intestines make strings for the lyre, and the smaller chords for the harp" ("Kinnim," Chap. III. m. 6).

The later history naturally tells only of the special occasions in which the people broke into song, but these serve to confirm the idea that worship through song had become a habit among the people. "There is the song of Jehoshaphat and his army, the chant of victory sung in faith before the battle, and itself doing battles in that the Lord fought for those who trusted Him, and they had nothing to do but divide the spoil and return to Jerusalem, with psalteries and harps and trumpets, into the house of the Lord. There is the song of Hezekiah, when he recovered from his sickness, and the Psalm of Jonah from the depths of the sea, made up from the memory of other Psalms sung in happier hours. There was many a song by the waters of Babylon, whispered low that the oppressors might not hear. There was the song of liberated Israel, at the dedication of the wall of the Holy City (another witness to the customs of the past), when the singers sang aloud and they all rejoiced; so that the joy of Jerusalem was heard afar off" all these serve to show how the lyric spirit prevailed among the people, ready, when touched by any deep emotion, to give rhythmic utterance to their prayer and praise.

It is with David, the minstrel King, however, that the stream of song suddenly grows broad and deep. Around him the chorus begins to gather, which has now grown to such a glorious multitude.

Ewald truly says: "His harp was full-stringed, and every angel of joy and of sorrow swept over the chords as he passed. For the hearts of a hundred men strove and struggled together within the narrow continent of his single heart. The Lord allowed him not to curtail his being by treading the round of one function. He cultivated his whole being, and filled his soul with wisdom and feeling. He brought him up in the sheep-pastures, that the groundwork of his character might be laid amongst the simple and universal forms of feeling. He took him to the camp and made him a conquerer, that he might be filled with nobleness of soul and ideas of glory. He placed him in a palace, that he might be filled with ideas of majesty and sovereign might. He carried him to the wilderness and placed him in solitude, that his soul might dwell alone in the sublime conceptions of God and His mighty works; and He kept him there for years, with only one step between him and death, that he might be schooled to trust and depend upon the providence of God." The Psalms formed at once the justification and inspiration of all the noble songs of the later history of Israel, to say nothing of lyric notes which are heard sounding through the pages of the Prophets. But most remarkable is it, that when we reach the New Testament we find no lyric book corresponding to the Psalter. There are distinct psalms, like the "Magnificat" and "Nunc Dimittis," kindled from the lyric fire of the Hebrew Psalter; and hints which indicate the presence of the lyric gift in the Apostolic Church, but there is no *Christian* Psalter in the New Testament, and the reason is not far to seek. It is not that the lyric fire has departed, but that the Old Testament Psalter has so sounded the deepest notes of the soul in joy and sorrow, in darkness and light, that it is adequate to the needs, not only of Jewish, but Christian hearts. Thus it was not for an age, but for all time. Just as the octave in music can express the loftiest conceptions of the composers of every age, from the simple Gregorian chant to the intricate music of Beethoven, so the Psalter, meeting the deepest needs of the soul, becomes the fitting vehicle through which Christian as well as Jewish feeling can find expression.

And so we find, as a matter of fact, that through by far the greater part of the history of the Church the Psalms have formed its worship-song; they have had a place in the services of every Chnrch of Christendom where praise has been offered. They have been said or sung in grand cathedral or lowly meeting-house, by white-robed priests and plain-clad Puritans. The hearts of Roman and Greek, Armenian and Anglican, no less than Puritan and Nonconformist, have been kindled into praise by the Psalms of David and his company. Edward Irving says: "From whatever point of view any Church hath contemplated the scheme of its *doctrine*, by whatever name they have thought good to designate themselves, and however bitterly opposed to each other in Church government or observance of rules, you will find them all, by harmonious consent, adopting the Psalms as the outward form by which they shall express the inward feelings of the Christian life."

And even those who refused to sing the Psalms in the form in which they are found in Scripture—who deemed it dangerous and even heretical so to do, have sung them in metrical versions from which much of their glory had departed. Until quite recently there were churches whose only hymnal consisted of these versions. Thus the Psalms have been at once an inspiration and a bondage: an *inspiration*, in that they have kindled the fire which has produced the hymnody of the entire Church; a *bondage*, because by stereotyping religious expression they robbed the heart of the right to express in its own words the fears, the joys, the hopes that the Divine spirit had kindled in their souls. Had there been no Psalter in the Canon of Scripture, the Church would have had no model for its song—no place at which to kindle its worship fire; but, on the other hand, its worshipping instinct would have compelled it to create a Psalter of its own, and so there would have been an earlier and fuller development of hymnody in the Church. The very glory and perfection of the Psalter made the Church for long ages content with the provision thus made for its worship, and so it discouraged all who else would have joined the company of the singers. And even those who at last ventured to join their company, did so timidly, and chiefly as adapters of the Psalms for public worship. George Wither, Sir Philip Sidney and his sister belong to this class. Even when Dr. Watts began to write, his hymns were used only as supplemental to the Versions; indeed, a large part of his compositions are themselves metrical renderings of the Psalms, though some of them are so alive with his peculiar genius as to deserve rank as original compositions.

Mighty indeed was the spell the Psalter exercised over the Church, and rightly so, for it is the heart-utterance of the noble men whose mission it was to give the world religion. And as we have not outgrown the art of Greece or the laws of Rome, so neither have we out-grown the worship-song of Israel. This is so deep and true that it expresses the longings and praise even of those who have sat at the feet of Christ and learnt of Him. And as in the most sacred moment of His life one of these Psalms served to express His deepest feelings, so they have inspired and expressed the feelings of His followers in all aftertime. It has been well said, "the Church has been singing these Psalms ever since, and has not yet sung them dry," and she will go on singing them until she takes up the new song in the heavenly city. It should be frankly admitted that there are elements in the Psalms distinctly Jewish, and expressive of the feeling of earlier days. There are imprecatory notes that are out of harmony with the gentler melody of Christ. These ought to be dropped as unsuitable to *Christian* worship; but as a whole the Psalms form the noblest treasury of sacred song, and their inspiration may be discerned in every hymn that is worthy of a place in the Church's worship. Her hymnody can never be understood apart from the Psalter, and it will be found that those whose hearts are steeped the most deeply therein have given to the Church the songs that she will not willingly let die.*

* For an admirable account of the parallellism and strophic arrangement of Hebrew poetry as well as of the music and psalmody of the Temple. *cf.* Prof. Frank Delitzsch's Commentary on the Psalms. Introduction (4th edition).

CHAPTER III.

HYMNS OF THE NEW TESTAMENT.

We turn next to the New Testament to discover in what relation sacred song stands to the practice and teaching of the Church founded by our Lord and His Apostles.

Here at once we may naturally expect that as Christianity arose among the Hebrew race, and did not break immediately with the past, neither ignore the grand truths held by the Fathers, because they were truths belonging to all time, so we must expect to find some of the old methods of worship, some presence of the old lyric spirit, showing themselves, and this more especially in the earlier days of its history.

It cannot, therefore, be deemed wonderful but rather a thing to be looked for, that when the hope of Israel neared fulfilment, a hope to which their political circumstances caused them to cling with a very passion of expectation, and which made every line of promise in the Old Testament thrill with new meaning and authority; if the spirit of sacred song descended again, as we find it did upon those who were waiting and praying for the "Consolation of Israel."

Note.—The Apocrypha belonging to the time between the close of the Old Testament and the opening of the Christian Era, contains several notable examples of sacred song, such as those of Tobit and Judith and the Benedicite.

Critics, indeed, have refused to believe that the "Magnificat" could have sprung from the lips of a simple peasant of Galilee, they have said the song is too lofty for so lowly a source—forgetting that some of the grandest strains of former days came from those little if anything superior in station; such as Hannah, to whose song that of Mary bears considerable resemblance.

But if the lyric spirit of which we have spoken was a peculiar gift of the Hebrew people, if the power to improvise be a reality clearly discernible through their history, surely it is not wonderful that a Hebrew maiden, whose mind was kindled by a prospect of the highest joy to which Hebrew motherhood could attain, a joy for which every woman of her nation had longed, the promise, the joy, that to her should be given the surpassing glory of becoming the mother of Messiah; that her heart should break forth into song, that her rapture should call forth all the poetry of her nature, and cast it into the forms consecrated by the sacred usages and instincts of her race. This song, which repeats the promises of the past with the assurance of a present realisation, is a preluding note that prepares for the great chorus of Christian song one day to be heard, and which will repeat through the ages the rapture, the trust, the praise of her words, "My soul doth magnify the Lord, and my spirit doth rejoice in God my Saviour."

Her song has scarcely died on her lips ere another voice is heard, the voice of a man, a priest whose lips had been closed through unbelief, but on whom when faith has sprung again in his heart, the spirit of praise and prophecy descends with all its accompaniment of lyric power—the Song of Zachariah, "Blessed be the Lord God of Israel. . . . This in turn is succeeded by another, the voice of one standing on the outermost edge of this mortal life, more subdued in tone but full of quiet confidence and expectant hope, "Lord, now lettest Thou Thy servant depart in peace." . . . A noble triad making up by their quality for the silence of other lips.

The New Testament contains no Book of Sacred Song; but then the fulness and spirituality of the Book of Psalms, its adaptations to express in prayer and praise the deepest emotions of the religious mind, rendered any other unnecessary, and it is not, therefore, surprising that neither Christ nor His apostles joined the company of singers, that no Christian David was given to the church.

Indeed, it was scarcely possible amid the disquiet, the contention, the troubles of the earlier years, when as yet Christian worshippers had no churches of their own, but rather found a place in the Synagogue or the Temple. Ere Christian life had crystallised to its proper forms, it was not possible that the service and song, the outcome and expression of that life should arise.

In the only two other references to singing in the Gospels—when Christ made His triumphant entry into Jerusalem, and ere He left it for the garden of Gethsemane—one (perhaps the same one) of the Psalms was used, otherwise the Gospels are silent as to sacred song.

There can be little doubt that singing formed a part of both the social and public worship of the Apostolic age. The disciples dismissed by the rulers in Jerusalem, came to their own company and lifted up their voice with one accord in a song, partly the inspiration of the moment, and partly from the book of Psalms (Acts iv. 24). In the Philippian dungeon, Paul and Silas prayed and *sang praises to God.* Paul exhorts both the Ephesians and Colossians to the use of psalms and hymns and spiritual songs.

Dr. Lightfoot regards "Psalms" as referring specially, though not exclusively, to the Psalms of David, which would early form part of the religious worship of the Christian brotherhood. "Hymns" would refer to a set form of words or spontaneous effusions of the moment of the Christians themselves, whilst the "spiritual songs" would extend the precept to all forms of song provided they were spiritual. Whilst St. Paul, in his Epistle to the Corinthians, declares that when they came together each one hath a psalm (1 Corinthians xiv. 26).

One of the earliest descriptions of the Christians contains the statement that "they sang hymns to Christ as God." But whether such hymns were Psalms adapted to the purpose and with a Christian application, or original compositions, we do not know. There is nothing in the record to decide the question, nor has any hymn of the Apostolic age come down to us. The threefold division of psalms and hymns and spiritual songs may indicate that in addition to the Old Testament Psalms, other compositions distinguished by the titles "hymns" and "spiritual songs" were used, but of this we cannot be certain.* The likelihood is that the new Christian feeling found expression in hymns of a simple kind addressed to Christ. Some have maintained that the rhythmic passages which are found in the Epistles are parts of hymns then in use.

The principal of these are the following: "Wherefore He saith, Awake, thou that sleepest, and arise from the dead, and Christ shall shine upon thee" (Ephesians v. 14). "And without controversy great is the mystery of godliness; He who was manifested in the flesh, justified in the spirit, seen of angels, preached among the nations, believed on in the world, received up in glory" (1 Timothy iii. 16). "Who is the blessed and only Potentate, the King of kings, and Lord of lords, who only hath immortality, dwelling in light unapproachable; whom no man hath seen, nor can see: to whom be honour and power eternal. Amen" (1 Timothy vi. 15). "Faithful is the saying: for if we died with Him, we shall also live with Him; if we shall deny Him, He also will deny us: if we are faithless, He abideth faithful, for He cannot deny Himself" (2 Timothy ii. 13). But it is not unlikely that such passages are due to impassioned emotion

* Dr. Morison (*Evangelical Repository*, June, 1856) says "hymns" and "spiritual songs" denote compositions more or less measured that were simply sung, whilst "psalms" denote the Psalms of David and other kindred lyrics that were *written to be sung to an instrumental accompaniment*. On the authority of Ephesians v. 19, he claims that instrumental music (in worship) has the sanction of the New Testament, and that it was practised in many of their assemblies, though it was probably confined for the most part to their more private meetings, and as persecution increased gradually disappeared. Dr. Neale says:—"From the brief allusions we find to the subject in the New Testament we should gather that the hymns and spiritual songs of the apostles were written in metrical prose."

which not unfrequently rises to rhythmic utterance, whilst the passage in 1 Cor. xiv. 26, forms a clear indication that the power to improvise, so apparent in the early history of Israel, prevailed in the times of the Apostles.

Of course these are utterly unlike hymns as we know them; but it must be remembered that it is all but certain that *metrical* compositions were not used until about the fourth century. Indeed, so late as the ninth century Walafrid Strabo warns us that by hymns he does not mean merely such metrical hymns as those of Hilary, Ambrose, Prudentius, or Bede, but such other acts of praise as are offered in fitting words and with musical sounds. Augustine lays down the same rule—any composition of a rhythmic character, whether in verse or not, which was capable of being sung, was reckoned a hymn. Looked at in the light of this rule, the passages in the Epistles already quoted seem likely to have been parts of the earliest hymns of the Church, for they have every quality, save metrical form, fitting them for such a use. The well-known "Gloria in Excelsis" may serve as a specimen of the kind of composition first of all used as hymns in the early Church.

The "Gloria in Excelsis" was in all probability the morning hymn of the Christians of early times, as the *Phos ilaron* preserved by St. Basil, which belongs to the first or second century, was their hymn for evening use. The latter, though less known, is as beautiful, perhaps in a poetic sense more beautiful, than the former. It has been effectively rendered in English by the following translation by Mr. Keble :—

"Hail! gladdening Light, of His pure glory poured,
Who is th' Immortal Father, heavenly blest,
Holiest of Holies—Jesus Christ our Lord!

Now we are come to the sun's hour of rest,
The lights of evening round us shine,
We hymn the Father, Son, and Holy Spirit Divine!

Worthiest art Thou at all times to be sung,
With undefiled tongue,
Son of our God, Giver of life, alone!
Therefore in all the world, Thy glories Lord we own." *

This is still the Vesper Hymn of the Greek Church.

How such hymns arose we know not. "Whether they sprang first to light in a burst of choral song, like that inspired hymn in the Acts; or were bestowed on the Church through the heavenly meditations of a solitary believer; or gradually, like a river, by its tributary streams, rose to what they are, we can perhaps never know."† We incline, however, to the idea that they were, in the first instance, improvised songs, and in aftertime brought to greater finish.

Thus the river which at first was but a tiny rill broadens and deepens until prophecy describes it as becoming like the mighty waves of the sea—"And I heard as it were the voice of a great multitude, and as the voice of many waters, and as the voice of mighty thunders saying Hallelujah! for the Lord our God, the Almighty reigneth. Let us rejoice and be glad, and let us give the glory unto him, for the marriage of the Lamb is come." "And I heard a voice from heaven as the voice of many waters, and as the voice of a great thunder, and the voice

* Lyra Apostolica, LXIII.
† "Voice of Christian Life in Song," p. 25.

which I heard *was* as the *voice* of harpers harping with their harps, and they sang, as it were, a new song before the throne."

The Revelation of St. John the Divine is full of glowing references to song as the highest expression of worshipping feeling, indicating that in the future as in the past, song is to be one of the noblest mediums for the ascription of praise. Do not the pictures in this book seem like glorified representations of the Temple at Jerusalem and its worship; and do they not as such justify the idea that song was in Herod's temple, as it had been in earlier times in Solomon's, a part of its ritual? So vivid a picture of choral worship would scarcely have risen in a mind that had not been accustomed to its earthly counterpart. Thus the Temple worship may have given form to the inspiration which moved in the heart of the Beloved Apostle, and led him to embody the thoughts kindled in his mind by means of symbols drawn therefrom in which song forms so conspicuous an element. Whilst it is not unworthy of notice that at times he rises above this symbolism and declares "I saw no Temple therein, for the Lord God Almighty and the Lamb are the Temple thereof."

CHAPTER IV.

HYMNS OF THE EARLY CHURCH.

As we have said in the last chapter, the "Gloria in Excelsis" gives us the best idea of the kind of hymn used in the age succeeding that of the Apostles. This, and the *Phōs ilaron* attributed to Athenagoras of the second century, and still in use in the daily office of the Greek Church, "probably represent in their rhythmic but unmetrical structure, many Christian hymns now lost. Of the existence of such hymns from the time of Pliny's well-known letter to Trajan we have abundant evidence."

As early as 269 A.D. it was made a charge against Paul of Samosata, that he had "put a stop to the psalms that were sung to our Lord Jesus Christ, as being innovations; the work of men of later times." This establishes the fact that such psalms must have been sung in the second century, and probably earlier still. The epilogue of Clement of Alexandria to his *Pædagogue* has usually been regarded as the first Christian hymn. In Dean Plumptre's translation, the first verse runs thus:—

Curb for the stubborn steed,
Making its will give heed;
Wing that directest right
The wild birds' wandering flight;
Helm for the ships that keep
Their pathway o'er the deep;
Shepherd of sheep that own
Their Master on the throne,
Stir up Thy children meek
With guileless lips to speak,
In hymns and songs Thy praise,
Guide of their infant ways.

O King of saints, O Lord!
Mighty, all-conquering Word;
Son of the Highest God,
Wielding His wisdom's rod;
Our stay when cares annoy,
Giver of endless joy;
Of all our mortal race,
Saviour of boundless grace,
O Jesus hear.

The fourth century, however, was the age in which hymns really established themselves in the regular services of the Church. And, strange to say, their establishment was due to the keen-sightedness of great men belonging to the orthodox party, who discerned the wide influence exerted by hymns in favour of the teaching of heretics, who made large use of them for the promulgation of their views. Bardesanes and his son Harmonius had introduced into Syria both the Greek metres and music, and by means of these had given currency and secured popularity for their particular views. To counteract this, Ephrem of Edessa wrote hymns on the Nativity, Baptism, Fasting, Passion, and Resurrection of our Lord, and set them to the music which had already become popular. He trained choirs of virgins to sing them, and on Sundays and festivals they were gathered in the church, and led by Ephrem himself, standing in their midst. Thus metrical hymnody became rooted in the services of the Syriac Church. In Constantinople, a like method was adopted against the Arians, who had been expelled from the churches by Theodosius, but who still met outside the walls, or in the open spaces of the city, marching in procession and singing their hymns. Chrysostom organised rival processions, which marched, bearing torches and crosses, and singing hymns. The

Empress Eudocia patronised the scheme, and provided means for its execution. It would seem that Chrysostom laid more stress, like a certain modern sect, on the torches, the crosses, the music, than on the words of the hymns.

Nor was it otherwise in the West. There, also, heresy gave birth to Christian hymnody. The story is told by Augustine, who, with his mother, Monica, was in Milan at the time. The Empress Justina ordered Ambrose, then the Bishop of the city, to give up one of the Basilicas for Arian worship. He refused, and was sentenced to exile—a sentence he refused to obey. The population of Milan, enthusiastic for their bishop, supported him in this refusal, and watched his house day and night, to protect him from the troops of the Empress. Ambrose formed these troops of watchers into bands of worshippers, and arranged for them a course of offices, in which hymns played an important part. This is the real source of the Offices for the various hours of the day and night which form so conspicuous an element in the Breviaries of the Western Church.

It is a fact of singular significance and great interest, that in the Syriac, the Greek, and the Latin churches, the action of the heretics should have given rise to the introduction of hymns as a part of the regular services of the Church. From the Syriac Church, few hymns have passed into our English hymnody;* but from the Greek; although none of the hymns of Chrysostom have come into English use—probably they were not worthy

* "Glad sight, the Holy Church," No. 351, in "Hymns Ancient and Modern," last edition but one, is from the Syriac; whilst others from the same source may be found in "The People's Hymnal," in Thrupp's collection, and in a recent volume by Dr. Bonar.

enough—the movement originated by him gave birth to a later school of hymnists; many of whose hymns, through the translations of Dr. Neale, have become deservedly popular among us. The results of the movement set on foot by Ambrose, on English hymnody have been far more direct, since several of the hymns composed by him, in their English form, are now sung, whilst the school of Ambrosian music has had considerable influence on that of modern times.

Turning now from the originating causes of these three schools of hymnody to the hymns themselves; (1) as to the Syriac hymns little need be said, since they have not exerted any perceptible influence on English hymnody. This is probably due to the language in which they were written, which has put them beyond the range of all save those versed in the tongues of the East. In Daniel's great book, they are represented in a German form. Dr. Burgess has translated them into English, and Mrs. Charles has rendered a few from the German version in Daniel. But, as they are seen in their English dress, they are singularly free from the gorgeous imagery so characteristic of the East. Doubtless they have been toned down by transference to our English speech. Some of them seem to us not unworthy of a place in our modern collections, since they are marked by a freshness and simplicity which are very pleasant.

Here is Ephrem's hymn on Palm Sunday, as translated by Mrs. Charles:—

He calls us to a day of gladness,
  Who came to us the King's own Son;
Go forth with boughs of palm to meet Him,
  And Him with loud hosannas own.

The angels are with us rejoicing.
  Angelic triumphs swell our song;
All nations in our joy uniting,
  Hosanna sounds on every tongue.

To Thee, O Lord, loud praise ascendeth,
  From every creature in its kind:
Thee, with an awed and quiv'ring motion,
  Exalteth every waving wind.

The heavens in their quiet beauty,
  Praise Thy essential majesty;
The heights rejoice from which Thou camest;
  The depths spring up to welcome Thee.

The sea exults to feel Thy footsteps,
  The land Thy tread, Lord, knoweth well;
Our human nature brings thanksgivings,
  Because Thy Godhead there doth dwell.

To-day the sun rejoicing shineth,
  With happy radiance tenfold bright,
In homage to the Sun of glory,
  Which brings to all the nations light.

The moon shall shed her fairest lustre
  O'er all the heavens her softest glow;
Thee on her radiant heights adoring,
  Who for our sakes hast stooped so low.

And all the starry hosts of heaven,
  In festive robes of light array'd,
Shall bring their festal hymns as offerings
  To Him who all so fair hast made.

To-day the forests are rejoicing,
  Each tree its own sweet anthem sings,
Because we wave their leafy branches
  As banners for the King of Kings.

To-day let all the brute creation,
  Rejoicing, be no longer dumb:
For lowly on the foal He sitteth,
  The Heavenly One to us has come.

Let every village, every city,
  In happy tumult sing His name;
Since even infant lips are shouting
  Blessed is He, the King who came.

Those who are curious as to Syriac hymnody should consult Dr. Burgess's translations of the hymns of Ephrem Syrus and other writers of his school.

(2) The hymns of the Greek Church, though somewhat allied to those of the Syriac, yet have in them enough

affinity to our Western ideas to be incorporated into our worship. Like the city in which they first appeared, they stand midway between the East and West, and have certain elements common to both; whilst the vast mass of hymns produced by this Church—Dr. Neale computes that out of the five thousand quarto pages of which the Greek office books consist, at least four thousand are poetry—has enabled men like Dr. Neale to select portions suited to our Western taste. Even then, however, it has been found necessary to subject such portions to a very free treatment, and to preserve their ideas rather than the forms in which they were cast. This is the more necessary since the great mass of the hymns of this Church are not in metrical form, but simply rhythmic and accentuated like the earliest Latin sequences.

Not until they fell under the skilful hand of Dr. Neale did they contribute their share to the now many-voiced song of the churches of England.

Through his centos from the hymns of the Eastern Church, we now have such well-known favourites as "The day is past and over" (585), probably by St. Anatolius (A.D. 458), which is to the scattered hamlets of Chios and Mitylene, what Bishop Ken's evening hymn is to the villages of our own land. "Christian dost thou see them" (413), a stichera for the second week of the great fast, by St. Andrew of Crete (660-732). "Art thou weary, art thou languid?" (520), by St. Stephen the Sabaite (725-794). "'Tis the day of Resurrection," by St. John Damascene (*circa* 780). This is the canon for Easter Day, and a modern traveller gives the following graphic account of its use at Athens. It is quoted in "Hymns of the Eastern Church," by Dr. Neale.

"As midnight approached, the Archbishop with his priests, accompanied by the King and Queen, left the church, and stationed themselves on the platform, which was raised considerably from the ground, so that they were distinctly seen by the people. Everyone now remained in breathless expectation, holding their unlighted tapers in readiness when the glad moment should arrive, while the priests still continued murmuring their melancholy chant in a low half-whisper. Suddenly a single report of a cannon announced that twelve o'clock had struck, and that Easter Day had begun; then the old Archbishop, elevating the cross, exclaimed in a loud, exulting tone: 'Christos anesti! Christ is risen!" and instantly every single individual of all that host took up that cry, and the vast multitude broke through and dispelled for ever the intense and mournful silence which they had maintained so long, with one spontaneous shout of indescribable joy and triumph: 'Christ is risen!—Christ is risen!' At the same moment, the oppressive darkness was succeeded by a blaze of light from thousands of tapers, which, communicating one from another, seemed to send streams of fire in all directions, rendering the minutest objects distinctly visible, and casting the most vivid glow on the expressive faces, full of exultation, of the rejoicing crowd; bands of music struck up their gayest strains; the roll of the drum through the town, and further on the pealing of the cannon, announce far and near these 'glad tidings of great joy,' while from hill and plain, from the sea-shore and the far-off olive-grove, rocket after rocket ascending to the clear sky, answer back with their mute eloquence that Christ is risen indeed, and told of other tongues that were repeating those blessed words, and other hearts that leaped for joy; everywhere men clasped each other's hands, and congratulated one another, and embraced with countenances beaming with delight, as though to each one separately some wonderful happiness had been proclaimed—and so in truth it was; and all the while, rising above the mingling of many sounds, each one of which was a sound of gladness, the aged priests were distinctly heard chanting forth a glorious old hymn of victory in tones so loud and clear that they seemed to have regained their youth and strength, to tell the world how 'Christ is risen from the dead, having trampled death beneath His feet, and henceforth they that are in the tombs have everlasting life.'"

All these differ widely from the hymns of the Latin Church, in that they are more vivid, and spring more directly out of Scripture events.

(3) It is generally admitted that the Western Churches owe the incorporation of metrical hymnody into their services to Ambrose, and the movement originated by him. Hymns may have been in use, in the West before his time, but all previous attempts were sporadic and fitful. Ambrose was the founder of a school of hymnody, from which no less than ninety-two examples have come down to us; of these twenty-one, or, at the lowest computation, that of the Benedictine Editors, twelve are from the pen of Ambrose himself. The hymns of this school, since they are more akin to our Western modes of thought, reached an earlier popularity in our midst than those from the Eastern or Greek Church. The picturesqueness of the Greek hymns, and the skilfulness of Dr. Neale's renderings

have, however, brought them of late into great prominence, and rendered them even more popular than those of the Latin Church. The strong ethical element in the hymns of the Ambrosian school, whilst it makes them, perhaps, more practically useful as aids to holy living, yet gives them a certain subdued tone which militates against their popularity. They are more akin to statuary—clear, sharp, cold—than, as the Eastern hymns are, to painting, with its richer colour and more vivid mode of portrayal, and so, like statuary, appeal less forcibly to the imagination. Professor F. M. Bird says:—"The Latin hymns of Ambrose and his successors form a school which may be said to have held possession of the Church of the whole of Europe for some 1200 years." This reached its highest point of excellence in the "Veni Creator," and "Veni Sancte Spiritus." The most notable hymns of the school of Ambrose which have established themselves by means of translations in our English hymnals are "We praise, we worship Thee, O God" (13), "O Jesu, Lord of heavenly grace" (558), and "Now that the daylight fills the sky" (554). These may suffice to indicate the subjects and style of this school. The "Te Deum" has usually been ascribed to Ambrose; the well-known tradition being that it broke forth in sudden inspiration from his lips as he was baptising Augustine; another form of the same tradition being that it was due to an inspiration common to both Ambrose and Augustine, which enabled the one to respond antiphonally to the verses uttered by the other. This, like the similar tradition concerning the Septuagint version of the Old Testament, can scarcely be regarded as a true account. The great authority, Daniel, seems to regard it as having sprung from an early Oriental hymn, or from fragments of many such hymns. It is probably the work of many minds and ages, in which Ambrose may have borne a part: it may have been that of arranging and perfecting the scattered fragments into a compact composition. The latest theory, however, respecting it is that it is later than the time of Ambrose, and probably of Gallican origin. Some there are who ascribe it to Hilary rather than Ambrose.

Spain, too, contributed its share to the early hymnody of the Church. The Mozarabic Breviary of the fifth century was no unworthy collection. Some idea of its contents may be gained from Mr. Ellerton's translation of one of its hymns:—

Sing Hallelujah forth in duteous praise,
O citizens of heaven, and sweetly raise
An endless Hallelujah.

Ye next, who stand before the Eternal Light,
In hymning choirs re-echo to the height
An endless Hallelujah.

The Holy City shall take up your strain,
And with glad songs resounding wake again
An endless Hallelujah.

In blissful antiphons ye thus rejoice
To render to the Lord with thankful voice
An endless Hallelujah.

Ye who have gained at length your palms in bliss,
Victorious ones, your chant shall still be this,
An endless Hallelujah.

There in one glad acclaim, for ever ring
The strains which tell the honour of your King,
An endless Hallelujah.

This is the rest for weary ones brought back,
This is the food and drink which none shall lack,
An endless Hallelujah.

While Thee, by Whom were all things made, we praise
For ever, and tell out in sweetest lays,
An endless Hallelujah.

Almighty Christ, to Thee our voices sing;
Glory for evermore to Thee we bring
An endless Hallelujah.

In these early, as in later, times, however, conflicts of considerable intensity arose concerning the introduction of hymns into the services of the Church. Some there were who doubted whether any but the words of Scripture should be used in worship. Others had grown so used to the Ambrosian hymns that, like the devotees of Watts or of the Scotch metrical psalms in a much later age, they resented the introduction of hymns from other sources. Indeed, it needed the decision of a Council to give them sanction; whilst in the 7th century, the Council of Toledo threatened with excommunication all in Spain or France who resisted the use of hymns in divine worship. Even as late as the 9th century, there were churches which would not admit metrical hymns into their offices. Thus the conflict raged, until at last hymns established themselves, either in metrical or rhythmic forms, as an integral and vital element in worship, and so played a great part in lifting the hearts of men to the Father of their spirits. The hymns of this earlier period are chiefly occupied with the events of our Lord's life; special stress being laid on His incarnation. There is an entire absence of that carnal element which in later, and especially in the latest times, came into prominence; so that the blood and wounds of Christ were regarded as though in themselves they possessed some mystic merit. This is so even in the hymns of the Eastern Church, which are so largely occupied with the actual scenes of our Lord's life; whilst in the Latin Church, it is the ethical side of the Christian faith which is thrown into special prominence. Indeed, the early literature of the Church—not only its hymns, but creeds and liturgies, are singularly free from those carnal conceptions of our Lord's work which came in later times into so much prominence, both in the Roman Church and what may be called the ultra-Evangelical section of the Protestant Church. Our modern hymnody is, to a large extent, reverting to this earlier type; occupying itself with the *facts* of our Lord's life as in the Eastern, and with the *ethical* side of the Gospel as in the Latin Church.

CHAPTER V.

MEDIÆVAL HYMNS.

There are two writers who form a kind of connecting link between early and mediæval hymnody—Venantius Fortunatus, who was born in 530, and died in 609 A.D.; and Gregory the Great, whose life extended from 550 to 604 A.D. Fortunatus, a child of the sunny south, in his early days was a kind of Troubadour: "the fashionable poet of his day," who wandered from castle to palace, appearing and singing his songs at marriages and festivals, fond of court revelry; but yet, so far as we can judge, one of the few who passed unscathed through the fires, and they were fierce, of the temptations of such a course in those times. Later in life he was consecrated a priest, and became almoner of the monastery at Tours, founded by Queen Rhadegunda, with whom he had been on very intimate terms, and to whom he addressed many of his poems. Still later in life he became Bishop of Poitiers. His hymns are such as we should expect from such a nature, and from the sunny land in which he spent his days. Three of these attained to great popularity. They have more in common with those of the Eastern Church than those of Ambrose and his school, and are more the product of the poet's imagination than of the moral nature which found so full an expression in the Ambrosian hymnody. One of these, the "Vexilla Regis prodeunt," well-known through Dr. Neale's translation, "The Royal Banners forward go," who calls it "one of the grandest in the treasury of the Latin Church," was written to commemorate the reception of certain relics of the true Cross by St. Gregory of Tours and St. Rhadegund, at the consecration of a church at Poitiers, and was originally intended for use as a processional hymn. This is Dr. Neale's translation of it:—

The Royal Banners forward go;
The Cross shines forth in mystic glow:
Where He in flesh, our flesh Who made,
Our sentence bore, our ransom paid.

Where deep for us the spear was dy'd,
Life's torrent rushing from His side,
To wash us in that precious flood
Where mingled water flowed, and Blood.

Fulfilled is all that David told
In true Prophetic song of old;
Amidst the nations God, saith he,
Hath reign'd and triumph'd from the Tree.

O Tree of Beauty! Tree of Light!
O Tree with royal purple dight!
Elect on whose triumphal breast
Those holy limbs should find their rest!

On whose dear arms, so widely flung,
The weight of this world's ransom hung:
The price of human kind to pay,
And spoil the Spoiler of his prey.

With fragrance dropping from each bough,
Sweeter than sweetest nectar Thou;
Decked with the fruit of peace and praise,
And glorious with triumphal lays.

Hail, Altar! hail, O Victim! Thee
Decks now Thy passion's victory;
Where Life for sinners death endured,
And life by death for man procured.

In the 14th century, the following verses were added when the hymn was appropriated to Passion-tide:—

[O Cross, our one reliance hail!
This holy Passiontide, avail
To give fresh merit to the Saint,
And pardon to the penitent.

To Thee, Eternal Three in one,
Let homage meet by all be done;
Whom by the Cross Thou dost restore,
Preserve and govern evermore.]

Another is the "Pange lingua gloriosi" ("Sing, my tongue, the glorious battle"), a hymn in which praise of the cross finds full expression, as witness the following verse:—

Bend thy boughs, O Tree of Glory!
  Thy relaxing sinews bend;
For awhile the ancient rigour
  That thy birth bestowed, suspend;
And the King of Heavenly Beauty
  On thy bosom gently tend!

His "Salve festa dies" ("Hail, festal day! ever exalted high") has for centuries been used as a hymn for Easter day, and is full of poetic vigour, as the following verses may show:—

The changing months, the pleasant light of days,
The shining hours, the rippling moments praise,
  Since God hath conquered hell, and rules the starry sky.

Countless the hosts Thou savest from the dead;
They follow free where Thou, their Lord, hast led.
  Hail, festal day! ever exalted high.

Gregory the Great is a personage of more interest to English folk than his contemporary Fortunatus, since to him we owe the mission of Augustine, by which Christianity was firmly planted in our land. His name is familiar to the youngest by the beautiful story which tells how, on going into the slave market at Rome, and marking the beauty of certain fair English youths, he exclaimed, "If they were Christians, they were not Angles but angels." A sight which probably prompted the despatch of the mission for the conversion of England to Christianity. Had our country been won to and remained faithful to a Christianity such as was seen in Gregory, the Reformation would have been little needed in our land. Gregory is one of the noblest figures in the history of the Church. To him we owe the Plain Song—the Gregorian tones which for centuries held their ground in the Church, and which to this day find many earnest defenders. Mone, in his great work, "Hymni Latini Medii Ævi," assigns to Gregory the "Veni Creator Spiritus," usually assigned to Charlemagne. Wackernagel is of the same opinion. Daniel, however, ascribes it, as it usually has been, to the great Emperor of the West. The question of its authorship must probably remain uncertain. Of its high popularity there can be no doubt. Daniel says it was appointed for use at the creation of a pope, the election of a bishop, the coronation of kings, the celebration of a synod, the elevation and translation of saints. It is the only hymn inserted in the Book of Common Prayer, where Bishop Cosin's version is adopted. It has been again and again translated. As it is so uncertain whether Gregory wrote it, we append another hymn by him, in the translation of an anonymous writer, which seems to us very beautiful:—

Now, when the dusky shades of night, retreating
  Before the sun's red banner, swiftly flee:
Now, when the terrors of the dark are fleeting,
  O Lord, we lift our thankful hearts to Thee,—

To Thee, Whose word, the fount of life unsealing,
  When hill and dale in thickest darkness lay,
Awoke bright rays across the dim earth stealing,
  And bade the eve and morn complete the day.

Look from the tower of heaven, and send to cheer us
  Thy light and truth to guide us onward still;
Still let Thy mercy, as of old, be near us,
  And lead us safely to Thy holy hill.

So, when that morn of endless light is waking,
  And shades of evil from its splendours flee,
Safe may we rise, the earth's dark breast forsaking,
  Through all the long bright day to dwell with Thee.

This is, perhaps, the place to speak of the Venerable Bede, rather than in the chapter on early English hymns, since, although an Englishman, and resident in England, he wrote all his hymns in the Latin tongue. His life extended from about 672 to 735 A.D. At seven years of age, he entered the monastery of Jarrow, where he remained till death called him to higher service. "There he read, wrote, and prayed, sang hymns to his Saxon harp, recorded the history of his people, and corresponded with friends in all parts of England and Europe; and there, as the last work of his busy life, he translated the Gospel of John into Anglo-Saxon, finishing it amid the sufferings of his last illness, and dying just as he had concluded the last chapter. 'Dearest master,' said his Amanuensis to him, 'there is only one thought left to write.' He answered, 'Write quickly.' Soon the writer replied, 'Now this thought also is written.' He answered, 'Thou hast well said. It is finished. Raise my head in thy hand, for it will do me good to sit opposite my sanctuary, where I was wont to kneel down to pray; that sitting I may call upon my Father.' So he seated himself on the ground in his cell, and sang the 'Glory to Thee, O God—Father, Son, and Holy Ghost,' and when he had named the Holy Ghost, he breathed his last breath." He wrote a long hymn, comparing the six days of the creation with the six days of the world. His hymn on the Ascension is full of quaint beauty, as will be seen from the following translation by Mrs. Charles:—

A hymn of glory let us sing:
New hymns throughout the world shall ring;
By a new way none ever trod,
Christ mounteth to the throne of God.

The apostles on the mountain stood,—
The mystic mount, in Holy Land;
They, with the virgin-mother, see
Jesus ascend in majesty.

The angels say to the eleven,
"Why stand ye gazing into heaven?
This is the Saviour,—this is He!
Jesus hath triumphed gloriously!"

They said the Lord should come again,
As these beheld Him rising then,
Calm soaring through the radiant sky,
Mounting its dazzling summits high.

May our affections thither tend,
And thither constantly ascend,
Where, seated on the Father's throne,
Thee reigning in the heavens we own!

Be Thou our present joy, O Lord!
Who wilt be ever our reward;
And, as the countless ages flee,
May all our glory be in Thee!

It is free from the objectionable and unscriptural elements of many hymns of the mediæval age, to which, in spirit, the monk of Jarrow scarcely belongs. Nearly a century later flourished Theodulph of Orleans (he died in 821 A.D.) whose hymn on Christ's entrance into Jerusalem is animated by a spirit very like to that of the Venerable Bede's on the Ascension. It was written at Metz, or as some say at Angers, during his imprisonment on a false accusation. On their way to the cathedral, the Emperor Louis and his court heard this hymn sung by choristers instructed by Theodulph. It procured his instant liberation. In Dr. Neale's translation it begins:—

Glory, and laud, and honour;

and until the seventeenth century, he says that the following quaint verse was included:—

Be Thou, O Lord, the rider,
And we the little ass,
That to God's holy city,
Together we may pass.

The two hymns that are best known beyond ecclesiastical circles, and that have made the greatest impression, both on literature and music, are the "Dies Iræ" and the "Stabat Mater," the former the most sublime, the latter the most pathetic of mediæval hymns. The "Dies Iræ" was written for private devotion in a lonely monastic cell, about 1250, by Thomas of Celano, the friend and biographer of St. Francis of Assisi. It has been truly said: "The secret of the irresistible power of the 'Dies Iræ' lies in the awful grandeur of the theme, the intense earnestness and pathos of the poet, the simple majesty and solemn music of its language, the stately metre, the triple rhyme, and the vowel assonances chosen in striking adaptation to the sense; all combining to produce an overwhelming effect, as if we heard the final crash of the universe, the commotion of the opening graves, the trumpet of the archangel that summons the quick and the dead, and as if we saw the King of tremendous majesty seated on the throne of justice and mercy, and ready to dispense everlasting life or everlasting woe." Goethe describes its effect upon the guilty conscience in the cathedral scene of "Faust." Sir Walter Scott introduces a portion of it into the "Lay of the Last Minstrel." It is at once the hope and despair of translators. Probably more attempts have been made to translate it than any other hymn. Dr. Irons' translation is perhaps the best, and has been most frequently chosen by hymnal editors. In our opinion it is quite unsuitable

—nor was it ever intended by its author—for public singing.

The "Stabat Mater," founded on John xix. 25, and Luke ii. 35, is by Jacobus de Benedictis, otherwise called Jacopone da Todi, a reformer before the Reformation, who came into conflict with Pope Boniface VIII., by whom he was imprisoned, and on whose death he was released. It has become the libretto to music by Palestrina, Pergolesi, Haydn, Rossini, and others.

The "Pange lingua gloriosi," by Thomas Aquinas, Dr. Neale says, contests the second place among those of the Western Church with the "Vexilla regis," the "Stabat Mater," the "Jesu dulcis memoria," and others, leaving the "Dies Iræ" in its unapproachable glory. Its materialistic conceptions are, in our judgment, fatal to poetic thought. That our readers may judge for themselves, we append the hymn as it stands in Dr. Neale's translation:—

Of the glorious Body telling,
  O my tongue its mysteries sing;
And the Blood, all price excelling,
  Which for this world's ransoming
In a generous womb once dwelling,
  He shed forth, the Gentiles' King.

Given for us, for us descending
  Of a Virgin to proceed,
Man with man in converse blending
  Scattered He the Gospel seed:
Till His sojourn drew to ending,
  Which He closed in wondrous deed.

At the last Great Supper seated.
  Circled by His brethren's band,
All the Law required, completed
  In the feast its statutes planned,
To the Twelve Himself He meted
  For their food with His own hand.

Word made Flesh, by Word He maketh
  Very Bread His Flesh to be:
Man in wine Christ's Blood partaketh,
  And if senses fail to see,
Faith alone the true heart waketh
  To behold the Mystery.

Therefore we, before it bending,
  This great Sacrament adore:
Types and shadows have their ending
  In the new Rite evermore:
Faith, our outward sense amending,
  Maketh good defects before.

Honour, laud, and praise addressing
  To the Father and the Son,
Might ascribe we, virtue, blessing,
  And eternal benison:
Holy Ghost, from Both progressing,
  Equal laud to Thee be done! Amen.

In the following hymn, "Adoro te devote, latens Deitas," Aquinas seems to take a more spiritual view of the Eucharist—it was probably the product of a higher mood:—

Humbly I adore Thee, hidden Deity,
Which beneath these figures art concealed from me;
Wholly in submission Thee my spirit hails,
For in contemplating Thee it wholly fails.

Taste and touch and vision in Thee are deceived:
But the hearing only may be well believed:
I believe whatever God's own Son declared:
Nothing can be truer than Truth's very Word.

On the Cross lay hidden but Thy Deity:
Here is also hidden Thy humanity:
But in both believing and confessing, Lord,
Ask I what the dying thief of Thee implored.

Though Thy Wounds, like Thomas, I behold not now,
Thee my Lord confessing, and my God, I bow:
Give me ever stronger faith in Thee above,
Give me ever stronger hope and stronger love.

O most sweet memorial of His death and woe,
Living Bread, Which givest life to man below,
Let my spirit ever eat of Thee and live,
And the blest fruition of Thy sweetness give!

Pelican of Mercy, Jesu, Lord and God,
Cleanse me, wretched sinner, in Thy Precious Blood:
Blood, whereof one drop for humankind outpoured
Might from all transgression have the world restored.

Jesu, Thou, whom thus veil'd, I must see below,
When shall that be given which I long for so,
That at last beholding Thy uncover'd Face,
Thou wouldst satisfy me with Thy fullest grace?

And of this whole period we may say, that where the writers depart from the spirituality of the Gospels, their muse fails them; where they are most spiritual they are most poetic. When they strive to express ideas foreign to the spirit of Christ—carnal conceptions of His work, veneration for His cross, the glory of His mother, the worship of relics—the poetic fire burns low, even if it does not quite expire. When they express ideas common to all Christian hearts, they rise to the truest poetry, since sacred poetry of the highest kind is but the expression of *universal* ideas.

The greatest of the mediæval hymn-writers, however, was Adam of St. Victor, who, if not a native of England, was of Brittany. It is impossible to say which, since he is described as "Brito," and this title may refer either to Brittany or Britain. The probability is, since he belonged to a monastery in France, and that most of the famous hymnists of the age were French, that he was also of that nation. At all events he studied in France. It is only quite recently that the great mass of his hymns was brought to light. For nearly seven centuries, a large part remained buried among forgotten manuscripts in the Abbey of St. Victor, in Paris. At the French Revolution, this abbey was dissolved as a religious foundation, its inmates dispersed, and its precious manuscripts removed to the National Library in the Louvre. Till the middle of the present century, only thirty-seven of his hymns had found their way into circulation; but then M. Gautier discovered about forty-eight in the Louvre Library, and published them; but as many of the great events of our Lord's life have no hymn to celebrate them, it is possible, and even likely, that many yet remain undiscovered. or have been either destroyed or lost. Adam of St. Victor is little known through English hymnals, and the reason is this--no translation can adequately represent his hymns. They abound in rhymes which cannot be rendered into English. Their glory is in their *style;* not in the variety of their subject, or picturesqueness of manner, but in the marvellously beautiful expression of his thought. But some idea may be gained of his merit from the praise bestowed upon him by the most competent judges. Rambach calls him "the Schiller of the Middle Ages;" Dr. Neale, "the greatest Latin poet, not only of mediæval, but of all ages," whilst in the preface to his "Mediæval Hymns" (to which I am much indebted in this work), he says, "It is a magnificent thing to pass along the far-stretching vista of hymns, from the sublime self-containedness of St. Ambrose to the more fervid inspiration of St. Gregory, the exquisite typology of Venantius Fortunatus, the lovely painting of St. Peter Damiani, the crystal-like simplicity of St. Notker, the Scriptural calm of Godescalcus, the subjective loveliness of St. Bernard, but all culminate in the full blaze of glory which surrounds Adam of St. Victor, the greatest of all." I give below a translation of one by him for St. Stephen's day, which is generally regarded as the finest he ever wrote:—

Yesterday, with exultation,
Join'd the world in celebration
  Of her promised Saviour's birth:
Yesterday the Angel-nation
Poured the strains of jubilation
  O'er the Monarch born on earth.

But to-day, o'er death victorious,
By his faith and actions glorious,
  By his miracles renown'd,
Dared the Deacon Proto-martyr,
Earthly life for Heaven to barter,
  Faithful midst the faithless found.

Forward, champion, in thy quarrel!
Certain of a certain laurel,
  Holy Stephen, persevere!
Perjur'd witnesses confounding,
Satan's Synagogue astounding
  By thy doctrine true and clear.

Lo! in heaven *thy* Witness liveth:
Bright and faithful proof He giveth
  Of His martyr's blamelessness.
Thou by name *a Crown* impliest;
Meetly then in pangs thou diest
  For the Crown of Righteousness!

For a crown that fadeth never,
Bear the torturer's brief endeavour;
  Victory waits to end the strife.
Death shall be thy birth's beginning,
And life's losing be the winning
  Of the true and better life.

Whom the Holy Ghost endueth,
Whom celestial sight embueth,
  Stephen penetrates the skies;
There God's fullest glory viewing,
There his victor strength renewing,
  For his near reward he sighs.

See, as Jewish foes invade thee,
See how Jesus *stands* to aid thee:
  Stands to guard His champion's death:
Cry that opened heaven is shown thee,
Cry that Jesus waits to own thee,
  Cry it with thy latest breath.

As the dying martyr kneeleth,
For his murderers he appealeth,
And his prayer their pardon sealeth,
  For their madness grieving sore;

Then in Christ he sleepeth sweetly,
Who His pattern kept completely,
And with Christ he reigneth meetly,
Martyr first-fruits, evermore!

To the end of the 11th and the first half of the 12th century (1091-1153) belongs Bernard of Clairvaux, who has been called "the last of the Apostles," and "the holiest monk that ever lived." To him we probably owe the long poem on the Name of Jesus which generally goes by the name "Jesus dulcis memoria." It is sometimes called the "Jubilus of St. Bernard," and by mediæval writers, the "Rosy Hymn." From this we have the three centos "Jesu, the very thought of Thee;" and "O Jesu King most wonderful," translated by Father Caswall; and "Jesu, Thou joy of loving hearts," translated by Dr. Ray Palmer—a well-loved trilogy; whilst Paul Gerhardt's hymn which begins in Dr. J. W. Alexander's translation "O Sacred Head, once wounded" is drawn from his "Salve Caput cruentatum," a poem of 350 lines, in which 50 lines are devoted to each of the limbs of our Lord. It is not absolutely certain that these and other poems ascribed to Bernard of Clairvaux were actually written by him; even Mabillon, the editor of his works, is doubtful as to his authorship of them, and many have shared his doubt; but Archbishop Trench, the editor of "Sacred Latin Poetry," a critic of large knowledge and fine insight, gives it as his opinion that they are from his pen, and says—"if he did not write them it is not easy to guess who could have written them; and, indeed, they bear profoundly the stamp of his mind, being only inferior in beauty to his prose." Positive proof may indeed be lacking, but the internal evidence is very strong for the authorship of the saintly Abbot of Clairvaux; and whilst the controversies in which he engaged with Abelard, the part he played in the Crusades, and his mystical sermons on the Canticles are well nigh forgotten save by students of ecclesiastical history, yet his hymns (if they are really his) are familiar and full of inspiration to multitudes, even of the most unlettered in our day. Thus the sacred Poet whose verses appeal to the *heart* is far surer of remembrance than the Theologue who discourses of doctrine which appeals only to the intellect, and is ever changing its forms.

To a period a little later belongs Bernard of Morlaix (the place of his birth), or as he is sometimes styled, of Clugny (the name of his monastery). Born though he was at Morlaix in Bretagne, he yet came of English parentage. Of his life, little is known save that he entered the Abbey of Clugny, of which Peter the Venerable was the head. To him we owe the hymn of three thousand lines, called sometimes "De contemptu mundi," and sometimes "Hora Novissima," from which so many centos have been drawn—the best known being "Jerusalem the golden," To Thee, O dear, dear country," and "Brief life is here our portion." Bernard attributed to a special inspiration of the Spirit of God the power to write so extended a hymn in such a difficult metre. It was written, strange to say, as a satire against the vices and follies of his age. It is remarkable that a *satire* should have given to the church some of her most popular hymns. The case is probably unique. The portions taken for translation by Dr. Neale are the more jubilant ones, and give no idea of the sadness and self abasement of the poem as a whole.

Of it, Dr. Neale says: "I have no hesitation in saying that I look on these verses of Bernard as the most lovely, in the same way that the 'Dies Iræ' is the most sublime, and the 'Stabat Mater' the most pathetic of mediæval poems."

It is curious that to one Bernard (of Clairvaux) we should owe some of the most prized of our hymns concerning Christ, and to another Bernard (of Morlaix or Clugny) the hymns most frequently sung concerning Heaven.

The "Veni Sancte Spiritus" ("Holy Spirit, Lord of Light"), the loveliest, in Archbishop Trench's opinion, of all the hymns in the whole circle of sacred Latin poetry, is admitted by all the great authorities to be by King Robert II. of France (997-1031), who was singularly addicted to church music, which he enriched, as well as hymnody, with many compositions of his own. It is said that "he placed himself, robed and crowned, among the choristers of St. Denis, and led the musicians in singing psalms and hymns of his own composition."

To this period belong those forms of hymns called Sequences. A specimen of these, familiar to all, may be found in the well-known "The strain upraise of joy and praise," translated from Godescalcus by Dr. Neale. I cannot do better than give Dr. Neale's beautiful account of the origin of Sequences:—

"It is well known that the origin of sequences themselves is to be looked for in the *Alleluia* of the Gradual, sung between the Epistle and Gospel. During this melody it was necessary that the deacon should have time to ascend from his place at the altar to the rood-loft, that he might thence sing the Gospel. Hence the prolongation of the last syllable in the Alleluia of the Gradual, in thirty, forty, fifty, or even a hundred notes; the *neuma* of which ritualistic writers speak so much. True, there was no sense in this last syllable and its lengthening out, but the mystical interpreters had their explanation: 'the way in which we praise God in our country is yet unknown.'

"And good people were content for some three hundred years with this service; and, as it has been very truly observed, the attempt itself, if one may use the expression, to explain the sound into sense, manifests a little of the rationalism with which the Eastern has always taunted the Western Church. But, towards the beginning of the eleventh century, there was a certain Swiss monk, by name Notker. The defects of every religious person were well known in the house where he resided, and a slight lisp in his speech gave him the surname of *Balbulus*. He had resided for some years in that marvellous monastery of S. Gall; the church of which was the pattern of all monastic edifices, till it was eclipsed by a church, the description of which now reads like a most glorious dream—Clugny. While watching the samphire gatherers on the precipitous cliffs that surrounded S. Gall, Notker had composed the world-famous hymn, 'In the midst of life we are in death.' But desirous of obtaining the best education which Christendom could afford, he afterwards betook himself to the monastery of Jumièges, and there formed an acquaintance with many of its monks. With one of them he had, it seems, a friendly discussion, whether the interminable *in* of the Alleluia might not be altered into a religious sense; a discussion which, for the time, had no result. But Jumièges, in common with so many other French monasteries, was desolated by the barbarian Normans. Whereupon Notker's friend, bethinking himself of S. Gall, took refuge in that great house; and the discussion which, years before, had commenced, was again carried on between the two associates. At length Notker determined to put words to the notes which had hitherto only interminably prolonged the Alleluia. He did so; and, as a first attempt, produced a sequence which began with the line—

'Laudes Deo concinat orbis universus,'

and which has lately been republished. He brought this, notes and all, on a parchment rolled round a cylinder of wood, to Yso, precentor of what we should now call the *Cantoris* side. Yso looked kindly on the composition, but said that he must refer it to Marcellus, the precentor on the *Decani* side. These two sang the sequence over together, and observed that sometimes two notes went to one syllable in a slur, sometimes three or four syllables went to one note in a kind of recitative. Yso thereupon was charged with the message that the verses would not answer their purpose. Notker, not much discouraged, revised his composition; and now, instead of (for the first line) *Laudes Deo concinat orbis universus*, he substituted *Laudes Deo concinat orbis ubique totus;* instead of the second line, *Coluber Adæ deceptor*, he now wrote *Coluber Adæ male-suasor;* which, as he himself tells us, when the good-natured Yso had sung over to himself, he gave thanks to God, he commended the new composition to the brethren of the monastery, and more especially to Othmar, Yso's brother by blood. Such then was the origin of sequences, at first called Proses, because written rather in rhythmical prose than with any attention to metre. St. Notker died about 912."

The introduction of such sequences into the worship of nearly all our English churches, furnishes one illustration, out of many which might be given, of the strange ways in which churches most remote from one another in doctrine and ritual, profit each other.

CHAPTER VI.

THE METRICAL PSALMS.

We have, in previous chapters, considered the hymns of the first ages of the Church and Mediæval times, although their introduction, in an English dress, to the hymnals of this country belongs to the later years of the present century. Those of the Latin Church were, doubtless, used in their original forms in the times before the Reformation, and came to our land in the Breviaries of the Roman Church, but those of the Eastern Church were used neither in their original nor translated forms till our own time. When England belonged to the Roman Church, her service of praise doubtless consisted of the Psalms in the Vulgate version, and the Breviary hymns in their original Latin. But when she threw off the yoke of Rome, the Psalms of the English Prayer Book, which were at first only *said*, began not long after through metrical versions, to be *sung*.* "Song has

* It should not be forgotten that the "said or sung" of the Prayer Book is a simple euphemism taken from the old Offices, and really meaning monotoned, which is equivalent to "said," or with inflexions which is equivalent to "sung." Even up to 1662 there remained a rubric by which not only the Psalms and Canticles but also the Lessons were directed to be "sung after the manner of distinct reading to a plain tune."

been a feature of every new up-springing of truth, or marked deliverance at the hand of God." The name of *Lollard*, indeed, was given to the witnesses for evangelical truth in the Low Countries, and in England and Scotland, from their habit of singing, and is connected with our word *lull*—to sing softly; they were *the sweet singers*. And the Reformation time, of which the Lollards were the heralds, was marked in relation to song by three closely connected features: (1) Their songs were in the mother tongue, instead of the Latin, in which before, all public worship had been conducted. (2) They assumed metrical form; and (3) they were for the use of the people at large, and not, as in the Roman Church, for the priests alone. This last feature was one of the great objects of the Reformers, and brought in its train the two preceding ones, since, for the people to sing, it was necessary that the songs should be in their native speech, whilst, for really united singing, metrical form was necessary. It is far more difficult for a congregation to chant Psalms than to sing them in metre, since, in the former, there is uncertainty as to how many syllables are to be given to the reciting note, whilst in the latter, each syllable is wedded to a corresponding note of the tune. Here lies the real motive which led to the rendering of the Psalms in metrical form. The Reformation was a people's movement, and so it demanded songs which the people could both understand and sing.

Before this time there existed Early Hymns, Carols both religious and secular, and translations of Breviary Hymns, but they did not come into church use, partly because of the apathy of the clergy, and partly because of the ignorance and indifference of the people.

The earliest of all the versions of the Psalms in the popular tongue was the celebrated one into French, of Clement Marot, a writer to whom even Edmund Spenser was indebted, who translated fifty Psalms, two being added by Calvin, and the rest by Theodore Beza. Goudimel, the first musician of his age, the master of Palestrina, an ardent Protestant, and one of the victims of St. Bartholomew, set these to music, drawing the airs from the popular songs of that time. This became the book of song in all French-speaking countries, attained great popularity, and aided greatly in the spread of the doctrines of the Reformation. "It was the book of song in the castle as well as the cottage; for recreation or at work; for the lady in the hall, the weaver at the loom, the peasant at the plough; the first lesson taught to children, the last words whispered to, or uttered by the dying man." Both the words and music of this collection exercised an important influence on the Scottish version of 1564.

Even before the Reformation time in England, Miles Coverdale had made metrical versions of certain of the Psalms, whilst the three brothers Wedderburn, in Scotland, had rendered a similar service by the issue of what is known as the *Dundee Psalms*. But the first complete, or nearly complete, metrical version into English, is that which goes by the name of Sternhold and Hopkins. Whilst most of the versions are by them, the remainder was gradually added by others. It was first published in London in parts, and afterwards, with additions, in Geneva, on account of the English-speaking refugees who had found shelter in that city. It was adopted as the version for use in the Church of England in 1562, and continued to be used for more than 235 years. About

350 editions of it were issued during that time; being gradually superseded in the Church of England by the version known as Tate and Brady's. It held its ground, however, among the Nonconformists until supplanted by the Psalms of Dr. Watts. In the Established Church until comparatively recent times, when hymns came into favour, the version of Tate and Brady continued to be sung. The Royal assent to Tate and Brady gave leave to adopt it, but did not impose it on the church, and it was more than a hundred years before it was generally adopted. So late as 1828 a new edition by Sternhold and Hopkins was issued for use. At that time hymn books were springing up in considerable numbers. Royal assent had indeed been given to other versions, *e.g.*, King James, George Wither, Patrick, and Blackmore. But the Church did not avail herself of it, partly because of their defects, and partly because of the unwillingness to make a change, and so Sternhold and Hopkins, and Tate and Brady held the field. Dr. Watts is the real connecting link between the age of the metrical versions and that of hymns, since his Psalms partake of the nature of both. The earlier versions were, in reality, the Psalms done into metre; Dr. Watts' are an accommodation of the Psalms to New Testament thought and language. Over the bridge erected by him, the English churches of all sections passed from the use of metrical Psalms to hymn-singing pure and simple—the prose translation being retained for recitation or chanting. In English Nonconformity, in some cases, Sternhold and Hopkins gave way to versions by Barton, Patrick,* who was himself a churchman, and others, but such versions had only a limited and local

* A selection from his Psalms was long used at the Charterhouse.

acceptance. At last, however, and about the same time, both in the Established and Nonconformist churches, the metrical versions gave way to hymns. This was not the case, however, in Scotland and the Presbyterian Church generally. There, the version of the Wedderburns prevailed over a limited area, and in an early time; but there, as in England, Sternhold and Hopkins was the first version generally used. But even in this, certain alterations were made; versions of certain Psalms being by other hands. While the 100th by Kethe, and the 124th by Whittingham, are common to the English and Scottish versions, and the 136th by Craig is substituted for Churchyard's version, additional versions by Craig of the 143rd and 145th were inserted from the Genevan edition. Sternhold and Hopkins, thus improved, was adopted by order of the General Assembly in 1564, and continued in use till 1650. The collection used in Presbyterian Churches, even to our own day, is due, however, to the action of the Westminster Assembly in 1643. The version selected by them was by Francis Rous, Provost of Eaton College, Oxford. The Assembly, however, could not agree on the matter, and hence the version of Rous gained no place in the churches of England; but the General Assembly in Scotland took up the matter where the Westminster divines had left it, and, with Rous's version for a basis, and with the addition of translations from the old Scottish Psalter, and after many alterations, the new collection was finally adopted by the Church of Scotland. From that time to the present, it has held its place in the worship of the Presbyterian section of the Church, both in Scotland and other lands, and there still remain a few who would restrict the song of the Church to these metrical Psalms. In a recent book (1886), the "Memoir of Henry Bazeley, the Oxford Evangelist," by the Rev. E. L. Hicks, M.A., there is an elaborate plea, by the subject of the memoir, for the exclusive use of the Psalms, as being the only inspired songs. Full of earnestness, however, as is this plea, it is unsupported by anything like reasonable argument, and is chiefly remarkable for the fact that a man trained in the University of Oxford, but who afterwards joined the Church of Scotland, should have grown narrow enough in thought to have put it forth. There are not wanting symptoms that its day is nearly over—only a selection from it is retained in the latest book, "Church Praise" of the English Presbyterian Church—and, in course of time, it will doubtless pass away altogether, before the nobler hymnody of the age; but for nearly 250 years it held its ground. It would be useless to argue the question of its defects. To the Scotch it is precious because of its early associations; but to the English, who regard it on its merits, whilst allowing that some versions of great beauty may be found in it, yet as a whole it seems utterly unworthy of retention in a time like our own, so rich in noble songs. It certainly has the great merit, in which Dr. Watts' version is the most deficient of all, that it adheres closely to the actual ideas of the Biblical Psalms. To the English mind, it is true, these ideas are, for the most part, presented in their least attractive form when stretched on the procrustean bed of modern metre. Still, it is one of the links with the Psalm-singing of the past; and from its historic and spiritual associations, ours shall not be the hand to touch it roughly. In the Nonconformist Churches of England, the transition from Psalm-singing in the versions of Sternhold and Hopkins, Patrick, Barton, and others, to hymn-singing was, as we have said, brought about by the labours of Dr. Watts, whose version of the Psalms forms a kind of connecting link between the two, partaking as they do of the characteristics of both. The elements in them drawn from the Book of Psalms connect them with the age of the metrical versions, whilst the elements drawn from the New Testament connect them with the hymn-singing era which followed, and of which Dr. Watts was the real pioneer.

Many other metrical versions of the Psalms were made in early times—by Sir Philip Sidney and his sister Mary, Countess of Pembroke, Bishop King, George Sandys, Lord Bacon of seven of the Psalms, and others; some of these were highly poetic, but not cast in a form suitable or public worship, and never came into use in the Church.

Those who desire to pursue the subject further should consult "The Story of the Psalters," by Henry Alexander Bell (Kegan Paul & Co., 1888) who gives an account of 123 complete versions of the Psalms, and specimens from each, of renderings of the 1st and 23rd Psalm. In the following table of editions now in the British Museum Library, the relative popularity of the principal versions is clearly seen:—

	1549 to 1600	1601 to 1650	1651 to 1700	1701 to 1750	1751 to 1800	1801 to 1868	Total
Sternhold	47	206	102	120	105	21	601
Tate & Brady	...	...	6	35	103	159	303
Scotch version	...	...	17	9	28	44	98
Watts	...	...	...	7	32	58	97
Wesley	...	...	...	2	8	3	13
King James	...	8	...	...	...	...	8
Barton	...	1	4	2	...	...	7
Patrick	...	...	3	4	...	...	7

CHAPTER VII.

EARLY ENGLISH HYMNS.

THERE are few, if any, English hymns to be found before the beginning of the seventeenth century. To the fifteenth century belong a few hymns addressed to the Virgin and Christ. These have been edited from the Lambert MS., No. 853, by Mr. Furnivall, for the Early English Text Society. One of these, on "The Sweetness of Jesus," is very tender and beautiful; another, on "The Love of Jesus," likens love to a fire which cleanses us from sin, and joins man to God. But since worship had not yet come to be offered through the vernacular, it is all but certain that such hymns were only for private reading and meditation.

Before the seventeenth century, there is much noble sacred English *poetry*, but few, if any hymns capable of being sung in the congregation. And these poems, as it has been well said, were "too subtle and fanciful ever to come home to the hearts of the people. They were written for a choice few to enjoy. They were full of those subtle allusions, half the pleasure of which consists in the ingenuity required to understand as well as to invent them. Such hymns could never be sung, like Luther's, by little children at Christmas, or become a nation's battle-song, or sweetly distil peace at moments when heart and flesh failed, and mortal effort was impossible; when the soul had lost its power to cling to anything. The verses of this period bear witness to the piety or the poetical power of the writers rather than to the faith of the times." This is true, especially when the general ignorance of the people of that time is taken into account. The spread of education has, however, now quickened intelligence, and made men capable of appreciating a style of hymn which, in earlier times, would have been beyond them. This will account for the presence, in our hymnals, of verses known in early times only to those of the literary class; whilst, in addition to this, it must be remembered that the habit of these earlier times was to look to one hymnist rather than to a multitude for the provision of hymns for worship. Indeed, the really hymn-singing age was not yet, and did not begin till the time of Watts. But still, scattered over the then existing English literature, there were the materials for a good, if not a large book of worship-song. It remained for our own age to search out and utilise these overlooked and neglected treasures.

The hymn, "O Lord, turn not Thy face from me," attributed by some to John Mardley, and by others to John Marckant, and belonging to about the middle of the 16th century, is probably the earliest really English hymn to be found in our present-day hymnals. Sir Egerton Brydges is inclined to attribute some versions of the Psalms in Sternhold and Hopkins signed M. to Mardley. The hymn to which we have referred is not without merit. It is usually given in the variation of Bishop Heber. Here is the original:—

O Lord, turn not Thy face from me,
 Who lie in woeful state,
Lamenting all my woeful life,
 Before Thy mercy-gate;

A gate which opens wide to those
 That do lament their sin:
Shut not that gate against me, Lord,
 But let me enter in.

And call me not to strict account.
 How I have sojourned here,
For then my guilty conscience knows
 How vile I shall appear.

So come I to Thy mercy gate,
 Where mercy doth abound;
Imploring pardon for my sin,
 To heal my deadly wound.

Mercy, good Lord, mercy I ask,
 This is the total sum;
For mercy, Lord, is all my suit:
 O let Thy mercy come.

George Sandys (1577-1643), is a much more notable contributor to hymnody. Dryden called him "the best versifier of his age." He wrote "a Paraphrase upon the Psalms of David, and upon the hymns dispersed throughout the Old and New Testaments," and poetical versions of the Song of Solomon, Job, and Ecclesiastes. The most notable of his renderings is of the 61st Psalm, beginning "Happy sons of Israel."

George Wither (1588-1667), wrote too much, it is true, but scattered over his writings are hymns that are likely to retain their place in the song of the Church. The best known are "Come, O come, with sacred lays;" "The Lord is King, and weareth," a version of the 93rd Psalm; and "Lord, living here are we," a hymn for the anniversary of marriage—quaint and beautiful, and not unlike to George Herbert. It is so little known that I append it:—

Lord, living here are we,
As fast united yet,
As when our hands and hearts by Thee
Together first were knit!
And in a thankful song
Now sing we will Thy praise,
For that Thou dost as well prolong
Our loving as our days.

Together we have now
Begun another year,
But how much time Thou wilt allow
Thou mak'st it not appear.
We therefore do implore
That live and love we may
Still so, as if but one day more
Together we should stay.

Let each of other's wealth
Preserve a faithful care,
And of each other's joy and health
As if one soul we were.
Such conscience let us make
Each other not to grieve,
As if we daily were to take
Our everlasting leave.

The frowardness that springs
From our corrupted kind,
Or from those troublous outward things
Which may distract the mind;
Permit Thou not, O Lord,
Our constant love to shake,
Or to disturb our true accord,
Or make our hearts to ache.

But let these frailties prove
Affection's exercise,
And that discretion teach our love
Which wins the noblest prize.
So time which wears away
And ruins all things else,
Shall fix our love on Thee for aye,
In whom perfection dwells.

Robert Herrick (born 1591) is better known by the secular poetry of his "Hesperides," than by his contributions to sacred song, which are included in "Noble Numbers," but his "Litany to the Holy Spirit," though containing verses ill adapted for public worship, as will be seen below, yet is in parts tender and beautiful.

In the hour of my distress,
When temptations me oppress,
And when I my sins confess,
Sweet Spirit, comfort me!

When I lie within my bed,
Sick in heart and sick in head,
And with doubts discomforted,
Sweet Spirit, comfort me!

When the house doth sigh and weep,
And the world is drowned in sleep,
Yet mine eyes the watch do keep,
Sweet Spirit, comfort me!

When the artless doctor sees
No one hope, but of his fees,
And his skill runs on the lees,
Sweet Spirit, comfort me!

When his potion and his pill,
Is of none or little skill,
Meet for nothing but to kill,
Sweet Spirit, comfort me!

When the passing-bell doth toll,
And the furies in a shoal
Come to fright a parting soul,
Sweet Spirit, comfort me!

When the tapers now burn blue,
And the comforters are few,
And that number more than true,
Sweet Spirit, comfort me!

When the priest his last hath prayed,
And I nod to what is said
Cause my speech is now decayed,
Sweet Spirit, comfort me!

When, God knows, I'm tossed about,
Either with despair or doubt,
Yet, before the glass be out,
Sweet Spirit, comfort me!

When the tempter me pursueth
With the sins of all my youth,
And half damns me with untruth,
Sweet Spirit, comfort me!

When the flames and hellish cries
Fright mine ears and fright mine eyes,
And all terrors me surprise,
Sweet Spirit, comfort me!

When the Judgment is revealed,
And that opened which was sealed,
When to Thee I have appealed,
Sweet Spirit, comfort me!

George Herbert, the model parish priest of Bemerton, is better known as a writer of sacred poetry—quaint and suggestive in character—than as a writer of hymns; but in his well-known book, "The Temple," verses so lovely are found, that, with slight alterations, they have been pressed into the service of the Church's song. Examples may be found in his rendering of the 23rd Psalm, beginning "The God of Love my Shepherd is," "Let all the world in every corner sing," and "Teach me, my God and King," called "The Elixir." We append the second of these:—

Let all the world in every corner sing
My God and King!
The heavens are not too high;
His praise may thither fly:
The earth is not too low;
His praises there may grow.
Let all the world in every corner sing
My God and King!

Let all the world in every corner sing
My God and King!
The Church with psalms must shout:
No door can keep them out:
But, above all, the heart
Must bear the longest part.
Let all the world in every corner sing
My God and King!

Parts of a poem called "Discipline," beginning "Throw away Thy rod," have been included in certain hymnals, but they are, in our judgment, not suited for singing, and are scarcely compatible with high thoughts of the Divine discipline of men.

Bishop Cosin finds a place among the hymnists by his rendering of the "Veni, Creator, Spiritus," beginning "Come, Holy Ghost, our souls inspire," incorporated into the Ordination Service of the English Prayer Book; the only hymn which has found a place in the venerable Liturgy of that Church.

Sir Thomas Browne (1605-1682), the well-known author of the "Religio Medici," is known in religious circles even better by his lovely Evening Hymn, "The night is come; like to the day," than he is by his famous book. As this hymn probably contains the germ out of which Bishop Ken's far better known Evening Hymn grew, I append it, that readers may judge for themselves to what extent Ken was indebted to the hymn of the learned Norwich physician :—

The night is come, like to the day
Depart not Thou, great God, away.
Let not my sins, black as the night,
Eclipse the lustre of Thy light.
Keep still in my horizon; for to me
The sun makes not the day, but Thee.
Thou, whose nature cannot sleep,
On my temples sentry keep;
Guard me 'gainst those watchful foes
Whose eyes are open while mine close.
Let no dreams my head infest
But such as Jacob's temples blest.
While I do rest, my soul advance;
Make my sleep a holy trance:
That I may, my rest being wrought,
Awake into some holy thought;
And with as active vigour run
My course as doth the nimble sun.
Sleep is a death;—O make me try,
By sleeping, what it is to die!
And as gently lay my head
On my grave as now my bed.
Howe'er I rest, great God. let me
Awake again at last with Thee;
And thus assur'd, behold I lie
Securely, or to wake or die.

These are my drowsy days: in vain
I do now wake to sleep again;
O, come that hour, when I shall never
Sleep again, but wake for ever!

John Milton (1608-1674), translated nine of the Psalms in metre. They are remarkable for fidelity to the original, as well as for their poetic beauty. The best known of these is of the 136th, "Let us with a gladsome mind." Not less worthy are his renderings of parts of the 82nd, 85th, and 86th Psalms, "The Lord will come, and not be slow," and of the 84th Psalm, "How lovely are Thy dwellings fair." These are so fine in quality, and distinctive in character, as to deserve rank as original compositions.

Bishop Jeremy Taylor (1613-1667), published in his book called "The Golden Grove," twenty-two "Festival Hymns," from which the one on "The Second Advent of Christ, or Christ coming to Jerusalem in triumph," has passed, in an altered form, into common use. In the original it begins, "Lord, come away," but in its altered form, "Descend to Thy Jerusalem, O Lord."

John Austin (died 1669), who belonged originally to the Church of England, but afterwards joined the Roman communion, issued a devotional manual, containing prayers and devout meditations for private and family use, under the title, "Devotions in the Ancient Way of Offices, containing Exercises for every day in the week, and every Holiday in the Year." It contained forty-three hymns, some of which are from his own pen, others are by Richard Crashaw. It received the rare honour of being adapted for the use of members of the English Church. This is not to be wondered at, since Austin's mind combined, in a very high degree, devoutness of feeling with deep insight into truth. He is one of the few men who reach through the letter to the spirit. Two of his hymns have, in recent times, been included in hymnals, and are likely to acquire a well-deserved popularity. "Blest be Thy love, dear Lord," is a hymn as true in thought as it is simple and tender in expression :—

Blest be Thy love, dear Lord,
That taught us this sweet way,
Only to love Thee for Thyself,
And for that love obey.

O Thou, our souls' chief hope!
We to Thy mercy fly;
Where'er we are, Thou canst protect,
Whate'er we need, supply.

Whether we sleep or wake,
To Thee we both resign;
By night we see, as well as day,
If Thy light on us shine.

Whether we live or die,
Both we submit to Thee;
In death we live, as well as life,
If Thine in death we be.

Whilst "Hark, my soul, how everything," is both poetically and lyrically lovely :—

Hark, my soul, how everything
Strives to serve our bounteous King;
Each a double tribute pays,
Sings its part, and then obeys.

Nature's chief and sweetest quire,
Him with cheerful notes admire;
Chanting every day their lauds
While the grove their song applauds.

Though their voices lower be,
Streams have too their melody;
Night and day they warbling run,
Never pause, but still sing on.

All the flowers that gild the spring
Hither their still music bring;
If Heaven bless them, thankful, they
Smell more sweet, and look more gay.

Only we can scarce afford
This short office to our Lord;
We, on whom His bounty flows,
All things gives, and nothing owes.

Wake! for shame, my sluggish heart,
Wake! and gladly sing thy part;
Learn of birds, and springs, and flowers,
How to use thy nobler powers.

Call all nature to thy aid,
Since 'twas He whole nature made;
Join in one eternal song,
Who to one God all belong.

Live for ever, glorious Lord!
Live, by all Thy works adored!
One in Three, and Three in One,
Thrice we bow to Thee alone!

The man who wrote such hymns as these must have been resting on those sublime truths which underlie even the corruptions of the Roman Church.

From Henry More, the Platonist (1614-1687), a few verses have passed through the adaptations of John Wesley, first into "Hymns and Sacred Poems," by John and Charles Wesley, and thence into the hymnals of different sections of the Methodist body. He belongs, however, to philosophy rather than hymnody.

Richard Baxter (1615-1691), produced a metrical version of the Psalms, which was published after his death, and also two volumes of poetry. From the latter, two hymns have passed into collections. "Lord, it belongs not to my care" is part of a larger hymn, consisting of eight verses of eight lines each, called "The Covenant and Confidence of Faith." It is so evidently the utterance of the heart, and so tenderly expressed, that it has won for itself a wide and deserved popularity among all sections of the Church. The finest verse is :—

Christ leads me through no darker rooms
  Than He went through before;
He that into God's kingdom comes,
  Must enter by His door.

"Ye holy angels bright," a Psalm of Praise, has merit, but lacks the distinctiveness and individuality of the former.

The well-known hymn "Jerusalem, my happy home" belongs to this period. Of its authorship little is known. It is contained in a MS. quarto volume number 15,225 in the British Museum, the date of which seems (from the internal evidence) to be about 1616. The hymn itself (which is entitled, "A Song," by F. B. P., to the tune "Diana") is probably of Queen Elizabeth's time. F. B. P. is usually regarded as standing for Francis Baker, Priest; but this is mere conjecture. In earlier days, it was attributed to David Dickson. Dr. Neale says :—"It was most impudently appropriated to himself, and mixed up with a quantity of his own rubbish, by one Dickson, a Covenanter." The hymn has undergone so many alterations at various times, that our readers may perhaps be glad to see it in its original form.

Hierusalem! my happie Home!
  When shall I come to thee?
When shall my sorrows have an end?
  Thy joyes when shall I see?

O happie harbor of the saints,
  O sweete and pleasant soyle,
In thee no sorrow may be found,
  Noe greefe, noe care, noe toyle!

In thee noe sicknesse may be seene,
  Noe hurt, noe ache, noe sore;
There is noe death, nor ugly devill,
  But Life for evermore.

Noe dampish mist is seene in thee,
Noe cold nor darksome night;
There everie soule shines as the sun;
There God Himselfe gives light.

There lust and lucre cannot dwell,
There envy bears no sway;
There is noe hunger, heate, nor colde,
But pleasure everie way.

Hierusalem! Hierusalem!
God grant I once may see
Thy endless joyes, and of the same
Partaker aye to bee!

Thy walls are made of pretious stones,
Thy bulwarkes diamondes square,
Thy gates are of right orient pearle,
Exceedinge riche and rare.

Thy turrettes and thy pinnacles
With carbuncles doe shine;
Thy verrie streets are paved with gould,
Surpassinge clear and fine.

Thy houses are of yvorie,
Thy windows crystal cleare;
Thy tyles are made of beaten gould;
—O God, that I were there!

Within thy gates nothinge doth come
That is not passinge cleane;
Noe spider's web, no durt, no dust,
Noe filthe may there be seene.

Ah! my sweete Home, Hierusalem,
Would God I were in thee!
Would God my woes were at an end,
Thy joyes that I might see!

Thy saints are crowned with glorie great,
They see God face to face;
They triumph still, they still reioyce;
Most happie is their case.

Wee that are heere in banishment
Continuallie doe moane;
We sigh and sobbe, we weepe and waile,
Perpetuallie we groane.

Our sweete is mixed with bitter gaule,
Our pleasure is but paine;
Our ioyes scarce last the lookeing on,
Our sorrowes still remaine.

But there they live in such delight,
  Such pleasure and such play,
As that to them a thousand yeares
  Doth seeme as yesterday.

Thy vineyardes and thy orchardes are
  Most beautifull and faire,
Full furnished with trees and fruits,
  Most wonderfull and rare.

Thy gardens and thy gallant walkes
  Continually are greene;
There growe such sweet and pleasant flowers
  As noe where else are seene.

There's nectar and ambrosia made
  There's muske and civette sweete;
There manie a fair and daintie drugge
  Are troden under feete.

There cinnamon, there sugar grows,
  There narde and balm abound:
What tounge can telle or harte conceive
  The ioys that there are found?

Quyt through the streetes, with silver sound,
  The Flood of Life do flowe;
Upon whose bankes, on everie syde,
  The Wood of Life doth growe.

There trees for evermore beare fruite,
  And evermore doe springe;
There evermore the angels sit,
  And evermore doe singe.

There David stands, with harpe in hands,
  As master of the queere;
Tenne thousand times that man were blest,
  That might this musicke heare!

Our Ladie singes *Magnificat*,
  With tune surpassinge sweete;
And all the Virginns beare their parte
  Sitting aboue her feete.

Te Deum doth Saint Ambrose singe,
  Saint Austine doth the like;
Ould Simeon and Zacharie
  Have not their songes to seeke.

There Magdalene hath left her mone,
  And cheerfullie doth singe
With blessed Saints, whose harmonie
  In everie street doth ringe.

Hierusalem! my happie Home!
Would God I were in thee!
Would God my woes were at an end,
Thy joyes that I might see!

Of the writers of the period covered by this chapter we may say generally, that none of them made hymn-writing a distinct object. It may be questioned whether any of them wrote hymns with the idea of their being sung in worship. Most of them are adaptations, either from poems, or verses written for private reading or meditation. They are sporadic utterances due to the lyric feeling which forced itself into expression. And the reason is evident: song, save in metrical versions of the Psalms, was unknown in the Church of those times. Sternhold and Hopkins monopolised the choir, and therefore there was no demand to create a supply of hymns. This accounts for their paucity during this period; and it also accounts for the great merit of most of those which were produced. They were not productions of men who wrote to order, but of those who could not help breaking into song. Quality, not quantity, is the characteristic of this period of hymnody, which bears the mark of the freshness and power so evident in the literature of that age.

CHAPTER VIII.

INCREASE OF THE HYMNIC FACULTY.

We are now nearing a period on which the coming glory of hymnody begins to cast its light. Foregleams of the hymn-singing ages now become visible. Of this period, George MacDonald, in his "England's Antiphon," says:—"We find ourselves now in the zone of *hymn*-writing. From this period, that is, from toward the close of the seventeenth century, a large amount of the fervour of the country finds vent in hymns: they are innumerable." John Mason, who died in 1694, is, perhaps, the first Englishman who set himself, with success, to produce hymns for actual use in worship. They were probably the first to be used in congregational worship in England. He wrote thirty-four songs of praise, six penitential hymns, and a version of the 86th Psalm. To these were added "Penitential Cries," chiefly by the Rev. Thomas Shepherd, an Independent minister, of Braintree. These, and the hymns included in W. Barton's "Psalms and Hymns" (1681), and his "Six Centuries of Select Hymns" (1688), formed the thin end of the wedge by means of which, at last, hymn singing found its way into the services of the Independents, who, therefore, are the true pioneers of hymn singing in England; but, at the same time, the first real hymn writer of merit belongs to the Established Church, for John Mason *is* a writer of great merit. This is evident from the fact that, although William Barton preceded him, none of Barton's hymns have established themselves in the favour of the Church. Mr. Enoch Watts, in a letter urging his brother to publish his hymns, rests his plea on the ground that "Mason now reduces this kind of writing to a sort of yawning indifference, and honest Barton chimes us asleep." The Church of later times has endorsed the second part of this plea by rejecting Barton's hymns, but it has repudiated the first part by retaining the finest of Mason's hymns, which are clearly growing in popularity. There are those in our day who prefer Mason to Watts himself. George MacDonald says of Mason's hymns:—"Dr. Watts was very fond of them; would that he had written with similar modesty of style!" Their popularity, even in those times, is seen in the fact that they passed through twenty editions. Montgomery says of his hymns:—"The style is a middle tint between the raw colouring of Quarles and the day-light clearness of Watts." Speaking of both Mason and Shepherd, George MacDonald says:—"In the writings of both we recognise a straightforwardness of expression equal to that of Wither, and a quaint simplicity of thought and form like that of Herrick; while the very charm of some of the best lines is their spontaneity. The men have just enough mysticism to afford them homeliest figures for deepest feelings." It seems to me that John Mason's style is best accounted for by two influences; one derived from George Herbert, whose poems, it is clear, he knew and loved, and the other from the fact that his purpose in writing his hymns was that they should be *sung*. The first accounts for his method of thought; the second for his style of verse. Deeper than both these influences, of course, was the devout and thoughtful nature of the man himself. To all these combined we owe his fine hymns, so increasingly prized, and which are fast recovering the place from which they were pushed by the hymns of Dr. Watts (which for so long held exclusive possession of the Independent Church). Rarely did Watts rise to the height of thought and beauty of expression which are found in Mason's hymns. Here are specimens:—

Now from the altar of our hearts
    Let incense-flames arise.
Assist us, Lord, to offer up
    Our evening sacrifice.

Awake! our love; awake! our joy,
    Awake! our heart and tongue;
Sleep not when mercies loudly call;
    Break forth into a song.

Minutes and mercies multiplied
    Have made up all this day;
Minutes came quick, but mercies were
    More fleet and free than they.

New time, new favours, and new joys
    Do a new song require:
Till we shall praise Thee as we would,
    Accept our hearts' desire.

Lord of our time, whose hand hath set
    New time upon our score;
Thee may we praise for all our time,
    When time shall be no more.

and what is, perhaps, his finest hymn, of which I quote the first three verses:—

Thou wast, O God, and Thou wast blest,
    Before the world began;
Of Thine eternity possest
    Before time's hour glass ran.
Thou needest none Thy praise to sing.
    As if Thy joy could fade;
Couldst Thou have needed anything,
    Thou couldst have nothing made.

Great and good God, it pleasèd Thee
Thy Godhead to declare;
And what Thy goodness did decree.
Thy greatness did prepare;
Thou spak st, and heaven and earth appeared
And answered to Thy call;
As if their Maker's voice they heard,
Which is the creature's all.

To whom, Lord, should I sing, but Thee,
The Maker of my tongue?
Lo, other lords would seize on me,
But I to Thee belong.
As waters haste into their sea,
And earth unto its earth,
So let my soul return to Thee,
From whom it had its birth.

So good a judge as George MacDonald regards this as one of the very finest hymns in the language. I once quoted the lines—

To whom, Lord, should I sing but Thee,
The Maker of my tongue,

to Mr. T. H. Gill, the well known hymnist, and shall never forget his ecstatic delight. The influence George Herbert exerted over Mason is seen in the hymn, "Blest day of God, most calm, most bright," which is clearly an echo of Herbert's "O day most calm, most bright." The influence of Herbert over Mason is as evident as that exerted by Mason over Watts. Had Mason's lot been cast in a later and hymn singing age, he would probably have reached a more perfect hymnic style. The compactness of his thoughts would then have taken on more lyric forms. But still, he deserves lasting honour as one of the very few who wrote fine hymns in English before the hymn singing era really began.

Thomas Shepherd (1665-1739), belongs to a somewhat later period, but should perhaps, be mentioned here, both because he belongs to the same school, and because his hymns were so closely associated with those of Mason. He wrote twenty "Penitential Psalms." His style is like that of Mason, but his verses lack his vigour and insight. He was originally a clergyman in Buckinghamshire, but joined the Independents, and became pastor of the church in which another great hymnist, Doddridge, afterwards ministered, at Northampton. His finest hymn contains the following verses—

Alas! my God, that we should be
Such strangers to each other!
O that as friends we might agree,
And walk and talk together!

Thou know'st my soul doth dearly love,
The place of Thine abode;
No music drops so sweet a sound
As these two words, *My God.*

If Henry Vaughan (1621-1695), the "Silurist's" lot had been cast in a hymn-singing age, he would have been almost sure to have written noble hymns, but there was then no musician waiting to wed his words to music, nor choir ready to sing them when thus wedded, and so he wrote only for men to *read.* Still, there is a rich mine of sacred *ideas* in his poetry, which only need setting by the skilful hymnist to shine in the crown of worship. Both Vaughan, and his predecessor, Herbert, with whom he has so much in common, might be to hymnists what Spenser is to the poets. Two of Vaughan's hymns have found their way into modern collections, viz.: "My soul, there is a countrie," and "Bright Queen of Heaven, God's Virgin Spouse," whilst his version of Psalm 121, beginning "Up to those bright and gladsome hills," has been included in several public school hymnals.

Samuel Crossman (1624-1683), has given us nine

hymns which have a certain lyric merit, but are not very healthy in tone. The best known are: "Jerusalem on high, my joy and city is," "My life's a shade, my days," and "My song is love unknown." They lack the vigour and insight of John Mason, and have a certain morbid tone of dissatisfaction with earth, which is, happily, passing from the faith of modern times.

The Earl of Roscommon's (died 1684) part in hymnody did not extend beyond a rendering of the *Dies Iræ*, which has acquired a certain fame, and was used commonly in England in his day. The two last lines of this—

My God, my Father, and my Friend,
Do not forsake me in my end—

were uttered by him just before he expired. Mr. Orby Shipley, in his "Annus Sanctus," says that, in all probability, it is wrongly attributed to the Earl.

To John Dryden (1623-1700) we owe the most popular rendering of the "Veni, Creator, Spiritus," of which we have spoken in an earlier chapter, beginning "Creator, Spirit, by whose aid." Much of the evidence points to him as the author of other renderings of ancient hymns, but it is not absolutely conclusive. He has been called "the most felicitous and the most reckless of English translators."

Bishop Thomas Ken, of whom Dryden's lines on the "Good Parson" are said to be a picture:—

Letting down the golden chain from high,
He drew his audience upward to the sky.
And oft with holy hymns he charmed the ears,
A music more melodious than the spheres;
For David left him, when he went to rest,
His lyre; and, after him, he sang the best.

Up to the present time, this would seem to be the popular judgment, since his Morning and Evening Hymns are probably the best known of any in English-speaking countries, and are included in nearly every collection, whilst the doxology with which they both close is certainly not only the finest, but the best known in the world. These hymns were first published by the author in the "Manual of Prayers, for the scholars of Winchester College," in 1625, and afterwards revised by him. It was in the first version the Evening Hymn began, "*Glory* to Thee, my God, this night." The Bishop afterwards altered it to "*All praise* to Thee, my God, this night." The hymn for Midnight, beginning "Lord, now my sleep does me forsake," has fine lines in it, but, as was natural, since it is very rarely people *sing* at that time, did not come into use like those for Morning and Evening. None of the other hymns in his "Christian Year" are worthy to be compared with these, nor have any of them attained to use in the Church.

It might perhaps be questioned whether the Morning and Evening Hymns were entirely original productions of Bishop Ken, on the ground that certain verses, in a more rugged version, are included in the "Verbum Sempiternum" of John Taylor, known as The Water Poet, which was republished in 1693, whilst the Winchester Manual, in which Ken's hymns are first found, did not appear till two years later, in 1695. These are the verses, as they appear in the "Verbum Sempiternum." A Prayer for the Morning:—

Glory to Thee, my God, who safe has kept,
And me refresh'd, while I securely slept;
Lord, this day guard me, lest I may transgress,
And all my undertakings guide and bless.

And since to Thee my vows I now renew,
Scatter my by-past sins as Morning Dew,
That so Thy glory may shine clear as day,
In all I either think, or do, or say.

Another from the Evening:—

Forgive me, dearest Lord, for Thy dear Son,
The many ills that I this day have done,
That with the world, my self, and then with Thee,
I, ere I sleep, at perfect peace may be.

Teach me to live that I may ever dread
The Grave as little as I do my bed;
Keep me this night, O keep me, King of Kings,
Secure under Thine own Almighty Wings.

But it is now known that Ken's hymns appeared earlier than 1695—in 1692—in a twelve-page pamphlet, of which the only known copy is in the Church House. It was a very common practice in that age, to insert hymns in religious books without any acknowledgment of the source whence they were taken. In the edition of the "Lama Sabacthani, or the Cry of the Son of God," a high Anglican book on the Passion, published in 1708, is inserted a mangled version of Dr. Watts' "When I survey the wondrous cross," which appeared in the first edition of his hymns in 1707; whilst in the 1701 edition of Bishop Joseph Hall's "Jacob's Ladder" are given several hymns, "Jerusalem, my happy home," and others from the pen of Mason, no acknowledgment of their authorship being appended. It has also been suggested, that Ken drew some of his materials from Flatman, who published a volume of poems and hymns in 1674, but a candid consideration of the hymn from which he is said to have borrowed does not support this suggestion. But whilst we must reject these charges of indebtedness, there can be little doubt that Ken was acquainted with the hymn of Sir Thomas Browne's, published in his "Religio Medici," and that unconsciously, in writing his Evening

Hymn, he was affected thereby. A comparison of the good Bishop's hymn with that of the Norwich physician, given on page 77, will reveal many similarities, both of thought and expression. The plagiarism, if such existed, was, however, probably quite unconscious. Those who desire to consider this question further, will find materials in an interesting chapter in Dean Plumptre's work, "The Life and Letters of Bishop Ken," of which, with great kindness, he permitted me to read the proofs.

Nahum Tate (1652-1715) and Nicholas Brady (1659-1726) are chiefly known by their translations of the Psalms into metre, which succeeded those of Sternhold and Hopkins, but in the appendix to their version of the Psalms are certain hymns, probably from the pen of one or other of them. The most important of these are "To God be glory, peace on earth," an English rendering of an ancient hymn, "While shepherds watched their flocks by night," and also "O God of Hosts, the mighty Lord," which, however, is a part of their Psalter, and also included therein, in its proper place. Some of their versions of the Psalms are deservedly retained as hymns in modern collections, especially "Through all the changing scenes of life" (Psalm xxxiv). Their versions of the Psalms as a whole, though less rugged than those of Sternhold and Hopkins (which they displaced), have little poetic merit, and could only have satisfied a commonplace age.

The Wesley family, to which hymnody owes so much, is represented in this age by Samuel, the father of John and Charles Wesley; himself the son of an earlier John Wesley. The one hymn we owe to him is "Behold the

Saviour of mankind." It was found written on a piece of music, which narrowly escaped destruction when his parsonage at Epworth was burnt down—a fire from which his son John was saved in an almost miraculous way. It is a somewhat dramatic hymn, and more after the manner of Watts than of his son, Charles Wesley.

The use of Joseph Stennett's (1663-1713) hymns has been confined, with one exception, chiefly to the Baptist body, to which he belonged. He wrote twelve hymns for believer's baptism—a theme on which we have never met with a really fine hymn, although there are many not specially written for it which are admirably suited to such a service. His hymn, beginning "Another six days' work is done," has some little merit for Sunday morning use. It consisted originally of fourteen verses, from which four are usually taken. The last verse, "Come, bless the Lord, whose love assigns," is by another hand.

The last name of the period, before Watts, is Joseph Addison (1672-1719), a great name in English literature, and, so far as style and taste are concerned, a notable name in hymnody; but he lacked the vision and faculty divine so essential to poetry of the highest order. Still, his hymns are far above the average. His rendering of the 19th Psalm, "The spacious firmament on high," was first given at the end of an article in the *Spectator*, No. 465, August 23rd, 1712, on "The right means to strengthen faith." That of the 23rd Psalm, "The Lord my pasture shall prepare," appeared in the same periodical, No. 441, July 26th, 1712. His hymn for travellers, "How are Thy servants blest, O Lord," in No. 489, Sept. 20th, 1712, at the end of a paper on "The Sea." "When rising from the bed of death," in No. 513, October 18th, 1712. His finest hymn, most full of feeling and lyric force, "When all Thy mercies, O my God," is appended to an article on "Praise to God," in No. 453, August 9th, 1712. It will thus be seen that all his hymns were published in the same year, 1712. Two of his hymns have been claimed as Andrew Marvell's by Captain Thompson, but there is no good ground for the claim.

In the period covered by this chapter, a distinct advance is observable toward hymn writing as distinguished from mere poetry. Hymns begin to assume a distinct style; they are less vehicles for thought and more for religious aspiration; they have grown simpler, both in form and substance, and more within the comprehension of simple folk. The foundations have thus been laid on which first Watts, then Wesley, and afterwards a multitude of builders will erect the great Temple of English Song.

CHAPTER IX.

THE FOUNDATIONS OF ENGLISH HYMNODY.

Isaac Watts is the real founder of English hymnody. What Ambrose was to the Latins; what Clement Marot was to the French; what Luther was to the Germans; that, and perhaps more, was Watts to the English. As Josiah Conder says:—"He was the first who succeeded in overcoming the prejudice which opposed the introduction of hymns into our public worship." In our hymn-singing age, it is difficult, especially for its younger members, to realise the strength and even violence of such a prejudice. So strong was it, so high did feeling run on the subject, that many a church was rent asunder by the proposal to introduce hymns; in some cases, even by the proposal to sing metrical versions of the Psalms. This was markedly the case among the Baptists. In the church of which Benjamin Keach was the pastor (the original of that to which Mr. Spurgeon ministered), when, after prolonged discussion, it was decided to introduce singing into its worship, "a minority took refuge in a songless sanctuary." In his "Truth Soberly Defined," published in 1698, Isaac Marlow, with considerable passion, maintained that the Church should not permit the introduction of singing into her services.

This appears to have been very closely connected with the Puritan prejudice against *forms* of prayer. The objection that was taken against *forms* in prayer was easily extended to *forms* in song. Regarded logically, they stand or fall together. And in many instances, the objection to forms was applied to *every* part of worship, even the reading of Scripture, which a century ago was not customary in the Congregational Churches in London.* But whilst the objection to forms of *prayer* remains among Nonconformists generally, that against forms of praise has long since died out; but in many quarters it died hard. In some Churches, however, the objection lay not against singing, for the metrical Psalms were sung, but against the singing of hymns. There was a feeling that the line must be drawn somewhere, and so it was drawn at hymns. It is very difficult to discover the usages in worship of the early Nonconformists. At my request, some of the Church books of the most ancient congregations, notably that at Stepney Meeting, have been searched by the kindness of friends, but no minutes can be found bearing on the subject. Even Dr. Stoughton, who probably knows more than any living man of the usages of the churches in England since the passing of the Act of Uniformity, can throw scarcely any light on the subject. The publication of various collections of hymns by W. Barton during the years between 1654 and 1688; the large sale of Mason and Shepherd's hymns (1691); the issue of a collection of "Divine Hymns," gathered from six authors, amongst whom were J. Mason and R. Baxter, in 1694; seem to point to the probability that hymns were used, at all

* *cf. Congregational Magazine* for 1833, p. 579.

events in some churches; but it is not decisive, since publication does not always imply adoption by the churches, and such collections may have been chiefly used for reading, or, as in the case of Matthew Henry's hymns (1695), for singing in the home. I cannot help thinking that such hymns, if used at all in public worship, could have been sung in very few churches, and that the great majority confined themselves to the singing of the metrical Psalms, in the versions of Sternhold and Hopkins, or Patrick, or Barton. If, however, Dr. Gibbons is to be relied on, *hymns* must have been in use in the closing years of the 17th century, for he says: "Mr. John Morgan, a minister of very respectable character, now living at Romsey, Hants, has sent me the following information: 'The occasion of the Doctor's (Watts) hymns was this, as I had the account from his worthy fellow-labourer and colleague, the Rev. Mr. Price, in whose family I dwelt above fifty years ago. The hymns which were sung at the Dissenting Meeting at Southampton [these were Barton's] were so little to the gust of Mr. Watts, that he could not forbear complaining of them to his father. The father bid him try what he could do to mend the matter. He did, and had such success in his first essay, 'Behold the glories of the Lamb,' that a second hymn was earnestly desired of him, and then a third and fourth, &c., till, in process of time, there was such a number of them as to make up a volume.'" But I cannot help thinking that the church at Southampton was exceptionally liberal in its spirit; evidence for which I see in the fact that they adopted the hymns of young Watts—a member of their own fellowship, and a prophet is not without honour, save in his own country—so readily, and without, so far as we know, opposition. That this is so seems to be proved by the fact that, in many cases, nearly half a century elapsed before some churches would admit even his versions of the Psalms into their worship. It must be remembered, too, that the fundamental principle of Independency permits no act of uniformity in relation to either doctrine or worship, but leaves each church free in both respects. This makes it the more difficult to discover its usage in the matter of singing than it is with bodies closely compacted, in which to discover the usage of one is to be sure of that of all.

When Watts's hymns began to find their way into favour, the more conservative regarded them, as Bradbury afterwards did, as "Watts's *Whims.*"* Whereas, in Germany, Luther's hymns were sung almost as soon as they were produced, it was thirty or forty years before those of Dr. Watts found their way into common use; and even then suspicions of heresy fastened about the churches that adopted them. It seems scarcely possible that little more than a century ago hymn-singing was scarcely known in our churches. Without it, those services must have been extremely dull; what with the long prayers and the long sermons, they must have been a great weariness to the flesh. There must surely have been a good many of the worshippers who, like Eutychus under Paul's long preaching, fell asleep. As to the hymnody of the time, Dr. Watts's lines would surely apply:—

> O what a wretched land is this,
> That yields us no supplies.

And it was this poverty which really gave birth to our modern hymnody, for, in the deepest sense, Dr. Watts is

---

* Walter Wilson's "History of Dissenting Churches in London," III, p. 527.

its founder. His versions of the Psalms and his original hymns supplanted all previous ones, and for many a long year held undisputed possession of the Nonconformist Church against all comers. This is a thing, so far as I know, perfectly unique in the history of the Church, and is not even paralleled by the case of Charles Wesley's hymns among the Methodists, since that collection contained hymns by both John and Charles Wesley, and a very few from other writers, as well as many translations from the German. But for more than a century, Watts remained undisputed master of the hymnody of the Independents. No other hymns than his were heard in any of the assemblies. No other writer ever ruled the Church in this way before. The Independent Churches became as superstitiously conservative in clinging to Watts's hymns as their forefathers had been in rejecting them, and using only the Psalms in metre. Even the Psalter—the hymn book of the Jewish Church—does not furnish a parallel, since that is the product, not only of many authors, but of many ages. Scripture itself has come to us through many minds; but for more than a century, Watts was the only hymnist of the Independent sanctuaries of our land; so venerated were his hymns and psalms, that in this very century there were persons who refused to sing any others, and actually sat down if any others were given out. This was both a gain and a loss—a gain in that, through him, hymns became a part of Divine worship; a loss in that his preeminence excluded the hymns of other writers, even those then in existence by George Herbert, John Milton, Richard Baxter, John Mason, to say nothing of those by writers of other lands, or the ancient hymns of the Church.

The unique position of Dr. Watts is due partly to the excellence and suitability of his hymns to the purposes of public worship, and partly to the nakedness of the land at the time he wrote. He is the pioneer of popular English hymnody. He broke new ground. For this he deserves to be kept in perpetual remembrance. This has, in my judgment, given his hymns a place higher than, as a whole, they deserve. This has covered a multitude of defects in them. As a matter of fact, he both soared very high and sank very low in hymn-writing. I know not where to look for more noble, and, at the same time, more unworthy hymns than are to be found in his pages. There are hymns by him that will last as long as the Church continues her worship-song—*e.g.*, "I'll praise my Maker with my breath," "Our God, our help in ages past," "When I survey the wondrous cross," "Hear what the voice from heaven proclaims," and others that might be named. These are a perpetual possession; but many, I may say most, of his hymns are destined to be, if they are not already, forgotten. Some of them, indeed, once sung in the Church cannot now be read without a smile. It is difficult to realise that verses in many of them could ever have been sung without a titter passing over the congregation. Take the following as illustrations. Here is a verse from his version of the 101st Psalm:—

I'll purge my family around,
  And make the wicked flee;
So shall my house be ever found
  A dwelling fit for Thee.

Here is a verse from Hymn 19 of the second book:—

He spoke, and straight our hearts and brains
  In all their motions rose;
Let blood (said He) flow round the veins,
  And round the veins it flows.

Here is a verse from Hymn 70 of the same book:—

If God His voice of tempest rears,
Leviathan lies still and fears;
Anon he lifts his nostrils high,
And spouts the ocean to the sky.

Here are a couple of verses from Hymn 100 of the same book:—

Christ is my light, my life, my care,
  My blessed hope, my heavenly prize;
Dearer than all my passions are,
  My limbs, my bowels, or my eyes.

The strings that twine about my heart,
  Tortures of racks may tear them off;
But they can never, never part
  With their dear hold of Christ, my love.

Here are the first and third verses of Hymn 2 of the second book:—

My thoughts on awful subjects roll,
  Damnation and the dead;
What horrors seize the guilty soul
  Upon a dying bed.

Then swift and dreadful she descends
  Down to the fiery coast,
Amongst abominable fiends,
  Herself a frightful ghost.

Ministering in a church in which the first verse of this hymn was being announced by the precentor, Mr. Paxton Hood (lover of Watts though he was) shouted, "No, my thoughts don't roll on awful subjects. Let us sing, 'Come, let us join our cheerful songs.'"

The fact is, Watts, responding to the call for hymns, wrote too much. No less than 515 psalms and hymns are found in the volume actually used in public worship, to say nothing of his sacred lyrics. It is not possible for any man, however gifted, to write so large a number of hymns of high quality, and with real distinctiveness of character and subject. It was even more difficult in his time than ours, since he was confined to a few metres—long, common, short, sevens, 113th and 148th metre are about the only ones he used. He never dreamt of the great variety of metre and style with which we are familiar. I question very much whether any man has ever written more than twenty-five or thirty hymns of sufficient merit and distinctive enough in theme and style to hold an abiding place in the hymnody of the Church. In my own collection I have included twenty-six from his pen, and after its publication I came across the following remark in Dr. Geo. MacDonald's "England's Antiphon:" "We cannot help wishing that he had written the twentieth part. How could any man write six hundred religious poems, and produce quality in proportion to quantity save in an inverse ratio?" This is just about the proportion I have retained. I think aftertimes will ratify this judgment. Those are the truest friends to the memory of Dr. Watts who only include the finest of his hymns in their collections. It is a vain effort to try to keep alive his didactic and inferior ones. They may be printed, but they will not be sung. The most recently published hymnal of the Congregational Church includes about sixty of his hymns, many of which are quite unsuited to the taste of the day. They only encumber the pages; and as so many nobler hymns are accessible in our churches, they will rarely, if ever, be sung. The day of rhymed prose is over, even when fathered by great names. Dr. Watts, with a modesty that is rare, once said that Charles Wesley's hymn on "Wrestling Jacob" was worth all he had ever written. This was an excess of modesty, but it reveals, perhaps, a feeling hidden in his mind that he had written too much. The fact is, Watts had a fatal facility of rhyming, and often mistook rhyme for poetry. He was not sufficiently critical of his work. But the critical faculty which he did not apply himself is being applied by others. In relation to his hymns, a process of spiritual selection is going forward which will render him known to posterity, not by five or six hundred, but by the surpassing excellence of some twenty-five or thirty, which will remain among the favourites of the Church at large.

Simon Browne (1680-1732) was a contemporary with Dr. Watts, and belongs to his school of hymn writing. He published, in 1720, "Hymns and Spiritual Songs, in Three Books, designed as a supplement to Dr. Watts." This is an indication of the fact that Watts's hymns had found their way into use in not a few churches, but that such churches had not as yet grown so conservative and exclusive as they afterwards became in relation to his hymns. Two of Browne's hymns are well known, and still hold a place in modern hymnals. The most popular is "Come, gracious Spirit, heavenly dove," which is not without merit; the other is "Lord, at Thy feet we sinners lie."

Alexander Pope (1688-1744), who fills so large a space in the poetic literature of England, used to be reckoned among the hymnists, on account of what has been called Pope's ode, "Vital spark of heavenly flame." This has been included in many hymnals, and was once a favourite at funeral services. It is an imitation of a poem composed, during his last hours, by the Emperor Adrian, beginning—

Animula, vagula, blandula,
Hospes, comesque corporis, etc.

To this, and to a fragment of Sappho, Pope confessed that he owed the inspiration which gave birth to "Vital spark of heavenly flame," the germ of which was sent for insertion in the *Spectator* in 1712. Soon after its receipt, Steele wrote to Pope, asking him to make an ode out of it suitable for music. He complied with this request, and sent "Vital spark" in the form we now possess it.

Samuel Wesley, junr. (1690-1739), the elder brother of John and Charles Wesley, who held aloof from the Methodist movement, which began only five years before his death, and of which they were the great leaders, and from which he did his best to turn them, was also a hymnist, and author of "Poems on Several Occasions." To the last, he adhered to the Church of England, as did his brothers, and was, indeed, a High Churchman of the type of that age. His best known hymn is "The Lord of Sabbath let us praise." Less known, but fairly good, are his hymns, "The morning flowers display their sweets," and "Hail! Father, whose creating call."

John Byrom (1691-1763), remarkable for his scientific attainments, belonged, in some degree, to the school of Mystics, but was probably kept from some of their excesses by his work in science. Two of his hymns, though greatly differing in style and substance, have attained to great popularity, and are still widely used. His hymn for Christmas Day, "Christians, awake, salute the happy morn," is very distinctive, and boldly lyrical; whilst "My spirit longeth for Thee"—as the reader may see—is terse and tender in a very high degree:—

My spirit longeth for Thee,
Within my troubled breast,
Though I unworthy be
Of so Divine a guest:

Of so Divine a guest
Unworthy though I be,
Yet has my heart no rest
Unless it come from Thee.

Unless it come from Thee,
In vain I look around;
In all that I can see
No rest is to be found:

No rest is to be found
But in Thy blessèd love:
O let my wish be crowned,
And send it from above;

He has given us very little, but that little is very good. Some of his verses anticipate, and set forth with great force the better theological thought of our own time. This is specially so in his "Meditation for Wednesday in Passion Week." George MacDonald speaks of his verses as "a well of the water of life, for its song tells of the love and truth which are the grand power of God."

Robert Seagrave (born 1693) wrote about fifty hymns, included in a collection prepared for his own congregation at Lorimer's Hall in 1742. He is remembered chiefly by one of these, "Rise, my soul, and stretch thy wings," which seems to me touched with the thought of Sir John Davies's remarkable philosophical poem, "Of the soul of man, and the immortality thereof."

Philip Doddridge (1702-1751) is one of the great names in hymnody. Remarkable for many things, his fame chiefly rests on his hymns. These were mostly written to gather up and set forth in rememberable form the teachings of his sermons. But whilst the sermons are forgotten, the hymns are remembered. They have been compared to "spiritual amber, fetched up and floated off from sermons long since lost in the depths of bygone time." During his life-time, they did not pass beyond manuscript, in which form they were passed about and read. They number 364. After his death, they were published under the title, "Hymns founded on Various Texts in the Holy Scriptures." In 1839, additional hymns were added, collected from his MSS., and called "Doddridge's Scripture Hymn Book." Some of these reach a very high point of excellence, whilst, as in the case of all voluminous hymn writers, very many are of no great value. The finest of all is "Hark! the glad sound, the Saviour comes." I should be disposed to rank this as one of the noblest hymns ever written, alike as to style and substance. There is a mingling of boldness and tenderness, a suitability and melody in its style, that stamp it as a masterpiece. One of the finest verses, however, is too often omitted—

On Him the Spirit, largely poured,
  Exerts its sacred fire;
Wisdom and might and zeal and love
  His holy breast inspire.

"Ye servants of the Lord" is a hymn of great directness, gradually rising to a fine climax at the close. "Grace! 'tis a charming sound" is a great favourite with many, and was probably suggested by a hymn of Esther Grünbeck of Gotha (1717-1796), beginning "Grace! grace! oh, that's a joyful sound." "My God, and is Thy table spread" was once inserted as a Communion Hymn in the Book of Common Prayer, and for a considerable period remained as part of the Prayer Book, in certain editions of which are two hymns by Doddridge, one each by Wesley, Sternhold, or J. Mardley, and Bishop Ken's Morning and Evening hymn abridged and altered. "O God of Bethel, by whose hand," sometimes attributed to Logan, is by Doddridge, and in his manuscript is dated January 16th, 1736-7. To whom the alterations in the hymn as usually printed are due is uncertain—they have been ascribed to Michael Bruce, but are known to be either Logan's or the revisers of the 1781 Scotch Paraphrases. "Interval of grateful shade," is a hymn of great beauty, set in a subdued and soothing key. It is a part of "an Evening Hymn (of 76 lines) to be used when composing one's self to sleep." In many of Doddridge's hymns which do not reach the highest excellence, there are found lines and verses of great beauty. His hymns appear to me to be a connecting link between Dr. Watts and Charles Wesley. They are akin to the Independent's in form, but to the Methodist's in their lyric force and fervour. Thus they possess the excellences of both. Many of them are likely to hold a permanent place in the song of the Church.

CHAPTER X.

THE LYRIC FIRE.

Song has nearly always proved a mighty influence in stirring the hearts of men in times of religious revival, and has also been felt to be a necessity for the full expression of the feelings aroused at such seasons. The Methodist Revival was no exception to this rule. Song had much to do both with the origination and expression of its feeling. And it was a providential thing that, in the person of the Brother of the real Leader of the movement, a man was at hand singularly fitted to provide the hymns that were needed.

To Charles Wesley we owe the largest contribution to the Church's treasury of song. Dr. Watts is usually regarded as a large contributor, but whilst his hymns number about six hundred, those of Charles Wesley number many thousands. Mr. Stevenson says six thousand; whilst a writer in McClintock and Strong's "American Cyclopædia" credits him, and rightly, with no less than seven thousand. The hymns and poems of John, Charles, and Samuel Wesley fill thirteen volumes in Dr. Osborn's edition; probably a larger number than could be gathered from all previous hymn writers put together. Charles Wesley is far and away the chief contributor to the volumes we have mentioned, and is the most fertile, and, taken altogether, probably the most brilliant of English hymnists. As in the case of Dr. Watts, however, we cannot help wishing that the number had been fewer, and the finish greater. Until almost recently, they practically held undisputed sway in the Methodist choir, since the hymn book issued by John Wesley in 1780, to which a supplement was added in 1831, and which continued in use till 1874, was, to all intents and purposes, the exclusive production of the Wesley family, of which by far the largest portion was contributed by Charles Wesley. His brother John, however, was the Editor of the collection, a task in which he showed great judgment. This secured the exclusion of the poorer of his brother's hymns. It would have been well for the fame of Dr. Watts if his hymns had been edited by an equally skilful hand.* This would have ensured the exclusion of such doggerel as we have quoted in a previous chapter. To the editorship of John Wesley is due the fact that the Wesleyan collection is of a far higher type than Dr. Watts's, which held a corresponding place in the Independent Church. The Wesleyan Hymnal contained, it is true, fragments from Gambold, Herbert, Watts, and translations from the German (these were by *John* Wesley), but the book is essentially a Wesley production.

The preface to this book is a curiosity of conceit. I do

* John Wesley's capacity as an editor is seen in the fact that he did not always import hymns from other sources in their entirety, but omitted verses unsuitable for singing; thus, from Watts' magnificent rendering of the 146th Psalm he omits the fifth verse, which contains the line, "But turns the wicked down to hell," which he evidently felt was scarcely a subject for praise.

not like to apply such an epithet to one so deservedly honoured as John Wesley; but the wisest err, and it cannot, I think, be rightly described in any milder language. The sixth paragraph reads as follows: "May I be permitted to add a few words with regard to the *poetry?* Then I will speak to those who are judges thereof with all freedom and unreserve. To these I may say, without offence: 1. In these hymns there is no doggerel; no botches; nothing put in to patch up the rhymes; no feeble expletives. 2. Here is nothing turgid or bombast on the one hand, or low and creeping on the other. 3. Here are no *cant* expressions; no words without meaning. Those who impute this to us know not what they say. We talk common-sense, both in prose and verse; and use no word but in a fixed and determinate meaning. 4. Here are, allow me to say, both the purity, the strength, the plainness suited to any capacity. Lastly, I desire men of taste to judge (these are the only judges) whether there be not, in some of the following hymns, the true spirit of poetry, such as cannot be acquired by art or labour, but must be the gift of nature. By labour, a man may become a tolerable imitator of Spenser, Shakespeare, or Milton, and may heap together pretty compound epithets, as pale-eyed, meek-eyed, and the like; but unless he *be born* a poet, he will never attain the genuine spirit of poetry."

Unbiassed critics will probably demur to this declaration—if not in relation to the Wesleyan Hymn Book, certainly in relation to Charles Wesley's hymns as a whole. Of certain of these (his hymns on the Nativity), even his brother once said: "Omit one or two of them, and I will thank you. They are namby-pambical." Such a criticism would apply to every large contributor to hymnody; and must, in the nature of things, apply to a man like Charles Wesley, who wrote hymns by the thousand. Even the noblest poets are best represented by a selection from their writings, and the smaller it is the more choice it is likely to be. But when this has been said, it may also be said, that amongst his writings are to be found some of the grandest hymns in the English language. For spontaneity of feeling, his hymns are pre-eminent. They are songs that soar. They have the rush and fervour which bear the soul aloft. They are more subjective, and grow more directly out of the personal experience of the writer than do the hymns of Watts, which sprang rather from the contemplation of the Divine facts and doctrines of Scripture. They are a kind of cardiphonia, caught from the beating of his own heart, and the observation of hearts kindled by the great movement in which he bore so large a part. The question has been debated again and again whether he or Watts bears off the palm in hymn writing. Comparisons are proverbially odious, but if a comparison *must* be made, in my judgment it must be in favour of Charles Wesley, especially for the lyric fervour of his hymns. Before him in time, Watts must, I think, be placed after him in order of merit, and this partly because his nature was not so fervid, nor was there so much in his course to kindle it. His wing was not so strong, and, therefore, his flight was not so high. And if, as I feel, the *lyric* should be the dominant note in hymns, the first place in the Christian choir must be assigned to the author of "O Thou Who camest from above," "O Love Divine, how sweet Thou art," "Head of the Church triumphant," "Hark! the herald angels sing," "Come, Holy Ghost, our hearts inspire," "Jesus, lover of my soul," "Soldiers of Christ, arise," "Come, let us join our friends above," "Thou hidden source of calm repose," "O for a thousand tongues to sing," "Christ, the Lord, is risen to-day," "O, what shall I do, my Saviour to praise," "Leader of faithful souls, and Guide," and perhaps greatest of all—probably the finest sacred lyric in the language—"Come, O Thou Traveller unknown." Isaac Watts is the founder of the choir, but in it Charles Wesley's is the noblest voice.

And the reasons for this pre-eminence are to be sought (first) in the lyric nature of the man himself, who could not help but sing—whose hymns are not the product of the mere student, but of a soul that naturally soared on the wings of praise; (secondly) in the religious influences which surrounded his early life. It is well known that both the Wesleys were at first deeply affected by the writings of William Law, the Mystic; and though in after years they threw aside his particular doctrines, yet his influence is discernible, more or less, in all their hymns. If William Law had not taught, Charles Wesley would not have sung as he did. A touch of mysticism, indeed, is necessary to hymns of the most spiritual and inspiring kind. A third influence may be found in his association with the Moravians, by whom both he and his brother were deeply impressed. Mr. Beecher, in the preface to his hymn book, says: "His hymns are only Moravian hymns resung. Not alone are the favourite expressions used, and the epithets they loved, but, like them, he beholds all Christian truths through the medium of confiding love. The *love element* of this school has never been surpassed."

And the fourth influence must be sought in the marvellous scenes amid which he moved, and the stirring work in which he bore a part. His hymns are the offspring of the Methodist revival almost as much as of the Methodist singer. Just as David's life is reflected in his Psalms, so Charles Wesley's career shines out through his stirring verses. All these things combine to make him the greatest hymn writer of England.

His brother John is as great as a translator as Charles is as an original hymnist. John came to know and love the hymns of Germany through his association with the Moravians. And it was probably during his voyages in their company that he turned many of their finest hymns into English. For congregational use, they are probably the finest translations in the English language, whilst they have the high honour of having opened to us the rich treasures of sacred song which Germany possesses. They are so good that they read like original English compositions. They have never yet been, and probably never will be, supplanted by other translations. What can be finer than his rendering of Paul Gerhardt's "Jesus, Thy boundless love to me," and "Commit thou all thy griefs," or Tersteegen's "Lo, God is here; let us adore," and "Thou hidden love of God, whose height," or Rothe's "O Lord, Thine everlasting grace," or Scheffler's "Thee will I love, my strength, my tower."* For such importa-

* I quote the first line of the *second* verse of this hymn, because the *first* verse—

"Now I have found the ground wherein
Sure my soul's anchor may remain,
The wounds of Jesus for my sin"—

is disfigured by the horrible imagery of an anchor cast in wounds. This has prevented the hymn from taking the high place which the rest of it so richly deserves, and, when the first verse is omitted, it is destined to receive.

tions we may be as thankful as for his brother's original productions. The choir opened by Watts is now full-voiced, and the music has ever since been growing richer and more varied. It is very pleasant to remember that these great and holy singers were brought into very close and blessed fellowship on the death-bed of John Wesley. The very last words that passed from his lips were those of Dr. Watts—"I'll praise my Maker with my breath," and it was as he was struggling to say, "I'll praise—I'll praise," that his spirit passed away to join "the choir invisible."

CHAPTER XI.

THE AGE OF ECHOES.

We have now reached a time in which the song of the Church finds expression through *many* voices. The lyric fervour of Watts and Wesley stirred the dormant flame of many a soul; whilst, at the same time, the place which hymns had won for themselves in the actual worship of the Church, has proved an additional influence to lead those with any hymnic gifts to its exercise. The demand had much to do with creating the supply. In earlier times, if hymns were written, no place was open for their use in worship. But now, hymn writers felt that their hymns might, if they approved themselves to the public taste, be used as the vehicle for worshipping feeling. This seems to me to account for the fact that a large number now entered the ranks of the hymnists, most of whom were men (together with a few women) touched by the new religious fervour, and associated with the churches in which hymns formed an important part of the worship. Many of these, it is true, were mere imitators of Watts and Wesley, especially the former, since he was far easier to imitate than the more lyric Methodist. These were mere echoes, and, like echoes, had neither the force nor fervour of the voices they prolonged. Still, here and there a distinct note was struck, vibrating with the individuality of the singer; but for the most part, until we reach the "Olney Hymns" of John Newton and William Cowper, there are but few hymnists of any great originality to be found.

Contemporary with the Wesleys was Joseph Grigg, who died in 1768. He wrote a few hymns, but is chiefly remarkable as having written, at ten years of age, the well-known "Jesus, and can it ever be," which first appeared in the *Gospel Magazine* for April, 1774, with the title, "Shame of Jesus conquered by love: by a youth of ten years." To the same author we owe another hymn of similar style and fervour, "Behold a Stranger at the door." He wrote altogether some forty hymns, but all save those we have mentioned have dropped out of sight.

Thomas Scott, a Presbyterian minister at Ipswich (who died about 1776), and who must not be confounded with the well-known Commentator of the same name, wrote many hymns and poems, but is now remembered only by two, the better known of which is "Hasten, O sinner, to be wise," a hymn of earnest invitation and warning against delay, and "Angels, roll the rock away."

William Hammond, B.A. (who died in 1783), at first a Calvinistic preacher, but in later life a member of the Moravian body, wrote and published "Psalms, Hymns, and Spiritual Songs." His hymn "Awake and sing the song" has found its way into a very large number of hymnals. There is in it considerable vigour. The verse, however—

"Sing till we feel our hearts
Ascending with our tongues;
Sing till the love of sin departs,
And grace inspires our songs"—

attributes to sacred song a power even greater than it possesses. His hymn beginning "Lord, we come before Thee now" is in a much more subdued and tender strain, and still retains a place in the Church's song.

James Grant (died 1785), a distinguished layman connected with the Church of Scotland, who wrote many hymns for use with Scotch melodies, for which he had a great affection, is now remembered, and even that remembrance is growing fainter, by one beginning "O Zion, afflicted with wave upon wave."

Daniel Turner, M.A. (1710-1798), Elizabeth Scott (circa 1764), John Needham, and Benjamin Wallin, fill too small a place in modern hymnody to demand more than the mention of their names.

Joseph Hart (1712-1768), minister of Jewin Street Independent Church, though possessing, in our judgment, little merit as a hymnist, has enjoyed a considerable popularity, especially with persons inclining to the Calvinistic view of Christianity, and his hymn book still finds purchasers and admirers. He is largely represented in "Our Own Hymn Book," edited by the Rev. C. H. Spurgeon for the use of his congregation at the Metropolitan Tabernacle. His Christian experience was of rather a striking nature, and is reflected in his hymns. The most popular, undoubtedly, is "Come, Holy Spirit, come," which is not without merit, though a good deal like other hymns addressed to the Holy Spirit. "Come ye sinners, poor and wretched," used to be a great favourite, but is so steeped in the extreme spirit of his day—a spirit which is now the exception rather than the rule—that its popularity is rapidly waning. It belongs to a class of hymns which are addressed, not to the Divine Being, but to the congregation, or rather to those who are supposed specially to need such exhortation. There is a kind of incongruity in such hymns which is increasingly felt, and which leads to their disuse in public worship.

To Dr. John Hawkesworth (1715-1773), compiler of the Parliamentary debates in the *Gentleman's Magazine*, we owe a hymn of some merit, "In sleep's serene oblivion laid;" to James Hutton (1715-1795), a cousin of Sir Isaac Newton, a bookseller, and deacon of the Moravian Church, a hymn of fine sentiment, "O teach us more of Thy blest ways;" and to Christopher Batty (1715-1797), "Captain of Thine enlisted host." All these three, it will be noted, were born in the same year.

Anne Steele (1716-1778), who, all her life, was a great sufferer, through an accident in childhood, and whose course was marked by many sorrows, has enjoyed considerable fame as a hymnist, not, in our judgment, quite justified by the quality of her productions. She is, perhaps, the first English woman who contributed hymns of any importance to the Church's treasury of song. Her hymn, "Father, whate'er of earthly bliss," is the expression of a life troubled as was hers, and is, indeed, remarkable for its tone of quiet resignation. In the original it begins with the verse, "When I survey life's varied scene." Touched with a similar spirit is her hymn, "Far from these narrow scenes of night."

John Berridge (1716-1793), vicar of Everton, and friend of Wesley and Whitfield, a quaint and racy preacher, published "A Collection of Divine Songs," but, on account of his adoption of Calvinistic views, repented of the publication, and whenever he met with a copy of it, committed it to the flames. In character and style of address, he was not unlike to John Newton. He altered and adapted certain of Charles Wesley's hymns. His hymn, "Jesus, cast a look on me," the first three verses of which consist of an altered version of Charles Wesley's "Lord, that I may learn of Thee," has a simplicity which is very pleasing. This and his Wedding Hymn, "Since Jesus freely did appear," are the only ones which have gained currency in hymnals.

John Cennick (1717-1755), originally one of Wesley's preachers, but afterwards an assistant of Whitfield, and finally a Moravian, the friend of Wesley and Whitfield, is a name of note among the hymnists. His hymns owe something to the revision of Charles Wesley and others, but they have a distinctiveness and lyric force which will probably ensure for them a lasting place in the Church's song. The best known is "Children of the heavenly King," which has found its way into a very large number of hymnals, both of the Established and Nonconformist Churches. The same may be said of "Jesus, my all, to heaven is gone," though it is not equal to the former. His Evening Hymn, "Ere I sleep, for every favour," is quaint and beautiful. His version of the *Te Deum*, commencing "We sing to Thee, Thou Son of God," before the original was commonly used in Nonconformist worship, was very popular in their assemblies. To him we owe the original of the hymn, to which so many writers contributed either alterations or additions, "Lo! He comes, with clouds descending," which in his version began, "Lo! He cometh; countless trumpets." In my judgment, Cennick possessed the genuine lyric fire, and, but for deficient culture, and the narrowness of the school of thought in which he lived, would have made still more valuable contributions to hymnody.

I cannot agree with the praise bestowed by James Montgomery and Robert Hall on the hymns of Benjamin Beddome, M.A. (1717-1795), pastor of the Baptist Church at Bourton-on-the-Water, Gloucestershire. The former praises him for preserving the unity of each hymn. This he does, but there is a didactic tone, and an absence of the lyric element, which are fatal faults in a hymn. This is partly due to the fact that they were written to be sung after his sermons, to which they are a kind of application. This is not the true office of hymns. The mind of their writers should not be occupied with the thought of the edification of the people, but of praise to God. This is the defect of most of his hymns, as will be seen even in his most popular, "Did Christ o'er sinners weep?" "Faith, 'tis a precious grace," and "Let party names no more." The fault is least evident in his Ordination hymn, "Father of mercies, bow Thine ear." He was the author of the large number of eight hundred and thirty hymns.

James Merrick, M.A. (1720-1769), a minister of the Church of England, but, on account of weak health, without pastoral charge, issued "The Psalms translated or paraphrased in English Verse," designed to supplant Tate and Brady, but the collection failed to secure royal sanction for its use in the Episcopal Church. His scholarship was equal to, but his poetic power sadly deficient for the task he undertook. His finest hymn —and it is a fine one—is "Eternal God, we look to

Thee." His version of the 122nd Psalm, beginning "The festal morn, my God, is come," a translation from Buchanan, is striking, but in parts rather inflated.

Dr. Thomas Gibbons (1720-1758), pastor of various Independent Churches, and tutor of the Dissenting Academy at Mile End, may be ranked with Merrick as possessing scholarship but not the poetic afflatus, although he fancied that he possessed it. His Missionary Hymn, "Great God, the nations of the earth," is not without merit, and held its place in a time when such hymns were not either plentiful or meritorious. It is a far finer hymn than the other by which he is remembered, "Now let our souls on wings sublime." He is one of the fading lights of hymnody.

Joseph Humphreys (born 1720), and Thomas Blacklock, D.D. (1721-1791), are forgotten names in hymnody, and need not detain us.

John Bakewell (1721-1819), a member of, and local preacher in, the Wesleyan Church, is remembered by one hymn which has had a wide popularity, "Hail! Thou once despiséd Jesus," which has merit, though not of the highest order.

Clare Taylor (died 1778), and John Fountain (died 1800), are now only represented by hymns in collections prepared more to represent their editors' theological views than with a view to poetic or lyric expression.

Andrew Kippis, D.D., F.R.S. (1725-1795), is more remarkable for his contributions to literature than to hymnody, but deserves to be remembered as the Editor of the first thoroughly popular Unitarian hymn-book, all previous ones having been for the worship of individual churches.

CHAPTER XII.

AN OASIS IN THE DESERT.

REMARKING on the fact that the hymns of earlier days seem to have been written by all kinds of persons except poets, James Montgomery says: "Cowper therefore stands alone among the mighty masters of the lyre, as having contributed a considerable number of approved and popular hymns for the purposes of public or private devotion." In the "Olney Hymns" of John Newton (1725-1807) and William Cowper (1731-1800), we come upon a veritable oasis in the wilderness, from which the Church has gathered and preserved with loving care many a flower of song. Newton's hymns are remarkable as being the productions of a man who, in early life, had exceedingly few educational advantages. To his vigorous nature, and the depth of his religious experiences, are due the high quality of his hymns. One example out of many afforded by hymnody, of the fact that scholarship has very little to do with the production of poetry. Scholarship may refine, but it does not create the poetic faculty. Newton disclaimed any pretension to the possession of the poetic gift, but he nevertheless possessed it, and, for the purposes of hymnody, in a remarkable degree: so remarkable, that a few of his hymns will bear comparison with those of his great friend and co-worker in the production of the "Olney Hymns,"

William Cowper. There are no hymns more popular among all sections of the Church than some of Newton's. This is largely due to the depth and vitality of his religious experience, which reached to regions far below the doctrinal forms in which it found expression. Scarcely a hymnal of any section of the Church can be mentioned which does not include some of his best known hymns. They may be found, not only in hymnals of the Evangelical type, but in those so widely separated in doctrinal matters as "Hymns Ancient and Modern" and Dr. Martineau's "Hymns of Praise and Prayer." His hymns indeed are alive with personal and vital religious feeling, and so are fitted to express the worshipping feeling of all Christian hearts. The best known is "How sweet the name of Jesus sounds," which some have thought must have been suggested by Bernard's "Jesu dulcis memoria." In all probability, Newton did not know of the earlier hymn of the saintly monk of Clairvaux, but wrote prompted solely by ardent love to Jesus Christ. Equally good, but in a different vein of feeling, is "Quiet, Lord, my froward heart," a hymn whose sentiment and style alike quiet and calm the restless spirit. His hymn for Parting, too often mutilated and made to begin with "For a season called to part," instead of, as it should, with "As the sun's enlivening eye," is of great excellence. "While with ceaseless course the sun" is a hymn of great solemnity and pathos. "Glorious things of thee are spoken" is in a very different and much bolder strain. I am disposed to regard those in his more subdued style as reaching to the highest point of excellence, and in them the affectionate characteristics which lay beneath a nature trained amid rugged scenes, and in so rough a life, find expression in hymns of a very tender and subdued type.

William Cowper, who co-operated with John Newton in the production of the "Olney Hymns," brought to his task the pathos and delicacy of touch of the true poet, although most of his hymns were written before his poetic power had reached its full development. Most of them are full of the characteristics of that sensitive and retiring poet, and enshrine his varying, though, for the most part, despondent moods. "Hark! my soul, it is the Lord"—Mr. Gladstone has made a fine translation of this hymn into Italian—and "O, for a closer walk with God," are in his more tender style; whilst "Jesus, where'er Thy people meet," written in a season of unusual joy, and "God moves in a mysterious way," said to have been written, though the evidence is not forthcoming, after a marvellous deliverance from purposed self-destruction, sound a bolder note. "Ere God had built the mountains," is, perhaps, his grandest hymn. "There is a fountain filled with blood" is, in certain quarters, greatly prized, but we cannot help regarding it as going far beyond Scriptural usage in its imagery, and not in harmony with Scripture fact in its reference to the dying thief. The retiring spirit of the poet finds very full expression in the hymn, "Far from the world, O Lord, I flee." From the little volume of "Olney Hymns" the Church has drawn a far larger number of hymns, and these greatly prized, than from many more voluminous collections. Its somewhat narrow theology is softened by the reality and tenderness of the religious experience of its authors, of both of whom it may be said, "They learnt in suffering what they taught in song."

CHAPTER XIII.

DIDACTIC HYMNISTS.

VASTLY different from the "Olney Hymns" in merit are most of the compositions of their contemporaries and immediate successors, in whom the didactic tone is very marked. Still, here and there a lyric note is heard.

William Mason, M.A. (1725-1797), vicar of Aston, one of the chaplains of George the Third, and biographer of Gray, did much for church music. His anthem, "Lord of all power and might," is still occasionally sung. He wrote a few hymns, one of which, "Again returns the day of holy rest," is of considerable merit.

Thomas Olivers (1725-1799), one of John Wesley's travelling preachers, who had but the scantiest education in youth, is represented in hymnals by one hymn in which there are verses of remarkable power, "The God of Abraham praise." The same may be said of Edward Perronet (1726-1792), whose "All hail the power of Jesu's name" is one of the most striking hymns in the language. It appeared with tune in *The Gospel Magazine*, 1779-80.

Dr. Samuel Stennett (1727-1795) and Bishop Horne (1730-1792) are amongst the hymnists whose productions are vanishing from hymnals.

Thomas Haweis, LL.B., M.D. (1732-1820), one of the chaplains of Lady Huntingdon, and rector of All Saints',

Aldwinkle, in Northamptonshire, was the author of "Carmina Christo," containing two hundred and fifty-six hymns. Three of his hymns are of considerable merit, and still retain a place in the song of the Church, "Enthroned on high, Almighty Lord," "O Thou from whom all goodness flows," which has a touch of genuine pathos in it, and "The happy morn is come," an Easter Hymn.

James Newton, M.A. (1733-1790), and Benjamin Francis (1734-1799), both ministers of the Baptist body, belong to the class of mediocrities whose hymns are fast fading from memory and use in the Church.

James Allen (1734-1804), a partial follower of the views of Glas and Sandeman, which, with some modifications, he preached in a chapel on his estate at Gayle, the editor and chief contributor to the "Kendal Hymn Book," was the author of "Glory to God on high," a hymn of great force and merit, and of "Sweet the moments, rich in blessing," a hymn very frequently used in earlier times at the Communion Service. It is, however, lacking in healthiness of feeling, and expressive of a rather sentimental and languishing type of devotion· This hymn was afterwards altered to its present form by W. W. Shirley, the brother-in-law of the Countess of Huntingdon, in 1772, who edited the 1780 edition of her collection.

Robert Robinson (1735 - 1790), the vigorous but eccentric Baptist minister at Cambridge, was the author of "Mighty God, while angels bless Thee," one of the most vigorous and distinctive hymns in the English tongue; and also (although doubts have been expressed as to his authorship), of "Come, Thou fount of every blessing," a noteworthy hymn, but marred by its doctrinal representation of the work of Christ.

Samuel Medley (1738 - 1799), minister of Baptist churches, first at Watford, and afterwards at Byrom Street, Liverpool, issued a considerable number of hymns on broadsides, which were afterwards collected into a volume. They are of no special merit, save two which are of great spirit and much lyric force, "Mortals, awake, with angels join," and "Awake, my soul, in joyful lays."

John Fawcett, D.D. (1739-1817), minister of the Baptist Church at Wainsgate, and afterwards at Hebden Bridge, published a collection of his hymns as a supplement to Dr. Watts's "Psalms and Hymns." They are of little worth, and even those which have passed into collections are fast going out of use. We may, however, except "Blest be the tie that binds," and "Thus far my God hath led me on," which have considerable merit.

Augustus Montague Toplady (1740-1778), vicar of Broad Hembury, Devonshire, is the author of "Rock of Ages, cleft for me," which is perhaps the most popular hymn in the language; at all events, it contests this honour with Bishop Ken's Evening Hymn. It was inserted in the *Gospel Magazine* for March, 1776, under the title, "A Living and Dying Prayer for the Holiest Believer in the World." The immediate purpose of the author in writing it was to protest against the possibility of entire sanctification in this life as he understood it to be taught by the Wesleys. This polemical purpose probably led Toplady to express, in the strongest possible forms, the doctrine which he opposed to that held, or which he supposed to be held, by the early Methodists.

The hymn is full of solemnity and pathos, and exerts a very wonderful power over the worshipper. Judged by a strictly literary standard, it is not equal to many a hymn which could be named, since its imagery is somewhat confused;* but judged by what is a true standard—its power to solemnise and move the heart—it takes a high place. Although Toplady wrote one hundred and thirty-three poems and hymns, this is the only one which has attained to great popularity. After this, perhaps his best hymns are: "Deathless principle arise," and "Your harps, ye trembling saints." "Jesus, at Thy command," is often attributed to him, but is probably by De Courcey.

Anna Lœtitia Barbauld (1743-1825), sister of the celebrated Dr. Aikin, whom she helped in his well-known work, "Evenings at Home," the authoress of many important works, and editor of the "British Novelists," and some of the English poets, belongs to a very different school to those we have considered, all of

* Since this paragraph was written, I notice that the Rev. John Hudson, in an article on "Church Hymns" in *The National Review* for August, 1888, writes of this hymn:—"It seems a medley of confused images, and accumulated, if not misapplied, metaphors—'cleft rock,' 'riven side,' 'to Thy cross I cling,' 'to the fountain fly.' What is the precise meaning of '*double* cure?' Is the curative agent or the thing cured *double? i.e.*, does it refer to 'water and blood,' or 'guilt and power' of sin? And surely, to 'cleanse' from power is an odd expression! The hymn itself does not make clear to the reader whence the writer took his idea 'Rock of Ages' is generally supposed to be taken from the marginal reading of Isaiah xxvi. 4, rendered by the Revisers, 'In the Lord Jehovah is an Everlasting Rock,' the idea being stability. But the second line, 'Let me hide myself in Thee,' would seem to be suggested by some such verse as Isaiah xxxii. 2, 'The shadow of a great rock in a weary land,' or by the incident in Moses' life recorded in Exodus xxxii. 22, 'I will put thee in a cleft of the rock, and will cover thee with My hand.' Whereas, again, the heading of the hymn, 'That rock was Christ,' would seem to imply an allusion to the history of the Israelites described in Exodus xvii. 6, Numbers xx. 11, and referred to in 1 Corinthians x. 4."

whom were of the strongly Evangelical type. She is one of the earliest Unitarian contributors to hymnody; a woman of great literary ability and vigour of mind. Her hymn, "How blest the righteous when he dies," an alteration from her "Sweet is the scene where virtue dies," is one of great beauty and delicacy of thought and expression.

Rowland Hill, M.A. (1744-1833), the eccentric but devoted minister of Surrey Chapel, published a collection of "Psalms and Hymns for Public Worship," in which some of his own were included. It is difficult to be certain which they were, as he did not append his name. "We sing His love who once was slain," is, however, known to be by him. It was written for Dr. Arne's tune "Rule, Britannia," and issued in the 1796 supplement to his collection.

Michael Bruce (1746-1767), who for a brief time before his early death was engaged in conducting a school, and whose hymns were published by John Logan as his own, was a hymnist of very considerable merit; the best of his hymns are "Where high the heavenly temple stands," and "Behold the mountain of the Lord." Logan may have slightly altered these, but there can be no doubt that, substantially, they were Bruce's compositions. With great effrontery, Logan also claimed as his own the fine hymn of Doddridge, "O God of Bethel, by whose hand," which he only altered.

Jonathan Evans (1749-1809), the founder and minister of an Independent Church at Foleshill, near Coventry, was the author of at least twenty-two hymns, but is only remembered by the well-known one, "Hark! the voice of love and mercy," first published in Dr. Burder's Coventry Collection in 1787. Some doubt has been felt as to his authorship of this hymn, as his name is not appended, but it is now generally admitted to be by him. It has enjoyed considerable popularity, and is, in some senses, a striking hymn.

John Morrison, D.D. (1749-1798), minister of the parish of Canisbay in Caithness, a member of the General Assembly for revising the Church Paraphrases of the Scottish Church, was a hymnist of great vigour. Two of his paraphrases, "The race that long in darkness pined," and "Come, let us to the Lord our God," are deservedly popular.

William Cameron (1751-1811), minister of Kirknewton in Mid Lothian, also belonged to the company of Paraphrasers, and for that collection prepared a version of Dr. Watts's hymn which begins "How bright those glorious spirits shine."

George Burder (1752-1832), minister of the West Orchard Independent Church at Coventry, and afterwards editor of the *Evangelical Magazine*, and secretary of the London Missionary Society, well known as the author of "Village Sermons," once extensively used by lay preachers, published three hymns of his own, in a selection intended for use as supplementary to Dr. Watts's "Psalms and Hymns." These have enjoyed considerable popularity, and though not remarkable for poetic excellence, are yet well adapted for the purposes of worship. The best is "Great the joy when Christians meet." "Lord, dismiss us with Thy blessing" has been attributed to him, but it appeared eleven years earlier, in 1773, in the Shawbury Collection, and is most likely, but not certainly, by John Fawcett.

John Ryland, D.D. (1753-1825), President of the Baptist College at Bristol, a post he held together with the pastorate of Broadmead Chapel in the same city, a well-known Baptist minister, was the author of many hymns. The one beginning "Thou Son of God, and Son of Man," is marked by great force, and warmth of expression. His favourite hymn was "O Lord, I would delight in Thee." It is full of a joyful trustfulness, and contains, in the following line, the fine thought that every creature good has its source in God—

> "No good in creatures can be found,
> But may be found in Thee."

Edmund Butcher (1757-1822), minister of a congregation in Leather Lane, Holborn, wrote more than a hundred hymns, amongst which his harvest hymn is found, beginning "Great God, as seasons disappear." It is a fine hymn, and has passed into a large number of collections.

John Dobell (1757-1840), an officer at Poole under the Board of Excise, is more remarkable as an Editor than as a Writer of hymns. In 1806 he issued "A New Selection of Seven Hundred Evangelical Hymns for Private, Family, and Public Worship, from more than two hundred of the best authors in England, Scotland, Ireland, and America." He spent many years in this work, and took great pains to ascertain the authorship of the hymns he included. On this account, his labours have been of great value to hymnologists. His hymn, "Now is the accepted time," which has passed into several other collections, is of no great value.

Sir James Edward Smith, M.D., F.R.S. (1759-1828), a Norwich physician, is more remarkable for his scientific labours, especially in natural history, than for his contributions to hymnody. Of the nine hymns from his pen, the best is "Adore, my soul, that awful name."

William Shrubsole (1759-1829), who held a post of importance in the Bank of England, is remembered by his Missionary Hymns, one of which, "Bright as the sun's meridian blaze," was written for the first meeting of the London Missionary Society, whilst his striking hymn, though somewhat hard in tone, "Arm of the Lord, awake! awake!" was published in "Missionary Hymns" (1795).

Alice Flowerdew (1759-1830) is the authoress of that exceedingly poetical hymn (sometimes ascribed to John Needham), "Fountain of mercy, God of love." It is probably founded on a hymn of Needham's.

Basil Woodd, M.A. (1760-1831), author of a new metrical version of the Psalms of David; James Upton (1760-1834); and Thomas Park, F.S.A. (1760-1835), fill too small a place in hymnody to deserve more than the mention of their names.

Joseph Swain (1761-1796), minister of a Baptist Church at Walworth, the author of the "Walworth Hymns," is remembered by a few hymns, among which we may mention: "Lift up your heads, ye gates," "For ever to behold Him shine," and "How sweet, how heavenly is the sight," which are not without merit.

Helen Maria Williams (1762-1827), a woman of great ability, was the authoress of a hymn of great originality and pathos, "While Thee I seek, protecting power."

William Goode, M.A. (1762 - 1816), successor to Romaine in the Church of St. Ann, Blackfriars, dissatisfied, like many others, with the versions of the Psalms then in existence, produced a new one, which, instead of surpassing its predecessors in excellence, fell below them. Only one of his versions has gained any popularity, that of the 74th, which begins "Thou gracious God and kind."

Job Hupton (1762-1849), one of the Countess of Huntingdon's preachers, and afterwards minister of the Baptist Church at Claxton, Norfolk, author of "Hymns and Spiritual Poems," is the author of "Come, ye saints, and raise an anthem." This hymn was rewritten by Dr. J. M. Neale and placed in parallel columns with the original in an article in the *Christian Remembrancer.* Dr. Neale's version begins thus—"Come, ye faithful, raise the anthem."

John Kent (1766-1843), a shipwright in the employ of the Government at Plymouth, was the author of "Original Gospel Hymns," which reached a tenth edition, and consisted of two hundred and sixty-four hymns. No less than twelve of these appear in "Our Own Hymn Book," edited by the Rev. C. H. Spurgeon.

Edmund Jones (circa 1777), Samuel Pearce, M.A. (1766-1799), Thomas Fanshaw Middleton, D.D., F.R.S., and the well known Amelia Opie (1796-1853), fill too small a place in hymnody to call for special mention.

The period covered by this chapter is not a remarkable one. It is little more than the afterglow of the brilliant sunset of Watts and Wesley. It includes a large number of names, and a few fine hymns; but, for the most part, the hymns are expressive of a religious fervour from which the freshness and individuality had departed. Nearly all the writers were men who had been touched, more or less, by the influence of the Methodist Revival. Most of them were Dissenters, or Churchmen so low in doctrine that, to a High Churchman, they differed little from Dissenters. The Baptists fill a very large place in the hymnody of this period. This was probably due to the fact that, though they were great admirers of Dr. Watts's Psalms and Hymns, they were less dominated by them than the Independents, to whose company Dr. Watts belonged. Whilst the earliest English hymnists were stronger in poetic thought than doctrinal precision, those of this period are more doctrinal and experimental than poetic. This is, indeed, with a few exceptions, one of the least poetic and lyric periods in the history of hymnody, and, apart from the Olney, and such hymns as "Rock of Ages," and "All hail the power of Jesu's name," comparatively few of its hymns are likely to retain a permanent place in the Church's song. It was, indeed, a dull age as regarded poetry generally. It was not till the latter part of the time that the poems of Wordsworth, Coleridge, Byron, Shelley, and Keats saw the light, and still later before their influence was widely felt. Hymnody is largely affected by the current poetry. But it is probable that the religious ideas of the age covered by this chapter prevented the poetry then in existence exerting its full influence on hymn writers. The range of reading of the ministry in Nonconformist churches (and to their ministers we owe the larger part of the hymns of this period), was more exclusively theological than in our day, and thus the poetic afflatus was little nourished, as now, by the study of poetry. In many a hymnist of succeeding times, we shall discover the true poet: men who not only gave themselves to the production of poetry, but even in their hymn writing worked with the poet's spirit. To this narrow range of sympathy and of reading is due the dulness and sameness which must strike everyone acquainted with any considerable number of the hymns of the age covered by this chapter.

CHAPTER XIV.

INCREASE OF POETIC ELEMENTS.

We now come to a time at which the influence of Isaac Watts, and, in a less degree, of Charles Wesley, over hymnody, has somewhat waned, and in which the influence of contemporary poetry begins to make itself felt in an increasing degree, whilst the more general culture of the age becomes apparent in the hymns that are produced. This is less evident in the earlier writers of this period, but becomes more so as the time goes on. To this we owe the variety of style and metre, the distinctiveness of theme, the greater finish, and the more poetic touches which distinguish our modern hymnody. These are not so apparent in the first writer of this period to which I refer (Thomas Kelly), but are markedly so in the second (James Montgomery), and others which follow.

Thomas Kelly (1769-1855), only son of Judge Kelly, of the Irish Bench, was driven from the Established Church of Ireland by the opposition of the then Archbishop of Dublin to Evangelical doctrine. At first Mr. Kelly's ministry was carried on in private houses; but, at length, York Street Chapel, Dublin, was erected for the exercise of his ministry, on what were virtually the lines of Independency. He was the author of a large number of hymns, larger even than Dr. Watts. His completed book contains seven hundred and sixty-seven. Like all voluminous hymn writers, there are many—most, we may say—that are not remarkable. But scattered over the volume there are hymns of great excellence. Of one of these, "We sing the praise of Him who died," Lord Selborne has said: "I doubt whether Montgomery ever wrote anything quite equal to this." This seems to me exaggerated praise, since James Montgomery must be ranked as one of the greatest of English hymnists. But still, at his best, Kelly is very good as a hymnist. Though we cannot subscribe to Lord Selborne's praise of the hymn he names, it is an exceedingly good one, fine in sentiment, and lyric in expression. In the Supplement to the "New Congregational Hymn Book," it was the subject of, perhaps, a more extraordinary alteration than any hymn which could be named, although many have suffered much at the hands of incompetent editors. In the original, the verse reads thus—

"Inscribed upon the cross we see,
In shining letters, GOD IS LOVE.
He bears our sins upon the tree,
He brings us mercy from above."

which was changed to the following—

"Inscribed upon the cross we see,
In crimson letters, darkly bright,
Of Holy Love the mystery,
For God is Love and God is Light."

The verse, as thus amended, is "darkly bright" indeed, but there is more of darkness than brightness. Quite equal to this hymn are—"The head that once was crowned with thorns," "Look, ye saints, the sight is glorious," and "We've no abiding city here," whilst his Evening Hymn, "Through the day Thy love has spared us," is one of the most tenderly beautiful for that season. Thomas Kelly deserves, and will probably long hold, a place of honour in the hymnody of the Church, but to doubt, as Lord Selborne has done, whether Montgomery ever wrote anything quite equal to his hymn on the Cross, shows an exaggerated estimate of Kelly, and a want of appreciation of Montgomery, who certainly holds a far higher place in the Christian Choir. He did not write nearly as many hymns as Kelly, probably because he had a much higher conception of what is essential to a good hymn. Would that this had been the case with hymnists generally, and that they had the grace to commit to the flames such of their hymns as were either echoes of previous ones, or but the mere rhymed prose, with which the hymnal stores of the Church are so sadly encumbered.

To scarcely any hymnist does this remark apply with less force than to James Montgomery (1771-1854), who came of a Moravian stock, and received his education at Fulneck, in Yorkshire. He had been designed for the ministry of that body, but was probably kept therefrom by a certain diffidence and shyness of nature which prevented him from even becoming a member of the Moravian Church till he was over forty years of age. To this peculiarity of his nature some of the excellences of his hymns may, perhaps, be ascribed. Too many of the hymnists have been of the bolder and more assertive type of character, and so their verses lack the tenderness and quiet reserve which add so much beauty to hymns. For variety, clearness, strength, suitability of form to subject, Montgomery's hymns have rarely, if ever, been excelled. An unusually large proportion of those he wrote has passed into use and favour. I found as many worthy of a place in public worship as in the far more voluminous productions of Dr. Watts. But for the prejudice in favour of Dr. Watts as the real founder of English hymnody—for which, indeed, he deserves high honour—Montgomery would, I believe, be ranked above him. Where can grander missionary hymns be found than his "O Spirit of the living God," and "Hark! the song of Jubilee." They move the heart like the sound of a trumpet. Where shall we find a nobler version of a Psalm than his of the 72nd, "Hail to the Lord's Anointed;" or if we turn to those of a more subdued type, how compact and yet tender is "When on Sinai's top I see;" how suggestive and impressive, "O where shall rest be found;" how pathetic, "According to Thy gracious word;" how comprehensive in its scope, how catholic in its sympathy, "Millions within Thy courts have met." In all these there is a unity of thought, a clearness of utterance, a purity of style, a healthiness of religious tone, ranking them amongst the choicest treasures of the Church's song. If Charles Wesley is more subjectively lyrical, Montgomery is more objectively clear and impressive. His writings did much to elevate and purify the taste of the Church in relation to hymnody. He seems to have been conscious that his real success had been as a hymnist rather than as a poet, since, when asked by a Whitby solicitor, "Which of your poems will live?" he replied, "None, sir; nothing, except, perhaps, a few of my hymns."

Mrs. Voke was an ardent friend of missions. Most of her hymns owe their origin to this feeling. Two of them, at a time when missionary hymns were much fewer in number and poorer in quality than they are now, were popular. One of these was "Ye messengers of Christ," and the other, "Behold the expected time draws near."

George Keith, a son-in-law of Dr. Gill, who is said to have written hymns as he listened to his father-in-law's sermons, is credited by Mr. Sedgwick, but on quite insufficient evidence, with the authorship of "How firm a foundation, ye saints of the Lord," a hymn of no great merit. It is really by Robert Keene, who compiled with Dr. Rippon the tune book to Dr. Rippon's "Selection of Hymns."

James Hogg (1772-1835), commonly known as the Ettrick Shepherd, one of Nature's geniuses, finds a place among the hymnists by one hymn, in which there are many poetic touches, "Lauded be Thy name for ever."

Harriet Auber (1773-1862), daughter of the rector of Tring, was the editor of "The Spirit of the Psalms," in which the deservedly popular hymn, "Our blest Redeemer, ere He breathed," with others of hers are found. It is one of the most beautiful hymns on "The Comforter" in the language. Her version of the 75th Psalm, beginning "That Thou, O Lord, art ever nigh," though not equal to the former, is of considerable merit.

John Cawood, M.A. (1775-1852), the perpetual curate of St. Ann's Chapel of Ease, Bewdley, was the author of at least seventeen hymns, of which one, "Almighty God, Thy word is cast," suitable to be sung after the sermon, is very practical, and adapted for its purpose.

Richard Mant, D.D. (1776-1848), Bishop of Dromore, was the author of "The Book of Psalms in an English Metrical Version," and "Ancient Hymns from the 'Roman Breviary' and Original Hymns" (1837); many of these hymns were inserted in his prose works.

Some of them are very vigorous, and marked by a certain grandeur of style. Perhaps the finest is "Bright the vision which delighted," which is often appropriately inserted in hymnals with the omission of the first verse, and beginning, "Round the Lord, in glory seated." His Litany, "Son of God, to Thee I cry," is a fine example of that class of composition; whilst there is a quiet restfulness about "There is a dwelling place above," which is very attractive. His Funeral Hymn, "For Thy dear saint, O Lord," has also not a little merit. The really anonymous hymn, "Praise the Lord, ye heavens adore Him," has often been ascribed, without proof, to Bishop Mant.

Thomas Campbell (1777-1844), the well-known author of "The Pleasures of Hope," and many stirring national poems, is represented in a few hymnals, by "When Jordan hush'd his waters still," which, as was to be expected, has poetic, but little hymnic merit. I have sometimes thought that the anxiety of editors to remove the charge that few great poets have contributed to hymnody, has sometimes led them to strain a point, so as to include in their collections verses by well-known authors which are not really hymns. In several recent hymnals there are compositions against which one would be disposed to write—a poem, but not a hymn. A distinction which may be briefly described in the following way. The *poem* dwells on a theme or a word, without designing it to be a vehicle of praise, or a medium for worship, whilst the *hymn proper* has one or both of these as its special purpose—it should be the lyric outburst of a worshipping spirit, calling and helping others to worship also.

Thomas Moore (1779-1852) is a considerable name in

poetry, and if his religious fervour had been stronger, might have been equally so in hymnody. In a literary and intellectual sense, he was singularly and most richly fitted for hymnic composition. He was deeply poetic; he had a wonderful command of rhythm; the music of his verse is lovely; and yet his hymns have never laid hold of the worshipping instinct. And the reason is probably to be found in a lack of spiritual fervour. Had a great religious movement taken hold of him, he would have been, I fancy, one of the greatest hymn writers of the world. As one regards the perfect mechanism of his hymns, the feeling rises in the heart, "O that the fire were there to set it in motion!" Having that fire, the hymns of many an inferior writer have grown into far greater favour. And yet we could hardly spare from our collections such hymns as "Thou art, O God, the life and light," with its exquisite poetry, or "O Thou who dry'st the mourner's tear," with its beautiful verse embodying the fine idea of Blanco White's noble sonnet, "Mysterious Night." Did Moore borrow the idea from Blanco White or Blanco White from Moore?—

> "Then sorrow, touch'd by Thee, grows bright
> With more than rapture's ray:
> As darkness shows us worlds of light
> We never saw by day."

His rendering of Miriam's song, "Sound the loud timbrel o'er Egypt's dark sea," used to be a great favourite, but is less so now that a tenderer spirit is in the ascendant in the Church.

Marianne Nunn (1779-1847) is well known by her hymn, "One there is above all others," a version of John Newton's beginning in the same way, adapted to be sung to a favourite Welsh tune.

Ralph Wardlaw, D.D. (1779-1853), occupies a considerable place in the theology, but a small one in the hymnody of his age. For a collection he edited, he wrote eleven hymns, of which the most widely known one is "Lift up to God the voice of praise," which has a force and crispness of utterance that are remarkable. To these characteristics, rather than to its poetic quality, its popularity is due.

Joseph Dacre Carlyle, B.D. (1759-1804), the learned Professor of Arabic at Cambridge, appended to a volume of poems, suggested by scenes in Asia Minor, three of a religious character. One of these is the hymn, "Lord, when we bend before Thy throne," intended for use before public worship, calling the heart to sincerity and penitence before God. It is a hymn of great reality and tenderness, and deservedly popular.

John Marriott (1780-1825), for a time Vicar of Church Lawford, in Warwickshire, was the author of the Missionary Hymn, "Thou, whose Almighty word," which justly holds a place in the first rank.

George Croly, LL.D. (1780-1860), acquired considerable reputation in literature, and wrote a good deal of sacred poetry, but of his "Psalms and Hymns for Public Worship," containing twenty Psalms and the same number of hymns, not one has established itself in the affections of the Church.

Gerard Thomas Noel, M.A. (1782-1851, elder brother of the devoted Baptist W. Noel), Vicar of Romsey, is remembered by a hymn often used at the Communion, "If human kindness meets return." It is full of a tender and subdued feeling, and admirably suited for such a service.

William Bengo Collyer, D.D., LL.D. (1782-1854), was a Congregational minister at Hanover Chapel, Peckham, and, like a few of his brethren in the ministry at that time, had a considerable reputation for attracting more fashionable folk than are usually found within the circle of Dissent. The Duke of Kent, and others of the royal blood, were occasional worshippers in his chapel. He belonged to a type which has left no representatives behind, but of which there were in his time not a few, including men like the Claytons, Thomas Adkins, of Southampton, Dr. Raffles, of Liverpool, and Dr. Morton Brown of Cheltenham. All of them were touched in their style of preaching by the influence of Dr. Johnson. Dr. Collyer published a collection of hymns for his own congregation, but those from his own pen are by no means remarkable. The best is "Return, O wanderer, return." He was one of the authors of that very composite hymn in its present form, "Great God, what do I see and hear," the original source of which was a hymn by Ringwaldt, of which Dr. Collyer saw the first verse in a translation by Jacobi. He thought it was Luther's. To it he added three verses; these have been considerably altered by other editors. It used to be often sung, but conceptions of the future life have so altered during recent years that it is now very rarely used. I have not heard it sung for at least twenty years.

Reginald Heber, D.D. (1783-1826), the greatly-beloved Bishop of Calcutta, is one of the few hymnists of an earlier time whose reputation is increasing rather than diminishing. Fault used to be found with his hymns because they "carried the poetic element to its utmost point." Josiah Miller says: "They are usually distinguished by a rhetorical flow, and an elevation of manner and imagery that threatens to take them out of the class of hymns, and rob them of that pious moderation we ordinarily expect to meet with in such productions." The pious moderation of which Mr. Miller speaks has been the curse of hymnody, and it will be found that such pious moderation will take the hymns marked thereby, before long, out of the Church's song; whilst the poetic element discernible in Heber's hymns is bringing them more and more into favour and use. I have an impression that a larger proportion of the hymns written by him are in actual use than is the case with any considerable writer. By use I mean, not what is commonly meant—their presence in hymnals—but their actual use in the worship of the Church. Insertion in a hymnal is one thing; singing by a congregation is quite another. A hymnist's true reputation rests on the latter, and not on the former, since very few editors have, as yet, had the courage to omit from their collections hymns which have passed out of use.* Heber's best known, and perhaps the most popular of all hymns for missionary services, is "From Greenland's icy mountains." The story of its production is as follows. On Whitsunday, 1819, the late Dr. Shipley, Dean of St. Asaph, and vicar of Wrexham, preached a sermon in Wrexham Church in aid of the Society for the Propagation of the Gospel in Foreign Parts. That day was also fixed upon for the commencement of the Sunday Evening Lectures to be

* Since writing this paragraph, I have learned from Mr. W. T. Brooke, that both he and the Rev. John Julian, the Editor of the "Dictionary of Hymnology," came to the conclusion that every hymn written by Heber is now in common use—a thing unique in hymnody.

established in that church, and the late Bishop of Calcutta (Heber), then rector of Hodnet, the Dean's son-in-law, undertook to deliver the first lecture. In the course of the Saturday previous, the Dean and his son-in-law being together at the vicarage, the former requested Heber to write "something for them to sing in the morning," and he retired for that purpose from the table where the Dean and a few friends were sitting, to a distant part of the room. In a short time the Dean enquired, "What have you written?" Heber, having then composed the three first verses, read them over "There, there; that will do very well," said the Dean. "No, no; the sense is not complete," replied Heber. Accordingly, he added the fourth verse; and the Dean being inexorable to his repeated request of "Let me add another! let me add another!" thus completed the hymn which has since become so celebrated. It was sung the next morning in Wrexham Church for the first time. Only one correction appears in the MS., that of the word "savage" to "heathen." Almost equal in popularity is his hymn for Trinity Sunday, "Holy, holy, holy, Lord God Almighty," a hymn of great beauty, and full of a rich lyric feeling. Its only fault, in my judgment, is the too metaphysical line, "God in Three Persons, blessed Trinity," due, in all probability, to the fact that it was written for Trinity Sunday. In hymns, dogma should take on the softened form of poetry, and be a pervading spirit —not a metaphysical declaration. Indeed, the doctrine of the Trinity finds much more spiritual expression in Scripture than in the creeds of the Church of which, when he wrote this line, the good Bishop's mind was evidently full. Quite equal in merit is "Hosanna to the living Lord," a glorious burst of praise, relieved, here and there, by strains of great solemnity and tenderness. "The Lord of might from Sinai's brow," is a hymn of great force and picturesqueness, unhappily disfigured by the line which tells of Christ meeting the Father's anger; a line due, not to the kindly spirit of the writer, but to the theology current in his time. "Lord of mercy and of might" is a litany solemn and grand. "The Son of God goes forth to war" is a most stirring hymn, marked in parts by very pathetic touches, and strikes quite a new note in hymnody. "Thou art gone to the grave, but we will not deplore thee," is one of the most prized of Funeral Hymns. Bishop Heber evidently thought that hymns should be more marked by poetic and literary grace than they usually are, since he compiled a small collection, containing what he thought the best of his own, together with others by Jeremy Taylor, Addison, Sir Walter Scott, Dean Milman, and others of a like character. In common with James Montgomery, he did much to elevate the standard of hymnody.

Bernard Barton (1784-1849) presents to us the strange spectacle of a member of the unsinging body of the Society of Friends as a contributor to the Church's song. From his poetical works, two hymns have been drawn of no little merit—"Lamp of our feet, whereby we trace," on the Bible, and "Walk in the light, so shalt thou know." One cannot help wishing that they had been addressed (as hymns should be) directly to God. The first is really a description of Scripture, and the second a persuasive to sincerity of life.

Henry Kirke White (1785-1806), is one of the small company of real poets who have contributed to hymnody.

It was concerning him that Byron used the striking image of the struck eagle, which

> "Viewed his own feather on the fatal dart,
> And winged the shaft that quivered to his heart."

His life was brought to a premature end by his excessive devotion to mathematical study. Strange to say, the fragment of the hymn by which he is best known, was found on the back of his mathematical papers—"Much in sorrow, oft in woe." It was afterwards completed by Frances Fuller Maitland, afterwards Mrs. Colquhoun. There is a singular delicacy and tenderness in his hymn for a family party at eventide, "O Lord, another day is flown." "Awake, sweet harp of Judah, wake," a much less known hymn, is in an altogether bolder style.

Sir Robert Grant (1785-1838), Governor of Bombay, wrote some twelve hymns, which were published after his death. From this small collection, three have acquired, and deservedly, great popularity. Perhaps the finest is "O worship the King," a jubilant hymn of praise, relieved by one verse in a tenderer strain, beginning "Frail children of dust." "Saviour, when in dust to Thee" is one of the finest hymns in the litany style in our language. His hymn, "When gathering clouds around I view," is very pathetic, but is, perhaps, too personal for use in public worship.

Andrew Reed, D.D. (1787-1862), minister of Wycliffe Chapel, but better known as the founder of three of the greatest Asylums in London, was the editor of "The Hymn Book," a too pretentious title, not justified by the quality of the book. To this collection he contributed nineteen, and his wife twenty-one hymns. One of his hymns, and perhaps only one, is of great merit, "Spirit

Divine, attend our prayers." It has deservedly passed into use in many sections of the Church, and is one of the most inspiring hymns we possess addressed to the Holy Spirit.

Thomas Raffles, D.D., LL.D. (1788-1863), enjoyed a great reputation as minister of Great George Street Chapel, Liverpool. He was one of the contributors to a small volume, "Poems by Three Friends," and issued a supplement to Watts's "Psalms and Hymns" for use in his own congregation. A few of his hymns passed into the "New Congregational Hymn Book," but none of them are likely to retain a place in the favour of the Church. They are little more than rhymed prose. Perhaps the best are "Lord, like the publican I stand," and "High in yonder realms of light," the latter written for Collyer's Collection in 1812.

Josiah Conder (1789-1855) did a great deal, both by the hymns he wrote and his editing of the hymns of other writers, to raise the standard of taste in hymnody. The issue of the "Congregational Hymn Book" under his editorship in 1836, marks a distinct step in advance. This was intended to be used as a supplement to Dr. Watts's "Psalms and Hymns," and thus Mr. Conder was relieved of the great difficulty meeting the editors of all hymnals for use in churches where Watts had been largely used, of making a selection from his writings. Very few have had the courage to reduce Dr. Watts's hymns within the narrower dimensions which, in the present state of hymnody, they rightly deserve to fill. Most of the Hymnals for use in Congregational and Baptist churches are spoilt by too large an infusion of the Watts element. Mr. Conder had not to face that problem, and so his task was easier. But still, for the age in which it was done, it is marked by great ability, and does great credit to his critical faculty. To it he contributed fifty-six hymns from his own pen: too large a number by one author; an error into which most editors who have been also hymnists have fallen. A hymn writer should scarcely undertake the task of editing a hymnal. A natural love for his own compositions is almost sure to lead him astray, as it did the late Rev. Paxton Hood and the Rev. Godfrey Thring; to both of whom, especially the latter, we are indebted for many noble hymns. Still, the general level of Mr. Conder's hymns is high; so high that we wonder they are not *more* used beyond the Church to which he belonged. He had the mastery of a considerable variety of style. In the more bold and jubilant strain, his best hymns are—"The Lord is King, lift up thy voice," "O give thanks to Him who made," and "Beyond, beyond the boundless sky." The last of these is a very distinctive and remarkable hymn on the omnipresence of God. In "O show me not my Saviour dying," there is a very striking mingling of minor and major tones. Perhaps this is his finest hymn. Fine specimens of his more subdued style may be found in "How shall I follow Him I serve," "Holy, holy Lord," "Day by day the manna fell," and "Heavenly Father, to whose eye;" whilst in "Head of the Church, our risen Lord," there is a fulness of meaning, finding expression through very few words, that is very remarkable. It is like a poetical collect. His Communion Hymn, "Bread of heaven, on Thee we feed," though by no means his best, has probably reached a greater general popularity than any other of his hymns.

Within the years 1791 and 1792 will be found the birth-dates of a company of hymnists filling a considerable place in hymnody, and whose hymns are still, and seem likely to remain, in constant use—Dean Milman, James Edmeston, Sir John Bowring, John Keble, and Henry Francis Lyte.

Henry Hart Milman (1791-1868), the learned and accomplished Dean of St. Paul's, was, like Josiah Conder, a large contributor to literature. His historical works once held a high place, and exerted a deep influence on the thought of the Church. But he is known to a far wider circle by his hymns than by his histories. His compositions are chiefly in the litany form. They have a certain grandeur and solemnity of style, but are somewhat lacking in spontaneity and lyric force. They are the work of the literary artist rather than of the sacred poet; of the finished scholar rather than the psalmist. Still, they possess a certain grandeur and pathos which make them impressive. "When our heads are bowed with woe," and "Lord, have mercy when we pray," are solemn litanies. "Ride on, ride on in majesty," is a striking rendering of the story of our Lord's entry into the beloved but doomed city of Jerusalem; whilst in "Lord, Thou didst arise and say," there is a union of tenderness and force which is very striking.

James Edmeston (1791-1867) was a very large contributor to hymnody, and wrote many hymns for the young. By far the most popular is "Saviour, breathe an evening blessing," which is marked by a tenderness of tone that renders it specially suitable as an Evening Hymn. It was written after reading "Salte's Travels in

Abyssinia," in which the following passage occurs: "At night, their short Evening Hymn, 'Jesus, forgive us,' stole through the camp." It deserves to be ranked with the still better-known Evening Hymns of Keble, Lyte, and Ellerton. Scarcely equal to it, but still of great merit, is his "Lead us, Heavenly Father, lead us," a prayer for Divine guidance and sympathy, written for the children of the London Orphan Asylum.

Sir John Bowring, LL.D., F.R.S. (1792-1872), who achieved a considerable reputation as a diplomatist, and as a scholar versed in the language and literature of many lands, was a member of the Unitarian Church; but in feeling, if not in doctrine, more allied to the Evangelical school. Few who sing his hymn, "In the cross of Christ I glory," would imagine that it came from such a source. After a lecture I once delivered on Hymnody, this hymn was quoted by a subsequent speaker as an example of one embodying doctrine which is usually regarded as being specially Evangelical. It *is* a noble hymn; equally fine in thought, feeling, and expression. Bowring's little book, "Matins and Vespers," though small in bulk, is rich in quality. To him we owe "From all evil, all temptation" (erroneously ascribed in the "New Congregational Hymn Book" to Bishop Mant), "God is love, His mercy brightens," and "Lead us with Thy gentle sway," all of them delightful hymns, and the subdued and pathetic utterance, "From the recesses of a lowly spirit." No one can, without prejudice, read hymns like these, and not feel that, beneath great diversities as to *doctrine*, there may be, and often is, a real unity of Christian *spirit*.

Born in the same year as Sir John Bowring, but passing away six years before him, was John Keble, who belonged to a school of religious thought most remote from that of the Unitarian. He was one of the leaders of the great Oxford movement, and did much, by his poetry, to help its progress. Keble was as remarkable for finish as Bowring for width of scholarship; and, speaking generally, it may be said that finish rather than strength is the characteristic of his poetry. Space will not allow me to speak of his poetry generally. His "Christian Year" has great merits and great defects. It deserves a high, though not, perhaps, so high a place as it has secured in popular estimation. He falls far below his early friend, Newman, in depth of thought and compactness of expression. Keble takes pages to set forth what Newman would compress into a few lines. Keble descends to details, leaving little for the imagination to fill in; whilst Newman utters suggestive words which draw the mind on to large fields of spiritual thought and feeling. Keble's principal poetical works were "The Christian Year," which attained to a circulation perhaps larger than any work of the kind in modern times, and from the profits of which Hursley Church was built; and the "Lyra Innocentium." Most of the hymns of Mr. Keble which have come into use have been taken from "The Christian Year." His Evening Hymn, "Sun of my soul, Thou Saviour dear," which is a selection of verses from the hymn as it stands in "The Christian Year," beginning "'Tis gone, that bright and orbed blaze," has, I fancy, in recent times supplanted, in common use, Bishop Ken's famous hymn for the same season, which excels it in vigour, but falls short of it in tenderness of thought and expression. His Morning Hymn, "O timely happy, timely wise," is, perhaps, equal in merit to the evening one, but is not nearly so widely known or greatly loved. One reason for this may be found in the fact that we are more disposed to hymn singing in the evening than in the morning, and that we are more moved by songs of the night than of the day. There are fine verses in "There is a book who runs may read," a hymn on the book of Nature; but perhaps the finest, and the key to all the rest, is a verse too often omitted—

"Two worlds are ours: 'tis only sin
Forbids us to descry
The mystic heaven and earth within,
Plain as the earth and sky."

"The livelong night we've toiled in vain," is a hymn well fitted to cheer desponding ministers of the kingdom of God. "The Voice that breathed o'er Eden" is one of the finest of Marriage Hymns. "Spirit of Christ, Thine earnest given," is in his noblest strain, and admirably suited for use after the Ordination Prayer at the consecration of men to the ministry of Christ.

Born in the year following that of Keble, but passing away twenty years before him, was Henry Francis Lyte, to whom we owe the Evening Hymn which competes with Keble's for the first place in the estimation of the Church. It would be difficult to say which is the more frequently used, Keble's "Sun of my soul," or Lyte's "Abide with me, fast falls the eventide;" probably their use is about equal. A particular interest gathers about the latter hymn, since it was the last penned by its author. Ordered abroad on account of his health, and with the shadow of death gathering and deepening around him, the good pastor of the little fishing town of Brixham, on the westerly side of Torbay, addressed words of tender farewell to his flock, administered the Communion for the last time, and then retired to the privacy of his own room. When, in the evening, he rejoined his family, he handed them "Abide with me," with music to which he had set it. The hymn, though not its accompanying music, has enshrined itself in the tenderest affections of the Church at large. By this he is best known, but a very large number of his hymns have grown into considerable popularity, notably the following—"Praise, my soul, the King of Heaven," marked by a lovely union of boldness and tenderness; "Jesus, I my cross have taken," a plaintive but resolute expression of devotion to the following of Christ. His "Spirit of the Psalms" contains many fine versions; specially good are those of the 65th, "Praise, Lord, for Thee in Zion waits," and of the 81st, "Sing to the Lord our might." His version of a hymn by Francis Quarles, beginning "Long did I toil, and knew no earthly rest," is of great beauty, and shows the noble use which might be made of some of the hymns of the early hymnists, which, though fine in thought, are too archaic in their mode of expression for use in their original forms.

Felicia Dorothea Hemans (1794-1835) is best known by her more distinctly poetical works, but the few hymns we owe to her make us wish that she had consecrated her powers more largely to this end. Her most widely known hymn, "Lowly and solemn be," I should rank as one of the very finest of that order in the language. It is plaintive and solemn, both in its thought and expression; the metre being exquisitely suited to the sentiment. It is taken from a funeral dirge which follows her poem, "The Funeral Day of Sir Walter Scott," and is the utterance of a heart moved and solemnised by the thought of death. Her verses on Christ in Gethsemane, "He knelt, the Saviour knelt and prayed," and those on the heralds of the birth of Christ, "O lovely voices of the sky," and for the death of a child, "Saviour, now receive him," are all marked by that gracefulness and tenderness which, alas! are so often conspicuous by their absence in hymnic compositions. These are likely to become more popular as the taste of worshippers becomes more cultivated.

Thomas Binney (1798-1874) is chiefly remembered as one of the most suggestive and inspiring preachers of his time; and the leader, it may be said, of a new style of preaching. He also did much to elevate the style and tone of worship in Nonconformist churches, by the example set in his services at the King's Weigh House Chapel, where for forty years he ministered, as well as by his suggestive little book, "The Service of Song in the House of the Lord." Under his direction, what is called "The Weigh House series of Tunes, Chants, and Anthems," was issued. He wrote some few hymns and poems, but, as a hymnist, he is almost exclusively remembered by "Eternal Light, Eternal Light," written about 1826. This hymn is one of remarkable originality and force, and is likely to be remembered even when his eloquent sermons are forgotten. It is said to have been conceived by its author during his ministry at Newport, in the Isle of Wight, on a brilliant starry night, which moved him deeply. A Sunday Evening Hymn by him, beginning "Holy Father, whom we praise," has found its way into a few collections, but has neither the distinctiveness nor beauty of "Eternal Light, Eternal Light."

Charlotte Elliott (1789-1871) is one of the most popular of lady hymnists. To her pen we owe a large number of hymns, the two most popular of which are "Just as I am, without one plea," and "My God and Father, while I stray." Scarcely a hymnal for general use is now published in which these hymns do not find a place. They are marked by so distinctive a style, and so pathetic a spirit, that they have a strange power over the heart. They are deeply Evangelical, not only in their sentiment, but, what is of more importance, in their feeling. There are other hymns by her far less known, but showing the same high qualities, and well deserving a place in the Hymnals of the Church. Amongst these, we should give a foremost place to "Christian, seek not yet repose." In this hymn, it is rather startling to find the idea of guardian angels, which has rarely been associated with the faith of Evangelical Churchmen, to which school Miss Elliott belonged. "Let me be with Thee where Thou art," "O, Holy Saviour, Friend unseen," "My God, is any hour so sweet," and "Leaning on Thee, my Guide, my Friend." Most of her hymns were written for those in sorrow or sickness, and are, perhaps, somewhat more suited for private than public worship. But their great excellence, their reality of tone, their pathos, have drawn many of them into more public use than was intended by their authoress.

John Harris, D.D. (1802-1856), attained to great reputation in his day as an eloquent preacher, a brilliant essayist, and a theological professor. He wrote a few hymns, for one of which he claims mention. "Light up this house with glory, Lord," is a composition of great merit, full of spiritual thought, expressed with much force and beauty.

John Hampden Gurney (1802-1862), rector of St. Mary's, Mary-le-bone, is an instance of a man who, without any great lyric or poetic power, had yet such a true idea of what a hymn should be, and such skill in working into good form the ideas of others, that the hymns he has given us are deservedly popular. They are all characterised by good taste, healthiness of Christian feeling, and suitability to public worship. "Lord, as to Thy dear cross we flee," is included in a large number of collections. "Through centuries of sin and woe" is a fine hymn for use in time of war, as is "Great King of nations, hear," in time of trouble. "Yes, God is good," is in a brighter strain. In several instances, notably in the following, Mr. Gurney wrought up to good purpose the work of previous hymnists—"Yes, God is good," by Eliza Lee Follen, and "We saw Thee not when Thou didst come." The latter, in its present form, is a very striking hymn.

Isaac Williams, B.D. (1802-1865), one of the contributors to the "Tracts for the Times," and, of course, belonging to the High Church party of which they formed the manifesto, is a contributor of considerable importance to sacred poetry by means of original and translated pieces; many of the latter have found their way into Hymnals of the High Church school. But one of his hymns, "Lord, in this Thy mercy's day," an extract from a poem of 110 stanzas in "The Baptistery," has passed into hymnals of a more evangelical and less ecclesiastical type; but it is scarcely in place in them, and has, in my judgment, a dogmatic tone which may be suitable in discourse, but is not in song. The following hymn from his pen is in a very different strain, and seems to me very lovely—

The child leans on its parent's breast,
Leaves there its cares, and is at rest;
The bird sits singing by his nest,
And tells aloud
His trust in God, and so is blest
'Neath every cloud.

He has no store, he sows no seed,
Yet sings aloud and doth not heed;
By flowing stream or grassy mead
He sings to shame
Men, who forget, in fear of need,
A Father's name.

The heart that trusts for ever sings,
And feels as light as it had wings;
A well of peace within it springs;
Come good or ill,
Whate'er to-day, to-morrow brings,
It is His will.

John Chandler, M.A. (1806-1876), is chiefly known by translations published in "Hymns of the Primitive Church," many of which are of great worth, and which have been largely drawn upon by editors of Church of England Hymnals. The best known are—"Christ is our Corner-stone," from the form in the "Paris Breviary;" "O Jesus, Lord of heavenly grace," from St. Ambrose; "As now the sun's declining rays," from Charles Coffin, in the "Paris Breviary;" "O Christ, our hope and heart's desire," from an Ambrosian Hymn of the 9th or 10th century; "'Tis for conquering kings to gain," from Charles Coffin in the "Paris Breviary;" "Thou brightness of the Father's face." Mr. Chandler deserves very high rank as a translator: a task almost as difficult as that of original composition.

Julia Anne Elliot, *nee* Marshall (died 1841), wife of the Rev. H. V. Elliott, clearly had great capacity for hymn composition. This is evident in her lovely Evening Hymn, "On the dewy breath of even," and "We love Thee, Lord, yet not alone."

Elizabeth Mills (1808-1829), wife of Thomas Mills, M.P., is remembered by the well-known hymn, "We speak of the realms of the blest," suggested by a passage in "Bridges on the 119th Psalm"—"We speak of heaven; but oh! to be there." It was written a few weeks before her death.

Sarah Adams, *nee* Flower (1805-1849), contributed thirteen pieces to "Hymns and Anthems," published by Charles James Fox in 1841. One of these, "Nearer, my God, to Thee," is amongst the most popular hymns in the language, and is an illustration, of which hymnody furnishes so many, that, beneath all diversities of theological thought, there is a real unity in all Christian hearts. Though Mrs. Adams belonged to the Unitarian Church, her hymn is sung in Trinitarian churches of every order. She also wrote "He sendeth sun, He sendeth shower," which is also of great beauty.

Henry Addiscott (1806-1860), minister of the Independent Church at Taunton, is only known to have written one hymn, "And is there, Lord, a cross for me," but it is so good in sentiment and spirit, and so distinctive, that both the hymn and its writer deserve remembrance.

Arthur Tozer Russell, B.C.L. (1806-1874), vicar of Holy Trinity Church, Wrockwardine Wood, Wellington, Shropshire, was a considerable contributor to literature, both by original and translated works. His work as a hymnist consisted chiefly of translations from the German, contributed to "Hymns for Public Worship and Private Devotion," edited by Mr. Ernest Bunsen. He also edited "Psalms and Hymns; partly original, partly translated; for the use of the Church of England."

This work is notable for its translations from the German. The original hymns by which he is known are—"We praise, we bless Thee; Lord, we confess Thee," and "Another year has fled, renew." These are both good hymns; the former marked by a subdued solemnity, and the latter by great tenderness. A hymn by him, beginning "O God of life, whose power benign," not without merit, but far inferior to those we have named, was included in "Hymns, Ancient and Modern," but omitted from the revised edition of that work.

Thomas Rawson Taylor (1807-1835), a Congregational minister in Sheffield, afterwards classical tutor in Airedale College, where his career was cut short by death when only 28 years of age, is chiefly remembered as the author of the well-known hymn, "I'm but a stranger here," which is marked by no little pathos, but goes a little too far in the direction of what George Eliot called "other-worldliness," when it speaks of earth as "a desert drear." The longing for another world is not quite healthy when it leads to disparagement of the present one, which is quite as truly of the divine appointment as that which is to succeed it. His hymn for the young, "There was a time when children sang," is in a far healthier strain, and deserves very high rank as one of the sweetest hymns for children in the language.

Richard Chenevix Trench, D.D. (1807-1886), vicar of Alverstoke, and afterwards of Itchenstoke, theological professor at King's College, London, Dean of Westminster, and Archbishop of Dublin, occupied a considerable place in the literary and theological world of his day. An eminently interesting writer, who gave a charm to every subject of which he wrote, he found a place among the hymnists only by reason of adaptations of certain of his poems for public worship. In the strictest sense, these versions are not really hymns, but the sentiments of the poems thus used, their largeness of view, their tenderness of thought, their beauty of expression, have led to their adaptation as hymns. If the real object of hymns be to quicken devotional and gracious feeling in those who sing them, then Dr. Trench's lines deserve the place they have obtained in public worship. Though he cannot be called a *great* poet, yet there is an indescribable charm about his poetry which would lead us to part with the works of *some greater* poets rather than his. "Let all men know that all men move" is a part of his poem, beginning "I say to thee, do thou repeat." "Make channels for the streams of love," is a rendering of his beautiful little poem on "The law of Love." We have often wondered that the good Archbishop never applied his poetic faculty to the production of hymns. He had every quality needful for a good and even a masterly hymnist. The reason may, perhaps, be found in the fact that, in his earlier days, when his poetic faculty was at its zenith, hymns were comparatively little used in the Church of which he was so distinguished an ornament.

Since writing the foregoing paragraph, I have been interested to find that his friend John Sterling entertained a like feeling. In the "Letters and Memorials" of Richard Chenevix Trench, just published, there is a letter written from Floriac, near Bordeaux, by Sterling, dated May 13, 1837, in which the following passage occurs:—"I hope you still find time to write poetry, and I have often thought of the importance of supplying English devotion with more genuine and satisfactory hymns than we now possess, in which, it seems to me, you might be of much use. I would work for the purpose myself if I thought there was any chance of my succeeding. [He did write one or two hymns of great freshness and beauty.] I wish you would try. You would influence millions whom poetry in any other form would never reach." In the half-century which has elapsed since John Sterling penned his letter, much progress has been made in the direction there indicated; and when poets feel that no nobler use can be made of their powers than in providing verses for use in public and private worship, the golden age of hymnody will have come.

Christopher Wordsworth, D.D. (1807-1885), his contemporary (they were born in the same year), successively Head Master of Harrow, Canon and Archdeacon of Westminster, and Bishop of Lincoln, a larger but less popular contributor to literature than Trench, though he came of a poetic stock, is far less remarkable as a poet than as a hymnist. He seems to have discerned more clearly than Dr. Trench the large place which hymns would fill, and the deep influence they would exert in the Church. This is clear from "The Holy Year," published by him with a view to supply suitable hymns for each and every occasion of the Ecclesiastical Year; in the preface to which he says: "A Church Hymn Book ought not to be content with supplying *general* hymns on martyrs, and *general* hymns on Apostles and Evangelists. These are like general exordiums of speeches—not appropriate to any. But something more is requisite in a Church Hymn Book. The peculiar teaching which each festival supplies, and the special expression of thankfulness which each festival prompts, ought to find a responsive echo in the hymn of each of the festivals of the Christian Year." Dr. Wordsworth set himself to supply the want he thus felt; and, steeped in knowledge of Scripture and Christian antiquities though he was, in our judgment his attempt is a failure, and that not from want of ability or zeal, but simply from lack of materials. He could not make bricks without straw. Some even of the Evangelists are mere names to us; of their character and history we *know* literally nothing. Hymns for the days consecrated to their memory must, in the nature of things, be either so vague as to have no special application, or be the result of untrustworthy traditions, or the play of fancy around their names. And so it comes to pass that, when Dr. Wordsworth had a good subject for his verse, his hymns are of the highest order; when a place in the Church Year had to be filled for which no trustworthy information could be found, his efforts end in failure. And even when such information was forthcoming the result was not much better, since it was a bit of versified history rather than a hymn. It is the fruitless attempt to provide hymns for each festival of the ecclesiastical year which, more or less, lowers the quality of every Church of England hymnal. The idea of an ecclesiastical year itself is not justified by either the teaching of the Apostles or the information contained in their writings. The connection of certain names with certain days rests on the flimsiest tradition, whilst the very attempt to teach any special lesson suggested by the lives of the Apostles is sure to lead to the didactic, which is the worst form hymns can assume.

It is the rarest thing to find such hymns with any lyric fire. But where Dr. Wordsworth is free from such trammels, he often rises to a great elevation of style and thought, marred here and there, it is true, by dogmatic rather than scripturally spiritual forms of expression. Yet the high quality of his best hymns makes us tolerate such minor defects. Very picturesque and beautiful is his "The Galilean fishers toil." "Gracious Spirit, Holy Ghost" is a lovely lyric expression of the grand ideas of St. Paul's great utterance on charity in his First Epistle to the Corinthians. Equally beautiful is the hymn so often used at the offertory, "O Lord of heaven, and earth, and sea." A noble outburst of song concerning the great multitude of the redeemed in heaven, is "Hark! the sound of holy voices, chanting at the crystal sea." His Evening Hymn is one of great tenderness and beauty, "The day is gently sinking to a close," marred in one point by the line, "The weary world is mouldering to decay," which seems to me morbid and ascetic rather than healthily Christian. His Sunday Morning Hymn, "O day of rest and gladness," is one of his happiest efforts, and has deeply enshrined itself in the affections of the Church at large. His Litany Hymn, "Father, we humbly pray," includes a vast number of objects in its petitions, which are couched in the most sincere and well expressed forms. When Dr. Wordsworth touches the great themes of the Gospel, or seeks to give expression to the deepest Christian feeling, he rarely fails. It is only when the ecclesiastical overpowers this deeper Christian feeling that his muse fails.

Joseph Anstice (1808-1836), first professor of Classical

Literature in King's College, London; to which he was appointed at the very early age of 22, was the author of fifty-four hymns, which "were all dictated to his wife during the last few weeks of his life, and were composed just at the period of the day (the afternoon) when he most felt the oppression of his illness; all his brighter morning hours being given to pupils up to the very day of his death." They were privately printed by his widow after his decease. Twenty-seven of these were included in "The Child's Christian Year," published in 1841, edited by Mrs. Frances Mary Yonge, mother of the well-known novelist, Miss C. M. Yonge, of Otterbourne, near Winchester. This little book was attributed to the Rev. John Keble, probably because of its title, and the preface, which was from his pen. Thus it came to pass that some of Mr. Anstice's hymns were often attributed, in error, to the author of "The Christian Year." In one or two of them there is a certain similarity to Mr. Keble's. The best known of his hymns are—"Lord, Thou in all things like wert made," which is usually altered to "In all things like Thy brethren, Thou," a forcible and yet tender rendering of the thought of the author of the Epistle to the Hebrews in chap. ii. 17. "Darkly rose the guilty morning," a striking hymn on the Crucifixion, as caused not only by those who actually brought it about, but by our sins, for which He was wounded. "O Lord, how happy should we be," a vision of, and longing for the blessedness of a life in which all our care should be cast upon God. His Harvest Hymn, "Lord of the harvest, once again," and his Evening Hymn, "Father by Thy love and power," are both of value, but have not the distinctiveness of those we have previously mentioned. We are disposed to give a high place to his little known hymn, "Sweet is the Spirit's strain," suggested by the great invitation of the Apocalypse, "The Spirit and the Bride say come." Hymns of this order are confessedly difficult to write without becoming sermons in disguise, and having a certain pharisaic tone of "we are the people" about them. This hymn avoids these perils, and is tender and beautiful in a very high degree. It is so little known that I append it—

Sweet is the Spirit's strain;
Breath'd by soft pleadings inly heard,
By all the heart's deep fountains, stirr'd
By conscience and the written word;
Come, wanderers, home again!

The Bride repeats the call;
By high thanksgiving, lowly prayer,
By days of rest and fostering care,
By holy rites, that all may share;
She whispers, Come! to all.

Let him who hears say, Come!
If thou hast been sin's willing slave,
If thou art risen from that grave,
Thy sleeping brethren seek to save,
And call the wanderers home.

And let all come who thirst;
Freely for every child of woe
The streams of living waters flow,
And whosoever will may go
Where healing fountains burst.

There, drink, and be at rest;
On Him who died for thee believe;
The Spirit's quickening grace receive;
No more the God who seeks thee grieve;
Be holy and be blest!

Had Professor Anstice's life been spared longer his hymns would probably have undergone careful revision, by which they would have been freed from the faults which here and there are evident. But when the circumstances under which they were produced are taken into account, they are seen to show great poetic and spiritual insight.

William Lindsay Alexander, D.D. (1808-1884), minister of Augustine Church, Edinburgh, and Professor of Theology in the Theological Hall of the Scotch Congregational Churches, was a large contributor to the Biblical and theological literature of his time. He wrote several hymns which were included in the "Augustine Hymn Book," prepared for the use of his own church. The only one likely to retain a place in hymnody is one for the aged, "I'm kneeling at the threshold," which, however, is only suitable for private use.

Jane Crewdson, *née* Fox (1809-1863), like many another hymnist, "learnt in suffering what she taught in song." During a long illness, she wrote several volumes of hymns and poems, from which two hymns of a pathetic kind have found their way into the song of the Church—"There is no sorrow, Lord, too light," and "O Saviour, I have nought to plead," but are, perhaps, more suitable for use in the home than in the Church.

Henry Alford, D.D. (1810-1871), well known for his edition of the Greek Testament, and as the catholic-spirited Dean of Canterbury, possessed a poetic power which found its best expression in verses of a religious kind. He wrote not a few hymns, most of which are wanting in lyric force; but in two that element is very conspicuous. "Come, ye thankful people, come," is probably the most popular Harvest Hymn now in existence, and deservedly finds a place in nearly every hymnal published in recent times, and is sung at the great majority of harvest festivals. "Forward be our watchword" is equally popular as a Processional Hymn, and when sung to Sir Arthur Sullivan's tune is singularly inspiring. It has suffered much at the hands of many editors, whose alterations have broken the continuity of its thought, and hidden the historic event—the passing of the Israelites into the Promised Land—out of which the hymn evidently grew in the author's mind. It was written to be sung at the Tenth Festival of Parochial Choirs of the Canterbury Diocesan Union, on the 6th June, 1871. It was accompanied with music from the Dean's pen, to which, however, it is rarely, if ever, sung now. The original text will be found in Appendix B to "The Life of Dean Alford." His Baptismal Hymn, "In token that thou shalt not fear," is striking, and very popular in churches where the sign of the cross is used in Baptism, although the use made of that symbol in the hymn is of such a kind that it might be used in other churches. His hymn, "Lo! the storms of life are breaking," is of great merit. "Ten thousand times ten thousand" is one of his most lyric hymns, and growing in popularity. Others might be mentioned, some of which touch on themes too much overlooked in hymns; but they have not the spontaneity of those we have named.

John Samuel Bewley Monsell, LL.D. (1811-1875), who, after holding various appointments in the Irish Church, became, in succession, vicar of Egham, and of St. Nicholas, Guildford, holds a distinguished place in the ranks of recent hymnists. His hymns were published in several volumes, the principal being—"Spiritual Songs," "Hymns of Love and Praise for the Church's Year," "Litany Hymns," and "Parish Musings." Some were included in the collection edited by him under the title of "The Parish Hymnal." Dr. Monsell possessed the lyric gift to an unusual extent. Many of his hymns are full of melody and tenderness. The verses in "Spiritual Songs" commended themselves to the venerable author of "The Christian Year," who gave them a careful revision. They were "written during a winter (1874) spent for the sake of health amid the orange and olive groves of Italy." To this, the tender and subdued feeling which characterises them may be partly due. They have since become deservedly popular. Here and there they are somewhat diffuse, and would have been improved by compression, but they have very high merit, and fill a considerable place in our best modern hymnals. I found no less than seventeen suitable and desirable for inclusion in my own Hymnal. Of a more joyful kind, I may mention the following as of great value—"Sing to the Lord a joyful song," and "God is Love, by Him upholden." Singularly tender and distinctive is "Birds have their quiet nest," perhaps his finest hymn, although "O worship the Lord in the beauty of holiness," is more widely known, and frequently sung. "To Thee, O dear, dear Saviour," "Labouring and heavy laden," "Lord of the living harvest," "The spring-tide hour brings leaf and flower," "Sing to the Lord of harvest," "O Love, divine and golden," are his finest efforts. The following hymn from his pen is so very fine, and so little known, that I quote it:—

Weary and sad, a wanderer from Thee,
By grief heart-broken, and by sin defiled;
O what a joy in sorrow 'tis to be
Conscious that I am still, O God, Thy child.

Strained were the cords of love by my sad will,
  I would have broke them had I had my way,
But, Lord, it was Thy love, not mine, that still
  Held my heart back, my tott'ring steps did stay.

And now the crumbs that from Thy table fall
  Are all I ask, more than is meet for me;
Yet kiss and banquet, ring and robe, are all
  Waiting me, Father, in my home with Thee.

Back to the door which ever open lay;
  Back to the table where the feast still stood;
Back to the heart which never, night or day,
  Forgat me in my most forgetful mood.

Drawn by Thy love, that found me when a child,
  And never for a moment let me go;
Still, still Thine own, though soiled and sin-defiled,
  I come, and Thou wilt make me clean, I know.

There feed me with Thyself, until I grow
  Into the stature of the life divine;
My right to plead, my privilege to know
  That Christ is God's, and I, O Christ! am Thine,

Feed me, and set me up upon the Rock
  Higher than I, my shelter and my stay
Against the rudest winter-tempest's shock,
  Against the fiercest sultry summer's day.

Thus let my life in ceaseless progress move,
  On into deeper knowledge, Lord, of Thee:
The length, the breadth, the height, the depth of Love,
  That first could care for, then did stoop to me.

Dr. Monsell deserves a very high place among our modern hymnists. His deep religiousness, his tenderness of spirit, his lyric nature, all combined to enable him to give the Church verses which have done much, and will probably do still more, to express and deepen her worshipping emotion. Whilst watching the restoration of his church at Guildford, a stone fell and struck him, and after lingering for some time, he succumbed to heart-disease, aggravated by the shock.

William Josiah Irons, D.D. (1812-1884), the High Church son of the well-known and eccentric minister of Camberwell Grove, who, in his day, was noted for the boldness of his Calvinism, a considerable contributor to theological literature, was, like his father, the author of many hymns, both original and translations. Some of these are of no little merit; but he is chiefly remembered by what is probably the best version, at all events for singing, of the *Dies Iræ*, which begins, "Day of wrath! O day of mourning." As no less than 160 translations are known to have been made of this hymn, some of them by remarkable men, it is no small distinction to have produced the most popular version. His hymn for Palm Sunday, "Is not this our King and Prophet?" and that beginning "Father of love, our Guide and Friend," seem to me of great beauty. I quote the former:—

"Is not This our King and Prophet?"—
  Ring Hosannas, wave the palm,
Let the children from the temple
  Echo back the people's psalm;
"Blessèd is the Son of David,"
  Blessèd is the Christ of God,
Welcome to the hill of Sion,
  Deck the pathway, strew the sod!

"Meek and lowly One," He cometh,
  And the anthem greets His ears;
Lo, the city lies before Him.
  But He sees it through His tears;
Looking from the Mount of Olives,
  Towers and marble temple rise;—
Is thy peace, O well-loved Salem,
  "Hid for ever from thine eyes?"

Sees He now, in solemn vision,
  Calvary "without the gate?"
Israel fallen—"house and city
  Left unto her desolate?"
Yes, O Saviour all-enduring!
  Thou wast watching every heart—
Which would love Thee, which forsake Thee.
  Which would do the traitor's part.

Pity, Lord, man's hollow praises,
  Then or now, which greet Thee thus;
"By Thy Cross, and by Thy Passion,"
  O have mercy yet on us!

Now Thou reignest with the Father,
And the Spirit evermore;
Lord, look down upon Thy servants,
Who repent, and would adore.

Robert Murray McCheyne (1813-1843), the greatly beloved minister of S. Peter's, Dundee, whose saintly life, which came to an end when he was only thirty years of age, exerted a wide and deep influence—an influence perpetuated by the publication of his memoir by the Rev. A. A. Bonar, which had an enormous circulation—finds, and will probably keep, a place among the hymnists, by the solemn and tender strains of the well-known hymn, entitled "I am debtor"—"When this passing world is done."

Edward Caswall (1814-1878) was one of the company of talented men forced from the Church of England to that of Rome by the condemnation of the "Tracts for the Times." He gave up his perpetual curacy at Stratford-sub-Castle, near Salisbury, and soon after was admitted to the Congregation of the Oratory, at Edgbaston, Birmingham, founded by Dr. J. H. Newman. He had a genius for poetic translation. During his student days at Oxford, he published "The Art of Pluck," a humorous imitation of Aristotle, which has gone through many editions, and is still a favourite with undergraduates at the University. In 1849 he issued the "Lyra Catholica," containing a large number of translations of hymns from the Breviary and Missal, with some from other sources. In 1858 he published "The Masque of Mary, and other poems," and in 1865, "A May Pageant, and other poems," but his chief successes are his translations, some of which have deservedly become popular, and are included in the Hymnals of nearly every section of the Church. The best known are "Jesus, the very thought of Thee," and "O Jesu, King most wonderful," from the "Jesu dulcis memoria," by Bernard of Clairvaux. These are of great excellence. Next in order of popularity comes his translation of Francis Xavier's hymn, "My God, I love Thee, not because," one of the noblest hymns in the language, save for the dogmatic declaration of the latter part of the first verse :—

> "Nor yet because who love Thee not
> Must burn eternally"—

but even that, if understood as setting forth, not the *eternity* of punishment, but that so long as love to God is absent from the soul, it must suffer, may be accepted as grandly true. So few, however, would understand it in that way, though the great-hearted Xavier may have thus meant it, that, on account of these two lines, it has been excluded from Hymnals where its otherwise noble teaching would have been gladly welcomed. "The sun is sinking fast," from a Latin original (probably of the 18th century), which has been lost, is of great tenderness, and is gradually finding its way into many hymnals. Most of the other translations by Father Caswall are confined to Hymnals of the High Church order.

Samuel Greg (1804-1877), the brother of the well-known W. R. Greg, author of the "Creeds of Christendom," but of a more believing, though by no means credulous turn of mind—a manufacturer, and large employer of labour, who did much for those in his employ, conducting services for them, and labouring hard for their mental and spiritual good—deserves mention for several hymns of great beauty, which were included in the books we owe to his pen. His hymn on "The Transfiguration," which he appended to his chapter on that event, in "Scenes in the Life of Jesus," is certainly the finest we possess on that theme, as may be seen below :—

Stay, Master, stay upon this heavenly hill:
A little longer, let us linger still;
With these three mighty ones of old beside,
Near to the Awful Presence still abide;
Before the throne of light we trembling stand,
And catch a glimpse into the spirit-land.

Stay, Master, stay! we breathe a purer air;
This life is not the life that waits us there:
Thoughts, feelings, flashes, glimpses come and go;
We cannot speak them—nay, we do not know;
Wrapt in this cloud of light we seem to be
The thing we fain would grow—eternally.

"No!" saith the Lord, "the hour is past,—we go;
Our home, our life, our duties lie below.
While here we kneel upon the mount of prayer,
The plough lies waiting in the furrow there!
Here we sought God that we might know His will;
There we must do it,—serve Him,—seek Him still."

If man aspires to reach the throne of God,
O'er the dull plains of earth must lie the road.
He who best does his lowly duty here,
Shall mount the highest in a nobler sphere:
At God's own feet our spirits seek their rest,
And He is nearest Him who serves Him best.

Few nobler hymns of trustful confidence in God can be found than the following one, which is included in a posthumous work from his pen, entitled "A Layman's Legacy." The close of it is singularly impressive :—

Slowly, slowly darkening,
  The evening hours roll on;
And soon behind the cloud-land
  Will sink my setting sun.

Around my path life's mysteries
  Their deepening shadows throw;
And as I gaze and ponder,
  They dark and darker grow.

But there's a voice above me
  Which says, "Wait, trust, and pray;
The night will soon be over,
  And light will come with day."

Father! the light and darkness
  Are both alike to Thee;
Then to Thy waiting servant,
  Alike they both shall be.

The great unending future,
  I cannot pierce its shroud;
Yet nothing doubt, nor tremble,
  God's bow is on the cloud.

To Him I yield my spirit;
  On Him I lay my load:
Fear ends with death; beyond it
  I nothing see but GOD.

Thus moving towards the darkness,
  I calmly wait His call;
Now seeing,—fearing nothing;
  But hoping, trusting—all!

Arthur Penrhyn Stanley (1815-1881), the pleasant son of a pleasant father, was one loved by all who knew him, even by those who most differed from his theological opinions. He raised the Deanery of Westminster to a height of renown it had never before reached. He wrote valuable works on the Holy Land, the Jewish and Eastern Churches, the Cathedral of Canterbury, of which he was once a Canon, and on the Abbey of Westminster, of which he was Dean. Although from his early days a lover of poetry—at Oxford he took the Newdigate prize for a poem on "The Gypsies"—and had a mind that was essentially rather poetic than dogmatic, yet fills a small place among the hymnists, and claims that place more from the catholicity of spirit, and picturesqueness of his hymns, than for their lyric and poetic qualities. Some of the finest lines in them are adaptations from Milton, Gray, and other of the great poets. Most of them grew out of the consideration of some of the great incidents in the life of our Lord, and set forth their most spiritual lessons for those of later days. They are chiefly in rather heavy measures, not greatly favoured by musicians—double long and sevens metres. But, with all their deficiencies, they are so full of "sweetness and light" that we could ill spare them from our collections. Perhaps the best is the hymn on "The Transfiguration," originally published in *Macmillan's Magazine*. In the same number, the Dean inserted the hymn by Samuel Greg on the same subject, which he declared to be far finer than his own. Our readers may judge for themselves by turning to page 175, where I have included it. I may take this opportunity of setting at rest a doubt that has been felt with regard to the true text of this hymn. In most Hymnals it begins "O, Master, it is good to be," and this is the reading of the hymn as printed in *Macmillan's Magazine*, but when I was compiling the New Testament part of "The Poets' Bible," Dr. Stanley was good enough to lend me his collection of all the hymns and poems he had printed, with his final revisions, and I there found that he had altered the first line of this hymn to "Lord, it is good for us to be." I therefore printed it thus in the volume I was then editing, and afterwards in my "Congregational Hymns." It is the more necessary to state this, since in "The Westminster Abbey Hymn Book," issued after his death, the hymn is made to begin "Master, it is good to be." I give the text as finally revised by the author:—

Lord, it is good for us to be
High on the mountain here with Thee,
Where stand revealed to mortal gaze
The great old saints of other days.
Who once received, on Horeb's height,
The eternal laws of truth and right,
Or caught the still small whisper, higher
Than storm, than earthquake, or than fire.

Lord, it is good for us to be
With Thee, and with Thy faithful three,
Here, where the Apostle's heart of rock
Is nerved against temptation's shock;
Here, where the Son of Thunder learns
The thought that breathes, the word that burns;
Here, where on eagle's wings we move
With him whose last, best creed is Love.

Lord, it is good for us to be
Entranced, enwrapt, alone with Thee,
Watching the glistening raiment glow
Whiter than Hermon's whitest snow,
The human lineaments that shine
Irradiant with a light Divine;
Till we too change from grace to grace,
Gazing on that transfigured face.

Lord, it is good for us to be
Here on the Holy Mount with Thee;
When darkling in the depths of night,
When dazzled with excess of light,
We bow before the heavenly Voice
That bids bewildered souls rejoice:
Though love wax cold, and faith be dim—
"This is my Son! O hear ye Him!"

The following are the most notable of Dr. Stanley's hymns, which are all marked by the characteristics I have already noted—"The Lord is come on Syrian soil," an Advent hymn; "He is gone beyond the skies," on the Ascension of Christ; "When the Paschal evening fell," for the Lord's Supper; and "Where shall we learn to die"—probably inspired by Montgomery's far finer hymn, "Go to dark Gethsemane"—which I append:—

Where shall we learn to die?
Go, gaze with steadfast eye
On dark Gethsemane,
Or darker Calvary,
Where, through each lingering hour,
The Lord of grace and power,
Most lowly and most High,
Has taught the Christian how to die.

When in the olive shade,
His long last prayer He prayed;
When on the cross to Heaven
His parting spirit given.

He showed that to fulfil
The Father's gracious will,
Not asking how or why,
Alone prepares the soul to die.

No word of angry strife,
No anxious cry for life;
By scoff and torture torn
He speaks not scorn for scorn;
Calmly forgiving those
Who deem themselves His foes,
In silent majesty
He points the way at peace to die.

Delighting to the last
In memories of the past;
Glad at the parting meal
In lowly tasks to kneel;
Still yearning to the end
For mother and for friend;
His great humility
Loves in such acts of love to die.

O by those weary hours
Of slowly ebbing powers,
By those deep lessons heard
In each expiring word;
By that unfailing love
Lifting the soul above,
When our last end is nigh,
So teach us, Lord, with Thee to die.

Frederick William Faber (1815-1863) stands in perfect contrast to Dr. Stanley, not only in theological belief and spirit, but in his faculty for hymn-writing. In Faber the lyric and poetic gift was present in abundant measure. He was, if report be true, as pleasant a man as Arthur Stanley, but one cast in an utterly different and far more ecclesiastical mould. Whilst Stanley was a man of the world (using that word in a good sense), delighting in all fair and gracious things, Faber was a man of the cloister, who viewed all things in the dim religious light which streams through windows bearing the coloured forms of haloed saints. Very different men, but both very lovely in their lives. As a hymnist,

Faber towers far above Stanley. Indeed, it would be difficult to find one who rises higher, or, I am bound to add, when dominated by some dogmatic or ecclesiastical tradition, sinks lower. It is difficult to believe that one who rises so high, into such a clear, pure vision of the love of God, could ever sink so low as, in some of his verses, he does. Some of his noblest hymns include verses before which the reader stands amazed. Now here do we see how a Church which has nourished the saintliest piety, yet throws a shadow over the mind deep as night. I have not the heart to quote any of the verses in which Faber sinks below his true self, lest it should make any of my readers prize less highly the glorious hymns which have come into use from his pen. He is truly one of the greatest hymnists of any age. The thought, the fervour, the poetic quality, which are all combined in his hymns, place him in that little circle which includes the chief singers of the Church—a circle to which nearly every section has contributed representatives. I question whether a finer hymn could be named than his "My God, how wonderful Thou art," which impious hands have too often marred by their senseless alterations or omissions. It is probably his finest hymn; but falling little below this are "O God, Thy power is wonderful":—

O God! Thy power is wonderful,
  Thy glory passing bright;
Thy wisdom, with its deep on deep,
  A rapture to the sight.

Yet more than all, and ever more,
  Should we Thy creatures bless,
Most worshipful of attributes,
  Thine awful holiness.

There's not a craving in the mind,
Thou dost not meet and still;
There's not a wish the heart can have
Which Thou dost not fulfil.

Thy justice is the gladdest thing
Creation can behold;
Thy tenderness so meek, it wins
The guilty to be bold.

All things that have been, all that are,
All things that can be dreamed,
All possible creations, made,
Kept faithful, or redeemed,—

All these may draw upon Thy power,
Thy mercy may command;
And still outflows Thy silent sea,
Immutable and grand.

O little heart of mine! shall pain
Or sorrow make thee moan,
When all this God is all for thee,
A Father all thine own?

"I worship Thee, sweet will of God" (often marred, and even spoilt, notably in the supplement to the "New Congregational Hymn Book"):—

I worship Thee, sweet Will of God!
And all Thy ways adore;
And every day I live, I long
To love Thee more and more.

I love to trace each print where Thou
Hast set Thine unseen feet;
I cannot fear Thee, blessèd Will,
Thine empire is so sweet.

I have no cares, O blessèd Will!
For all my cares are Thine;
I live in triumph, Lord! for Thou
Hast made Thy triumphs mine.

Man's weakness, waiting upon God,
Its end can never miss,
For men on earth no work can do
More angel-like than this.

Ride on, ride on triumphantly,
Thou glorious Will! ride on;
Faith's pilgrim sons behind Thee take
The road that Thou hast gone.

He always wins who sides with God,
To him no chance is lost;
God's will is sweetest to him when
It triumphs at his cost.

Ill, that He blesses, is our good,
And unblest good is ill;
And all is right that seems most wrong,
If it be His sweet Will!

The following is exquisite in its tenderness and simplicity of expression:—

Thy home is with the humble, Lord,
The simplest are the best;
Thy lodging is in child-like hearts;
Thou makest there Thy rest.

Dear Comforter! Eternal Love!
If Thou wilt stay with me,
Of lowly thoughts and simple ways,
I'll build a house for Thee.

Who made this beating heart of mine,
But Thou, my heavenly Guest?
Let no one have it, then, but Thee,
And let it be Thy rest.

Thy sweetness hath betrayed Thee, Lord!
Great Spirit! is it Thou?
Deeper and deeper in my heart,
I feel Thee resting now.

"Souls of men, why will ye scatter," in which occur the following verses, so marvellous as coming from the lips of a man in the exclusive communion of Rome:—

"There's a wideness in God's mercy,
Like the wideness of the sea;
There's a kindness in His justice
Which is more than liberty.

For the love of God is broader
Than the measures of man's mind,
And the heart of the Eternal
Is most wonderfully kind."

"Sweet Saviour, bless us ere we go," only marred by the idea of death as *a dark night;* "I wish to have no wishes left." These are his finest hymns. Others are more popular, such as "O Paradise, O Paradise," and "The Pilgrims of the night," but they are not so healthily Christian, and, if I mistake not, owe much of their popularity to the attractive music to which they have been wedded. His hymn, which in Protestant collections begins "Dear Jesus, ever at my side," is a hymn to the Guardian Angel, and begins "Dear Angel, ever at my side," and, beautiful as it is, is not properly applicable, in some of its particulars, when addressed to Jesus instead of the Guardian Angel. "O come and mourn with me awhile," is profoundly pathetic, but, as it stands in the original, is in parts too intent upon the physical agony of our Lord, notably in the following verse—

> "Come, take thy stand beneath the Cross,
> And let the Blood from out that Side
> Fall gently on thee, drop by drop;
> Jesus, our Love, is crucified!"

For use beyond his own Church, it has been found necessary, in nearly every case, to omit stanzas from this hymn. Still, the points of harmony are more and deeper than those of discord, and hence Dr. Faber will ever hold a place of honour in the universal song of the Church. It should be added that, in 1849, he established the Brotherhood of S. Philip Neri at King William Street, Strand, since removed to the well-known Oratory at Brompton.

John Mason Neale, D.D. (1818-1866), was as near to Dr. Faber in his theological and ecclesiastical sympathies as a man could well be who did not actually belong to the Roman Church. But for one or two points of doctrine, he would probably have entered that communion. To the lay mind, those points are scarcely perceptible. Their discussion would be out of place here. But he was, if I may judge from report, as beautiful and Christ-like in character as Dr. Faber. No Church, indeed, has a monopoly of saintliness, or a patent for its production. Judged by their doctrines, Neale and Stanley, though they belonged to the same Church, were wide as the poles asunder, but judged by their likeness of spirit to Christ, they were very closely united. Dr. Neale's services to Christian Hymnody were as great, in the matter of translations and adaptations of ancient, as were those of Dr. Faber in the production of original hymns. For the English-speaking people, indeed, he unearthed and prepared for use the great stores of hymnody buried in the office books of the Eastern, and, in less degree, of the Mediæval and Latin Churches. For this task he was richly endowed, both with learning and poetic taste. Beside this, he wrote many original hymns, especially for children, which are of no little merit. Personally, I do not rank them as high as some hymnologists, but his eminence in hymnody is chiefly due to the exquisite way in which he adapted (for his work was far more than translation), the verses scattered through the voluminous Office Books of the Ancient Churches, for use in the English Church. For this he deserves lasting remembrance and honour, since it was a work to which he devoted much time, immense pains, and great talent. As proof of this, it will be sufficient to name the most popular of his renderings—"Art thou weary, art thou languid," from St. Stephen the Sabaite; "The day is past and over," probably by St. Anatolius; "'Tis the day of resurrection," by St. John Damascene; "O happy band of pilgrims," by St. Joseph of the Studium; "Alleluia! song of sweetness," from a hymn of the 14th or 15th century; "All glory, laud, and honour," by Theodulph, of Orleans; "The strain upraise, of joy and praise," probably by Godescalcus; and his well-known translation of the "Hora Novissima," from which the centos, "Brief life is here our portion," "For thee, O dear, dear country," and "Jerusalem the golden," have been taken. All these have passed into hymnals used in every section of the Church, whilst many more have found their way into churches of the Anglican type, in the pages of "Hymns Ancient and Modern," "The People's Hymnal," "The Hymnary," &c. Of his original hymns, in my opinion, the best are—"O Lord of hosts, whose glory fills," and "The day, O Lord, is spent." "The foe behind, the deep before," is more of a poem than a hymn, and whilst in parts striking, is rather confused in the way in which it treats and applies the Exodus of Israel, which is its subject. Dr. Neale seems to me to have always needed some previous fire at which to kindle his torch; when that could be found his success was indeed great.

Anne Brontë (1820-1849), a member of the talented family to which we owe such striking works, finds a place among the hymnists by the following hymns—"Oppressed with sin and woe," which she calls "Confidence;" "Believe not those who say," six verses from "The Narrow Way;" "Spirit of Faith! be thou my guide," a selection from "The Three Guides;" and "I hoped that with the brave and strong," the last verses she ever wrote. All are touched with that melancholy but strenuous tone which pervaded her life. There is in it that unmistakable note of reality and conviction which ever gives power to hymns.

Edwyn Paxton Hood (1820-1885), a versatile and voluminous author. His hymns suffer, as did his books, from the haste with which all his work was done. Still, when this has been said, it must be acknowledged that his hymns are marked by an originality and freshness which are so often lacking in such productions. They were thrown off when he was moved by some scene, or event, or expression, which moved him deeply. In my judgment, the following are the most noteworthy, and strike a new note in hymnody. The one I quote was suggested by a scene he witnessed when the waves were dashing over the breakwater at Portland, bringing to his mind the words of our Lord concerning the house on the sand and on the rock. Unfortunately, its verses are somewhat irregular in metre; this, perhaps, lends force to them, but renders it more difficult for them to be wedded to music:—

Saviour and master,
These sayings of Thine,
Help me to make them
Doings of mine;
Words that like beams
Of humanity shine.
By them let me build up
The holy, divine.

Not on the sand, Lord!
Oh, not on the sand;
On the rock, on the rock,
Let my heritage stand.
Beyond the floods raging,
Beyond the rude storm,
Where the rain cannot injure,
Nor lightning deform.

Up on the rock, Lord!
Up high on the rock,
I have reeled, I have trembled
Beneath the rude shock.
To the Rock of the ages,
To Thee, Lord, to Thee!
From the storm and the tempest
I flee, Lord, I flee!

Not on the sand, Lord!
Oh, not on the sand:
On the rock, on the rock,
Let my heritage stand.
Saviour and Master,
These sayings of Thine,
Help me to make them
Doings of mine.

His well-known hymn for children, "God, who hast made the daisies," is well suited for their use, but might have been wrought into a closer unity of idea. His hymn, "Heart-broken and weary, where'er thou may'st be," is marked by great depth of feeling, but its form is not equal to its emotion. It is, however, a great favourite with many. The same remarks apply to "Sing a hymn to Jesus." Had Mr. Hood received the advantages of academic training in his early days, the loss of which he so deeply regretted, he would probably have been one of the most popular hymnists of his time. He possessed unmistakable genius, but was not sufficiently careful and critical of his own work.

Sir Henry Williams Baker, Bart. (1821-1877), is chiefly remarkable as one of the Editors of that phenomenally successful collection, "Hymns Ancient and Modern." In my judgment, he had little original power as a hymnist, but some of his hymns have become popular from their inclusion in the collection already named. His best hymns are—"O God of love, O King of peace," "How welcome was the call," "Lord, Thy word abideth," "There is a blessed home." But they are the work of a man familiar with hymns rather than of the original hymnist. The same remark applies to his translations—they owe much to previous workers.

Thomas Toke Lynch (1818-1871) is as remarkable for originality as Sir H. W. Baker was for the absence of it.

Indeed, he is one of the most original and poetic hymnists that could be named. His little volume, "The Rivulet," which raised such a storm in the theological atmosphere of the Free Churches, is pure, fresh, sparkling—true to its name. It conveys truth, as did the Parables of our Lord, by means of the sights and sounds of nature. It is like a breath from the hills, rather than, as so many hymns are, from the study, or the cloister, or the hall of theology. It is the work of the poet, not of the divine. It was not meant to exclude other hymns from his congregation, but only as a supplement to Dr. Watts, and so to add to the somewhat solid provision of that book, some fresher strains. And the marvel of "The Rivulet" is that so great a sufferer as its author was all his days should have been able to produce such buoyant and inspiring verses. It is a lark-like song, which cheers the soul even of the sad and sombre. It was so original, that the folk who can only recognise truth in the doctrinal dress to which they have been accustomed, called it heresy, and did their best to cast and keep it out of the Synagogue. In relation to such, Mr. Lynch relieved his mind by the production of "Songs Controversial, by Silent Long; fifteen songs, uttering a new protest." As these are unknown to the majority of readers in our day, I quote one which he called "A Negative Affair; showing that when a man palms off his negative 'stuff' upon the public as Christian, there is always somebody acute enough to detect the imposition"—

When sugar in the lump I see,
  I know that it is there:
Melt it, and then I soon suspect
  A negative affair;
Where is the sugar, sir? I say,
  Let me both taste and see;

Sweetness instead of sugar, sir,
You'll not palm off on me.

Don't tell me that the sugar-lumps
When dropt in water clear,
That they may make the water sweet,
Themselves must disappear:
For common sense, sir, such as mine,
The lumps themselves must see;
Sweetness instead of sugar, sir,
You'll not palm off on me.

For instance, sir, in every hymn
Sound doctrine you must state
As clearly as a dead man's name
Is on his coffin-plate;
Religion, sir, is only fudge,—
Let's have theology;
Sweetness instead of sugar, sir,
You'll not palm off on me.

These lines may still be commended to all those who would insist that hymns should be a vehicle for theological rather than religious expression. For a time, Mr. Lynch's detractors succeeded. But all such successes are short-lived. Years after its publication, when Mr. Miller, in 1869, published his "Singers and Songs of the Church," he could only name six hymns by Mr. Lynch as having passed into Hymnals, but to-day he would have largely to extend the list. "The Baptist Hymnal" (1879) contains eleven, "Congregational Hymns" (1884), fourteeen, and the "Congregational Church Hymnal" nine of his hymns. Even now, however, they have not passed, with one exception—"Gracious Spirit, dwell with me"—into Church of England Hymnals, which, up to the present, have been rather shy of really poetic hymns, preferring those of a more markedly doctrinal type. Its hymns, for the most part, are more akin to the Creeds than the Parables and the Sermon on the Mount, with which Mr. Lynch's have so much more affinity. But the time will come when Mr. Lynch's hymns will be sung as freely in stately churches as they are now in Dissenting Conventicles, and they will do much to remove the charge of Dean Stanley as to the "uniform pedestrian style which is unfortunately familiar to English Churchmen in the vast mass of the hymns contained in 'Hymns Ancient and Modern,'" and will give freshness to the song of the Episcopal Church. I quote the following, which are little known, as illustrations of the freshness of his style, and of his habit of dealing with aspects of truth seldom, if ever, dealt with in hymns:—

Where is thy God, my soul?
Is He within Thy heart;
Or ruler of a distant realm
In which thou hast no part?

Where is thy God, my soul?
Only in stars and sun;
Or have the holy words of truth
His light in every one?

Where is thy God, my soul?
Confined to Scripture's page;
Or does His Spirit check and guide
The spirit of each age?

O Ruler of the sky,
Rule Thou within my heart:
O, great Adorner of the world,
Thy light of life impart.

Giver of holy words,
Bestow Thy holy power,
And aid me, whether work or thought
Engage the varying hour.

In Thee have I my help,
As all my fathers had;
I'll trust Thee when I'm sorrowful,
And serve Thee when I'm glad.

The following contains a terse exposition of true Christian Socialism:—

O Lord, Thou art not fickle;
  Our hope is not in vain;
The harvest for the sickle
  Will ripen yet again.

But though enough be given
  For all the world to eat,
Sin with Thy love has striven
  Its bounty to defeat.

Were men to one another
  As kind as God to all,
Then no man on his brother
  For help would vainly call.

On none for idle wasting
  Would honest labour frown;
And none, to riches hasting,
  Would tread his neighbour down.

No man enough posseses
  Until he has to spare;
Possession no man blesses
  While self is all his care.

For blessings on our labour,
  O, then, in hope we pray,
When love unto our neighbour
  Is ripening every day.

What a delightful introduction to the reading or exposition of Scripture is found in the following lines :—

Christ in His Word draws near;
Hush, moaning voice of fear,
    He bids thee cease;
With songs sincere and sweet
Let us arise, and meet
Him who comes forth to greet
    Our souls with peace.

Rising above thy care,
Meet Him as in the air,
    O weary heart:
Put on joy's sacred dress;
Lo, as He comes to bless,
Quite from Thy weariness
    Set free thou art.

For works of love and praise
He brings thee summer days,
    Warm days and bright;
Winter is past and gone,
Now He, salvation's Sun,
Shineth on every one
    With mercy's light.

From the bright sky above,
Clad in His robes of love,
'Tis He, our Lord:
Dim earth itself grows clear.
As His light draweth near:
O let us hush and hear
His holy word.

How exquisitely the spirit of the Kingdom of God is set forth, by illustrations drawn from the natural world, in the lyric utterance below:—

Lift up your heads, rejoice,
Redemption draweth nigh;
Now breathes a softer air,
Now shines a milder sky;
The early trees put forth
Their new and tender leaf;
Hushed is the moaning wind
That told of winter's grief.

Lift up your heads, rejoice,
Redemption draweth nigh;
Now mount the laden clouds,
Now flames the darkening sky.
The early scattered drops
Descend with heavy fall,
And to the waiting earth
The hidden thunders call.

Lift up your heads, rejoice,
Redemption draweth nigh;
O note the varying signs
Of earth, and air, and sky:
The God of glory comes
In gentleness and might,
To comfort and alarm,
To succour and to smite.

He comes, the wide world's King;
He comes, the true heart's Friend;
New gladness to begin,
And ancient wrong to end;
He comes, to fill with light
The weary waiting eye:
Lift up your heads, rejoice,
Redemption draweth nigh.

The most popular of Mr. Lynch's hymns up to the present time, however, are the following:—"Gracious Spirit, dwell with me," "O where is He that trod the sea,"

"Now have we met that we may ask," "Dismiss me not Thy service, Lord," "The Lord is rich and merciful," "How calmly the evening once more is descending," "Love me, O Lord, forgivingly," "Oft when of God we ask." "The Rivulet" also contains many poems not suitable for public worship, but admirably adapted to freshen the religious life. For my own part, I should put that work above Mr. Keble's "Christian Year" for the spontaneity of its poetry.

James Drummond Burns (1823-1864), like Mr. Lynch, was a sufferer for many years from illness, and, like him, was richly gifted with poetic power. His hymns are amongst the most pathetic and tender of recent production. A man of rare refinement and saintly character, showing that the Presbyterian Church, usually supposed to foster only the more vigorous and even hard type of character, numbers among its members men who deserve to be ranked with those nurtured in more cloistral ways. I should assign a very high place to such hymns as "Still with Thee, O my God," "O Thou whose tender feet have trod," and "Thou, Lord, art Love, and everywhere," which has so often been maugled by editors that I quote it as penned by the author;—

Thou, Lord, art Love—and everywhere
   Thy name is brightly shown,
Beneath, on earth Thy footstool fair,
   Above, in heaven Thy throne.

Thy word is Love—in lines of gold
   There mercy prints its trace;
In Nature we Thy steps behold,
   The Gospel shows Thy face.

Thy ways are Love—though they transcend
   Our feeble range of sight,
They wind through darkness to their end,
   In everlasting light.

Thy thoughts are Love, and Jesus is
  The living voice they find;
His love lights up the vast abyss
  Of the Eternal Mind.

Thy chastisements are Love—more deep
  They stamp the seal divine;
And by a sweet compulsion keep
  Our spirits nearer Thine.

Thy heaven is the abode of Love—
  O blessèd Lord, that we
May there, when time's dim shades remove
  Be gathered home to Thee;

There with Thy resting saints to fall
  Adoring round Thy throne;
Where all shall love Thee, Lord, and all
  Shall in Thy love be one.

whilst almost equal are—"Not, Lord, unto that mount of dread," "As helpless as a child who clings," and "At Thy feet, our God and Father." His hymn on Samuel, "Hushed was the evening hymn," is one of the loveliest for children, in the language, and deserves to rank with, even if it does not excel, the best of Mrs. C. F. Alexander's. It may be unknown to some of my readers, and I therefore quote it:

  Hushed was the evening hymn,
  The Temple courts were dark;
  The lamp was burning dim
  Before the sacred ark;
When suddenly a voice divine
Rang through the silence of the shrine.

  The old man, meek and mild,
  The priest of Israel, slept;
  His watch the Temple child,
  The little Levite kept:
And what from Eli's sense was sealed,
The Lord to Hannah's son revealed.

  Oh! give me Samuel's ear,
  The open ear, O Lord,
  Alive and quick to hear
  Each whisper of Thy word:
Like him to answer at Thy call,
And to obey Thee first of all.

Oh! give me Samuel's heart,
A lowly heart that waits,
When in Thy house Thou art,
Or watches at Thy gates.
By day and night, a heart that still
Moves at the breathing of Thy will.

Oh! give me Samuel's mind,
A sweet, unmurmuring faith,
Obedient and resigned
To Thee in life and death;
That I may read with child-like eyes
Truths that are hidden from the wise.

Some of Mr. Burns' translations from the German are of great merit, as may be seen from the following rendering of a hymn by Joachim Neander:—

Heaven and earth, and sea and air,
Still their Maker's praise declare;
Thou, my soul, as loudly sing,
To thy God thy praises bring.

See the sun his power awakes,
As through clouds his glory breaks;
See the moon and stars of light,
Praising God in stillest night.

See how God this rolling globe
Swathes with beauty like a robe;
Forests, fields, and living things,
Each its Maker's glory sings.

Through the air Thy praises meet,
Birds are singing clear and sweet;
Fire, and storm, and wind, Thy will
As Thy ministers fulfil.

The ocean waves Thy glory tell,
At Thy touch they sink and swell;
From the well-spring to the sea,
Rivers murmur, Lord, of Thee.

Ah! my God, what wonders lie
Hid in Thine infinity!
Stamp upon my inmost heart
What I am, and what Thou art.

Adelaide Anne Procter (1825-1864), the daughter of B. W. Procter, better known as Barry Cornwall, under which *nom de plume* his poems were published, was the authoress of the well-known and delightful "Legends and Lyrics," to which, after her death, her friend Charles Dickens prefixed a beautiful and touching sketch of her life, in which the following touching incident is recorded: "In the spring of the year 1853, I observed, as conductor of the weekly journal, *Household Words*, a short poem among the proffered contributions, very different, as I thought, from the shoal of verses perpetually seething through the office of such a periodical, and possessing much more merit. Its authoress was quite unknown to me. She was one Miss Mary Berwick, whom I had never heard of; and she was to be addressed by letter, if addressed at all, at a circulating library in the western district of London. Through this channel, Miss Berwick was informed that her poem was accepted, and invited to send another. She complied, and became a regular and frequent contributor. Many letters passed between the journal and Miss Berwick, but Miss Berwick herself was never seen. How we came gradually to establish, at the office of *Household Words*, that we knew all about Miss Berwick, I have never discovered. But we settled somehow, to our complete satisfaction, that she was governess in a family; that she went to Italy in that capacity, and returned; and that she had long been in the same family. We really knew nothing whatever of her, except that she was remarkably business-like, punctual, self-reliant, and reliable, so I suppose we insensibly invented the rest. For myself, my mother was not a more real personage to me, than Miss Berwick, the governess, became. This went on until December, 1854, when the Christmas number, entitled 'The Seven Poor Travellers,' was sent to press. Happening to be going to dine that day with an old and dear friend distinguished in literature as

Barry Cornwall, I took with me an early proof of that number, and remarked, as I laid it on the drawing-room table, that it contained a very pretty poem, written by a certain Miss Berwick. Next day brought me the disclosure that I had so spoken of the poem to the mother of its writer, in its writer's presence, and that the name had been assumed by Barry Cornwall's eldest daughter—Miss Adelaide Anne Procter." In recent years, when Editors came to see that poetic character did not disqualify, but rather fitted verses for inclusion in their collections, many hymns have been drawn from these volumes for the worship of the Church, and have acquired a great popularity, which is ever increasing. Some of these have very great merit, notably the following, which I print in order to bring them under the notice of future Editors of Hymnals. The first she calls "Thankfulness":—

* Our God, we thank Thee, who hast made
The earth so bright,
So full of splendour and of joy,
Beauty and light;
So many glorious things are here,
Noble and right!

We thank Thee, too, that Thou hast made
Joy to abound;
So many gentle thoughts and deeds
Circling us round,
That in the darkest spot of earth
Some love is found.

We thank Thee *more* that all our joy
Is touched with pain;
That shadows fall on brightest hours,
That thorns remain;
So that earth's bliss may be our guide,
And not our chain.

For Thou who knowest, Lord, how soon
Our weak heart clings,
Hast given us joys, tender and true,
Yet all with wings,
So that we see, gleaming on high,
Diviner things!

* In the original, the singular number is used.

We thank Thee, Lord, that Thou hast kept
The best in store;
We have enough, yet not too much,
To long for more;
A yearning for a deeper peace,
Not known before.

We thank Thee, Lord, that here our souls,
Though amply blest,
Can never find, although they seek,
A perfect rest—
Nor ever shall, until they lean
On Jesus' breast!

The following, called "The Pilgrims," is well known through Henry Leslie's exquisite musical setting:—

The way is long and dreary,
The path is bleak and bare,
Our feet are worn and weary,
But we will not despair;
More heavy was Thy burden,
More desolate Thy way,
O Lamb of God! who takest
The sin of the world away,
Have mercy upon us.

The snows lie thick around us,
In the dark and gloomy night;
And the tempest wails above us,
And the stars have hid their light;
But blacker was the darkness
Round Calvary's cross that day;
O Lamb of God! who takest
The sin of the world away,
Have mercy upon us.

Our hearts are faint with sorrow,
Heavy and hard to bear;
For we dread the bitter morrow,
But we will not despair;
Thou knowest all our anguish,
And Thou wilt bid it cease:
O Lamb of God! who takest
The sin of the world away,
Give us Thy peace!

The next is her poem entitled "The Peace of God"—

We ask for Peace. O Lord!
Thy children ask Thy peace;
Not what the world calls rest,
That toil and care should cease.

That through bright sunny hours
Calm life should fleet away,
And tranquil night should fade
In smiling day;—
It is not for such Peace that we would pray.

We ask for Peace, O Lord!
Yet not to stand secure,
Girt round with iron pride,
Contented to endure:
Crushing the gentle strings
That human hearts should know,
Untouched by others' joy,
Or others' woe;—
Thou, O dear Lord, wilt never teach us so.

We ask Thy Peace, O Lord!
Through storm, and fear, and strife,
To light and guide us on,
Through a long, struggling life;
While no success or gain
Shall cheer the desperate fight,
Or nerve, what the world calls
Our wasted might,—
Yet pressing through the darkness to the light.

It is Thine own, O Lord;
Who toil while others sleep,
Who sow with loving care
What other hands shall reap:
They lean on Thee entranced,
In calm and perfect rest:
Give us that Peace, O Lord,
Divine and blest,
Thou keepest for those hearts who love Thee best.

The last is, perhaps, more suitable for private than public worship:—

I do not ask, O Lord, that life may be
A pleasant road;
I do not ask that Thou wouldst take from me
Aught of its load.

I do not ask that flowers should always spring
Beneath my feet;
I know too well the poison and the sting
Of things too sweet.

For one thing only, Lord, dear Lord, I plead:
Lead me aright,
Though strength should falter, and though heart should bleed,
Through Peace to Light.

I do not ask, O Lord, that Thou shouldst shed
Full radiance here;
Give but a ray of peace, that I may tread
Without a fear.

I do not ask my cross to understand,
My way to see;
Better in darkness just to feel Thy hand
And follow Thee.

Joy is like restless day: but peace divine
Like quiet night;
Lead me, O Lord, till perfect day shall shine
Through Peace to Light.

I am bound to say that a want of discernment of what really constitutes a hymn has led certain Editors to include some pieces from Miss Procter's works, very beautiful in themselves, but more fit for private reading than public worship. This is an error in judgment which needs to be guarded against. But, on the other hand, verses cannot be too *poetic* for use in worship, if they are *really hymns*. This is a lesson which Church of England Editors need to learn. They have not learnt it yet, as may be seen by the fact that they have not, so far as my knowledge goes, included a single hymn from this gifted authoress in their collections.* Congregations would thank them if they did, and they have good right to complain that, as yet, they have not done so. There is only one drawback to some of her hymns—that they are not metrically uniform, but they are so good that composers should arrange their music to suit them.

Frances Ridley Havergal (1836-1879), a devoted and saintly woman, the daughter of the hymnist and musician, the Rev. W. H. Havergal, M.A., had a great gift of lyric expression, and much facility in its use, to which her deeply religious nature constantly moved her. She was a very prolific writer of hymns and religious poems, which have had a very wide circulation, and exerted

* Since the first Edition of this book appeared, Miss Procter has found a place in several hymnals of the Church of England.

a great influence. They have done much to foster that warmer and more consecrated type of religion which is one of the remarkable features of our time, and is the real barrier against the spirit of scepticism which is so common, whilst they show how independent of dogmatic formularies is the religious life. Some of her hymns touch a very high point of vigour and excellence, whilst others are rather diffuse and weak in texture. The finest are the following—"Lord, speak to me, that I may speak," "O Saviour, precious Saviour," "Golden harps are sounding," "Take my life, and let it be," "Tell it out among the heathen" (a noble missionary hymn), and "Another year is dawning," a hymn for the New Year, of great tenderness :—

Another year is dawning,
  Dear Master, let it be,
In working or in waiting,
  Another year with Thee.

Another year of leaning
  Upon thy loving breast,
Of ever-deepening trustfulness,
  Of quiet, happy rest.

Another year of mercies,
  Of faithfulness and grace;
Another year of gladness
  In the shining of Thy face.

Another year of progress,
  Another year of praise,
Another year of proving
  Thy presence "all the days."

Another year of service,
  Of witness for Thy love;
Another year of training
  For better work above.

Another year is dawning,
  Dear Master, let it be,
On earth, or else in heaven
  Another year for Thee!

Among the minor contributors to the hymnody of this period, I may class together, in alphabetical, rather than chronological order—

William Hiley Bathurst (1796-1877), vicar of Barwick-in-Elmet, Yorkshire, who published, in 1830, "Psalms and Hymns for Public and Private Use." Two of his hymns are of merit, "O, Saviour, may we never rest," and "Jesus, Thy Church, with longing eyes."

To John Ernest Bode (1816-1874), we owe the fine hymn of consecration, which is specially suitable to occasions of Adult Baptism (far more suitable than most hymns written specially for that service), or the reception of members into the fellowship of the Church :—

O Jesus I have promised
  To serve Thee to the end ;
Be Thou for ever near me,
  My Master and my Friend !
I shall not fear the battle
  If Thou art by my side,
Nor wander from the pathway
  If Thou wilt be my Guide.

O let me hear Thee speaking
  In accents clear and still,
Above the storms of passion
  The murmur of self-will.
O speak ! to re-assure me,
  To hasten or control ;
O speak ! to make me listen,
  Thou Guardian of my soul.

O let me see Thy features,
  The look that once could make
So many a true disciple
  Leave all things for Thy sake ;
The look that beamed on Peter,
  When he Thy name denied ;
The look that draws Thy loved ones
  Close to Thy piercèd side.

O Jesu ! Thou hast promised,
  To all who follow Thee,
That where Thou art in glory,
  There shall Thy servant be ;

And, Jesu, I have promised,
  To serve Thee to the end;
O give me grace to follow
  My Master and my Friend!

James Baldwin Brown, B.A. (1821-1884), the eloquent and original minister of the Brixton Independent Church, the whole spirit of whose life is gathered up and concentrated in the following striking hymn:—

Thou, who our faithless hearts canst read,
  And know'st each weakness there;
Poor, trembling, faint, with Thee we plead,
  O turn not from our prayer.

We cannot grasp from hour to hour
  The truths Thy gospel saith;
Then aid us by Thy heavenly power,
  And so increase our faith.

That we may trust Thy guardian care,
  When no kind hand we see;
That we may lift our souls in prayer
  Undoubtingly to Thee.

Help us to gaze on things unseen
  By eyes of mortal sight;
To pierce through earth's dark veil, and gleam
  Some beams of heavenly light.

Thy glorious presence may we see,
  When earth's last tie is riven;
In faith then trust our souls to Thee,
  Till we awake in heaven.

George Burden Bubier (1823-1869), Professor of Theology and Philosophy at Spring Hill College, Birmingham, who compiled a Sunday School Hymn Book of unusual excellence, to which he contributed eleven hymns, deserves remembrance for a few hymns which remind us somewhat of Dr. Byrom's—"I would commune with Thee, my God," "Great is Thy mercy, Lord," "My God, I love Thee for Thyself," "A fitly spoken word," and "Blest be the God of love."

William Gaskell, M.A. (1805-1884), minister of Cross Street Unitarian Chapel, Manchester, and husband of the celebrated authoress of that name, a man of fine Christian character and spirit, wrote a few hymns of singular delicacy of thought and beauty of expression, which richly deserve even wider acceptance than they have yet received. I quote one of his hymns, that readers may judge for themselves :—

Though lowly here our lot may be,
  High work have we to do,
In faith, O Lord, to follow Thee,
  Whose lot was lowly too.

Our days of darkness we may bear,
  Strong in our Father's love;
We lean on His almighty arm,
  And fix our hopes above.

Our lives enriched with gentle thoughts
  And loving deeds may be,
As streams that still the nobler grow,
  The nearer to the sea.

To duty firm, to conscience true,
  However tried and pressed,
In God's clear sight high work we do,
  If we but do our best.

Thus may we make the lowliest lot
  With rays of glory bright:
Thus may we turn a crown of thorns
  Into a crown of light.

"O God, who know'st how frail we are," is also of great merit.

William Freeman Lloyd (1791-1853), one of the secretaries of the Sunday School Union, and Editor of various magazines for the young, was the author of the hymn of trust, "My times are in Thy hand."

Alfred James Morris (1814-1868), minister of Holloway Congregational Church, and author of many original religious works, wrote a few hymns, the best of which—and it is very good—is "Blest Saviour, let me be a child." It was included in his book for children, "The Shepherd and His Lambs," a hymn suitable to young and old alike. Here it is :—

Blest Saviour, let me be a child,
A little child of Thine;
Thou hast on infant spirits smiled,
O kindly smile on mine.

Make me a child in simple ways,
In heart more simple still;
Believing all the Father says,
And doing all His will.

Give me a nature pure and true,
My evil one control;
And day by day Thy grace renew
The childhood of my soul."

May this sweet spirit ne'er depart,
'Midst all my joys and cares;
And may I be a child in heart,
Although a man in years.

William Pennefather, M.A. (1816-1873), the founder of the Mildmay Conference, was the author of two hymns of great excellence, which are not nearly so well known as they richly deserve to be, that I quote them. The first, on Pentecost, is one of the finest we possess on that subject:—

Oh Lord! "with one accord,"
We gather round Thy throne,
To hear Thy holy Word,
To worship Thee alone.
Now send from heaven the Holy Ghost,
Be this another Pentecost!

We have no strength to meet
The storms that round us lower
Keep Thou our trembling feet
In every trying hour;
More than victorious shall we be
If girded with Thy panoply.

Where is the mighty wind
That shook the holy place,
That gladdened every mind,
And brightened every face,
And where the cloven tongues of flame
That marked each follower of the Lamb?

There is no change in Thee,
Lord God the Holy Ghost,
Thy glorious Majesty
Is as at Pentecost!

O may our loosened tongues proclaim,
That Thou, our God, art still the same!

And may that living wave,
That issues from on high,
Whose golden waters lave
The throne eternally,
Flow down in power on us to-day,
And none shall go unblessed away!

The second is remarkable for the terseness and force of its expression. In this respect it is a model:—

Jesus! stand among us
In Thy risen power,
Let this time of worship
Be a hallowed hour.

Breathe the Holy Spirit
Into every heart,
Bid the fears and sorrows
From each soul depart.

Thus, with quickened footsteps,
We'll pursue our way,
Watching for the dawning
Of th' Eternal Day!

Greville Phillimore, M.A. (1821-1884), one of the Editors of "The Parish Hymn Book," and vicar of Down Ampney, in Gloucestershire, wrote a few hymns of more than average merit. Indeed, one, "O Lord of health and life, what tongue can tell," is of great excellence.

William Morley Punshon (1824-1881), an eloquent preacher of the Methodist Church, published a volume of poems called "Sabbath Chimes," in which there is the following hymn for Sunday Evening of remarkable beauty and tenderness:—

We rose to-day with anthems sweet,
To sing before the mercy-seat,
And ere the darkness round us fell,
We bade the grateful vespers swell.

Whate'er has risen from heart sincere,
Each upward glance of filial fear,
Each true resolve, each solemn vow,
Jesus our Lord! accept them now.

O let each following Sabbath yield
For our loved work an ampler field,
A sturdier hatred of the wrong,
A stronger purpose to grow strong.

Whate'er beneath Thy searching eyes
Has wrought to spoil our sacrifice,
'Mid this sweet stillness while we bow,
Jesus our Lord! forgive us now.

And teach us erring souls to win,
And hide their multitude of sin;
To tread in Christ's long-suffering way,
And grow more like Him day by day.

So as our Sabbaths hasten past,
And rounding years bring nigh the last;
When sinks the sun behind the hill,
When all the weary wheels stand still;

When by our bed the lovedones weep,
And death-dews o'er the forehead creep,
And vain is help or hope from men;
Jesus our Lord! receive us then.

George Wade Robinson (1838-1877), a devoted minister of the Congregational Church, had a considerable power, both of poetic thought and expression, as will be evident to all who have read his little book, "Songs in God's World," from which, with some slight transposition, I took the following verses for inclusion in my "Congregational Hymns." They are marked by the tenderness and pathos which characterised all his writings—due, it may be, in part, to the shadow, ever deepening around him, of that coming death, which, at so early an age, closed his earnest career:—

Strangers and pilgrims here below,
In want, in weakness, and in woe,
To whom, O Jesus, should we go,
To whom but unto Thee?

To whom, when hating what is ill,
We find our strength unequal still
To do, although we love, Thy will,
To whom but unto Thee?

To whom, with all our faults and fears,
With all our toils and all our tears,

Pouring them into loving ears,
To whom but unto Thee?

To whom, when all around appears
Against us, and too anxious fears
Look trembling up the coming years,
To whom but unto Thee?

To whom, when gloomy Death appals,
And the cold shadow darkly falls
Along our happy household walls,
To whom but unto Thee?

Emily Taylor (1795-1872), a member of the Unitarian Church, and Editor of "Memories of some Contemporary Poets," was the authoress of "Come to the house of prayer," and a very suggestive hymn descriptive of the loss that would arise to believers if the gifts of God were ours, but we without the power to approach Him in prayer. The idea is so beautiful, and its expression so unique in hymnody, that I venture to quote it:—

O Source of good! around me spread,
Ten thousand thousand blessings lie;
By night Thy mercy guards my head—
By day I feel Thee ever nigh.

Yet if to taste Thy gifts were all
Thy bounteous hand bestowed on me;—
No leave upon Thy name to call,
And gain access by prayer to Thee;

How would my spirit, sorrowing,
'Mid all those gifts have sighed,—to feel
It knew not the refreshing spring
That ceaseless flows to soothe and heal.

No chain to bind the wandering soul,
No link connecting earth and heaven,
No Father's pitying kind control,
No child repenting and forgiven!

But now the voice of prayer is heard,
When strength departs and comforts flee;
And man may act upon that word—
"Seek, and He shall be found of Thee."

William Whiting (1825-1878), choirmaster of Winchester College, was the author of what is certainly the most popular hymn for "those at sea." It *is* a good hymn, but its popularity is partly due, I fancy, to the music to which it was wedded in "Hymns Ancient and Modern." There are hymns whose constant use is as much due to this cause as to their intrinsic merit. No other hymn from Mr. Whiting's pen has gained currency in the Church.

Sarah Williams was the gifted authoress of many poems, which she published under the *nom de plume* of "Sadie." Her early death cut short the promise of a career of considerable usefulness in literature. The following lines from her pen seem to me singularly tender and beautiful. I quote them in the hope that they may catch the eye of Hymnal Editors, and lead to their inclusion in future collections, as I happen to know that, where used, they have become greatly beloved. Three verses are omitted, as unsuitable for public worship.

Because I knew not when my life was good,
And when there was a light upon my path,
But turned my soul perversely to the dark—
    O Lord, I do repent.

Because I held upon my selfish road,
And left my brother wounded by the way,
And called ambition duty, and pressed on—
    O Lord, I do repent.

Because I spent the strength Thou gavest me
In struggle which Thou never didst ordain,
And have but dregs of life to offer Thee—
    O Lord, I do repent.

Because I was impatient, would not wait,
But thrust my impious hand across Thy threads,
And marred the pattern drawn out for my life—
    O Lord, I do repent.

Because Thou hast borne with me all this while,
Hast smitten me with love until I weep,
Hast called me as a mother calls her child—
    O Lord, I do repent.

It will be evident, from what I have written, that the middle of the present century has been remarkable for the production of a large number of hymns, of a very high order of merit. Probably no age has been more

P

fruitful in this respect. I question whether, in any period of the same length, so many fine hymns have been written. This is to be ascribed to many causes, not merely to the large place which hymns now fill in the worship of the Church, but to the revived religious life, the superior culture, the widely spread poetic gift and spirit, as well as to the increase of musical culture, all of which have exerted a great influence. What, in earlier times, took ages to produce, has been produced almost within the limits of a generation. Indeed, the Church would not be ill supplied with song if she were dependent on the productions of the last half century It has been in hymnody as fruitful as the Elizabethan age was in dramatic works. We have scarcely yet realised the wealth of our recent hymnody; since hymnists rarely reach their true position till time has removed them from our gaze. Age does not soften hymns as it does pictures, but it enables us to regard them with less of prejudice, whilst use familiarises, and helps us to realise their beauty. Many an old hymn, through usage or the lapse of time, gains a glory it does not deserve Many a new hymn is not valued as it should be through lack of these. There is no gift for which the Church deserves to be more profoundly grateful than for the great succession of singers who have of late enriched her song, and so ennobled her worship. These, in days to come, will reach their true place, and their age be regarded as among the classic ones of hymnody.

CHAPTER XV.

RECENT HYMNISTS.—I.

BORN 1796—1820.

THERE must surely be to the hymn-writer a deep joy in knowing that his verses have kindled the hearts of multitudes to worship, and risen on the wings of music to the ear of heaven. I can conceive of few things that would waken more real, though it may be quiet, satisfaction. Bishop Ken deemed it would be an addition to his happiness in the happier world, if he should know that his devotional poems were answering on earth the purpose for which he had piously composed them:—

And should the well-meant songs I leave behind,
With Jesus' lovers an acceptance find,
'Twill heighten e'en the joys of heaven to know,
That in my verse the saints hymn God below.

It has not always fallen to the lot of even the noblest hymnists to reap this reward during life, for not till they had passed away did their verses enter into the worship-song of the Church. The worth of many a noble hymn has not been discovered until its author had gone over to the majority. But many an author in our day has had the joy of knowing that his hymns have been warmly welcomed by the Church, and that they have risen in choral song from the lips of devout worshippers. There are many hymnists, happily still spared to us, who must rejoice in the thought that scarcely a Sunday passes in which their hymns do not both kindle and express the devout feelings of men in a multitude of churches in this and other English-speaking lands, many of them being widely separated in doctrine, in ritual, in ecclesiastical forms, from that to which they themselves belong. In many a case hymns are sung in assemblies in whose worship their authors would scarcely care to join, and whose doctrines they heartily condemn. The words of Dean, and Bishop, and Cardinal, are used in lowly conventicles where their stately canonicals would seem quite out of place, whilst, on the other hand, the hymns of many an unadorned Layman belonging to the simpler Free Churches are sung by white-robed choristers and priests under the fretted roofs of venerable cathedrals. Thus one touch of (what is better than nature) grace makes the whole Church kin. Thus the hymns of the Presbyterian Bonar, and the Independent Watts, have passed into use and are sung as parts of a richly ornate service; whilst, on the other hand, hymns by Cardinal Newman, Bishop Christopher Wordsworth, and Father Caswall have found their way into the simple services of village chapels. There is no bond of union stronger or more spiritual than that furnished by hymns which have sprung out of hearts kindled to lyric expression by the vision of Christ and His peerless work on behalf of men. Thus Christian feeling is proved to be mightier and more important in securing unity than the particular formulas which the minds of men have fashioned for its expression. For nowhere is the real unity, underlying all diversity, of the Church more clearly revealed than in the hymnody of these modern days. There are no helpers in the great work of quickening and deepening religious life whose aid is more precious than those whose love reaches its noblest expression in sacred song. Of late years the Church has been blessed with a large number of such helpers. Perhaps in no age has the number been so large, or the quality of the songs they have given us so high. From all quarters such songs have come; from laymen like George Rawson and Chatterton Dix, from the clergy of every rank, from the humble curate or country pastor to the right reverend bishop and the princely cardinal; nay, even woman has had no mean place in this high work, for in many a church where women's voices may not be heard in *speech*, they are heard in holy song (as in the hymns by Miss Havergal and Miss Elliott in "Hymns Ancient and Modern"). Thus the lyric fervour sets at nought all ecclesiastical restrictions, all doctrinal exclusivenesses. Thus may we catch gleams of the time when the whole Christian company shall be gathered, if not into one *fold*, yet into one *flock*, under the great Shepherd, Christ. For of that time so greatly desired, and often sought in such foolish ways, the truest heralds are the hymnists whose hearts are touched by the spirit of Christ.

It is only bare justice to say that of living hymnists, the Established Church furnishes the greater number; amongst these must, of right, be included, some who now belong to the Roman Communion; but whose hymns were written before they left the church of their fathers.

Sir Edward Denny (born 1796), is one of the few

writers of hymns belonging to that section of the Church, known as "The Brethren." His hymns are, of course, imbued by the special doctrines of that sect, and this unfits most of them for general use in the Church at large; but in some, the Christian and lyric nature of their author overpowers his doctrinal prepossessions, and such hymns from his pen are of great force and merit. Examples of this may be found in his hymn :—

What grace, O Lord, and beauty shone
Around Thy steps below;
What patient love was seen in all
Thy life and death of woe.

For ever on Thy burden'd heart
A weight of sorrow hung;
Yet no ungentle, murmuring word
Escaped Thy silent tongue.

Thy foes might hate, despise, revile,
Thy friends unfaithful prove,
Unwearied in forgiveness still,
Thy heart could only love.

Oh! give us hearts to love like Thee,
Like Thee, O Lord, to grieve
Far more for others' sins, than all
The wrongs that we receive.

One with Thyself, may every eye
In us, Thy brethren, see
The gentleness and grace that spring
From union, Lord, with Thee.

And in his really fine Missionary Hymn :—

Light of the lonely pilgrim's heart,
Star of the coming day,
Arise, and with Thy morning beams,
Chase all our griefs away:

Come, blessèd Lord, bid every shore
And answering island sing
The praises of Thy royal Name,
And own Thee as their King.

Bid the whole earth, responsive now
To the bright world above,

Break forth in rapturous strains of joy,
  In memory of Thy love.

Lord, Lord, Thy fair creation groans,
  The air, the earth, the sea,
In unison with all our hearts,
  And calls aloud for Thee.

Come, then, with all Thy quickening power,
  With one awakening smile,
And bid the serpent's trail no more
  The beauteous realms defile:

Thine was the cross, with all its fruit
  Of grace and peace divine;
Be Thine the crown of glory now,
  The palm of victory Thine.

Here again we see how the Christian spirit stretches over all dividing and narrowing enclosures of doctrinal forms.

The first quarter of the present century is remarkable as having given to us some of the most notable hymnists which the Church has ever possessd. In this respect it is one of the golden ages of hymnody, only equalled by one or two similar periods.

Matthew Bridges (born 1800), originally a member of the Anglican, but now of the Roman Church, is a writer with a great lyric gift, which in my judgment he has allowed to be marred by the carnal views of Christian truth prevalent in the church to which he now belongs. It is not so with all the hymnists of that Communion (with Cardinal Newman, for example, whose mind seizes the more spiritual aspects of Christianity); but it is so with Mr. Bridges, as may be seen from the following hymn; magnificent in some of its parts, but in others carnal and sensuous to the last degree. This is specially so in the third and fifth verses, which lay stress on the physical rather than the spiritual offering of our Lord:—

Crown Him with many crowns,
  The Lamb upon His throne;
Hark! how the heavenly anthem drowns
  All music but its own.

Awake, my soul, and sing
  Of Him who died for thee;
And hail Him as thy matchless King,
  Through all eternity.

Crown Him the Virgin's Son,
  The God incarnate born;
Whose arm those crimson trophies won
  Which now His brow adorn.

Fruit of the mystic rose,
  As of that rose the stem;
The Root, whence mercy ever flows,
  The Babe of Bethlehem.

Crown Him the Lord of Love:
  Behold His hands and side,
Rich wounds, yet visible above,
  In beauty glorified.

No angel in the sky
  Can fully bear that sight,
But downward bends his burning eye
  At mysteries so bright.

Crown Him the Lord of peace,
  Whose power a sceptre sways
From pole to pole, that wars may cease
  And all be prayer and praise.

His reign shall know no end,
  And round His pierced feet
Fair flowers of Paradise extend
  Their fragrance ever sweet.

Crown Him the Lord of years,
  The Potentate of time,
Creator of the rolling spheres,
  Ineffably sublime.

Glazed in a sea of light,
  Whose everlasting waves
Reflect His form, the Infinite,
  Who lives and loves and saves.

Crown Him the Lord of heaven,
  One with the Father known;
And the blest Spirit through Him given,
  From yonder triune throne.

All hail! Redeemer, hail!
  For Thou hast died for me;
Thy praise shall never, never fail,
  Throughout eternity.

John Henry Newman (1801-1894), filled a very distinguished place in the intellectual, ecclesiastical, theological thought of his age. His early religious life was fostered by the somewhat narrow evangelicalism which prevailed in the earlier years of this century; gradually he passed to a type of Christianity which is now described as Anglican, and after lingering and hesitating for some time on the borderland which separates High Anglicanism from Romanism, moved, as is clear from the self-revelation of his inner life in his marvellous book "Apologia pro vita sua," by the idea that there is and can be only one *visible* church, he entered the fold which it must be confessed has the best claim to fulfil that supposed requirement. Such an idea of the church is, to my way of thinking, not only utterly unscriptural, but utterly unspiritual, but when it takes possession of the mind there can, in the nature of things, be no resting place but in the Roman Communion. The forces which fix a man's ecclesiastical position are, however, too subtle to be fully analysed, and may leave the moral and spiritual character to a large extent untouched. It is curious to notice how two men, the offspring of the same parents, both of exceptional ability and nobility of character, should be so widely severed as John Henry and Francis William Newman; the first becoming a Cardinal of the Roman Catholic church, and the second a prominent and eloquent apostle of Theism. Strange to say, both have laid bare much of their inner spiritual history. The first in the book to which I have already referred, "Apologia pro vita sua," and the second in "Phases of Faith, or Passages from the History of my Creed." The Cardinal has been one of the most voluminous and powerful writers of our time, and is indeed one of the greatest masters of a noble English style. Some passages in his sermons are poems in all but form. But he is known to a far larger circle by his hymn "Lead, kindly light, amid the encircling gloom," which is now one of the most deservedly popular in the English language. Those who desire to see the effects which high culture may have on hymn-production should compare it with the hymn on the same subject, "Guide me, O Thou great Jehovah!" by the Welsh writer, W. Williams (probably the only Welsh hymn, which has found its way into popular use, in English), but which has been largely supplanted by the more poetic hymn of Cardinal Newman. The story of its composition is told as follows in the "Apologia" *—

"I got to Castro-Giovanni, and was laid up there for nearly three weeks. Towards the end of May I set off for Palermo, taking three days for the journey. Before starting from my inn in the morning of May 26th or 27th, I sat down on my bed and began to sob bitterly. My servant, who had acted as my nurse, asked what ailed me. I could only answer, 'I have a work to do in England.' I was aching to get home; yet for want of a vessel I was kept at Palermo for three weeks. I began to visit the churches, and they calmed my impatience, though I did

* "Apologia pro vita sua," p. 99 (1864).

not attend any services. I knew nothing of the Presence of the Blessed Sacrament there. At last I got off in an orange boat, bound for Marseilles. We were becalmed a whole week in the Straits of Bonifacio. Then it was that I wrote the lines 'Lead, kindly Light,' which have since become well known. I was writing verses nearly the whole time of my passage; at length I got to Marseilles, and set off for England. The fatigue of travelling was too much for me, and I was laid up for several days at Lyons. At last I got off again, and did not stop night or day till I reached England, and my mother's house. My brother had arrived from Persia only a few hours before. This was on the Tuesday. The following Sunday, July 14th, Mr. Keble preached the Assize Sermon in the University Pulpit. It was published under the title of 'National Apostasy.' I have ever considered and kept the day as the start of the religious movement in 1833."

Another hymn of great force and beauty from his pen is the following, which forms "The fifth choir of Angelicals," in his greatest poem, "The Dream of Gerontius."

Praise to the Holiest in the height,
And in the depth be praise:
In all His words most wonderful,
Most sure in all His ways!

O loving wisdom of our God!
When all was sin and shame,
A second Adam to the fight
And to the rescue came.

O wisest love! that flesh and blood,
Which did in Adam fail,
Should strive afresh against their foe,
Should strive and should prevail.

O generous love! that He, who smote
In man for man the foe,

The double agony in man
  For man should undergo.

And in the garden secretly,
  And on the cross on high,
Should teach His brethren, and inspire
  To suffer and to die.

Praise to the Holiest in the height,
  And in the depth be praise:
In all His words most wonderful,
  Most sure in all His ways.

The hymn called "Desolation," written, like "Lead, kindly Light," at the time of his great doubt and anxiety in 1833, "off Sardinia," though not quite suitable for public worship, is exquisitely beautiful and suggestive:—

O say not thou art left of God,
Because His tokens in the sky
Thou canst not read; this earth He trod
To teach thee He was ever nigh.

He sees beneath the fig-tree green
Nathaniel con His sacred lore;
Shouldst thou the closet seek, unseen
He enters through the unopened door.

And when thou liest, by slumber bound,
Outwearied in the Christian fight,
In glory, girt with saints around,
He stands above thee through the night.

When friends to Emmaus bend their course,
He joins, although He holds their eyes:
Or, shouldst thou feel some fever's force,
He takes thy hand, He bids thee rise.

Or, on a voyage, when calms prevail,
And prison thee upon the sea,
He walks the waves, He wings the sail,
The shore is gained, and thou art free.

Dr. Newman has translated many hymns from the Latin Breviary, and as was to be expected from such a man, they are models of what translations should be. The following is a fine example:—

Now that the sun is gleaming bright,
  Implore we, bending low,

That He, the uncreated Light,
  May guide us as we go.

No sinful word, nor deed of wrong,
  Nor thoughts that idly rove.
But simple truth be on our tongue,
  And in our hearts be love.

And while the hours in order flow,
  O Christ, securely fence
Our gates, beleaguered by the foe,
  The gate of every sense.

And grant that to Thine honour, Lord,
  Our daily toil may tend;
That we begin it at Thy Word,
  And in Thy favour end.

Dr. Newman was one of the chief contributors to the "Lyra Apostolica," where his verses appear under the signature of a Greek *delta*, and in 1868 he gathered his poems together and published them under the modest title—"Verses on various occasions." This is one of the most beautiful and suggestive volumes of religious poetry in the language. Those on Scripture Character are full of fine insight, expressed in the most terse and vigorous language. I may be permitted to travel a little out of the path marked out for myself in these pages, and quote the one on "Moses," which, though not a hymn, is only one degree removed therefrom.* This may lead readers to seek further acquaintance with Dr. Newman's suggestive verses.

Moses, the patriot fierce, became
  The meekest man on earth,
To show us how love's quick'ning flame
  Can give our souls new birth.

Moses, the man of meekest heart,
  Lost Canaan by self-will,

* By his kind permission, I have been enabled to introduce the finest of his scripture poems into my work, "The Poets' Bible" (Ward, Lock & Co.).

To show, where grace has done its part,
  How sin defiles us still.
Thou who hast taught me in Thy fear,
  Yet seest me frail at best,
O grant me loss with Moses here,
  To gain his future rest.

James Martineau (born 1805), the most distinguished preacher of the age in the Unitarian body, one of the greatest philosophers, and certainly the most eloquent, of his time, has edited two hymnals for the use of his own section of the Church, and written, though without appending his name to them, two or three hymns of great beauty. The one quoted below was included in my "Congregational Hymns" without any ascription of authorship. On receiving the volume Prof. F. M. Bird, the most erudite hymnologist of America, wrote to me saying he believed the hymn was by James Martineau, and urging me to ask him. I appended his name in the copy I was revising, and on the printers suddenly calling for copy for a new edition, I sent them the volume in which I had appended his name to the hymn. I had previously written to ask him if the hymn was from his pen, and he replied that he was not at liberty to relieve it of its anonymity. Forgetful of the fact that his name had been added to the hymn, the new edition came out ascribing the authorship to him. I then called to explain the circumstance, and he told me that the hymn had been written nearly forty years before, and he fancied that some German hymn had been running in his head at the time he composed it, and so he scarcely liked to claim it as his own. Probably only the suggestion came from a German source, and to all intents and purposes the hymn is by him. At all events, it is very fine, as my readers will see:—

Thy way is in the deep, O Lord!
 E'en there we'll go with Thee:
We'll meet the tempest at Thy word,
 And walk upon the sea.

Poor tremblers at His rougher wind,
 Why do we doubt Him so?
Who gives the storm a path, will find
 The way our feet shall go.

A moment may His hand be lost,
 Drear moment of delay!
We cry, "Lord, keep the tempest-tost,"
 And safe we're borne away.

The Lord yields nothing to our fears,
 And flies from selfish care;
But comes Himself, where'er He hears
 The voice of loving prayer.

O happy soul of faith divine!
 Thy victory how sure!
The love that kindles joy is thine,
 The patience to endure.

Come, Lord of peace! our griefs dispel,
 And wipe our tears away:
'Tis Thine, to order all things well,
 And ours to bless Thy sway.

One other hymn is also ascribed to him; very striking, but scarcely so suitable for public worship. It begins "A voice upon the midnight air."

George Rawson (1807-1889), is a man whose leisure hours have been largely occupied with meditation on sacred themes. I am told that his Bible is neatly annotated with his own devout musings as well as by illustrations drawn from a wide range of reading. But every now and then his thoughts have found expression in verse. His first songs saw the light under the signature, "A Leeds Layman," and for a long time he refused permission to append his name to his hymns, so that they appeared anonymously; but at last, what had been before an open secret to the few, ceased to be a secret at all, and in nearly every hymnal of a truly eclectic character one, or even more, hymns from his pen appeared with his name appended. Still later, in 1877, all the hymns he had then written were collected and published under the title "Hymns, Verses, and Chants," by George Rawson. Quite recently (1885) a little volume called "Songs of Spiritual Thought" was issued by the Religious Tract Society, containing a selection of hymns from the former volume, together with others written since its publication. I have before me the original volume with the additions, in the venerable author's own handwriting, of all the hymns he has since produced, together with improved readings of some of the earlier ones. I am bound to say, that with one or two exceptions, the earlier are finer than the later hymns. The best fruits are from the tree of middle life. Very rich and diversified they are. Indeed, diversity of style and treatment is one of the characteristics of this little volume. There is an entire absence of the monotony which renders the collected hymns of so many of the earlier hymnists unattractive. Each hymn seems like an idea which has possessed the author's mind, and then gradually taken on its appropriate dress. Standing first in the volume are Mr. Rawson's renderings of certain of the Psalms. Some of these are but variations from renderings by other hands. There are three versions of the twenty-third Psalm; in one of these, it is evident that the beautiful one of Francis Rous in the

Scotch Psalter is ringing in the author's ears. Dr. Watts's version of the 148th Psalm must have been in his mind when he wrote his version of the same Psalm; but Mr. Rawson's is far the finer of the two, indeed, it is one of the grandest versions of a Psalm in our English tongue.

Praise ye the Lord! immortal quire,
In heavenly heights above,
With harp and voice and souls of fire,
Burning with perfect love.

Shine to His glory, worlds of light!
Ye million suns of space,
Fair moons and glittering stars of night,
Running your mystic race!

Ye gorgeous clouds, that deck the sky
With crystal, crimson, gold,
And rainbow arches raised on high,
The light of light unfold!

Lift to Jehovah, wintry main,
Your grand white hands in prayer;
Still summer seas, in dulcet strain
Murmur hosannas there!

Do homage, breezy ocean floor,
With many-twinkling sign;
Majestic calms, be hushed before
The Holiness Divine.

Storm, lightning, thunder, hail and snow,
Wild winds that keep His word,
With the old mountains far below,
Unite to bless the Lord.

His name, ye forests, wave along:
Whisper it, every flower;
Birds, beasts, and insects, swell the song
That tells His love and power.

And round the wide world let it roll,
Whilst man shall lead it on;
Join every ransomed human soul,
In glorious unison!

Come, aged man! come little child!
Youth, maiden, peasant, king--
To God in Jesus reconciled,
Your hallelujahs bring!

The all-creating Deity,
Maker of earth and heaven!
The great redeeming Majesty,
To Him the praise be given

When we pass from his versions of certain of the Psalms to his hymns, the work is, of course more original, save in one or two instances where the hymn is clearly suggested by one from another author. This is the case with his lovely hymn full of a quiet earnestness, written in 1853, which begins "In the dark and cloudy day." A poet-artist, who has been fortunate enough to win the benediction of John Ruskin, says that this hymn brought to him some of the sweet repose George Herbert is wont to give.

In the dark and cloudy day,
When earth's riches flee away.
And the last hope will not stay,—
My Saviour, comfort me.

When the secret idol's gone,
That my poor heart yearned upon,
Desolate, bereft alone,
My Saviour, comfort me.

Thou who wast so sorely tried,
In the darkness crucified,
Bid me in Thy love confide:
My Saviour, comfort me.

In these hours of sad distress,
Let me know He loves no less,
Bid me trust His faithfulness;
My Saviour, comfort me.

Not unduly let me grieve,
Meekly the kind stripes receive,
Let me humbly still believe;
My Saviour, comfort me.

So it shall be good for me
Much afflicted now to be,
If Thou wilt but tenderly,
My Saviour, comfort me.

Beautiful as it is, it is not equal to Herrick's Litany, as

our readers may see if they refer to page 75 of this work, which surely must have been in Mr. Rawson's mind at the time he wrote the foregoing hymn. Most akin in form and spirit to the hymn I have quoted is what is perhaps Mr. Rawson's best-known one, a Litany to the Comforter; of which, the Hon. Roden Noel says, "It is a hymn one prizes greatly." Indeed, the Litany form seems specially suited to Mr. Rawson's genius.

Come to our poor nature's night,
With Thy blessed inward light,
Holy Ghost, the infinite;
    Comforter Divine.

We are sinful—cleanse us, Lord,
Sick and faint—Thy strength afford,
Lost—until by Thee restored.
    Comforter Divine.

Orphans are our souls, and poor,
Give us from Thy heavenly store,
Faith, love, joy, for evermore,
    Comforter Divine.

Like the dew Thy peace distil;
Guide, subdue our wayward will,
Things of Christ unfolding still,
    Comforter Divine.

Gentle, awful, holy Guest,
Make Thy temple in each breast;
There Thy presence be confessed,
    Comforter Divine.

With us, for us, intercede,
And with voiceless groanings plead,
Our unutterable need,
    Comforter Divine

In us 'Abba, Father,' cry,
Earnest of the bliss on high;
Seal of immortality,
    Comforter Divine.

Search for us the depths of God;
Upwards by the starry road,
Bear us to Thy high abode,
    Comforter Divine.

But whilst Mr. Rawson often owes his inspiration to the hymns of previous writers, he is far from being a mere imitator. In his writings we notice some of the most distinctive and original notes in modern hymnody. Subjects and treatment are both new and quite his own. What can be finer or more suited to the theme than his verses on Pastor Robinson's advice to the Pilgrim Fathers? "He charged us, if God should reveal anything to us by any other instruments of His, to be as ready to receive it as any truth by his ministry; for he was very confident the Lord had more light and truth yet to break forth out of His holy word."

We limit not the truth of God,
  To our poor reach of mind,
By notions of our day and sect,
  Crude, partial, and confined;
No, let a new and better hope
  Within our hearts be stirred;
The Lord hath yet more light and truth
  To break forth from His word.

Who dares to bind to his dull sense,
  The oracles of heaven,
For all the nations, tongues, and climes,
  And all the ages given;
That universe, how much unknown!
  That ocean unexplored!
The Lord hath yet more light and truth
  To break forth from His word.

Darkling our great forefathers went
  The first steps of the way:
'Twas but the dawning, yet to grow
  Into the perfect day.
And grow it shall; our glorious Sun
  More fervid rays afford;
The Lord hath yet more light and truth
  To break forth from His word.

The valleys past, ascending still,
  Our souls would higher climb,
And look down from supernal heights
  On all the bygone time.

Upward we press; the air is clear,
  And the sphere-music heard;
The Lord hath yet more light and truth
  To break forth from His word.

O Father, Son, and Spirit, send
  Us increase from above;
Enlarge, expand all Christian souls
  To comprehend Thy love!
And make us all go on to know,
  With nobler powers conferred,
The Lord hath yet more light and truth
  To break forth from His word.

What verses more appropriate to be sung when a valiant soldier of Christ has finished the fight and gone to his reward than the following?—

Captain and Saviour of the host
  Of Christian chivalry;
We bless Thee for our comrade true,
  Now summoned up to Thee.

We bless Thee for his every step
  In faithful following Thee;
And for his good fight fought so well,
  And crowned with victory.

We thank Thee that the wayworn sleeps
  The sleep in Jesus blest;
The purified and ransomed soul
  Hath entered into rest.

We bless Thee that his humble love
  Hath met with such regard:
We bless Thee for his blessedness,
  And for his rich reward.

Our age is rich in hymns for Sunday evening. Some of our modern hymnists, indeed, have been happiest in their hymns for this season. Its sacredness seems to have stirred all their poetic power. But for quiet tenderness and pathos the verses which follow are excelled by none.

Thou who hast known the careworn breast,
  The weary need of sleep's deep balm,
Come Saviour, ere we go to rest,
  And breathe around Thy perfect calm.

Thy presence gives us childlike trust,
  Gladness and hope without alloy,
The faith that triumphs o'er the dust,
  And gleamings of eternal joy.

Stand in our midst, dear Lord, and say,
  'Peace be to you this evening hour;
Then all the struggles of the day
  Vanish before Thy loving power.

Blest is the pilgrimage to heaven,
  A little nearer every night;
Christ to our earthly darkness given,
  Till in His glory there is light.

Full of a healthy spiritual feeling and with a metre and rhythm singularly bright and appropriate is the following:

Walking with Thee, my God,
  Saviour benign;
Daily confer on me
  Converse divine;
Jesus in Thee restored,
Brother and Holy Lord,
  Let it be mine.

Walking with Thee, my God,
  Like as a child
Leans on his father's strength,
  Crossing the wild;
And by the way is taught
Lessons of holy thought,
  Faith undefiled.

Darkness and earthly mists,
  How do they flee,
Far underneath my feet,
  Walking with Thee:
Pure is that upper air,
Cloudless the prospect there,
  Walking with Thee.

Walking in reverence
  Humbly with Thee,
Yet from all abject fear
  Lovingly free:
E'en as a friend with friend,
Cheered to the journey's end,
  Walking with Thee!

Then Thy companions here
  Walking with Thee,
Rise to a higher life,
  Soul liberty.
They are not here to love,
But to the home above,
  Taken by Thee.

Gently translated, they
  Pass out of sight;
Gone! as the morning stars
  Flee with the night:
Taken to endless day!—
So may I fade away
  Into Thy light.

It was to be expected that such a nature as Mr. Rawson's would be specially moved by what is certainly the most tender and pathetic of all the services of the church—the Supper of the Lord—and some of his finest hymns have been written for this holy feast of remembrance. The hymn by which he is perhaps most widely known is one out of many he has written for that service. This has reached far beyond the bounds of the Church to which Mr. Rawson belongs, and is sung in churches widely severed from his own in their conception of that ordinance. It appears in an altered, but certainly not improved form in "Church Hymns." I do not like the fifth verse, since it points to a *physical* resurrection of the body, for which there is no warrant in Scripture.

By Christ redeemed, in Christ restored,
We keep the memory adored,
And show the death of our dear Lord
  Until He come.

His body, broken in our stead,
Is here, in this memorial bread.
And so our feeble love is fed
  Until He come.

The streams of His dread agony,
His life-blood shed for us, we see:
The wine shall tell the mystery,
Until He come.

And thus that dark betrayal-night
With the last advent we unite,
By one blest chain of loving rite,
Until He come.

Until the trump of God be heard,
Until the ancient graves be stirred,
And with the great commanding word,
The Lord shall come.

O blessed hope! with this elate,
Let not our hearts be desolate,
But strong in faith, in patience, wait
Until He come.

I have already said that his later hymns lack the distinctiveness and vigour of the best of his earlier ones. An exception must, however, be made in the case of one hymn, likewise a Communion hymn, which he was good enough to send me in MS., and which appeared first of all in my own hymnal. It is intended for use after the service.

Like the first disciples
In their strange glad hour.
We have seen the Master
In His risen power.

In this rite have owned Him,
As the Christ adored:
In His living presence,
We have seen the Lord.

O that face of suffering,
Wounded hands and side,
Say to each—'I loved thee,
And for thee I died.'

Hear His voice of triumph,
Death's dark reign is o'er,
I am He that liveth,
Liveth evermore.

My death hath redeemed you,
Now for you I live,
Uttermost, eternal,
Is the love I give.

'Lo! I'm with you always
Till the ages cease.'
Lord, we rest believing;
Lord, in Thee is peace.

Such hymns as these are likely to hold a permanent place in the hymnody of the churches in which they are already used, and to find their way into other communions, since they are full of a true Christian feeling, expressed in forms that are at once poetic and devout.

Horatius Bonar, of Edinburgh (1808-1889), who is one of the most popular of recent hymnists, presents to us the strange spectacle of an author whose hymns have passed into use in nearly every section of the Church, but whose own congregation refused to allow them to be sung, and rigidly adhered to the Scottish Psalms and Paraphrases. Whilst equally remarkable is the fact, that, though he belonged to a strongly Calvinistic body, his hymns abound in the most ecstatic assertions of the universal love of God. Here, as in so many other cases, the heart was wiser than the head—the poet than the theologian. When the soul soars the highest, the limitations of earth sink out of sight. Just as the Unitarian whose heart is kindled by the lyric fire, sees more in Christ than his reasoning theological brother of the same church, so the strong Calvinist, when moved in heart to poetic expression, sees that "the love of God is broader than the measures of man's mind." We are safer with the poet than the theologian. Take, as an illustration of this, the following from Dr. Bonar:—

O love of God, how strong and true!
Eternal, and yet ever new,
Uncomprehended and unbought,
Beyond all knowledge and all thought!

O love of God, how deep and great!
Far deeper than man's deepest hate;
Self-fed, self-kindled like the light,
Changeless, eternal, infinite!

O heavenly love, how precious still,
In days of weariness and ill,
In nights of pain and helplessness,
To heal, to comfort, and to bless!

O wide-embracing, wondrous love,
We read thee in the sky above,
We read thee in the earth below,
In seas that swell, and streams that flow!

We read thee best in Him who came
To bear for us the cross of shame,
Sent by the Father from on high,
Our life to live, our death to die.

We read thee in the tears once shed
Over doomed Salem's guilty head,
In the cold tomb of Bethany,
And blood drops of Gethsemane.

We read thy power to bless and save,
E'en in the darkness of the grave;
Still more in resurrection light,
We read the fulness of thy might.

O love of God, our shield and stay
Through all the perils of our way;
Eternal love, in thee we rest,
For ever safe, for ever blest!

The most widely known and loved of his hymns are—"I heard the voice of Jesus say," called "A Voice from Galilee;" "A few more years shall roll," probably suggested by two lines in Peter Abelard's hymn—

Illic nec Sabbato
Succedit Sabbatum,
Perpes laetitia
Sabbatizantium.

"Thy way, not mine, O Lord," "I lay my sins on Jesus," "Calm me, my God, and keep me calm," "Lord, give me light to do Thy work," "Go, labour on, spend and be spent;" "When the weary, seeking rest," modelled on the pattern of Solomon's prayer at the dedication of the Temple. But the following richly deserve notice. This is very fine, in substance and expression:—

Bear Thou my burden, Thou who bear'st my sin;
Both are too heavy, Lord, for me to bear;
Oh, take them, call them Thine; yes, Thine, though mine;
And give me calm repose in hours of fear and care.

Let me not fret because of evil men;
Smooth Thou each angry ripple of my soul;
Reviled, O let me not revile again,
And ever let Thy hand my rising warmth control.

Let not my peace be broken when the wrong
Conquers the right, but let me still wait on;
The day of right is coming, late, but long,
Long right beneath the sway of the all-righteous One.

When truth is overborne and error reigns,
When clamour lords it over patient love.
Give the brave calmness which from wrath refrains,
Yet from the steadfast course declines one foot to move.

When love no refuge finds but silent faith,
When meekness fain would hide its heavy head,
When trustful truth, shunning the words of wrath,
Waits for the day of right, so long, so long delayed;

Beneath the load of crosses and of cares,
Of thwarted plans, of rude and spiteful words;
O bear me up, when this weak flesh despairs,
And the one arm which faith can lean on is the Lord's.

As is this, touched with the same spirit:—

Not what I am, O Lord, but what Thou art!
That, that alone, can be my soul's true rest;
Thy love, not mine, bids fear and doubt depart,
And stills the tempest of my tossing breast.

It is Thy perfect love that casts out fear:
I know the voice that speaks the "It is I";
And in these well-known words of heavenly cheer
I hear the joy that bids each sorrow fly.

Thy name is Love! I hear it from yon cross;
Thy name is Love! I read it in yon tomb;
All meaner love is perishable dross,
But this shall light me through time's thickest gloom.

It blesses now, and shall for ever bless,
It saves me now, and shall for ever save;
It holds me up in days of helplessness,
It bears me safely o'er each swelling wave.

Girt with the love of God on every side,
Breathing that love as heaven's own healing air,
I work or wait, still following my Guide,
Braving each foe, escaping every snare.

'Tis what I know of Thee, my Lord and God,
That fills my soul with peace, my lips with song;
Thou art my health, my joy, my staff, my rod,
Leaning on Thee, in weakness I am strong.

I am all want and hunger; this faint heart
Pines for a fulness which it finds not here;
Dear ones are leaving, and, as they depart,
Make room within for something yet more dear.

More of Thyself, O show me, hour by hour,
More of Thy glory, O my God and Lord;
More of Thyself, in all Thy grace and power;
More of Thy love and truth, Incarnate Word.

This is brief, but beautiful:—

O Love that casts out fear,
O Love that casts out sin,
Tarry no more without,
But come and dwell within.

True Sunlight of the soul,
Surround me as I go;
So shall my way be safe,
My feet no straying know.

Great Love of God, come in,
Well-spring of heavenly peace,
Thou Living Water, come,
Spring up, and never cease.

Bold and lyric is:—

Speak, lips of mine,
And tell abroad
The praises of thy God.
Speak, stammering tongue,
In gladdest tone,
Make His high praises known.

Speak, sea and earth,
Heaven's utmost star,
Speak from your realms afar,
Take up the note,
And send it round
Creation's farthest bound.

Speak, heaven of heavens,
Wherein our God
Has made His bright abode.
Speak, angels speak,
In songs proclaim
His everlasting name.

Speak, son of dust,
Thy flesh He took,
And heaven for thee forsook.
Speak, child of death,
Thy death He died;
Bless thou the Crucified.

One of his most beautiful and poetic hymns is:—

Light of the world! for ever, ever shining;
There is no change in Thee;
True Light of life, all joy and health enshrining,
Thou canst not fade nor flee.

Thou hast arisen; but Thou declinest never:
To-day shines as the past;
All that Thou wast, Thou art, and shalt be ever;
Brightness from first to last!

Night visits not Thy sky, nor storm, nor sadness;
Day fills up all its blue:
Unfailing beauty, and unfaltering gladness,
And love for ever new!

Light of the world! undimming and unsetting,
O shine each mist away!
Banish the fear, the falsehood, and the fretting,
Be our unchanging day!

Strong, and yet tender, is:—

Through good report and evil, Lord!
Still guided by Thy faithful word,
Our staff, our buckler, and our sword,
We follow Thee.

In silence of the lonely night,
In fullest glow of day's clear light,
Through life's strange windings, dark or bright,
We follow Thee.

Great Master! point Thou out the way,
Nor suffer Thou our steps to stray;
Then in the path that leads to day,
We follow Thee.

Thou hast passed on before our face;
Thy footsteps on the way we trace;
O keep us, aid us by Thy grace,—
We follow Thee.

Whom have we in the heaven above?
Whom on this earth, save Thee, to love?
Still in Thy light we onward move,
We follow Thee.

A very inspiring hymn is:—

Shall this life of mine be wasted?
Shall this vineyard lie untilled?
Shall true joy remain untasted,
And the soul abide unfilled?
Shall the God-given hours be scattered,
Like the leaves upon the plain?
Shall the blossoms die unwatered
By the drops of heavenly rain?

Shall the heart still spend its treasures
On the things that fade and die?
Shall it court the hollow pleasures
Of bewildering vanity?
No, we were not born to trifle
Life away in dreams of sin;
No, we must not, dare not stifle
Longings such as these within.

Swiftly moving upward, onward,
Let our souls in faith arise,
Calmly gazing skyward, sunward,
Let us fix our steadfast eyes

Where the cross, God's love revealing,
  Sets the fettered spirit free;
Where it sheds its wondrous healing,
  There, O soul, thy rest shall be.

Then no longer idly dreaming
  Shall we fling our years away;
But, each precious hour redeeming,
  Wait for the eternal day.
God, the Father of creation,
  Son, the Saviour of mankind,
Spirit of illumination,
  Make us Thine in heart and mind.

The following yearning intercession for children is very beautiful:—

Father, our children keep!
We know not what is coming on the earth;
Beneath the shadow of Thy heavenly wing,
O keep them, keep them, Thou who gav'st them birth.

Father, draw nearer us!
Draw firmer round us Thy protecting arm;
O clasp our children closer to Thy side,
Uninjured in the day of earth's alarm.

Them in Thy chambers hide!
O hide them and preserve them calm and safe,
When sin abounds, and error flows abroad,
And Satan tempts, and human passions chafe.

O keep them undefiled!
Unspotted from a tempting world of sin;
That, clothed in white, through the bright city-gates,
They may with us in triumph enter in.

Some of his Communion hymns are finely adapted to that service, notably the following:—

Here, O my Lord, I see Thee face to face;
Here would I touch and handle things unseen;
Here grasp with firmer hand the eternal grace,
And all my weariness upon Thee lean.

Here would I feed upon the bread of God;
Here drink with Thee the royal wine of heaven;
Here would I lay aside each earthly load;
Here taste afresh the calm of sin forgiven.

This is the hour of banquet and of song,
This is the heavenly table spread for me:

Here let me feast, and feasting, still prolong
The brief bright hour of fellowship with Thee.

Too soon we rise: the symbols disappear:
The feast, though not the love, is past and gone;
The bread and wine remove, but Thou art here,
Nearer than ever, still my Shield and Sun.

Feast after feast thus comes and passes by,
Yet, passing, points to the glad feast above,
Giving sweet foretaste of the festal joy,
The Lamb's great bridal feast of bliss and love.

Dr. Bonar has written many works in prose, but he will be remembered by his hymns, many of which are likely to keep a permanent place in the Church's song.

Jane Borthwick (born 1813), is known chiefly as joint authoress with her sister, Mrs. Findlater, of "Hymns from the Land of Luther," one of the finest collections of translation from the German we possess in the English tongue. But she possesses, as most good hymn translators do, real poetic faculty of her own. A translation is a poor affair if the original does not pass through a poet's mind before it appears in its new language. That Miss Borthwick has such a mind is clear from the following hymn; one of the most tender and pathetic of its kind in existence:—

Thou knowest, Lord, the weariness and sorrow
  Of the sad heart that comes to Thee for rest;
Cares of to-day, and burdens for to-morrow,
  Blessings implored, and sins to be confessed;
  We come before Thee at Thy gracious word,
  And lay them at Thy feet: Thou knowest Lord.

Thou knowest all the past; how long and blindly
  On the dark mountains the lost wanderer strayed;
How the good Shepherd followed, and how kindly
  He bore it home, upon His shoulders laid;
  And healed the bleeding wounds and soothed the pain,
  And brought back life, and hope, and strength again.

Thou knowest all the present; each temptation,
Each toilsome duty, each foreboding fear;
All to each one assigned of tribulation,
Or to belovèd ones, than self more dear;
All pensive memories, as we journey on,
Longings for vanished smiles and voices gone.

Thou knowest all the future; gleams of gladness
By stormy clouds too quickly overcast;
Hours of sweet fellowship and parting sadness,
And the dark river to be crossed at last;
O what could hope and confidence afford
To tread that path; but this, Thou knowest, Lord?

Thou knowest, not alone as God, all knowing;
As Man, our mortal weakness, Thou hast proved;
On earth, with purest sympathies o'erflowing,
O Saviour, Thou hast wept, and Thou hast loved;
And love and sorrow still to Thee may come,
And find a hiding-place, a rest, a home.

Therefore we come, Thy gentle call obeying,
And lay our sins and sorrows at Thy feet,
On everlasting strength our weakness staying,
Clothed in Thy robe of righteousness complete,
Then rising and refreshed we leave Thy throne,
And follow on to know as we are known.

Equally good, but in quite another strain is:—

Come, labour on!
Who dares stand idle on the harvest-plain,
While all around him waves the golden grain?
And to each servant does the Master say,
'Go work to-day.

Come, labour on!
Claim the high calling angels cannot share,
To young and old the Gospel-gladness bear;
Redeem the time; its hours too swiftly fly,
The night draws nigh.

Come, labour on!
The enemy is watching night and day,
To sow the tares, to snatch the seed away;
While we in sleep our duty have forgot,
He slumbered not.

Come, labour on!
Away with gloomy doubts and faithless fear!
No arms so weak, but may do service here;
By hands the feeblest can our God fulfil
His righteous will.

Come, labour on!
No time for rest, till glows the western sky,
While the long shadows o'er our pathway lie,
And a glad sound comes with the setting sun—
'Servants, well done!

Come, labour on!
The toil is pleasant, and the harvest sure,
Blessèd are those who to the end endure;
How full their joy, how deep their rest shall be,
O Lord, with Thee!

The following hymn from C. J. P. Spitta may be taken as a specimen of her translations:—

We praise and bless Thee, gracious Lord,
Our Saviour, kind and true,
For all the old things passed away,
For all Thou hast made new.

New hopes, new purposes, desires,
And joys, Thy grace has given;
Old ties are broken from the earth,
New ties attach to heaven.

But yet, how much must be destroyed
How much renewed must be,
Ere we can fully stand complete
In likeness, Lord, to Thee!

Thou, only Thou, must carry on
The work Thou hast begun;
Of Thine own strength Thou must impart,
In Thine own ways to run.

Ah! leave us not; from day to day
Revive, restore again;
Our feeble steps do Thou direct,
Our enemies restrain.

So shall we faultless stand at last,
Before Thy Father's throne;
The blessedness for ever ours,
The glory all Thine own.

"Jesus, still lead on," from the German of Count Zinzendorf is too well-known to need quoting. As a specimen of her sister's (Sarah Findlater) genius for translation, I quote her rendering of Gerhardt

Tersteegen's magnificent hymn often sadly marred by editors:—

Lord our God, in reverence lowly,
The hosts of heaven call Thee 'holy,'
From cherubim and seraphim,
From angel phalanx, far extending,
In fuller tones is still ascending
The 'holy,' 'holy,' of their hymn;
The fount of joy Thou art,
Ever filling every heart,
Ever! Ever!
We, too, are Thine, and with them sing,
'Thou, Lord, and only Thou, art King.'

Lord, there are bending now before Thee,
The elders with their crownèd glory,
The first born of the blessèd band;
There, too, earth's ransomed and forgiven
Brought by the Saviour safe to heaven,
In glad unnumbered myriads stand;
Loud are the songs of praise
Their mingled voices raise,
Ever! Ever!
We, too, are Thine, and with them sing,
'Thou, Lord, and only Thou, art King.'

They sing in sweet and endless numbers
The wondrous love that never slumbers,
And of the wisdom, power, and might,
The truth and faithfulness abiding,
And over all Thy works presiding.
But they can scarcely praise aright;
For all is never sung,
Even by seraph's tongue,
Never! Never!
We, too, are Thine, and with them sing,
'Thou, Lord, and only Thou, art King.'

Oh! come, reveal Thyself more fully,
That we may learn to praise more truly;
Make every heart a temple true,
Filled with Thy glory overflowing,
More of Thy love each morning showing,
And waking praises loud and new;
Here let Thy peace divine
Over Thy children shine,
Ever! Ever!
And glad or sad, we joining sing,
'Thou, Lord, and only Thou, art King.'

Both sisters prefer to be known under the signature H. L. L. (Hymns from the Land of Luther), but I believe I am right in ascribing those I have named as I have done.

Henry Downton (1818-1885), for many years Chaplain of the English Church at Geneva, and after Rector of Hopton, Norfolk, is the author of many hymns, and translations from the French, chiefly of Vinet, which he has gathered into a little volume, "Hymns and Verses, Original and Translated." He possesses, in very marked degree, the faculty for hymn composition. He has been most successful in verses written for the opening and close of the year. One of these, "For Thy mercy and Thy grace," has become very popular, whilst another, which I quote below, is on the high road to a like popularity, which it richly deserves. I omit the first four lines, which seem to me to mar the general effect of the hymn.

Sing we, brethren, faithful-hearted,
Lift the solemn voice again
O'er another year departed
Of our threescore years and ten.

Lo, a theme for deepest sadness,
In ourselves with sin defiled;
Lo, a theme for holiest gladness,
In our Father reconciled.

In the dust we bend before Thee,
Lord of sinless hosts above;
Yet in lowliest joy adore Thee,
God of mercy, grace, and love.

Gracious Saviour! Thou hast lengthened
And hast blessed our mortal span,
And in our weak hearts hast strengthened
What Thy grace alone began.

Still, when danger shall betide us,
  Be Thy warning whisper heard;
Keep us at Thy feet, and guide us
  By Thy Spirit and Thy word.

Let Thy favour and Thy blessing
  Crown the year we now begin;
Let us all, Thy strength possessing,
  Grow in grace and vanquish sin.

Storms are round us, hearts are quailing,
  Signs in heaven and earth and sea;
But, when heaven and earth are failing,
  Saviour, we will trust in Thee.

Thomas Hincks (born 1818), a minister of the Unitarian Church, who has acquired a considerable reputation for his scientific researches, has written a few hymns, which were first included in a collection called "Vespers," prepared for the congregation at Mill Hill Chapel, Leeds, to which he formerly ministered. They resemble the hymns of many writers of his own section of the Church in America: in their subdued feeling, their gracefulness of expression, and a certain refined and spiritual love for the place of worship. The finest is the following:—

Heavenly Father, by whose care
Comes again this hour of prayer,
In the evening stillness, we
Grateful raise our hearts to Thee;
To our spirits, as we bend,
Peace and holy comfort send.

Gladly we Thy presence seek:
Father! to our spirits speak:
Call us from the world away;
Still our passions' reckless play;
On our inner darkness shine;
Bend our wayward will to Thine.

In this quiet eventide
May our souls with Thee abide,
Own Thy presence, feel Thy power,
Through this consecrated hour;
And from peaceful vesper-prayer
Purer, stronger spirits bear.

George Rundle Prynne (born 1818), vicar of St. Peter's, Plymouth, wrote several hymns for a collection he edited, under the title, "A Hymnal, suited for the Services of the Church, together with a selection of Introits." The one notable hymn, which has since passed into many collections, is "Jesu, meek and gentle," equally suitable for use by adults and children. His hymns have recently been included in "The Soldier's Dying Vision, and other Poems."

James Hamilton (1819-1896), vicar of Doulting, Shepton Mallet, has written several hymns, which are chiefly used in churches of the Anglican order. One for midnight services is of great beauty. In the original, the third line of the first verse reads

"We deck Thine altar, Lord, with light,"

but, in order to adapt it to churches in which there is no altar, I ventured to alter the line as it stands below—an alteration since adopted in other Hymnals:—

Across the sky the shades of night
  This winter's eve are fleeting:
We come to Thee the Life and Light,
  In solemn worship meeting:
And as the year's last hours go by,
We lift to Thee our earnest cry,
  Once more Thy love entreating.

Before Thee, Lord, subdued we bow,
  To Thee our prayers addressing;
Recounting all Thy mercies now,
  And all our sins confessing;
Beseeching Thee, this coming year,
To hold us in Thy faith and fear,
  And crown us with Thy blessing.

And while we kneel, we lift our eyes
  To dear ones gone before us;
Safe housed with Thee in Paradise,
  Their spirits hovering o'er us:

And beg of Thee, when life is past,
To re-unite us all, at last,
And to our lost restore us.

We gather up, in this brief hour,
The memory of Thy mercies;
Thy wondrous goodness, love, and power,
Our grateful song rehearses:
For Thou hast been our Strength and Stay
In many a dark and dreary day
Of sorrow and reverses.

In many an hour, when fear and dread
Like evil spells have bound us,
And clouds were gathering overhead,
Thy Providence hath found us:
In many a night when waves ran high,
Thy gracious Presence drawing nigh
Hath made all calm around us.

Then, O great God, in years to come,
Whatever fate betide us,
Right onward through our journey home
Be Thou at hand to guide us:
Nor leave us till, at close of life,
Safe from all perils, toil, and strife,
Heaven shall unfold and hide us.

William Cowper, in his "Table Talk," says that Nature seldom—

Vouchsafes to man a poet's just pretence—
Fervency, freedom, fluency of thought,
Harmony, strength, words exquisitely sought;
Fancy that from the bow that spans the sky,
Brings colours, dipp'd in heav'n, that never die;
A soul exalted above earth, a mind
Skill'd in the characters that form mankind.

* * * * *

'Twere new, indeed, to see a bard all fire,
Touch'd with a coal from heav'n, assume the lyre,
And tell the world, still kindling as he sung,
With more than mortal music on his tongue;
That He who died below, and reigns above,
Inspires the song, and that His name is Love.

If such characteristics be rare in the poet, they are still more rare in the hymnist. It would be difficult, perhaps impossible, to name a hymnist in whom such transcendent qualities are united. But many of these qualities—fervency, freedom, fluency of thought—are very conspicuous, and are, indeed, the prominent qualities in the hymns of Thomas Hornblower Gill. Indeed, before I made his personal acquaintance, or knew anything of his spiritual history, I was struck with the freedom, and yet the fervency of his song; the breadth of his thought, and yet the truly evangelical tone which pervaded it. This was a puzzle to me, and in my first interview with him, I expressed my surprise. The story of his life which he then narrated, at once removed the mystery from my mind, as it will do from that of others who may have read his hymns with a similar perplexity. He was born at Birmingham, on the 10th February, 1819, and educated at the well-known King Edward's Grammar School, in that town, under Dr. Jeune, who afterwards became Bishop of Peterborough. He took a distinguished place in the school, and would have passed thence to the University of Oxford, but his conscientious religious scruples prevented him subscribing to the articles of the Church of England, without which the University could not then be entered. This led to his becoming for the rest of his life a student-recluse, giving himself up chiefly to classical and historical studies. Such a life has been, of course, singularly devoid of outward incident. All that can be chronicled is connected with the production and publication of his various works. The real interest of his life centres, however, in the singular and almost unique influences which have combined to form his character, and determine his thinking.

Here is to be found the true clue to the strange combination of breadth of thought with the fervency and evangelical character of his hymns. He was trained in the Priestley School of Unitarianism which had its head-quarters in his native town, where Dr. Priestley exercised his ministry. Later in life a breath of warm evangelical feeling passed over him. This was closely connected with, and largely fostered by, an acquaintance with the hymns and lyrics of Dr. Watts, of whom he is an ardent admirer. If I understand him rightly, he came of a Puritan stock, but his immediate ancestors had fallen under the influence of Unitarianism, in which he was brought up. Indeed, he calls himself a Puritan of the Puritans, and when he wants to describe himself more fully he calls himself "An Emersonian Puritan." The careful reader of his hymns will discern the freshness and freedom from restraint, so characteristic of the Unitarian school of thought with the fervour and passionate devotion to be observed in Puritan circles. These two distinctive features of his hymns, features so rarely combined, are fully accounted for by his ancestry and training. The late Dr. Freeman Clarke, of America, used to call him "A more-intellectual Charles Wesley." This is a little too eulogistic, but is on the whole a happy description, since there is in his hymns much of the fire of the great Methodist singer, with an intellectual vigour and subtlety of thought which are only here and there to be found in the hymns of Charles Wesley, to whom, however, he is not equal in force and directness of diction. Those who may desire to gain a fuller insight into the spiritual history of this remarkable hymnist will find much of his thought and feeling reflected in the life he has written of his friend Franklin Howarth, who passed through an experience very like to his own. The volume was published in 1883, under the title "The Triumph of Christ—Memorials of Franklin Howarth," by T. H. Gill. This seems to me a kind of oblique biography of himself. Besides this he has published "The Fortunes of Faith, or Church and State," a poem of considerable length, with much of the fire of youth against Church Establishments (1841); "The Anniversaries—poems in commemoration of Great Men and Great Events" (1858); "The Golden Chain of Praise" (1869); "The Papal Drama," an historical essay (1866), and "Luther's Birthday" (hymns) (1883.) He is now engaged on "A History of the Germans," which he scarcely expects to finish. He also edited the second hymn-book issued by the late George Dawson, of Birmingham. Altogether he has written over 200 hymns, 165 of these were published in "The Golden Chain of Praise," of which an enlarged edition was issued in 1895. His friend, Dr. R. W. Dale, of Birmingham, was a great admirer of his hymns, and introduced no less than 40 into his collection called "The English Hymn Book." Half that number were included in "The Baptist Hymnal," eleven in my own "Congregational Hymns," and the same number in Dr. Martineau's "Hymns of Praise and Prayer," whilst in Dr. Odenheimer and F. M. Bird's "Songs of the Spirit," there are 23, one of these, "Lord God, by whom all change is wrought," having been written for that work. Up to the present time, and with one exception—"O mean may seem this house of clay," his hymns have been confined to collections used in the Free Churches, which desire suggestiveness of thought, and rely, for the deepening of spiritual life more upon the power of truth over the mind than upon external ritual. But in the Free Churches they are becoming increasingly known and valued. The following are the most popular, "O mean may seem this house of clay," our double kindred to Emmanuel as suggested by "The second man was the Lord from heaven," and "as we have borne the image of the earthy, we shall also bear the image of the heavenly"—

O mean may seem this house of clay,
Yet 'twas the Lord's abode;
Our feet may mourn this thorny way,
Yet here Immanuel trod.

This fleshly robe the Lord did wear,
This watch the Lord did keep,
These burdens sore the Lord did bear,
These tears the Lord did weep.

* * * *

Our very frailty brings us near
Unto the Lord of heaven;
To every grief, to every tear,
Such glory strange is given.

But not this fleshly robe alone
Shall link us, Lord, to Thee;
Not only in the tear and moan
Shall the dear kindred be.

We shall be reckoned for Thine own,
Because Thy heaven we share,
Because we sing around Thy throne,
And Thy bright raiment wear.

* * * *

O mighty grace, our life to live,
To make our earth divine:
O mighty grace, Thy heaven to give,
And lift our life to Thine.

Yes, strange the gift and marvellous
By Thee received and given!
Thou tookest woe and death for us,
And we receive Thy heaven.

"Our God! our God! Thou shinest here" is a noble hymn suggested by the words of John Milton—"The power of Thy grace is not passed away with the primitive times, as fond and faithless men foolishly imagine, but Thy kingdom is now at hand, and Thou standing at the door." This is one of his finest and most characteristic hymns—

Our God! our God! Thou shinest here,
Thine own this latter day:
To us Thy radiant steps appear:
We watch Thy glorious way.

Thou tookest once our flesh; Thy face
Once on our darkness shone:
Yet through each age new births of grace
Still make Thy glory known.

Not only olden ages felt
The presence of the Lord;
Not only with the fathers dwelt
Thy Spirit and Thy word.

Doth not the Spirit still descend
And bring the heavenly fire?
Doth not He still Thy Church extend,
And waiting souls inspire?

Come, Holy Ghost! in us arise;
Be this Thy mighty hour!
And make Thy willing people wise
To know Thy day of power!

Pour down Thy fire in us to glow,
Thy might in us to dwell;
Again Thy works of wonder show,
Thy blessed secrets tell.

Bear us aloft, more glad, more strong,
On Thy celestial wing,
And grant us grace to look and long
For our returning King.

He draweth near, He standeth by,
He fills our eyes, our ears;
'Come, King of grace," Thy people cry,
"And bring the glorious years!"

Closely allied to the foregoing is a hymn on the passage in Zech. viii. 21, "Let us go to seek the Lord":—

O saints of old! not yours alone
These words most high shall be;
We take the glory for our own;
Lord! we are seeking Thee.

Not only when ascends the song,
And soundeth sweet the Word;
Not only "midst the Sabbath throng,"
Our souls would seek the Lord,

We mingle with another throng,
And other words we speak;
To other business we belong,
But still our Lord we seek.

We would not to our daily task
Without our God repair;
But in the world Thy presence ask,
And seek Thy glory there.

Would we against some wrong be bold,
And break some yoke abhorred;
Amidst the strife and stir behold
The seekers of the Lord;

* * * *

When on Thy glorious works we gaze,
We fain would seek Thee there:
Our gladness in their beauty raise
To joy in Thee, First Fair!

O everywhere, O every day,
Thy grace is still outpoured;
We work, we watch, we strive, we pray;
Behold Thy seekers, Lord!

The sweetness of subjection to Christ is delightfully set forth in the following hymn—

Dear Lord and Master mine,
Thy happy servant see!
My Conqueror! with what joy divine!
Thy captive clings to Thee!

I love Thy yoke to wear,
To feel Thy gracious bands,
Sweetly restrainèd by Thy care,
And happy in Thy hands.

No bar would I remove,
No bond would I unbind;
Within the limits of Thy love
Full liberty I find.

I would not walk alone,
But still with Thee, my Lord;
At every step my blindness own,
And ask of Thee the road.

The weakness I enjoy
That casts me on Thy breast;
The conflicts that Thy strength employ,
Make me divinely blest.

Dear Lord and Master mine,
Still keep Thy servant true:
My Guardian and my Guide Divine,
Bring, bring Thy pilgrim through.

My Conqueror and my King,
Still keep me in Thy train;
And with Thee Thy glad captive bring,
When Thou return'st to reign.

Mr. Gill is a passionate lover of nature, upon which he looks with most religious gaze, finding therein "Parables of God," as will be seen from the two hymns which follow, which seem to me equally beautiful. The first is on "The Witness of Earth to Heaven."—

What sweetness on Thine earth doth dwell!
How precious, Lord, these gifts of Thine!
Yet sweeter messages they tell,
These earnests of delights divine.

Yes! glory out of glory breaks,
More than the gift itself is given;
Each gift a glorious promise makes:
Thine earth doth prophesy of heaven.

These mighty hills we joy to climb,
These happy streams we wander by,
Reveal the eternal hills sublime—
Of God's own river prophesy.

These odours blest, these gracious flowers,
These sweet sounds that around us rise,
Give tidings of the heavenly bowers,
Prelude angelic harmonies.

These vernal hours, what news they bring!
What tidings these bright summers tell!
They fore-announce the eternal spring,
Foreshow the Light Ineffable.

* * * *

Lord, from Thy gifts to Thee we rise,
But with more strength we soar above,
Upon these glorious prophecies,
These earnests of Thy dearer love.

The second is on the "Divine Renewer," suggested by "Thou renewest the face of the earth," and "Be renewed in the spirit of your mind":—

The glory of the spring, how sweet!
  The new born life, how glad!
What joy, the happy earth to greet,
  In new bright raiment clad.

Divine Renewer! Thee I bless;
  I greet Thy going forth:
I love Thee in the loveliness
  Of Thy renewèd earth.

But O these wonders of Thy grace,
  These nobler works of Thine,
These marvels sweeter far to trace,
  These new births more divine!

These sinful souls Thou hallowest,
  These hearts Thou makest new,
These mourning souls by Thee made blest
  These faithless hearts made true:

This new-born glow of faith so strong
  This bloom of love so fair;
This new-born ecstasy of song
  And fragrancy of prayer!

Creator, Spirit, work in me
  These wonders sweet of Thine!
Divine Renewer, graciously
  Renew this heart of mine;
Still let new life and strength upspring,
  Still let new joy be given!
And grant the glad new song to ring
  Through the new earth and heaven.

His New Year's hymn strikes a new and quite original note, and is full of life and tenderness:—

Break, new-born year, on glad eyes break!
  Melodious voices move!
On, rolling Time! thou canst not make
  The Father cease to love.

The parted year had wingèd feet;
  The Saviour still doth stay:
The New Year comes: but, Spirit sweet
  Thou goest not away.

Our hearts in tears may oft run o'er;
  But, Lord, Thy smile still beams;
Our sins are swelling evermore;
  But pardoning grace still streams.

Lord! from this year more service win,
  More glory, more delight;
O make its hours less sad with sin,
  Its days with Thee more bright!

Then we may bless its precious things
  If earthly cheer should come,
Or gladsome mount on angel wings
  If Thou shouldst take us home.

* * * *

Space will not permit me to give further illustrations. These will suffice to show that Mr. Gill, lover and student of Dr. Watts though he be, is, to use Goethe's distinction, no mere *echo*, but a *voice*. His hymns, as to their substance, seem to me, marked by the following characteristics: (1) A remarkable absence of, and even opposition to, all antiquarian and sacerdotal ideas of Christianity, being rather filled with the conception that the Spirit of God is working as really and as mightily now as in the first age of the Church's history. (2) A keen and searching discernment between the spirit and letter of the gospel; and (3) By often really profound thought on Scripture themes. As to their style, I may notice (1) A certain quaintness of expression, reminding the reader of George Wither or John Mason, but rendered clearer by his study and appreciation of Dr. Watts. (2) Great warmth of feeling, leading to the use of very expressive epithets, but kept within due bounds, save in exceptional cases, by a taste singularly pure and chaste. (3) Often there is to be noticed a happy adaptation of metre and rhythm to the subject of the hymn. In some cases the tune gave birth to the hymn. Mr. Gill is only kept from reaching the very highest place as a hymnist by too great subtlety of thought and expression. This renders many of his hymns more suitable for private reading than public praise.

The value of Mr. Gill's hymns is largely due to the fact to which he calls attention in the preface to "The Golden Chain of Praise," that they enshrine the spiritual experience of their author; to this is due their living force. They are not the product of the mere thinker or rhymer, but of one impelled by great spiritual impulses. Mr. Gill rarely, if ever, wrote unless moved thereto by what he does not hesitate to call "inspiration."

In an extract from an unpublished autobiography which he has been good enough to communicate to me, he says "I fully believe in tides of song which we cannot command and cannot restrain; in seasons of inspiration which come and go, not at our bidding, wherein the soul, in the fullest possession and happiest exercise of all its powers, is yet borne along by a power beyond itself. More than twice or thrice have I been borne along on such a tide. I have known three or four such seasons, and have vainly striven to prolong them. Then, hymns have streamed forth day after day, week after week; not without the diligent co-operation of all my powers, but with their unforced, free, gladsome, almost unconscious co-operation. At other times I have set myself to write hymns, and with some effort have accomplished the task; but the task was not worth accomplishing—the song had no life, no power, no glow.

"These seasons of inspiration had their rise in some high and happy estate of the soul, in some new revelation of spiritual truth, in some ascent of the spirit into a diviner region; on one occasion in the concurrence of a bright outward experience with a blessed inward stir. Each new birth of grace was attended by a fresh stream of song. Between these seasons I have now and then produced a strain, not without worth, but these gushes of song lay apart from the great tides whereof I have spoken."

Here lies the secret of Mr. Gill's power, moved himself as he produced his hymns, they move others to fresher and more spiritual worship.

CHAPTER XVI.

RECENT HYMNISTS.—II.

BORN 1821 ET SEQ.

Edward Hayes Plumptre (1821-1891), Dean of Wells, the accomplished scholar, to whom we owe such valuable work in many departments—as translator: of Dante, Æschylus, Sophocles; as poet: "Lazarus," "Master and Scholar," "Things Old and New"; as theologian: "The Spirits in Prison"; as biographer: "The Life and Letters of Bishop Ken"; as biblical critic: many works on parts of both the Old and New Testament—has written a few hymns, which only lack the lyric fire to make them excellent. Were that present, and were they a little more condensed, they would be even more valuable than they are. Dr. Plumptre, however, takes more space to move in than a hymn affords. The finest, and most lyric of his productions, is the following, which seems to me to stand apart from all his others:—

Rejoice, ye pure in heart,
Rejoice, give thanks and sing
Your festal banner wave on high,
The Cross of Christ your King.

With all the angel-choirs,
  With all the saints on earth,
Pour out the strains of joy and bliss,
  True rapture, noblest mirth.

Your clear hosannas raise,
  And hallelujahs loud,
Whilst answering echoes upward float,
  Like wreaths of incense-cloud.

With voice as full and strong
  As ocean's surging praise,
Send forth the hymns our fathers loved,
  The psalms of ancient days.

Yes, on, through life's long path,
  Still chanting as ye go,
From youth to age, by night and day,
  In gladness and in woe.

Still lift your standard high,
  Still march in firm array,
As warriors through the darkness toil,
  Till dawns the golden day.

At last the march shall end,
  The wearied ones shall rest,
The pilgrims find their Father's house,
  Jerusalem the blest.

Then on, ye pure in heart,
  Rejoice, give thanks, and sing;
Your festal banner wave on high,
  The Cross of Christ your King.

Praise Him who rules on high,
  Whom heaven and earth adore,
Praise Father, Son, and Holy Ghost,
  One God for evermore.

Next in merit I should place the following, for a Time of Pestilence:—

Thine arm, O Lord, in days of old
  Was strong to heal and save;
It triumphed o'er disease and death,
  O'er darkness and the grave:
To Thee they went, the blind, the dumb,
  The palsied and the lame,
The leper with his tainted life,
  The sick with fevered frame;

And lo, Thy touch brought life and health,
  Gave speech, and strength, and sight;
And youth renewed and frenzy calmed
  Owned Thee, the Lord of Light.
And now, O Lord, be near to bless,
  Almighty as of yore,
In crowded street, by restless couch,
  As by Gennesareth's shore.

Though love and might no longer heal
  By touch, or word, or look;
Though they who do Thy work must read
  Thy laws in Nature's book:
Yet come to heal the sick man's soul,
  Come, cleanse the leprous taint;
Give joy and peace where all is strife,
  And strength where all is faint.

Be Thou our great Deliverer still,
  Thou Lord of life and death,
Restore and quicken, soothe and bless
  With Thine almighty breath:
To hands that work and eyes that see
  Give wisdom's heavenly lore,
That whole and sick, and weak and strong,
  May praise Thee evermore.

His other hymns are admirable in sentiment, but not nimble enough in their movement.

Francis Turner Palgrave (1824-1897), whose hymns strike a new note, is the eldest son of Sir Francis Palgrave, the well-known historian, and his wife Elizabeth, from whom he derives his second name. He was born in Great Yarmouth on the 28th of September, 1824. From 1838 to 1843 he spent at the Charterhouse School, whence he passed to Balliol College, Oxford, of which he became a scholar in 1842. In 1846 he was elected Fellow of Exeter College, and in 1847 took a first class in the classical schools. Leaving the University of Oxford, Mr. Palgrave was engaged for a considerable time in the Education Department of the Privy Council, from which he retired in 1884.

During that time he was private secretary to Earl Granville, who was then Lord President. In the following year he was elected Professor of Poetry in the University of Oxford.

The following works have proceeded from his pen:—"Idylls and Songs" (1854), "Art Catalogue of the Great Exhibition" (1862), "Essays on Art" (1869), and "Lyrical Poems" (1871). He has also edited "The Golden Treasury of English Lyrics" (1861), "Sir Walter Scott's Poems, with Life" (1867), "Chrysomela—a selection from Herrick," and "The Visions of England" (1881), and "The Treasury of Sacred Song" (1889). He is best known, however, by his collection of English lyrics, which is a model of editing, and appeared in 1867, followed by enlarged editions in 1868 and 1870. His object was "To try and write hymns which should have more distinct matter for thought and feeling than many in our collections offer, and so, perhaps, be of a little use and comfort to readers." His hymns admirably fulfil this purpose. To those who are familiar with the monotony and dulness of the vast mass of hymns, it is a great relief to turn to Mr. Palgrave's with their distinctiveness of theme, their marked individuality, and delicacy of phrasing. The exaggerated tone, expressive of feelings far above the range of ordinary mortals, so often found in hymns, is conspicuous by its absence, and in its place there is what Mr. Keble, in the preface to his "Christian Year," calls "a sober standard in matters of practical religion." Then his hymns are expressive of the feelings which are characteristic of the Christian heart in our own day—its difficulties, its perplexities, its longings. Professor Palgrave seems to me to have a singularly true idea of what a hymn should be, and how poetry and religious feeling should be blended in its production. If I may quote from a letter addressed by him to myself, "The main reason for the inferiority of hymns to ordinary lyrics lies, I think, simply in the fact that the true end of poetry is *Pleasure*, not *Instruction.* It may and should often *teach*, but always through such pleasure as this fine art can give. Hence, the didactic element which hymns always do and ought to include is very apt to lower the poetical quality. The strict laws of poetry are in fact inapplicable in this region, and it is only a critic who has no sympathy with the object of hymns can complain that these laws are more or less set aside." But it is quite clear from Mr. Palgrave's own hymns that he regards the poetic as an essential element in every hymn worthy of the name—that the didactic purpose should be suffused with keen and high emotion which is sure to take on lyric forms; whilst in hymns of pure worship the didactic element falls quite into the background. The stronger the lyric element, the more will the hymn bear the soul aloft. And the more cultivated taste of the present day is not satisfied with the mere rhymed prose which passed current in earlier days, but demands verse in which the religious feeling is so strong that it naturally takes on lyric forms. Hence, the hymns most frequently sung in our day are those which are the product of the vision and faculty divine. In this respect the advance is very evident. Sternhold and Hopkins had to give way to Isaac

Watts. Watts was largely eclipsed by the more lyric Charles Wesley, whilst all but the finest of *his* have had to yield to the selected ones of many a poetic hymnist of our own time. The age, too, demands verses which shall express *its own* feelings and not those of a bygone time. And those hymnists are the most popular who, being in deepest sympathy with the real feelings of the age, are able to give these the fullest and most lyric expression. Amongst these, Professor Palgrave's hymns deserve a place of high honour for their sobriety of thought, their fidelity to the actual feeling of the time, their refined and yet poetical expression. Here and there he fails in melodiousness of utterance or in suitability of metre, but these defects are so slight that I do not care to dwell on them.

Perhaps the best known of his hymns are those for Morning and Evening; the former beginning "Lord God of morning and of night," and the latter, "O Light of life, O Saviour dear," both of which conclude with the fine doxology (second only in merit to the well-known one of good Bishop Ken)—

> Praise God, our Maker and our Friend;
> Praise Him through time, till time shall end,
> Till psalm and song His name adore
> Through heaven's great day of evermore.

The child's hymn "Thou that once on mother's knee," is one of the few really fine children's hymns in the language. The above are too well-known for it to be necessary to quote them; but others which are only gradually finding their way into use and favour are not so well known, and I will therefore append them.

How true, how free from other-worldliness is the

conception of the kingdom of God in the following hymn suggested by our Lord's saying, "For behold the kingdom of God is within you":—

O Thou not made with hands,
Not throned above the skies,
Not walled with shining walls,
Nor framed with stones of price,
More bright than gold or gem,
God's own Jerusalem.

Where'er the gentle heart
Finds courage from above;
Where'er the heart forsook
Warms with the breath of love;
Where faith bids fear depart,
City of God! thou art.

Thou art where'er the proud
In humbleness melts down;
Where self itself yields up;
Where martyrs win their crown;
Where faithful souls possess
Themselves in perfect peace.

Where in life's common ways
With cheerful feet we go;
Where in His steps we tread
Who trod the way of woe;
Where He is in the heart,
City of God! thou art.

Not throned above the skies
Nor golden-walled afar;
But where Christ's two or three
In His name gathered are;
Be in the midst of them,
God's own Jerusalem.

How accurately, and yet how tenderly, the difficulty and longing of our day for faith in the unseen Christ is expressed in the following verses, "Faith and sight in the latter days":—

Thou say'st 'Take up thy cross,
O man, and follow me;
The night is black, the feet are slack,
Yet we would follow Thee.

But O dear Lord, we cry,
That we Thy face could see!
Thy blessèd face one móment's space—
Then might we follow Thee!

Dim tracts of time divide
Those golden days from me;
Thy voice comes strange o'er years of change;
How can we follow Thee?

Comes faint and far Thy voice
From vales of Galilee;
Thy vision fades in ancient shades;
How should we follow Thee?

O heavy cross—of faith
In what we cannot see;
As once of yore Thyself restore
And help to follow Thee!

If not as once Thou cam'st
In true humanity,
Come yet as guest within the breast
That burns to follow Thee.

Within our heart of hearts
In nearest nearness be:
Set up Thy throne within Thine own:—
Go, Lord! we follow Thee.

How true is the abasement of spirit before the thought of God in this terse and yet pathetic hymn which he calls "Through and through":—

Infelix, quis me liberabit?

We name Thy Name, O God,
As our God call on Thee,
Though the dark heart meantime
Far from Thy ways may be.

And we can own Thy law,
And we can sing Thy songs,
While the sad inner soul
To sin and shame belongs.

On us Thy love may glow,
As the pure midday fire
On some foul spot looks down;
And yet the mire be mire.

Then spare us not Thy fires,
The searching light and pain;

Burn out our sin; and last,
With Thy love heal again.

Touched with a like spirit, but yet suffused with faith, is the hymn which follows; "Lost and Found," in which the real influence of sin is seen and traced out with rare insight—

Though we long, in sin-wrought blindness,
From Thy gracious paths have strayed,
Cold to Thee and all Thy kindness,
Wilful, reckless, or afraid;
Through dim clouds that gather round us
Thou has sought, and Thou hast found us.

Oft from Thee we veil our faces,
Children-like, to cheat Thine eyes;
Sin, and hope to hide the traces;
From ourselves, ourselves disguise;
'Neath the webs enwoven round us
Thy soul-piercing glance has found us.

Sudden, 'midst our idle chorus,
O'er our sin Thy thunders roll,
Death his signal waves before us,
Night and terror take the soul;
Till through double darkness round us
Looks a star,—and Thou hast found us.

O most merciful, most holy,
Light Thy wanderers on their way;
Keep us ever Thine, Thine wholly,
Suffer us no more to stray!
Cloud and storm oft gather round us;
We were lost, but Thou hast found us.

How full of emotion, how picturesque in its description of the course of our Lord is this "Litany to the name of Jesus"—

Thrice-holy Name!—that sweeter sounds
Than streams which down the valley run,
And tells of more than human love,
And more than human power in one;
First o'er the manger-cradle heard,
Heard since through all the choirs on high;—
O Child of Mary, Son of God,
Eternal, hear Thy children's cry!
While at Thy blessèd Name we bow,
Lord Jesus, be amongst us now!

Within our earth-dimmed souls call up
The vision of Thy human years;
The mount of the transfigured form;
The garden of the bitter tears;
The cross upreared in darkening skies;
The thorn-wreathed head; the bleeding side;
And whisper in the heart, 'For you.
For you I left the heavens, and died.'
    While at the blessèd Name we bow,
    Lord Jesus, be amongst us now!

Ah! with faith's surest inmost eye
The riven rock-hewn bed we see,
Untreasured of its heavenly guest,—
Triumphant over Death in Thee!
And O! when Thou, our Saviour Judge,
Again shall come in glory here,
With love upon Thy children look,
And bid us read our pardon clear!
    While at the blessèd Name we bow,
    Lord Jesus, be amongst us now!

These are but examples of Professor Palgrave's styles. The reader will see how varied and distinctive they are. Their author seems never to write until some distinct idea has possessed his mind, and then with the deep earnestness of a Christian soul, and the skill and taste of the accomplished scholar, the idea clothes itself with apt and beautiful expression. Like a true artist, Mr. Palgrave is reticent in utterance. His collected hymns are all included in a tiny pocket volume of 51 pages, but nothing is included which is without worth. If I am not greatly mistaken there is in store for many of his hymns a growing popularity, since they are well calculated to foster and keep alive a piety, not of a noisy kind, but after the manner and spirit of the Great Master, Christ.

William Walsham How (1823-1897), who for many years was the devoted Bishop of Bedford—why that title should have been given to a see which had nothing to do with Bedford, but was chiefly composed of the East End of London, is a mystery to the unecclesiastical mind!—but who afterwards occupied the newly constituted see of Wakefield, contributed an unusually large number of fine hymns to the store of church song. His published volume, in which he collected his scattered hymns, contains fifty-four, and scarcely a hymn is to be found in it without merit. Its perusal forces on the mind the conclusion, that the standard of hymnody has been greatly raised during recent years. A considerable proportion of the hymns in this volume have passed into general use. The best known are the following—they are too well known to need quotation—"We give Thee but Thine own," a fine hymn for use at the offertory; "O Jesu, Thou art standing," a forcible and yet pathetic hymn on Jesus at the door; "For all the saints who from their labour rest," a thanksgiving for departed saints." All these are included in "Hymns Ancient and Modern." His hymns for certain seasons of the natural year seem to me very felicitous. Here is the one on summer:—

Summer suns are glowing over land and sea,
Happy light is flowing bountiful and free.

Everything rejoices in the mellow rays,
All earth's thousand voices swell the psalm of praise.

God's free mercy streameth over all the world,
And His banner gleameth everywhere unfurled.

Broad and deep and glorious as the heaven above
Shines in might victorious His eternal love.

Lord, upon our blindness Thy pure radiance pour,
For Thy lovingkindness makes us love Thee more.

And when clouds are drifting dark across our sky,
Then, the veil uplifting, Father, be Thou nigh.

We will never doubt Thee, though Thou veil Thy light,
Life is dark without Thee; death with Thee is bright.

Light of light! shine o'er us on our pilgrim way,
Go Thou still before us to the endless day.

This is his hymn for autumn:—

The year is swiftly waning;
The summer days are past:
And life, brief life, is speeding;
The end is nearing fast.

The ever-changing seasons
In silence come and go;
But Thou, Eternal Father,
No time or change canst know.

O pour Thy grace upon us,
That we may worthier be,
Each year that passes o'er us,
To dwell in heaven with Thee.

Behold the bending orchards
With bounteous fruit are crowned;
Lord, in our hearts more richly
Let heavenly fruits abound.

Oh, by each mercy sent us,
And by each grief and pain.
By blessings like the sunshine,
And sorrows like the rain—

Our barren hearts make fruitful
With every goodly grace,
That we Thy name may hallow,
And see at last Thy face.

This is his hymn for winter:—

Winter reigneth o'er the land,
Freezing with its icy breath,
Dead and bare the tall trees stand;
All is chill and drear as death.

Yet it seemeth but a day
Since the summer flowers were here,
Since they stacked the balmy hay,
Since they reaped the golden ear.

Sunny days are past and gone:
So the years go, speeding fast,
Onward ever each new one
Swifter speeding than the last.

Life is waning, life is brief;
Death, like winter, standeth nigh;
Each one, like the falling leaf,
Soon shall fade, and fall, and die.

But the sleeping earth shall wake,
And the flowers shall burst in bloom,
And all nature rising break
Glorious from its wintry tomb.

So, Lord, after slumber blest,
Comes a bright awakening,
And our flesh in hope shall rest
Of a never-fading spring.

The following, on "It is I, be not afraid," is very tender:—

When the dark waves round us roll,
And we look in vain for aid,
Speak, Lord, to the trembling soul,—
"It is I; be not afraid."

When we dimly trace Thy form
In mysterous clouds arrayed,
Be the echo of the storm,—
"It is I; be not afraid."

When our brightest hopes depart,
When our fairest visions fade,
Whisper to the fainting heart,—
"It is I; be not afraid."

When we weep beside the bier,
Where some well-loved form is laid,
O may then the mourner hear,—
"It is I; be not afraid."

When with wearing, hopeless pain,
Sinks the spirit sore dismayed,
Breathe Thou then the comfort-strain—
"It is I; be not afraid."

When we feel the end is near,
Passing into death's dark shade,
May the voice be strong and clear,—
"It is I; be not afraid."

One of the best hymns on the Word of God is the following:—

O Word of God Incarnate,
O Wisdom from on high,
O Truth unchanged, unchanging,
O Light of our dark sky;
We praise Thee for the radiance
That from the hallowed page,
A lantern to our footsteps,
Shines on from age to age.

The Church from Thee, her Master,
Received the gift Divine;
And still that light she lifteth
O'er all the earth to shine.
It is the golden casket
Where gems of truth are stored;
It is the heaven-drawn picture
Of Thee, the living Word.

It floateth like a banner
Before God's host unfurled
It shineth like a beacon
Above the darkling world;
It is the chart and compass,
That o'er life's surging sea,
'Mid mists and rocks and quicksands,
Still guides, O Christ, to Thee

O make Thy Church, dear Saviour,
A lamp of burnished gold,
To bear before the nations
Thy true light, as of old.
O teach Thy wandering pilgrims
By this their path to trace,
Till, clouds and darkness ended,
They see Thee face to face.

Of his hymns for children I will speak in the chapter on that subject. Useful as has been Bishop How's work in other directions, he will probably be longest remembered by the hymns he has contributed to the worship of the Church.

Godfrey Thring (born 1823), late rector of Alford-with-Hornblotton, Somerset, is one of the most considerable contributors to hymnody of our time. A large proportion of his hymns have passed into actual use. "The Church of England Hymn Book," edited by him, which touches a higher literary and poetic level than any other specially prepared for that church, contains fifty-nine hymns from his pen; to say nothing of verses added to hymns by other writers. This is too large a number to be inserted in a single collection from the same pen, and forms the defect of the book; still it must be acknowledged that most of his hymns are of great merit. His Evening Hymn, in its amended form, is, perhaps, one of his finest. In it, the first line of the second verse spoke of "Our life is but a fading dawn." This was afterwards altered to "Our life is but an autumn day," which is an improvement, since the dawn does not fade, but grows to the perfect day. Mr. Stopford Brooke says the alteration was made at his suggestion, but Mr. Thring has no recollection of such a suggestion. I quote the hymn in its amended form:—

The radiant morn hath passed away,
And spent too soon her golden store
The shadows of departing day
    Creep on once more.

Our life is but an autumn day,
Its glorious noon how quickly past:—
Lead us, O Christ, Thou Living Way,
    Safe home at last.

Oh! by Thy soul-inspiring grace
Uplift our hearts to realms on high;
Help us to look to that bright place
    Beyond the sky;—

Where light, and life, and joy and peace
In undivided empire reign,
And thronging angels never cease
    Their deathless strain;—

Where saints are clothed in spotless white,
And evening shadows never fall.
Where Thou, Eternal Light of Light
Art Lord of all.

Equally beautiful and most picturesque is "Fierce raged the tempest o'er the deep," which in few words calls up the whole scene of the stilling of the tempest. It is far finer than the ancient hymn, on the same subject, by St. Anatolius "Fierce was the wild billow." His Sunday morning hymn is very lovely:—

Hail, sacred day of earthly rest,
From toil and trouble free;
Hail, quiet spirit, bringing peace
And joy to me.

A holy stillness, breathing calm
On all the world around,
Uplifts my soul, O God, to Thee,
Where rest is found.

No sound of jarring strife is heard,
As weekly labours cease;
No voice, but those that sweetly sing
Sweet songs of peace.

All earthly things appear to fade,
As, rising high and higher,
The yearning voices strive to join
The heavenly choir.

For those who sing with saints below,
Glad songs of heavenly love,
Shall sing, when songs on earth have ceased,
With saints above.

Accept, O God, my hymn of praise
That Thou this day hast given,
Sweet foretaste of that endless day
Of rest in heaven.

"Saviour, blessed Saviour" is very lyric, but would have been improved by compression. The following is a very happy and spiritual, rendering of the idea of the coming of Christ:—

Jesus came—the heavens adoring—
Came with peace from realms on high;
Jesus came for man's redemption,
Lowly came on earth to die:
Hallelujah! Hallelujah;
Came in deep humility.

Jesus comes again in mercy,
When our hearts are bowed with care;
Jesus comes again in answer
To an earnest, heart-felt prayer;
Hallelujah! Hallelujah!
Comes to save us from despair.

Jesus comes to hearts rejoicing,
Bringing news of sins forgiven;
Jesus comes in sounds of gladness,
Leading souls redeemed to heaven;
Hallelujah! Hallelujah!
Now the gate of death is riven.

Jesus comes in joy and sorrow
Shares alike our hopes and fears;
Jesus comes, whate'er befalls us.
Glads our hearts, and dries our tears;
Hallelujah! Hallelujah!
Cheering e'en our failing years.

Jesus comes on clouds triumphant,
When the heavens shall pass away;
Jesus comes again in glory;—
Let us then our homage pay,
Hallelujah! ever singing,
Till the dawn of endless day.

His hymn on the "Holy Spirit" is both beautiful and original in conception:—

Hear us, Thou that broodedst
O'er the watery deep,
Waking all creation
From its primal sleep;
Holy Spirit, breathing
Breath of life divine,
Breathe into our spirits,
Blending them with Thine.
Light and Life Immortal!]
Hear us as we raise
Hearts, as well as voices,
Mingling prayer and praise.

When the sun ariseth
  In the cloudless sky,
May we feel Thy presence,
  Holy Spirit, nigh;
Shed Thy radiance o'er us,
  Keep it cloudless still,
Through the day before us,
  Perfecting Thy will.
    Light and Life Immortal! etc.

When the fight is fiercest
  In the noontide heat,
Bear us, Holy Spirit,
  To our Saviour's feet,
There to find a refuge
  Till our work is done
There to fight the battle
  Till the battle's won.
    Light and Life Immortal! etc.

If the day be falling
  Sadly as it goes,
Slowly in its sadness
  Sinking to its close,
May Thy love in mercy
  Kindling, hear it die,
Cast a ray of glory,
  O'er our evening sky.
    Light and Life Immortal! etc.

Morning, noon, and evening,
  Whensoe'er it be,
Grant us, gracious Spirit,
  Quickening life in Thee;
Life, that gives us, living,
  Life of heavenly love.
Life, that brings us, dying,
  Life from heaven above.
    Light and Life Immortal! etc.

To him we owe what is probably the finest version for *singing* of Luther's "Ein feste burg ist unser Gott." Carlyle's version is ruggedly good, but not adapted for worship.

Walter Chalmers Smith (born 1824), minister of the Free High Church, Edinburgh is widely known by his published poems—"Olrig Grange," "Hilda among the Broken Gods," "North Country Folk," "Kildrostan," "The Bishop's Walk," &c., which are among the finest produced in recent years in Scotland. In 1867 Dr. Smith published a small volume, "Hymns of Christ and the Christian Life," and though he afterwards regretted its publication, it contains fine materials, which only need revision and slight alterations to render their metre correct, to make noble hymns for worship. Two of these were subjected to this at my request by Dr. Smith, and included in my "Congregational Hymns." They have already become favourites in the churches in which that collection is used. Readers may judge whether they are not of high excellence. The first is on "The King Eternal, Immortal, Invisible":—

Immortal, invisible, God only wise,
In light inaccessible hid from our eyes,
Most blessèd, most glorious, the Ancient of Days,
Almighty, victorious, Thy great name we praise.

Unresting, unhasting, and silent as light,
Nor wanting, nor wasting, Thou rulest in might;
Thy Justice like mountains high soaring above;
Thy clouds which are fountains of goodness and love.

To all, life Thou givest—to both great and small;
In all life Thou livest, the true life of all;
We blossom and flourish as leaves on the tree,
And wither and perish—but nought changeth Thee.

To-day and to-morrow with Thee still are Now;
Nor trouble, nor sorrow, nor care, Lord, hast Thou;
Nor passion doth fever, nor age can decay,
The same God for ever that was yesterday.

Great Father of Glory, pure Father of Light,
Thine angels adore Thee, all veiling their sight!
But of all Thy rich graces this grace, Lord, impart,
Take the veil from our faces, the veil from our heart.

All laud we would render; O help us to see,
'Tis only the splendour of light hideth Thee;
And so let Thy glory, Almighty, impart,
Through Christ in the story, Thy Christ to the heart.

The second on "The Lord reigneth, let the earth rejoice" is equally fine; the third verse especially is as musical as it is picturesque:—

Lord, God Omnipotent,
  Lord God alone,
High o'er the firmament
  Planting Thy Throne,
Curtained about with light,
Under Thy feet a bright
  Pavement of stars,
No shade of darksome night
  Thy glory mars.

Sun, moon, and stars fulfil
  Their times by Thee;
Angels to do Thy will
  Fleet lightnings be;
Rain, hail, and frost and snow,
And all the winds that blow,
  Are at Thy nod;
Oceans and tempests know
  Their mighty God.

Thou breathest on the earth,
  And there is spring,
Leaf buds come bursting forth,
  All the birds sing,
Flocks on the hills are seen
Herds on the meadows green,
  Forests rejoice,
All that had silent been
  Lifts up its voice.

Thou art our fortress strong,
  Our sun and shield,
Thou art our triumph-song
  On battle field:
By Thee we vanquish still
World foe and carnal will,
  All hell's array;
Thou wilt Thy plan fulfil,
  Plot as they may.

Lord God Omnipotent,
 'Bide with Thy flock;
O keep them, when they faint,
 Safe on the Rock;
Show them Thy tender grace,
And the light of Thy face
 To them accord:
Praise to Thy holiness,
 Praise to the Lord.

This hymn offers a fine opportunity for a musician to wed to noble music.

George MacDonald (born 1824), widely known as a writer of fiction, pervaded by strong religious conviction, and by means of which he has deeply influenced the theological thought of the present age, carrying the ideas which mark the school of Thomas Erskine, Macleod Campbell, and Frederick Denison Maurice, into a far wider circle than their works ever reached, has written a good deal of poetry marked by fine religious insight, but scarcely brought to sufficient clearness of expression to become popular. At the request of the Editors of "Hymns and Sacred Songs for Sunday Schools and Social Worship" (1873), he wrote several hymns which have since undergone careful revision, and been included in his "Works of Fancy and Imagination" (10 vols.). These are highly poetic, touched with a fine Christian mysticism and dealing with aspects of truth which ordinary hymnists have rarely discerned, and certainly have not expressed in their writings. The finest of his hymns are the following, which as they are known only to a limited circle, and have passed into few hymnals, I quote. The first shall be one on "The Son of Man":—

O Son of Man—Thy name by choice—
  Our hope, our joy, our life,
Make us like Thee, whose gentle voice
  Was never heard in strife.

Holy and harmless, undefiled,
  On earth Thou wert alone;
Come from the depths of heaven, a child,
  To make the lost Thine own.

To be a glory in our night,
  And bring us from above,
The way heaven's children live all bright,
  With self-forgetting love.

In all things like Thy brethren made,
  O teach us how to be
With meekness, gentleness, arrayed,
  In all things like to Thee.

The second is on "Blessed are the poor in spirit, for theirs is the kingdom of heaven":—

Our Father, hear our longing prayer,
  And help this prayer to flow,
That humble thoughts, which are Thy care,
  May live in us and grow.

For lowly hearts shall understand
  The peace, the calm delight,
Of dwelling in Thy heavenly land,
  A pleasure in Thy sight.

Give us humility, that so
  Thy reign may come within,
And when Thy children homeward go,
  We too may enter in.

Hear us, our Saviour! ours Thou art,
  Though we are not like Thee;
Give us Thy Spirit in a heart
  Large, lowly, trusting, free.

The finest, certainly the most poetic, is one which lays stress on the fact that "The meek inherit the earth":—

A quiet heart, submissive, meek,
  Father, do Thou bestow,
Which more than granted will not seek
  To have, or give, or know.

Each little hill then holds its gift
  Forth to my joying eyes;
Each mighty mountain will uplift
  My spirit to the skies.

Lo, then the running water sounds
  With gladsome secret things!
The silent water more abounds,
  And more the hidden springs.

Sweet murmurs then the trees will send,
  To hold the birds in song;
The waving grass its tribute lend
  Low music to prolong.

The sun will cast great crowns of light,
  On waves that anthems roar;
The dusky billows break at night
  In flashes on the shore.

Yea, every lily's shining cup,
  The hum of hidden bee,
The odours floating mingled up,
  With insect revelry,—

All hues, all harmonies divine,
  The holy earth about,
Their souls will send forth into mine,
  My soul to widen out.

And thus the great earth I shall hold
  A perfect gift of Thine,
Richer by these, a thousand-fold,
  Than if broad lands were mine.

With the increase of spiritual insight in the Church, such hymns as these are sure to be more largely appreciated and used.

Lawrence Tuttiett (1825-1897), of St. Andrews, N.B., was gifted with a peculiar power of tender expression, and his hymns have a certain distinctness of thought, which makes them of great value. This will be evident from the examples I quote below; no two are at all alike. In his most tender style is the following:—

O Jesu, ever present,
  O Shepherd, ever kind,
Thy very Name is music
  To ear, and heart, and mind.

It woke my wondering childhood
  To muse on things above;
It drew my harder manhood
  With cords of mighty love.

How oft to sure destruction
  My feet had gone astray,
Wert Thou not, patient Shepherd,
  The Guardian of my way.

How oft in darkness fallen,
  And wounded sore by sin,
Thy Hand has gently raised me,
  And healing balm poured in.

O Shepherd good, I follow
  Wherever Thou wilt lead;
No matter where the pasture
  With Thee at hand to feed.

Thy voice, in life so mighty,
  In death shall make me bold;
O bring my ransomed spirit
  To Thine eternal fold.

The following hymn on the coming of Christ the Judge, is very searching and powerful with a strain of subdued tenderness running through it:—

O quickly come, dread Judge of all;
For awful though Thine Advent be,
All shadows from the truth will fall,
And falsehood die in sight of Thee:
O quickly come: for doubt and fear
Like clouds dissolve when Thou art near.

O quickly come, great King of all;
Reign all around us, and within:
Let sin no more our souls enthral,
Let pain and sorrow die with sin:
O quickly come: for Thou alone
Canst make Thy scattered people one.

O quickly come, true Life of all,
For death is mighty all around;
On every home his shadows fall,
On every heart his mark is found:
O quickly come: for grief and pain
Can never cloud Thy glorious reign.

O quickly come, true Light of all;
For gloomy night broods o'er our way;
And weakly souls begin to fall
With weary watching for the day:
O quickly come: for round Thy throne
No eye is blind, no night is known.

The following is a very spiritual and yet strongly ethical hymn:—

O grant us light, that we may know
  The wisdom Thou alone canst give;
That truth may guide where'er we go,
  And virtue bless where'er we live.

O grant us light, that we may see
  Where error lurks in human lore,
And turn our doubting minds to Thee,
  And love Thy simple word the more.

O grant us light, that we may learn
  How dead is life from Thee apart;
How sure is joy for all who turn
  To Thee an undivided heart.

O grant us light, in grief and pain,
  To lift our burdened hearts above,
And count the very cross a gain,
  And bless our Father's hidden love.

O grant us light, when soon or late
  All earthly scenes shall pass away,
In Thee to find the open gate
  To deathless home and endless day.

Probably the most popular of his hymns is that for the New Year:—

Father, here we dedicate
  All our time to Thee,
In whatever worldly state
  Thou wouldst have us be;
Not from trouble, loss, or care
  Freedom would we claim;
This alone shall be our prayer,
  "*Glorify Thy name.*"

Can a child pretend to choose
  Where or how to live?
Can a Father's love refuse
  What is best to give?

More Thou grantest every day
  Than the best can claim;
Nor withholdest aught that may
  "*Glorify Thy Name.*"

If in mercy Thou wilt spare
  Joys that yet are ours,
If our future life may bear
  Some few brighter flowers;
Let our glad hearts, while they sing,
  Thee in all proclaim;
And whate'er this year may bring,
  "*Glorify Thy Name.*"

If we must, in grief and loss,
  Thy behest obey,
If beneath the shadowing cross
  Lies our homeward way,
We will think what Thy dear Son
  Once for us became,
And repeat, till life is done,
  "*Glorify Thy Name.*"

John Ellerton, M.A. (1826-1893), vicar of White Rothing, was, in my judgment, one of, if not the very greatest of modern hymnists. He is not quite so lyric as Bishop Walsham How, nor gifted with so popular a style as Dr. Bonar, nor so delicate and statuesque as Cardinal Newman, nor so pathetic as George Rawson, nor so quaint as Thomas Hornblower Gill, but for the union of strength and tenderness he is excelled by no hymnist of our day. He had, too, at his command, a variety of style and subject which is a very rare gift among the contributors to the hymnody of the Church. The best known of his hymns is that for Sunday evening, "Saviour again to Thy dear Name we raise," which is as tenderly spiritual as it is ethically strong. It is too well known to require quoting, and is sung perhaps as frequently as the hymns for the same season by Ken, Lyte, or Keble. Deeply solemn and impressive is his hymn on the Crucifixion: —

Throned upon the awful Tree,
King of grief, I watch with Thee;
Darkness veils Thine anguished face,
None its lines of woe can trace,
None can tell what pangs unknown
Hold Thee silent and alone.

Silent through those three dread hours,
Wrestling with the evil powers,
Left alone with human sin,
Gloom around Thee and within,
Till the appointed time is nigh,
Till the Lamb of God may die.

Hark that cry that peals aloud
Upward through the whelming cloud!
Thou, the Father's only Son,
Thou, His own Anointed One.
Thou dost ask him—"Can it be?
Why hast Thou forsaken Me?"

Lord, should fear and anguish roll
Darkly o'er my sinful soul,
Thou, who once wast thus bereft
That Thine own might ne'er be left—
Teach me by that bitter cry
In the gloom to know Thee nigh.

The most powerful of his hymns, however, is that on "All live unto Him," which is at once a protest against the unworthy ideas of death, which have so often prevailed, and an assertion of the fact that life follows at once, and not after a long interval of sleep, on departure from the present world:—

God of the living, in whose eyes,
Unveiled Thy whole creation lies;
All souls are Thine; we must not say
That those are dead who pass away;
From this our world of flesh set free,
We know them living unto Thee.

Released from earthly toil and strife,
With Thee is hidden still their life;
Thine are their thoughts, their works, their powers,
All Thine, and yet most truly ours;
For well we know, where'er they be,
Our dead are living unto Thee.

Not spilt like water on the ground,
Not wrapped in dreamless sleep profound,
Not wandering in unknown despair
Beyond Thy voice, Thine arm, Thy care;
Not left to lie like fallen tree;
Not dead, but living unto Thee.

Thy word is true, Thy will is just;
To Thee we leave them, Lord, in trust;
And bless Thee for the love which gave
Thy Son to fill a human grave,
That none might fear that world to see,
Where all are living unto Thee.

O Breather into men of breath,
O Holder of the keys of death,
O Giver of the life within,
Save us from death, the death of sin;
That body, soul, and spirit, be
For ever living unto Thee.

It is strange that the writer of such a hymn should have also written the well-known "Now the labourer's task is over," with its refrain, "Leave we now Thy servant sleeping," which is in direct contradiction to the far nobler idea of death contained in the line "Not wrapped in dreamless sleep profound." His Sunday morning hymn is cast in a very firm and rousing key:—

This is the day of Light!
Let there be light to-day!
O Dayspring, rise upon our night,
And chase its gloom away.

This is the day of Rest!
Our failing strength renew;
On weary brain and troubled breast
Shed Thou Thy freshening dew.

This is the day of Peace!
Thy Peace our spirits fill;
Bid Thou the blasts of discord cease:
The waves of strife be still.

This is the day of Prayer!
Let earth to heaven draw near;
Lift up our hearts to seek Thee there,
Come down to meet us here.

This is the First of days!
Send forth Thy quickening breath,
And wake dead souls to love and praise,
O Vanquisher of Death!

I am inclined to reckon his other hymns for Sunday evening, though not so well known, yet as equal in merit and perhaps more original than the one named. The assertion of the continuance of worship; the failing note of one land being taken up by the opening one of others is exceedingly fine in the following hymn :—

The day Thou gavest, Lord, is ended,
The darkness falls at Thy behest;
To Thee our morning hymns ascended,
Thy praise shall hallow now our rest.

We thank Thee that Thy Church unsleeping,
While earth rolls onward into light,
Through all the world her watch is keeping,
And rests not now by day or night.

As o'er each continent and island
The dawn leads on another day,
The voice of prayer is never silent,
Nor dies the strain of praise away.

The sun, that bids us rest, is waking
Our brethren 'neath the western sky,
And hour by hour fresh lips are making
Thy wondrous doings heard on high.

So be it, Lord; Thy throne shall never,
Like earth's proud empires, pass away;
But stand, and rule, and grow for ever,
Till all Thy creatures own Thy sway.

Whilst the following is charming, as a close to the Worship of the Sabbath :—

The Lord be with us as we bend
His blessings to receive;
His gift of peace upon us send,
Before His courts we leave.

The Lord be with us as we walk
Along our homeward road;
In silent thought, or friendly talk,
Our hearts be still with God.

The Lord be with us till the night
  Shall close the day of rest;
Be He of every heart the Light,
  Of every home the Guest.

And when our nightly prayers we say,
  His watch He still shall keep,
Crown with His grace His own blest day,
  And guard His people's sleep.

His National Hymn is well worthy of the theme. The description of England as "A garden fenced with silver sea" is very happy, probably suggested by Shakespeare's line—"This precious stone set in a silver sea."

Praise to our God, whose bounteous hand,
Prepared of old our glorious land;
A garden fenced with silver sea:
A people prosperous, bold, and free.

Praise to our God; through all our past
His mighty arm hath held us fast;
Till wars and perils, toils and tears,
Have brought the rich and peaceful years.

Praise to our God; the vine He set
Within our coasts is fruitful yet;
On many a shore her seedlings grow;
'Neath many a sun her clusters glow.

Praise to our God: His power alone
Can keep unmoved our ancient throne,
Sustained by councils wise and just,
And guarded by a people's trust.

Praise to our God, who still forbears,
Who still this guilty nation spares;
Who calls us still to seek His face,
And lengthens out our day of grace.

Praise to our God; though chastenings stern,
Our evil dross should throughly burn;
His rod and staff, from age to age.
Shall rule and guide His heritage!

One of the best hymns for a mid-day service in the week is from his pen—

Behold us, Lord, a little space
  From daily toil set free,
And met within this peaceful place,
  To rest awhile with Thee.

Around us rolls the ceaseless tide
  Of business, toil, and care;
And scarcely dare we turn aside
  For one brief hour of prayer.

Yet these are not the only walls
  Wherein Thou may'st be sought;
On homeliest work Thy blessing falls,
  In truth and patience wrought.
Thine is the forge, the loom, the mart,
  The wealth of land and sea;
The worlds of science and of art,
  Revealed and ruled by Thee.

Then let us prove our heavenly birth
  In all we do and know;
And own that King of all the earth
  Art Thou, and not Thy foe.
Work shall be prayer, if all be wrought
  As Thou wouldst have it done;
And prayer, by Thee inspired and taught,
  Itself with work be one.

His translations are quite equal to his original hymns. I may instance as very successful efforts in this difficult task the following:—the well-known "Sing Hallelujah forth in duteous praise," from the Mozarabic Breviary of the 5th century; "Welcome happy Morning, age to age shall say," from Venantius Fortunatus; whilst the following, from an anonymous Latin author, is finely expressed:—

O Strength and Stay upholding all creation,
  Who ever dost Thyself unmoved abide,
Yet day by day the light in due gradation
  From hour to hour through all its changes guide;

Grant to life's day a calm unclouded ending,
  An eve untouched by shadows of decay,
The brightness of a holy deathbed blending
  With dawning glories of the Eternal day.

It should be added that not only has Mr. Ellerton done fine work as a hymnist and translator, but he has also done much, by his editorial labours, to lift hymnody to a higher level.

Stopford Augustus Brooke (born 1832), formerly the eloquent minister of Bedford Chapel, Bloomsbury, whose departure from the Church of England, for theological reasons, created so much stir, is a man of a highly poetic temperament. In his student days, at Trinity College, Dublin, he carried off the prize for English verse, and has also published two volumes—"Riquet of the Tuft" and "Poems," the latter of which has, in my judgment, great poetic merit. Mr. Brooke prepared, for the use of his own congregation, a collection called "Christian Hymns," in which he dealt in a very free way with the hymns of other writers, adapting them to express his own views of Christian truth. In some instances, he took the hymns of Charles Wesley and other hymnists, and inserted in them a few lines of his own; in other cases, he wrote a hymn and made it to open with a line or two from other sources. In no collection with which I am acquainted has an editor treated the original texts of other writers with such freedom. The purist in such matters is horrified at the result, but one ignorant of the originals may be disposed to say that the collection is of considerable value. Some of the hymns from Mr. Brooke's own pen are exquisitely beautiful. The finest is the following, of which I give the best verses:—

When the Lord of Love was here,
Happy hearts to Him were dear,
Though His heart was sad;

Worn and lonely for our sake,
Yet He turned aside to make
All the weary glad.

Meek and lowly were His ways,
From His loving grew His praise,
From His giving, prayer:
All the outcasts thronged to hear,
All the sorrowful drew near
To enjoy His care.

When He walked the fields, He drew
From the flowers, and birds, and dew,
Parables of God;
For within His heart of love
All the soul of man did move,
God had His abode.

Fill us with Thy deep desire,
All the sinful to inspire,
With the Father's life:
Free us from the cares that press
On the heart of worldliness,
From the fret and strife.

Lord, be ours Thy power to keep
In the very heart of grief,
And in trial, love.
In our meekness to be wise,
And through sorrow to arise
To our God above.

Nearly, though not quite equal, is the following:—

Immortal Love, within whose righteous will
Is always peace;
O pity me, storm-tossed on waves of ill,
Let passion cease;
Come down in power within my heart to reign,
For I am weak, and struggle has been vain.

The days are gone, when far and wide my will
Drove me astray;
And now I fain would climb the arduous hill,
That narrow way
Which leads through mist and rocks to Thine abode;
Toiling for man and Thee, Almighty God.

Whate'er of pain Thy loving hand allot,
I gladly bear;

Only, O Lord, let peace be not forgot,
Nor yet Thy care,
Freedom from storms, and wild desires within,
Peace from the fierce oppression of my sin.

So may I, far away, when evening falls
On life and love,
Arrive at last the holy, happy halls,
With Thee above,
Wounded yet healed, sin-laden yet forgiven,
And sure that goodness is my only heaven.

To Miss Leeson we owe verses one, two, and six, to Mr. Brooke the remaining verses, of the following beautiful hymn for children :—

In the dark and silent night,
Blessèd Lord, be Thou my light,
So shall nothing me affright. Hallelujah!

Safely shadowed 'neath Thy wing,
Help Thy little one to sing
Glory to the heavenly King. Hallelujah!

All is still; the evening star
Rides upon its golden car;
In its light Thy glories are. Hallelujah!

And the moon, whose gentle ray
Glimmers like a softer day,
Seems to whisper, "Watch and pray." Hallelujah!

Softly nestled like a dove,
I am happy in Thy love;
Angels watch me from above. Hallelujah!

Angels sing, and so would I,
While upon my bed I lie,
Praise my Father silently. Hallelujah!

As a specimen of the way in which Mr. Brooke has dealt with and completed the work of other writers, I give the following, the nucleus of which is a hymn of Lamartine's, to which Mr. Whittier lent a new tenderness by his translation, and Mr. Brooke completed, with, as I think, certain lines of Charles Wesley running in his mind at the time he did his work :—

Mysterious Spirit, unto whom
Is known my sad and earth-bound frame;
Thou whom my soul, 'midst doubt and gloom,
Adoreth with a perfect flame;
Give me the speed of bird or wind,
Or torrent rushing to the sea,
That soaring upwards I may find
My resting place in Thee.

Thoughts of my soul, how swift ye go,
Swift as the eagle's wing of fire
Or arrows from the lightning's bow,
To God, the goal of my desire!
The weary tempest sleeps at last,
The torrent in the sea finds rest;
Let me not always be outcast,
Lord! take me to Thy breast.

My prayer hath pierced to God—the life,
The resurrection power is mine:
From sin and grief, from pain and strife,
I rise on wings of love divine;
Swifter than torrent, tempest, light,
I fly to my serene abode,
And on the last and holiest height,
Find rest and joy in God.

Mr. Brooke's mind is so steeped in the works of the English poets, that it must be very difficult to separate himself, in his hymn writing, from their influence, although in some of his hymns—for example, the first I have quoted—I do not trace any such influence. That, and others, seem to be quite original.

William Tidd Matson (born 1833), a minister of the Congregational Church possesses considerable mastery of the art of hymn composition, and has written many hymns for music which already existed. In this task he has been very successful; but this is an inversion of the true order—music should be written for words, not words for music. Sense should come before sound. Still, bearing in mind the conditions under which many of his hymns have been produced, they are very creditable performances, as may be seen by the following, both of which were written to be sung to German chorales :—

God is in His temple,
The Almighty Father!
Round His footstool let us gather :—
Him with adoration
Serve, the Lord most holy,
Who hath mercy on the lowly,
Let us raise
Hymns of praise,
For His great salvation :—
God is in His temple!

Christ comes to His temple:
We, His word receiving,
Are made happy in believing.
Lo! from sin delivered!
He hath turned our sadness,
Our deep gloom to light and gladness!
Let us raise
Hymns of praise,
For our bonds are severed :—
Christ comes to His temple!

Come and claim Thy temple,
Gracious Holy Spirit!
In our hearts Thy home inherit :—
Make in us Thy dwelling;
Thy high work fulfilling,
Into ours Thy will instilling;
Till we raise
Hymns of praise,
Beyond mortal telling,
In the eternal temple!

This is his best. The metre of the music rendered his task in the following more difficult, but still it is a clever piece of work :—

Glory, glory to God in the Highest!
Angels in chorus joyfully cry;
Glory, glory to God in the Highest!
Trembling and weak our voices reply:
Fain would we echo their anthem above,
Fain would we sing to the fountain of love

Glory to God in the Highest!
What though but feebly our accents arise,
Deigning to hearken, He bends from the skies;
Glory to God in the Highest!

Glory, glory to God in the Highest!
Bright beaming stars of midnight proclaim,
Glory, glory to God in the Highest!
All nature peals forth in praise to His name,
Warbles the woodland, and whispers the breeze,
Roar out the torrents and tempest-tossed seas,
Glory to God in the Highest!
Loudly creation still ceaseless prolongs,
Praise to her Maker in all her glad songs,
Glory to God in the Highest!

Glory, glory to God in the Highest!
Joining the choir, our tribute we bring;
Glory, glory to God in the Highest;
Mortals, break silence, gratefully sing,
Reigning in majesty, thronèd above,
Yours is the royallest gift of His love—
Glory to God in the Highest!
Spread through creation, His grandeur we trace,
Only in man He revealeth His grace,
Glory to God in the Highest!

His best-known hymn is "Lord, I was blind: I could not see," which consists of a series of antitheses which are effective, but a little too sharply and even hardly drawn.

Lord, I was blind: I could not see
In Thy marred visage any grace;
But now the beauty of Thy face
In radiant vision dawns on me.

Lord, I was deaf: I could not hear
The thrilling music of Thy voice;
But now I hear Thee and rejoice,
And all Thy uttered words are dear.

Lord, I was dumb: I could not speak
The grace and glory of Thy Name;
But now, as touched with living flame,
My lips Thine eager praises wake.

Lord, I was dead: I could not stir
My lifeless soul to come to Thee;
But now, since Thou hast quickened me,
I rise from sin's dark sepulchre.

Lord, Thou hast made the blind to see,
The deaf to hear, the dumb to speak,
The dead to live; and lo, I break
The chains of my captivity.

The following is a very good hymn of an ethical type, but with a very weak ending:—

Teach me, O Lord, Thy holy way,
And give me an obedient mind,
That in Thy service I may find
My soul's delight from day to day.

Guide me, O Saviour, with Thy hand,
And so control my thoughts and deeds,
That I may tread the path which leads
Right onward to the blessèd land.

Help me, O Saviour, here to trace
The sacred footsteps Thou hast trod,
And meekly walking with my God,
To grow in goodness, truth, and grace.

Guard me, O Lord, that I may ne'er
Forsake the right, or do the wrong;
Against temptation make me strong,
And round me spread Thy sheltering care.

Bless me in every task, O Lord,
Begun, contiuued, done for Thee;
Fulfil Thy perfect work in me;
And Thine abounding grace afford.

Richard Frederick Littledale (1833-1890), some ot whose hymns appeared under the signature A. L. P (a London Priest), and who was one of the chief editors of "The People's Hymnal" prepared for the High Anglican section of the Church, both as an original hymnist and a translator, has done excellent work. One of the most vigorous and lyric hymns of thanksgiving for rain after drought is the following. It is so lyric that it almost sings itself:—

O sing to the Lord,
   Whose bountiful hand
Again doth acord
   His gifts to the land.

His clouds have shed down
  Their plenteousness here,
His goodness shall crown
  The hopes of the year.

In clefts of the hills
  The founts He hath burst,
And poureth their rills
  Through valleys athirst.

The river of God
  The pastures hath blest,
The dry, withered sod
  In greenness is drest.

And every fold
  Shall team with its sheep,
With harvests of gold
  The fields shall be deep.

The vales shall rejoice
  With laughter and song,
And man's grateful voice
  The music prolong.

So too may He pour
  The Last and the First,
His graces in store
  On spirits athirst.

Till, when the great Day
  Of Harvest hath come,
He takes us away
  To garner at home.

Almost equal is his hymn for those at sea :—

O God, who metest in Thine hand
  The waters of the mighty sea,
And barrest ocean with the sand
  By Thy perpetual decree;

What time the floods lift up their voice
  And break in anger on the shore,
When deep to deep calls with the noise
  Of waterspouts and billows' roar;

When they who to the sea go down,
  And in the waters ply their toil,
Are lifted on the surge's crown,
  And plunged where seething eddies boil;

Rule then, O Lord, the ocean's wrath,
  And bind the tempest with Thy will;
Tread, as of old, the water's path,
  And speak Thy bidding, "Peace, be still."

So with Thy mercies ever new
  Thy servants set from peril free,
And bring them, Pilot, wise and true,
  Unto the port where they would be.

And when there shall be sea no more,
  Save that of mingled flame and glass,
Where goes no galley sped by oar,
  Where gallant ships no longer pass,

When dawns the Resurrection morn,
  Upon that shore, O Jesu, stand,
And give Thy pilgrims, faint and worn,
  Their welcome to the Happy Land.

The following translation of a hymn for the Burial of a Child, from the Paris Missal is admirable:—

Let no tears to-day be shed,
Holy is this narrow bed.
  Hallelujah!

Death eternal life bestows,
Open heaven's portal throws.
  Hallelujah!

And no peril waits at last
Him who now away hath past.
  Hallelujah!

Not salvation hardly won,
Not the meed of race well run;
  Hallelujah!

But the pity of the Lord
Gives His child a full reward.
  Hallelujah!

Grants the prize without the course;
Crowns without the battle's force.
  Hallelujah!

God, who loveth innocence,
Hastes to take His darling hence.
  Hallelujah!

Christ, when this sad life is done,
Join us to Thy little one.
  Hallelujah!

And in Thine own tender love,
Bring us to the home above.
Hallelujah!

Sabine Baring Gould (born 1834), Vicar of Lew Trenchard, Devonshire, an accomplished and prolific author, has written but few hymns, but those are of a very high order. To him we owe one of the most beautiful and deservedly popular children's hymns in the language, "Now the day is over"; whilst for adults he has written the stirring processional "Onward, Christian soldiers." To him we also owe the fine rendering of Ingemann's Danish hymn, "Through the night of doubt and sorrow." These are all too well known to need quotation.

William Chatterton Dix (born 1837) has been cited by Lord Selborne as an example of the fact that the power of hymn writing still exists in our day. A citation true but needless, since our lot has been cast not in an age in which the lyric fire burns lower, but rather brighter, than in any preceding age. Mr. Dix is a highly gifted hymn writer. Some of his less known compositions are touched by the High Church spirit, to which section he belongs, but the best are too deeply Christian to show any special theological or ecclesiastical bias. The most popular is the well known "As with gladness men of old," revised by the author at the suggestion of the Editors of "Hymns Ancient and Modern." Nearly equal, however, is the following—a most successful hymn of invitation—the most difficult subject to treat in verse without a preaching, if not a pharisaic tone, making those who sing to pose as saints singing to sinners. This danger Mr. Dix has successfully avoided, as my readers may see :—

"Come unto Me, ye weary,
   And I will give you rest,"
O blessèd voice of Jesus,
   Which comes to hearts oppressed.
It tells of benediction,
   Of pardon, grace, and peace,
Of joy that hath no ending,
   Of love which cannot cease.

"Come unto Me, dear children,
   And I will give you Light."
O loving voice of Jesus,
   Which comes to cheer the night.
Our hearts were filled with sadness,
   And we had lost our way,
But morning brings us gladness,
   And songs the break of day.

"Come unto Me, ye fainting,
   And I will give you Life."
O peaceful voice of Jesus,
   Which comes to end our strife.
The foe is stern and eager,
   The fight is fierce and long,
But Thou hast made us mighty,
   And stronger than the strong.

"And whosoever cometh
   I will not cast him out."
O patient love of Jesus,
   Which drives away our doubt;
Which calls us, very sinners,
   Unworthy though we be
Of love so free and boundless,
   To come, dear Lord, to Thee!

But the most perfect in the melody of its words—the hymn is musical, even as it is read—is his Harvest hymn. I do not know where one more perfect and melodious could be found :—

To Thee, O Lord, our hearts we raise
In hymns of adoration,
To Thee bring sacrifice of praise
With shouts of exultation;
Bright robes of gold the fields adorn,
The hills with joy are ringing,
The valleys stand so thick with corn
That even they are singing.

And now, on this our festal day,
Thy bounteous Hand confessing,
Upon Thine altar, Lord, we lay
The first-fruits of Thy blessing;
By Thee the souls of men are fed
With gifts of grace supernal,
Thou, who dost give us earthly bread,
Give us the Bread Eternal.

We bear the burden of the day,
And often toil seems dreary;
But labour ends with sunset ray,
And rest comes for the weary;
May we, the angel-reaping o'er,
Stand at the last accepted,
Christ's golden sheaves for evermore
To garners bright elected.

Oh, blessèd is that land of God,
Where saints abide for ever;
Where golden fields spread far and broad,
Where flows the crystal river:
The strains of all its holy throng
With ours to-day are blending;
Thrice blessèd is that harvest-song
Which never hath an ending.

Parts of this hymn have been very happily woven into Sir John Stainer's fine anthem, "Ye shall dwell in the land."

Samuel John Stone (born 1839), who is now Rector of All Hallows, London Wall, has written many hymns, some of which have acquired a world-wide popularity. The hymn by which he is best known is "Weary of earth, and laden with my sin," which appeared first of all in "*Lyra Fidelium, Twelve Hymns on the Apostles' Creed*" (1866). It is the hymn on Article X, "The Forgiveness of Sins." Since its first publication, it has been slightly altered by the author. The last lines originally read—

> Like that sweet nard let my devotion prove,
> Greatly forgiven, how I greatly love.

which now reads—

> Like Mary's gift let my devotion prove,
> Forgiven greatly, how I greatly love.

Next in popularity to this is "The Church's one foundation," which is the hymn on Article IX in *Lyra Fidelium*, "The Holy Catholic Church, the Communion of Saints." But of still greater merit is the following hymn for the close of the year:—

> The old year's long campaign is o'er
> Behold a new begun;
> Not yet is closed the holy war,
> Not yet the triumph won.
> Out of his still and deep repose
> We hear the old year say:
> "Go forth again to meet your foes,
> Ye children of the day!
>
> "Go forth! firm faith in every heart,
> Bright hope on every helm,
> Through that shall pierce no fiery dart,
> And this no fear o'erwhelm.
> Go in the spirit and the might
> Of Him who led the way;
> Close with the legions of the night,
> Ye children of the day."
>
> So forth we go to meet the strife,
> We will not fear nor fly;
> Love we the holy warrior's life,
> His death we hope to die.
> We slumber not, that charge in view,
> "Toil on while toil ye may,
> Then night will be no night to you,
> Ye children of the day."

Lord God, our Glory, Three in One,
Thine own sustain, defend;
And give, though dim this earthly sun,
Thy true light to the end;
Till morning tread the darkness down,
And night be swept away,
And infinite, sweet triumph crown
Thy children of the day.

Nearly equal, too, is the following:—

Dark is the sky that overhangs my soul,
The mists are thick that through the valley roll,
But as I tread, I cheer my heart and say,
" When the day breaks the shadows flee away."

Unholy phantoms from the deep arise,
And gather through the gloom before mine eyes;
But all shall vanish at the dawning ray,—
" When the day breaks the shadows flee away."

I bear the lamp my Master gave to me,
Burning and shining must it ever be,
And I must tend it till the night decay,—
" Till the day break, and shadows flee away."

He maketh all things good unto His own,
For them in every darkness light is sown;
He will make good the gloom of this my day,—
Till that day break, and shadows flee away.

He will be near me in the awful hour
When the last foe shall come in blackest power;
And He will hear me when at last I pray—
" Let the day break, the shadows flee away!"

In Him, my God, my Glory, I will trust:
Awake and sing, O dwellers in the dust!
Who shall come, will come, and will not delay,—
His day will break, those shadows flee away!

Mr. Stone is the author of " The Knight of Intercession," and also of the hymn used at the Thanksgiving Service for the recovery of the Prince of Wales, at St. Paul's.

To Gerald Moultrie (1829-1885) we owe the following fine rendering of the magnificent Midnight Hymn of the Greek Church, which deserves quotation, both on account of the impressiveness of the original and the admirable way in which it has been translated :—

Behold, the Bridegroom cometh in the middle of the night,
And blest is he whose loins are girt, whose lamp is burning bright;
But woe to that dull servant, whom his Master shall surprise
With lamp untrimmed, unburning, and with slumber in his eyes.

Do thou, my soul, beware, beware lest thou in sleep sink down,
Lest thou be given o'er to death, and lose the golden crown;
But see that thou be sober, with a watchful eye, and thus
Cry—Holy, Holy, Holy God, have mercy upon us.

That Day, the Day of Fear, shall come; my soul, slack not thy toil,
But light thy lamp, and feed it well, and make it bright with oil;
Thou knowest not how soon may sound the cry at eventide,
"Behold, the Bridegroom comes. Arise! Go forth to meet the Bride."

Beware, my soul; take thou good heed, lest thou in slumber lie,
And, like the foolish, stand without, and knock, and vainly cry;
But watch, and bear thy lamp undimmed, and Christ shall gird thee on
His own bright Wedding Robe of Light—the Glory of the Son.

Ada Cross, *née* Cambridge (born 1844), is the authoress of two volumes, entitled "Hymns on the Litany" and "Hymns on the Holy Communion," from which several of great beauty have passed into recent hymnals. One for Sunday morning, "The dawn of God's dear Sabbath," and another for the Communion, "Jesu, great Redeemer, source of life divine," are of great merit, and are now widely known.

Elizabeth Charles, *née* Rundle (died 1897), was the well-known authoress of "The Schönberg Cotta Family," and many stories of a religious historical type. Her book "The Voice of Christian Life in Song" is an admirable contribution to that subject, and contains many good translations of the hymns of other lands. I have already quoted (p. 51) an example, in her rendering of one of the hymns of the Venerable Bede. But she has written some admirable original hymns, most of them included in her volume of poems "The Three Wakings"; these are both original and suggestive. As they are not widely known, I will quote what are in my judgment the best. The following is full of spiritual insight into the work which the Cross is intended to effect in our hearts:—

Never further than Thy cross,
  Never higher than Thy feet;
Here earth's precious things seem dross,
  Here earth's bitter things grow sweet.

Gazing thus our sin we see,
  Learn Thy love while gazing thus;
Sin which laid the cross on Thee,
  Love which bore the cross for us.

Here we learn to serve and give,
  And, rejoicing, self deny;
Here we gather love to live,
  Here we gather faith to die.

Symbols of our liberty
  And our service here unite;
Captives, by Thy cross set free,
  Soldiers of Thy cross we fight.

Pressing onwards as we can,
  Still to this our hearts must tend;
Where our earliest hopes began,
  There our last aspirings end.

Till amid the Hosts of Light,
  We in Thee redeemed, complete,
Through Thy cross made pure and white,
  Cast our crowns before Thy feet.

Her hymn for the Communion lifts our eyes from the dead to the living Christ in a very striking way:—

Around a table, not a tomb,
  He willed our gathering-place to be;
When going to prepare our home,
  Our Saviour said—"Remember Me."

We kneel around no sculptured stone,
  Marking the place where Jesus lay;
Empty the tomb, the angels gone,
  The stone for ever rolled away.

Nay! sculptured stones are for the dead!
  Thy three dark days of death are o'er;
Thou art the Life, our living Head,
  Our living Light for evermore;

Of no fond relics, sadly dear,
  O Master! are Thine own possest;
The crown of thorns, the cross, the spear,
  The purple robe, the seamless vest.

Nay, relics are for those who mourn
  The memory of an absent friend;
Not absent Thou, nor we forlorn!
  "With you each day until the end!"

Thus round Thy table, not Thy tomb,
  We keep Thy sacred feast with Thee;
Until within the Father's home
  Our endless gathering-place shall be.

The following may be objected to, as not being in the strictest sense a hymn, but it is so rousing, so full of a large sympathy, that both Bishop Bickersteth in his "Hymnal Companion to the Book of Common Prayer," and I, in my "Congregational Hymns," could not resist the temptation to stretch a point, so as to include it. My readers shall judge whether we were wise or not in so doing:—

Is Thy cruse of comfort wasting? rise and share it with another,
And through all the years of famine it shall serve thee and thy brother.

Love divine will fill thy storehouse, or thy handful still renew;
Scanty fare for one will often make a royal feast for two.

For the heart grows rich in giving; all its wealth is living grain;
Seeds which mildew in the garner, scattered, fill with gold the plain.

Is thy burden hard and heavy? do thy steps drag wearily?
Help to bear thy brother's burden; God will bear both it and thee.

Numb and weary on the mountains, wouldst thou sleep amidst the snow?
Chafe that frozen form beside thee, and together both shall glow.

Art thou stricken in life's battle? Many wounded round thee moan;
Lavish on their wounds thy balsams, and that balm shall heal thine own.

Is the heart a well left empty? None but God its void can fill;
Nothing but a ceaseless fountain can its ceaseless longings still.

Is the heart a living power? self-entwined, its strength sinks low;
It can only live in loving, and by serving love will grow.

Anna Lætitia Waring is remarkable for the quiet trustfulness of the hymns which have proceeded from her pen. This is their distinctive excellence, their mechanism is somewhat faulty; the accent and rhythm might be improved, but the spirit that breathes through them is so deeply and truly Christian, that these minor defects are almost forgotten. A strict judge would perhaps pronounce them more suitable for times of quiet meditation than for those of public worship, but their quieting power has overridden critical considerations, and drawn them into a large number of hymnals for church use. The most popular is the widely-known "Father, I know that all my life," but quite equal are the less known:—

My heart is resting, O my God,
I will give thanks and sing;
My heart is at the secret source
Of every precious thing:
Now the frail vessel Thou hast made
No hand but Thine shall fill;
For the waters of this world have failed,
And I am thirsty still.

I thirst for springs of heavenly life,
And here all day they rise;
I seek the treasure of Thy love,
And close at hand it lies;

And a new song is in my mouth
  To long-loved music set,
Glory to Thee for all the grace
  I have not tasted yet.

Glory to Thee for strength withheld,
  For want and weakness known;
And the fear that sends me to Thyself
  For what is most my own:
I have a heritage of joy
  That yet I must not see;
But the hand that bled to make it mine
  Is keeping it for me.

My heart is resting, O my God,
  My heart is in Thy care;
I hear the voice of joy and health
  Resounding everywhere:
"Thou art my portion," saith my soul,
  Ten thousand voices say,
And the music of their glad Amen
  Will never die away.

And:—

Sweet is the solace of Thy love,
  My heavenly Friend to me,
While through the hidden way of faith
  I journey home with Thee,
Learning by quiet thankfulness
  As a dear child to be.

Though from the shadow of Thy peace
  My feet would often stray,
Thy mercy follows all my steps,
  And will not turn away;
Yea, Thou wilt comfort me at last,
  As none beneath Thee may.

O there is nothing in the world
  To weigh against Thy will:
E'en the dark times I dread the most,
  Thy covenant fulfil;
And when the pleasant morning dawns,
  I find Thee with me still.

Then in the secret of my soul,
  Though hosts my peace invade,
Though through a waste and weary land
  My lonely way be made,
Thou, even Thou, wilt comfort me—
  I need not be afraid.

Still in the solitary place
  I would awhile abide,
Till with the solace of Thy love
  My heart is satisfied;
And all my hopes of happiness
  Stay calmly at Thy side.

Whilst perhaps the most tenderly trustful of all is:—

Go not far from me, O my Strength,
  Whom all my times obey;
Take from me anything Thou wilt,
  But go not Thou away;
And let the storm that does Thy work
  Deal with me as it may.

On Thy compassion I repose,
  In weakness and distress;
I will not ask for greater ease,
  Lest I should love Thee less:
O 'tis a blessèd thing for me
  To need Thy tenderness,

Thy love has many a lighted path
  No outward eye can trace;
And my heart sees Thee in the deep,
  Though darkness cloud Thy face,
And communes with Thee 'mid the storm,
  As in a secret place.

When I am feeble as a child
  And flesh and heart give way,
Then on Thy everlasting strength,
  With passive trust I stay,
And the rough wind becomes a song,
  The darkness shines like day.

There is no death for me to fear,
  For Christ, my Lord, hath died;
There is no curse in this my pain,
  For He was crucified;
And it is fellowship with Him
  That keeps me near His side.

John Page Hopps, Minister of the Free Christian Church, Croydon, and a leader of the more emotional section of the Unitarian Church, possesses in a very high degree the faculty for hymn writing. He discerns what too many of those who belong to his section of the church fail to discern; that the Church is not a school of philosophy, where the intellect alone should be called into play, but that whilst the intellect should be appealed to, the heart should not be overlooked, and that worship should not be mere meditation, but a service, kindling mind and heart alike for the conflict and work of life. Having this idea of worship, Mr. Hopps's hymns are not as many proceeding from English Unitarians—mere poems appealing to the mind, but full of lyric fire and tenderness. Like those of Sir John Bowring, they are full of the evangelical *spirit*, if the doctrine which usually goes under that name be wanting. That this is so is clear from a fact communicated to me by a friend, that his Missionary Hymn, which I quote below, is more frequently sung than any other at the Monthly Prayer Meetings held at the Mission House of the London Society. In my opinion it is one of the finest hymns of its class ever written. The union of tenderness and boldness is very striking:—

Father, let Thy kingdom come.—
  Let it come with living power;
Speak at length the final word,
  Usher in the triumph hour.

As it came in days of old,
  In the deepest hearts of men,
When Thy martyrs died for Thee,
  Let it come, O God, again.

Tyrant thrones and idol shrines,
  Let them from their place be hurled;
Enter on Thy better reign,—
  Wear the crown of this poor world.

O what long, sad years have gone,
  Since Thy Church was taught this prayer!
O what eyes have watched and wept
  For the dawning everywhere!

Break, triumphant day of God!
Break at last, our hearts to cheer;
Throbbing souls and holy songs
Wait to hail Thy dawning here.

Empires, temples, sceptres, thrones,—
May they all for God be won!
And, in every human heart,
Father, let Thy kingdom come.

In a very different strain, but well suited to its subject is his hymn for winter:—

Cold and cheerless, dark and drear,
Wintry days and night appear;
But they all in order stand:
This is still God's goodly land.

Wind, and ice, and shrouding snow
At Thy bidding come and go;
Clouds obscure or planets shine,
But they serve Thee, and are Thine.

Flowers have faded from the plain,
But their mother-roots remain;
In the chilly earth they lie,
Waiting for the warmer sky.

Leaves and flowers and golden grain
God will bring all back again;
They shall come in beauty drest—
This is but their time of rest.

Thee we praise, then, Father dear,
E'en for winter, dark and drear;
All things lie within Thy mind,
Ever loving, ever kind.

One of the best hymns for children is the following from his pen. A large number of hymns of this class are, to use John Wesley's phrase, "namby-pambical," and not calculated to leave any real moral or spiritual influence on the mind of a child; but this hymn can scarcely fail to influence both the heart and life of the child for good. It has deservedly passed into most of the best hymnals for children, and is used in churches and schools of widely different theological prepossessions.

Father, lead me day by day,
Ever in Thine own sweet way;
Teach me to be pure and true,
Show me what I ought to do.

When in danger, make me brave;
Make me know that Thou canst save:
Keep me safe by Thy dear side;
Let me in Thy love abide.

When I'm tempted to do wrong,
Make me steadfast, wise, and strong;
And when all alone I stand,
Shield me with Thy mighty hand.

When my heart is full of glee,
Help me to remember Thee,—
Happy most of all to know
That my Father loves me so.

When my work seems hard and dry,
May I press on cheerily;
Help me patiently to bear
Pain and hardship, toil and care.

May I see the good and bright,
When they pass before my sight;
May I hear the heavenly voice
When the pure and wise rejoice.

May I do the good I know,
Be Thy loving child below,
Then at last go home to Thee,
Evermore Thy child to be.

The following hymn, suitable for use on behalf of children, is a perfect little gem, and can scarcely be read without emotion. I once quoted it to a friend, and the feeling, which he was unable to repress, was a striking witness to its pathos.

God bless the little children,
The faces sweet and fair,
The bright young eyes, so strangely wise,
The bonny silken hair.

God love the little children,—
The angels at the door;
The music sweet of little feet
That patter on the floor.

God help the little children,
Who cheer our saddest hours,
And shame our fears for future years,
And give us winter flowers.

God keep the little children
Whom we no more can see;
Fled from their nest, and gone to rest,
Where we desire to be.

It should be added that Mr. Hopps has edited "Hymns, Chants, and Anthems," a selection in excellent taste, but erring, as his own hymns do not, somewhat in the direction of being in parts a collection of *poems* rather than as it should have been, exclusively of hymns suitable to be sung.

CHAPTER XVII.

RECENT HYMNISTS.—MINOR CONTRIBUTORS.

Among minor contributors to hymnody may be mentioned, in alphabetical rather than chronological order, the following :—

Alfred Ainger, Reader at the Temple, and Canon of Bristol, whose Life and Edition of the works of Charles Lamb are so well known, to whom we owe a little hymn, terse in expression, and true in sentiment :—

O Lord! with toil our days are filled,
They rarely leave us free;
O give us space to seek for grace
In happy thoughts of Thee.

Yet hear us, little though we ask:
Oh! leave us not alone;
In every thought, and word, and task,
Be near us, though unknown.

Still lead us, wandering in the dark;
Still send us heavenly food,
And mark, as none on earth can mark,
Our struggle to be good.

Alfred Barry, formerly Principal of King's College, London, and until recently Bishop of Sydney, whose hymn for Sunday morning, though not equal to some for that season, is yet far above the average :—

As Thou didst rest, O Father, o'er nature's finished birth,
As Thou didst in Thy work rejoice, and bless the new-born earth,

So give us now that Sabbath rest, which makes Thy children free,
Free for the work of love to man, of thankfulness to Thee.

But in Thy worship, Father, O lift our souls above,
By holy word, by prayer and hymn, by eucharistic love;
Till e'en the dull cold work of earth, the earth which Christ hath trod,
Shall be itself a silent prayer, to raise us up to God.

So lead us on to heaven, where in Thy presence blest
"The wicked cease from troubling, and the weary are at rest."
Where faith is lost in vision, where love hath no alloy,
And through eternity there flows the deepening stream of joy.

To Thee, who giv'st us freedom, our Father and our King;
To Thee, the Risen Lord of life, our ransomed spirits sing;
Thou fill'st the Church in earth and heaven, O Holy Ghost—to Thee
In warfare's toil, in victory's rest, eternal glory be.

John Stuart Blackie (1809-1895), widely known as, for many years, the accomplished, but slightly eccentric Professor of Greek in the University of Edinburgh, who is said to have made his students *speak* this melodious and nervous language in his classes, has not only written much in prose, but also a good deal in verse, chiefly of a secular kind (if such a distinction may be permitted), but in his "Lays and Legends of Ancient Greece" occurs the following hymn, written on his marriage tour, which is permeated by the boldness and breeziness which characterise his unique personality, and is as different from the dull commonplace of many of the didactic hymn writers, as his well-loved Scotch mountains are from the monotonous levels of Essex. When sung to F. C. Maker's noble tune "Windermere," it freshens a congregation like a breeze from the heather-clad hills the author loves so well:—

Angels holy,
High and lowly,
Sing the praises of the Lord!
Earth and sky, all living nature,
Man, the stamp of thy Creator,
Praise ye, praise ye, God the Lord!

Sun and moon bright,
Night and moonlight,
Starry temples azure-floored;
Cloud and rain, and wild wind's madness,
Sons of God that shout for gladness,
Praise ye, praise ye, God the Lord!

Ocean hoary,
Tell His glory,
Cliffs, where tumbling seas have roared!
Pulse of waters, blithely beating,
Wave advancing, wave retreating,
Praise ye, praise ye, God the Lord!

Rock and highland,
Wood and island,
Crag, where eagle's pride hath soared;
Mighty mountains, purple-breasted,
Peaks cloud-cleaving, snowy-crested,
Praise ye, praise ye, God the Lord!

Rolling river,
Praise Him ever,
From the mountain's deep vein poured;
Silver fountain, clearly gushing,
Troubled torrent, madly rushing,
Praise ye, praise ye, God the Lord!

Bond and free man,
Land and sea man,
Earth, with peoples widely stored,
Wanderer lone o'er prairies ample,
Full-voiced choir, in costly temple
Praise ye, praise ye, God the Lord!

Praise Him ever,
Bounteous Giver;
Praise Him, Father, Friend, and Lord,
Each glad soul its free course winging,
Each glad voice its free song singing:
Praise the great and mighty Lord!

Abel Gerald Wilson Blunt (born 1827), the Vicar of Chelsea, has written a few hymns of merit, the best of which, it may also be added, the best yet written for the purpose, is one for Flower Services. It would be difficult to excel it:—

Here, Lord, we offer Thee all that is fairest,
Bloom from the garden, and flowers from the field;
Gifts from the stricken ones, knowing Thou carest
More for the love than the wealth that we yield.

Send, Lord, by these to the sick and the dying,
Speak to their hearts with a message of peace:
Comfort the sad, who in weakness are lying,
Grant the departing a gentle release.

Raise, Lord, to health again those who have sickened,
Fair be their lives as the roses in bloom;
Give of Thy grace to the souls thou hast quickened,
Gladness for sorrow, and brightness for gloom.

We, Lord, like flowers, must bloom and must wither,
We, like these blossoms, must fade and must die;
Gather us, Lord, to Thy bosom for ever,
Grant us a place in Thy home in the sky.

Robert Brown Borthwick (1840-1894), formerly Vicar of All Saints', Scarborough, was more conspicuous for his labours as an Editor of both hymns and tunes, than for his original contributions to hymnody, but one of his hymns, for the Lord's Supper, beginning "O Holy Jesu, Prince of Peace," though lacking the compactness of thought and expression necessary to a really popular hymn, is yet of very considerable merit.

William Bright, M.A. (born 1824), Canon of Christ Church, Oxford, is the author of a small volume of "Hymns and Poems," from which the following hymn for Sunday evening of great excellence has passed into many collections:—

And now the wants are told, that brought
Thy children to Thy knee;
Here lingering still, we ask for naught,
But simply worship Thee.

The hope of heaven's eternal days
Absorbs not all the heart,
That gives Thee glory, love, and praise,
For being what Thou art.

O wondrous peace, in thought to dwell
On excellence divine;
To know that naught in man can tell
How fair Thy beauties shine.

O Thou, above all blessing blest,
O'er thanks exalted far,
Thy very greatness is a rest
To weaklings as we are.

For when we feel the praise of Thee
A task beyond our powers,
We say, "A perfect God is He,
And He is fully ours."

All glory to the Father be
All glory to the Son,
All glory, Holy Ghost, to Thee,
While endless ages run.

Ellen Elizabeth Burman is the authoress of a hymn which has the rare merit of insisting that it is far more difficult to *live* than to *die* well. It was included in her "Poetical Remains," 1862. It is a hymn that would have satisfied George Eliot, whose dislike of "other-worldliness" was so pronounced, and who is usually credited with that (which, however, was S. T. Coleridge's) expressive phrase:—

Teach me to live! 'Tis easier far to die—
Gently and silently to pass away—
On earth's long night to close the heavy eye,
And waken in the glorious realms of day.

Teach me that harder lesson—how to live
To serve Thee in the darkest paths of life;
Arm me for conflict now, fresh vigour give,
And make me more than conqueror in the strife.

Teach me to live Thy purpose to fulfil;
Bright for Thy glory let my taper shine:
Each day renew, remould the stubborn will,
Closer round Thee my heart's affections twine.

Teach me to live for self and sin no more,
But use the time remaining to me yet,

Not mine own pleasure seeking as before,
Wasting no precious hours in vain regret.

Teach me live! No idler let me be,
But in Thy service hand and heart employ,
Prepared to do Thy bidding cheerfully—
Be this my highest and my holiest joy.

Teach me to live—my daily cross to bear,
Nor murmur though I bend beneath its load;
Only be with me; let me feel Thee near;
Thy smile sheds gladness on the darkened road.

Teach me to live and find my life in Thee,
Looking from earth and earthly things away;
Let me not falter, but untiringly
Press on, and gain new strength and power each day.

Teach me to live! with kindly words for all,
Wearing no cold repulsive brow of gloom,
Waiting with cheerful patience till Thy call
Summons my spirit to its heavenly home.

A lady, who desires to preserve her anonymity, and to be known only as E. B., is the author of two or three hymns, one of which, for Evening, deserves to be ranked with the many favourite ones we possess for that season. It has very high qualities, and is remarkable both for the vigour of its thought and the tenderness of its style. I append the finest verses—the fourth is very remarkable:—

Father, now the day is over,
As the sun sinks in the west,
Ere the night creep slowly round us,
Ere soft slumber be our guest,
Let us bless Thee that to-day
Thou, our God, hast been our stay.

Lord, we need no earthly temple,
For, where we Thy love have found,
All Thy humblest creatures teach us
Where we are is holy ground:
Lord, we need no holier place
Than where we Thy love can trace.

For the love of friends we bless Thee,
Who to-day our joys have shared,
Whose true hearts, spread out before us,
Have Thy love to us declared;
For each thought of truth and love
They have echoed from above.

For the mystic bond which binds us
Each to each, and all to Thee,
And with all the past entwines us,
In the world's long harmony;
For each striving human soul
Which is part of Thy great whole.

Pour Thy spirit, Lord, upon us,
Guard us in unconscious sleep;
Be that Spirit ever with us
While death-slumbers o'er us creep;
And, our life's long journey past,
We are safe with Thee at last!

Samuel Childs Clarke, vicar of Thorverton, Devon, is one of the many helpers which our time has had to a better psalmody, and for this he will be chiefly remembered; but two of his hymns are so distinctive as to deserve record. One of these is a Harvest Hymn, beginning, "Great Giver of all good, to Thee again," and the other a Festival one, "O Thou who dwellest in eternity."

Frances Power Cobbe (born 1822) is well-known by her contributions to periodical literature, and her published volumes, many of which are eloquent defences of Theism. She has also edited the works of Theodore Parker. Miss Cobbe has, however, written one hymn, so beautiful that it deserves quotation:—

God draws a cloud over each gleaming morn,—
Wouldst thou ask why?
It is because all noblest things are born
In agony.

Only upon *some* cross of pain or woe
God's Son may lie:
Each soul redeemed from self and sin must know
Its Calvary.

Yet we must crave neither for joy nor grief;
God chooses best:
He only knows our sick soul's best relief,
And gives us rest.

More than our feeble hearts can ever pine
For holiness,
That Father in His tenderness divine,
Yearneth to bless.

He never sends a joy not meant in love,
Still less a pain;
Our gratitude the sunlight falls to prove;
Our faith, the rain.

In His hands we are safe. We falter on
Through storm and mire:
Above, beside, around us, there is One
Will never tire.

What though we *fall*,—and bruised and wounded lie,
Our lips in dust!
God's arm shall lift us up to victory!
In Him we trust.

For neither life nor death, nor things below,
Nor things above,
Can ever sever us, that we should go
From His great love.

George Thomas Coster (born 1835), now minister of the Congregational Church at Stroud, has from his student days been addicted to poetic composition, for which, especially in relation to the interpretation of Scripture character, he possesses a decided genius. He has published "Lorrine, and other poems," "The Lay of St. Peter," "Hymns and Poems," and "Red Roofs," whilst he is represented in my "Poets' Bible" by fine poems on "Esau at the grave of Isaac," &c. Many of his hymns are above the average, but the Missionary Hymn which I append is very distinctive and charming, and should be a favourite at the services for which it was written :—

From north and south, and east and west,
When shall the peoples, long unblest,
All find their everlasting rest,
O Christ, in Thee?

When shall the climes of ageless snow
Be with the Gospel light aglow,
And all men their Redeemer know,
O Christ, in Thee?

When on each southern balmy coast,
Shall ransomed men, in countless host,
Rise, heart and voice, to make sweet boast,
O Christ, in Thee?

O when in all the orient lands,
From cities white and flaming sands,
Shall men lift dedicated hands,
O Christ, to Thee?

O when shall heathen darkness roll
Away in light, from pole to pole,
And endless day by every soul
Be found in Thee?

Bring, Lord, the long-predicted hour,
The ages' diadem and flower,
When all shall find their Refuge, Tower,
And Home in Thee!

His hymn for Sabbath use at sea, though not equal to the former, has some fine touches in it :—

Lord of the sea! afar from land
We still within Thy presence stand:
Now grant us grace to worship Thee,
And keep our Sabbath on the sea.

Be banished care, be banished fear!
Our hearts into calm waters steer;
So may they rest although we roam,
And on the deep be still at home.

Be calm without and calm within,
And all our worship free from sin;
And as of Thee Thy servants hear,
O let us feel that Thou art near!

Thy blessing, gracious Lord, we crave;
Thou oft didst sail the Hebrew wave;—
Sail with us now that, joyful, we
May keep our Sabbath on the sea.

Thine is the sea, as Thine the land;
We still within Thy presence stand;
In Thy blest Spirit's light may we
Find mercy's gate upon the sea!

It is strange that Mr. Coster's hymns should have been so overlooked by most Editors of Hymnals prepared for use in that section of the Church to which he belongs.

John Brooke Greenwood, of Manchester (born 1828), has written many hymns and short religious poems, which appeared in various magazines. One of these was included in the "Annus Sanctus," edited by the Rev. Orby Shipley, on the principle that no hymn or poem should be admitted to its pages, save those written by members of the Roman Communion. In this collection is included "The Return of the dove," with the initial S., of which Mr. Greenwood, a member of the Congregational Church, is the author. Astonished to find it there I set myself to unravel the mystery, and found that Mr. Greenwood's verses came into the hands of a relation of his belonging to the Roman Church, who gave them to her priest; through him they found their way into a Roman Catholic newspaper. Mr. Shipley finding them there concluded they were by a member of that communion, and included them in his "Annus Sanctus," where they figure among the verses of monks, priests, bishops, and cardinals. After this, who shall say that a heretic may not have some slight chance of heaven? I quote two hymns by Mr. Greenwood, which seem to me to be his best efforts. The first, a Marriage Hymn, is becoming a favourite for that service:—

Crown with Thy benediction
  This sacrament of love;
And make this hallowed union
  Foretaste of heaven above:
Let pure and perfect gladness,
  Let pure and perfect rest,
And peace that knows no sadness,
  Thy presence, Lord, attest.

As once in Eden's springtime,
  As once at Cana's feast,
So consecrate this Bridal—
  Be Thou its Guest and Priest!
With sunshine wreathe the altar,
  Chase every cloud away,
Nor let their voices falter
  Who plight their troth to-day.

God bless the Bride and Bridegroom,
  And fill with joy their life;
Keep them, through all its changes,
  True husband, faithful wife!
If Thou wilt smile upon them,
  They shall not need the sun:
This thought their hearts rejoicing—
  Henceforth, not twain but one.

With Thy great love befriend them,
  The love that casts out fear;
And make a rainbow round them
  For every falling tear:
Till, all their sheaves well-garnered,
  Heaven's harvest-home they raise,
Where love, that knows no ending,
  Inspires more perfect praise.

The second, a Baptismal hymn, is very tender, and admirably suited to that service:—

What shall we render, Lord, to Thee
  Who hast enriched our lives with love,
And in our midst has set this child
  To link our hearts to things above?

We thank Thee, Lord, that Thou hast given
  Such answer to our hopes and fears·
Has sent this little one from heaven,
  Glad recompence for all our tears.

To nestle dove-like, in our home,
And fill our lives with joy and light;
Make sunshine when the shadows come,
And parents' hearts to Thee unite.

To wean our souls from self and sin,
To nobler uses, higher claims;
A life of service that shall win
Thy benediction on its aims.

Baptize our households from above,
O gentle Shepherd of the sheep!
And, with Thy ministry of love,
Our tender nurslings safely keep.

We bring our little ones to Thee;
Their angels always see Thy face:
The Everlasting arms shall be
Our children's quiet resting place.

Thomas Hughes (1823-1896), known in every English-speaking country as the author of "Tom Brown's School Days," is the author of one hymn, written at the request of the Hon. Mrs. Norton, for "Lays of the Sanctuary," a poetical collection published for a charitable purpose, but it is so good, and so gathers up and expresses the inmost spirit of the author, that it deserves mention and quotation. Mr. Hughes told me that he never attempted to write another hymn. It is such a hymn as his dear friend Charles Kingsley would have rejoiced to sing:—

O God of Truth, whose living word
Upholds whate'er hath breath,
Look down on Thy creation, Lord,
Enslaved by sin and death.

Set up Thy standard, Lord, that we,
Who claim a heavenly birth,
May march with Thee to smite the lies
That vex Thy groaning earth.

Ah! would we join that blest array,
And follow in the might
Of Him the Faithful and the True,
In raiment clean and white!

We fight for truth, *we* fight for God,
Poor slaves of lies and sin !
He who would fight for Thee on earth,
Must first be true within.

Then, God of Truth, for whom we long,
Thou who wilt hear our prayer,
Do Thine own battle in our hearts,
And slay the falsehood there.

Still smite ! still burn ! till naught is left
But God's own truth and love ;
Then, Lord, as morning dew come down,
Rest on us from above.

Yea, come ! then, tried as in the fire,
From every lie set free,
Thy perfect truth shall dwell in us,
And we shall live in Thee.

John Julian (born 1839), Vicar of Wincobank, Sheffield, is best known as Editor of the "Dictionary of Hymnology," published by Mr. John Murray, to which he has devoted years of labour, and is the standard work of reference on that subject, but he has written two or three hymns which have a certain merit, but lack that inexpressible something—spontaneity—the vision and faculty divine, which make words to glow, and kindle other minds. They are not sufficiently quick in their movement to be effective, they are the work of the hymnologist rather than the poet, but yet the refrain of the following hymn is very impressive :—

O God of God ! O Light of Light !
Thou Prince of Peace, Thou King of Kings ;
To Thee, where angels know no night,
The song of praise for ever rings :—
To Him who sits upon the throne,
The Lamb once slain for sinful men,
Be honour, might ; all by Him won ;
Glory and praise ! Amen, Amen.

Deep in the Prophets' sacred page,
Grand in the Poets' wingèd word,
Slowly in type, from age to age,
Nations beheld their coming Lord;
    Till through the deep Judean night,
    Rang out the song, "Goodwill to men';
    Hymned by the firstborn sons of light,
    Re-echoed now—'Goodwill,' Amen.

That life of truth, those deeds of love,
That death of pain, 'mid hate and scorn;
These all are past, and now above,
He reigns our King! once crowned with thorn.
    "Lift up your heads, ye heavenly gates,"
    So sang His hosts, unheard by men;
    "Lift up your hearts, for you He waits,"
    "We lift them up! Amen, Amen!"

Nations afar, in ignorance deep;
Isles of the sea. where darkness lay;
These hear His voice, they wake from sleep,
And throng with joy the upward way,
    Thy cry with us, "Send forth Thy light,"
    O Lamb, once slain for sinful men;
    Burst Satan's bonds, O God of Might,
    Set all men free! Amen, Amen.

Sing to the Lord a glorious song,
Sing to His name, His love forth tell;
Sing on, heaven's host, His praise prolong;
Sing, ye who now on earth do dwell:—
    Worthy the Lamb for sinners slain,
    From angels, praise; and thanks from men.
    Worthy the Lamb, enthroned to reign,
    Glory and power! Amen, Amen.

The same kind of remark applies to his Christmas hymn for children, "Sweetly sang the angels in the clear calm light."

Mary Fawler Maude (born 1848) deserves mention for the terse and striking hymn, "Thine for ever, God of love."

Eliza Fanny Morris, *née* Goffe (born 1821), was the authoress of a little work, "The Voice and the Reply"

(1858), in the second part of which is found the hymn, "God of pity, God of grace," by which she is now well known. It is called "The Prayer in the Temple." She has written other hymns, but none of them equal to the one I have named.

Charles Edward Mudie (1818-1891), the founder of the well-known library which goes under his name, has written a few poems chiefly sacred, which have been collected and published under the title "Stray leaves." The one hymn which has passed into many collections, and become very popular among the Free Churches, is the following, which has great merit:—

I lift my heart to Thee,
Saviour Divine,
For Thou art all to me,
And I am Thine.
Is there on earth a closer bond than this—
That 'my Beloved's mine, and I am His'?

Thine am I by all ties;
But chiefly Thine,
That through Thy sacrifice
Thou, Lord, art mine.
By Thine own cords of love, so sweetly wound
Around me, I to Thee am closely bound.

To Thee, Thou bleeding Lamb,
I all things owe;
All that I have and am,
And all I know.
All that I have is now no longer mine,
And I am not mine own,—Lord, I am Thine.

How can I, Lord, withhold
Life's brightest hour
From Thee; or gathered gold,
Or any power?
Why should I keep one precious thing from Thee,
When Thou hast given Thine own dear self for me?

I pray Thee, Saviour, keep
Me in Thy love,
Until death's holy sleep
Shall me remove
To that fair realm, where, sin and sorrow o'er,
Thou and Thine own are one for evermore.

Some writers are forced into the company of hymnists, who never expected to be. Harriet Parr (better known under her *nom de plume* of Holme Lee) is an example of this. In 1856 she wrote, for Charles Dickens, a portion of the Christmas story "The wreck of the Golden Mary." The narrative which connects the various parts together is that the "Golden Mary" on her voyage to California, encounters an iceberg, and is wrecked. The crew and passengers take to their boats, and, to while away the time, relate their experiences. Poor Dick Tarrant tells his tale, and then says: "What can it be that brings all these old things over in my mind? There's a child's hymn I and Tom used to say at my mother's knee when we were little ones, keeps running through my thoughts. It's the stars, may be. There was a little window by my bed that I used to watch them at—a window in my room at home in Cheshire; and if I was ever afraid, as boys will be after reading a good ghost story, I would keep on saying it till I fell asleep." "That was a good mother of yours, Dick; could you say that hymn now, do you think? some of us would like to hear it." "It's as clear in my mind at this minute, as if my mother was here listening to me," said Dick, and he repeated:—

Hear my prayer, O heavenly Father,
Ere I lay me down to sleep;
Bid Thine angels, pure and holy,
Round my bed their vigil keep.

Great my sins are, but Thy mercy
Far outweighs them every one;
Down before the cross I cast them,
Trusting in Thy help alone.

Keep me, through this night of peril,
Underneath its boundless shade;
Take me to Thy rest, I pray Thee,
When my pilgrimage is made.

None shall measure out Thy patience
By the span of human thought:
None shall bound the tender mercies
Which Thy holy Son hath wrought.

Pardon all my past transgressions,
Give me strength for days to come;
Guide and guard me with Thy blessing
Till Thine angels bid me home.

It was first included in the "Congregational Hymn Book." Little did the authoress dream that her verses would be put to such a use, and become as they have, so deservedly popular. This is the only hymn we owe to her pen.

Catherine Pennefather, *née* King, to whose husband we owe several hymns of great beauty, has written one of great tenderness, which expresses the purpose which has marked the life work of its author, "Not now, my child, a little more rough tossing."

To Folliott Sandford Pierpoint (born 1835)—who must not be confounded with the American, John Pierpont—we owe one of the most delightful hymns of thankfulness in the language. The refrain, in the original, ran thus: "Christ, our God, to Thee we raise," but by most editors, it has been changed to the version I append:—

For the beauty of the earth,
For the beauty of the skies,
For the love which from our birth
Over and around us lies;
Father, unto Thee we raise
This, our sacrifice of praise.

For the beauty of each hour
Of the day and of the night,
Hill and vale, and tree and flower,
Sun and moon, and stars of light;
Father, unto Thee we raise
This, our sacrifice of praise.

For the joy of ear and eye,
For the heart and mind's delight,
For the mystic harmony
Linking sense to sound and sight;
Father, unto Thee we raise
This, our sacrifice of praise.

For the joy of human love,
Brother, sister, parent, child,
Friends on earth, and friends above,
For all gentle thoughts and mild;
Father, unto Thee we raise
This, our sacrifice of praise.

For each perfect gift of Thine
To our race so freely given,
Graces human and divine,
Flowers of earth, and buds of heaven;
Father, unto Thee we raise
This, our sacrifice of praise.

For Thy Church that evermore
Lifteth holy hands above,
Offering up on every shore
Its pure sacrifice of love;
Father, unto Thee we raise
This, our sacrifice of praise.

Richard Hayes Robinson (1842-1892), of Bath, is the author of the beautiful little hymn, "Holy Father, cheer our way."

Christina Georgina Rossetti (1830-1897), the sister of Dante Gabriel and William Michæl Rossetti, is better known as a poet than as a hymnist. Her poems take very high rank, and often remind us of those of the greatest poetess of England—Elizabeth Barrett Browning.

I question whether Miss Rossetti ever wrote verses with a view to use in worship, but the exquisite beauty of some of her shorter poems has led some editors to include them in their collections. They are, however, more suited to private than public worship, as may be seen from the following specimen:—

I would have gone; God bade me stay:
I would have worked; God bade me rest:
He broke my will from day to day,
He read my yearnings, unexpressed,
    And said them nay.

Now I would stay; God bids me go:
Now I would rest; God bids me work.
He breaks my heart, tossed to and fro,
My soul is wrung with doubts that lurk
    And vex it so.

I go, Lord, where Thou sendest me;
Day after day I plod and moil:
But, Christ, my God, when will it be
That I may let alone my toil
    And rest with Thee?

Jane Euphemia Saxby, *née* Browne (born 1811), the author of "The Dove on the Cross," is numbered among the hymnists by the following exquisite hymn, which appeared in the volume I have named:—

Show me the way, O Lord,
    And make it plain;
I would obey Thy Word,
    Speak yet again;
I will not take one step until I know
Which way it is that Thou wouldst have me go.

O Lord, I cannot see:
    Vouchsafe me light:
The mist bewilders me,
    Impedes my sight:
Hold Thou my hand, and lead me by Thy side;
I dare not go alone,—be Thou my Guide.

I will be patient, Lord,
 Trustful and still;
I will not doubt Thy Word;
 My hopes fulfil:
How can I perish, clinging to Thy side,
My Comforter, my Saviour, and my Guide?

Charles Smith (born 1844) is the author of two hymns, one of which especially deserves mention. It was written at my suggestion for "The Book of Praise for Children," which at the time, I was compiling. Its author made many attempts, and at last almost gave up the task in despair, when a sudden inspiration enabled him to write the following hymn, which is quite original in conception, and expressed with great beauty. It was afterwards revised for insertion in "Congregational Hymns," where it appears as quoted below. The comparison of the path of duty to a shining golden street is particularly happy:—

Lord! when through sin I wander
 So very far from Thee,
I think in some far country,
 Thy sinless home must be;
But when with heartfelt sorrow
 I pray Thee to forgive,
Thy pardon is so perfect,
 That in Thy heaven I live.

That heaven, Lord, so surrounds me,
 That when I do the right,
The saddest path of duty
 Is lightened by its light:
I know not what its glories
 Before Thy throne must be,
But here Thy smiling presence
 Is heaven on earth to me.

To love the right and do it,
 Is to my heart so sweet,
It makes the path of duty
 A shining golden street:

Give me Thy strength, O Father,
  To choose this path each day,
Then heaven within, about me,
  Shall compass all my way.

The other is a hymn for children on "Joy and Sorrow alike from God," and is of merit, though not equal to the one I have quoted.

George Hunt Smyttan (1825-1870) has shown the use which may be made of Scripture incident, when rightly treated, in the sharply-cut hymn:—

Forty days and forty nights
  Thou wast fasting in the wild;
Forty days and forty nights
  Tempted and yet undefiled.

Sunbeams scorching all the day,
  Chilly dewdrops nightly shed;
Prowling beasts about Thy way;
  Stones Thy pillow, earth Thy bed.

Lord, if Satan, vexing sore,
  Flesh or spirit should assail,
Thou hast vanquished him before;
  Grant we may not faint or fail.

So shall we have peace divine;
  Holier gladness ours shall be;
Round us, too, shall angels shine,
  Such as ministered to Thee.

Keep, O keep us, Saviour dear,
  Ever constant by Thy side;
That with Thee we may appear
  At th' eternal Eastertide.

David Thomas (1813-1894), for many years minister of the Congregational Church at Stockwell, for whose use he compiled "The Biblical Liturgy," and Editor of *The Homilist*, has written several hymns, which were included in the "Liturgy" I have named. One of these is pathetic and tender in no ordinary degree:—

Shew pity, Lord, for we are frail and faint;
We fade away, O list to our complaint!
We fade away, like flowers in the sun;
We just begin, and then our work is done.

Shew pity, Lord, our souls are sore distressed;
As troubled seas, our natures have no rest;
As troubled seas that surging beat the shore,
We throb and heave, ever and evermore.

Shew pity, Lord, our grief is in our sin:
We would be cleansed, O make us pure within!
We would be cleansed, for this we cry to Thee;
Thy word of love can make the conscience free.

Shew pity, Lord, inspire our hearts with love;
That holy love which draws the soul above;
That holy love which makes us one with Thee,
And with Thy saints, through all eternity.

Henry Twells (born 1832), rector of Waltham, Melton Mowbray, will be long remembered, and deservedly, by his hymn for Sunday evening, one of the finest we possess, "At even ere the sun was set." Scarcely a hymnal now appears in which this is not included.

CHAPTER XVIII.

GERMAN HYMNS.

GERMANY holds a place of pre-eminence for her *hymns*. In sacred *poetry*, she has had no writers at all to be compared with John Milton, George Herbert, Henry Vaughan, John Keble, and a host of others that might be named. Probably *now* our store of English Hymnody is equal, but before the present century it was far inferior to that of Germany. The reasons for this pre-eminence are twofold: the much earlier period (two or three centuries) at which the Germans began to cultivate hymn-writing, and their greater love for music, so that no sooner was a hymn written than it was at once set to music and its life and influence secured. "As far back as we hear anything of the German race, we hear of their love for song. They sang hymns, we are told, in their heathen worship, and lays in honour of their heroes at their banquets, and their heaven was pictured as echoing with the songs of the brave heroes who had died in battle."* Their love of music was not, however, checked or diverted from a religious use by Calvinism, which had but a very slight hold of the German mind. The more strongly churches have been influenced by the

* Winkworth's "Christian Singers of Germany," p. 6.

theology of Calvin, the less disposed have they been to admit Art, whether in the form of Music, Poetry, or Painting, as a handmaid to their worship. And so we find, that, whilst England was content with such versions of the Psalms as Sternhold and Hopkins, Germany possessed a noble collection of hymns in the vernacular. Mrs. Charles, in her "Voice of Christian Life in Song," attempts to explain the Calvinistic dislike to hymns in public worship in the following way:—"None of the strictly Calvinistic communities have a hymn-book dating back to the Reformation. It cannot, surely, be their doctrines which caused this; many of the best-known and most deeply-treasured hymns of Germany and England have been written by those who receive the doctrines known as Calvinistic. Nor can it proceed from any peculiarity of race, or deficiency in popular love of music and song. French and Scotch national character are too dissimilar to explain the resemblance; whilst France has many national melodies and songs, and Scotland is peculiarly rich in both. Is not the cause, then, simply the common ideal of external ecclesiastical forms which pervaded all the churches reformed on the Genevan type? The intervening chapters of ecclesiastical history were, as it were, folded up, as too blotted and marred for truth to be read to profit in them; and, next to the first chapter of Church History in the Acts of the Apostles, was to stand, as the second chapter, the history of the Reformed Churches. Words were to resume their original Bible meaning; nothing was to be received that could not be traced back to the Divine hand. Ecclesiastical order was to be such as St. Paul had established, or had found established; clearly to be traced, it was believed, in the

Acts and Apostolical Epistles. And, since the inspiration which glowed on the gifted lips of apostolic days existed no longer, and the "psalms and hymns and spiritual songs" in which St. Paul had delighted formed no part of the New Testament canon, recourse must be had to an older liturgy, inspired throughout, at once most human and most divine. Thus the Book of Psalms became the hymn-book of the Reformed Churches; adapted to grave and solemn music, in metrical translations whose one aim and glory was to render into measures which could be sung the very words of the Hebrew Psalms."

This seems to me a very insufficient explanation of the matter, since such a position would have led them to confine all their worship—prayers and sermons, as well as hymns—to Bible forms. This they did not do. It seems to me that the Calvinist had a rooted dislike to the aid of Art, whether in poetry, or music, or architecture, in the service of religion. In his mind, there lay an other-worldliness of a very pronounced type, so that although he dilated on the song and music of heaven, he would not admit these to any place in the Church on earth. The more rigid of the Calvinists excluded song of every kind, even that drawn from scripture sources, from worship.

The hymnody of Germany sprang from very small beginnings, and only gradually came into existence. In the earliest times, whilst the land was under the sway of Rome—there, as in England—hymns filled but a small place in worship; and those that were used had been drawn from Latin writers chiefly of the Gregorian or Ambrosian schools. In the earliest times of the German Church "the only part which the people were allowed to take in the services of the Church was to sing, or rather to shout, the 'Kyrie Eleison' in the Litany, and that only at extraordinary seasons, such as processions, pilgrimages, the transposition of relics, funerals, the consecration of churches, and other similar occasions."* "These words were frequently repeated, sometimes two or three hundred times in one service, and were apt to degenerate into a kind of scarcely articulate shout, as is proved by the early appearance, even in writing, of such forms as 'Kyrieles.' But soon after Notker had created the Latin Sequence, the priests began to imitate it in German, in order to furnish the people with some intelligible words in place of the mere outcry to which they had become accustomed. They wrote irregular verses, every strophe of which ended with the words 'Kyrie Eleison,' from the last syllables of which these earliest German hymns were called *Leisen*."† The earliest of these which has been handed down to us is on Peter, which runs as follows:—

Our dear Lord of grace hath given
To St. Peter power in heaven,
That he may uphold alway,
All who hope in him, and say
Kyrie eleison!
Christe eleison!

Therefore must he stand before
The heavenly kingdom's mighty door;
There will he an entrance give
To those who shall be bid to live:
Kyrie eleison!
Christe eleison!

Let us to God's servant pray,
All, with loudest voice to-day,
That our souls, which else were lost,
May dwell among the heavenly host:
Kyrie eleison!
Christe eleison!

* Kurtz's "Church History," vol. i, p. 547.
† Winkworth's "Christian Singers of Germany," p. 28.

This was the humble beginning of German Hymnody. Somewhat later, in the twelfth century, much of the native feeling found expression through the Minnesingers, whose songs were in the vernacular, and of a much more finished character. Many of these, though not distinctly religious, were yet touched with Christian feeling; some were distinctly religious, and did much to meet and satisfy the craving for lyric and musical expression on the part of the people. The *Leisen*, too, came into more general use, and grew to a greater finish, as may be seen from the following verses, afterwards adopted by Luther as part of his own hymns:—

Christ the Lord is risen,
Out of Death's dark prison,
Let us all rejoice to-day,
Christ shall be our hope and stay:
　　Kyrie eleison.
　　　　Alleluia, Alleluia, Alleluia!
Let us all rejoice to-day:
Christ shall be our hope and stay.
　　Kyrie eleison.

Many of the great Latin hymns were translated into German, and found their way into occasional use, and a large number of religious poems were composed. M. Wackernagel has collected nearly 1,500 pieces by 85 authors, belonging to the time before the Reformation. Some of these were composed for different classes and occasions—such as pilgrims, boatmen, &c., or to be sung in battle. The oldest German Easter Hymn belongs to the twelfth century.

To the heretical sects of the time is due both the composition of much of the religious poetry, and, as in the case of the Syriac and Greek churches, its introduction into the public worship of the Church. The school of Mystics, to which Tauler belonged, by the impetus it gave to the study of the Bible (the first complete version of it into German was by a Mystic—Matthias of Beheim), prepared the way for a nobler hymnody; and to this, I fancy, is due the fact that many of the early hymns are little more than Bible narrative in verse — the form of that verse being due to the influence exerted by the Volkslied, or popular song of the time, which was largely in the ballad style. The following are specimens, which, by reason of their simplicity and freshness, seem to me very beautiful:—

The first is on the Incarnation—

A ship comes sailing onwards
  With a precious freight on board;
It bears the only Son of God,
  It bears the Eternal Word.

A precious freight it brings us,
  Glides gently on, yet fast;
Its sails are filled with Holy Love,
  The Spirit is its mast.

And now it casteth anchor,
  The ship hath touched the land:
God's Word hath taken flesh, the Son
  Among us men doth stand.

At Bethlehem, in the manger,
  He lies, a babe of days;
For us He gives Himself to death,
  O give Him thanks and praise.

Whoe'er would hope in gladness
  To kiss this Holy Child,
Must suffer many a pain and woe
  Patient like Him and mild;

Must die with Him to evil
  And rise to righteousness,
That so with Christ he too may share
  Eternal life and bliss.

The second is on the Resurrection—

There went three damsels ere break of day,
To the Holy Grave they took their way;
They fain would anoint the Lord once more
As Mary Magdalene did before. Alleluia.

The damsels each to other made moan,
"Who will roll us away the stone,
That we may enter in amain
To anoint the Lord as we are fain?"

Full precious spices and salve they brought,
But when they came to the spot they sought,
Behold the grave doth open stand,
An angel sitteth on either hand.

"Ye maidens, be not filled with fear
He whom ye seek, He is not here;
Behold the raiment white and fair
Which the Lord was wrapped in, lieth there.

"Ye maidens, do not here delay,
Ye must to Galilee away;
To Galilee ye now must go,
For there the Lord Himself will show."

But Mary Magdalene could not depart,
Seeking the Lord, she wept apart;
What saw she in a little while?
She saw our Lord upon her smile.

In garb and wise He met her there
As were He a gardener, and did bear
A spade within His holy hand,
As would He dig the garden land.

"O tell me, gentle Gardener thou,
Where hast thou laid my Master now?
Where thou hast hidden Him bid me know,
Or my heart must break beneath its woe."

Scarce could He speak a single word,
Ere she beheld it was the Lord;
She kneeleth down on the cold bare stone,
She hath found her Lord, and she alone.

"Touch me not, Mary Magdalene,
But tell the brethren what thou hast seen;
Touch me not now with human hand,
Until I ascend to my Father's land." Alleluia.

Some of the popular songs of the time, too, were themselves adapted to a religious use, so that, in some cases, the religious supplanted, in public esteem, the secular versions. The following is an adaptation of the song of a wandering artisan, beginning "Innsbruck, I must forsake thee":—

O World, I must forsake thee,
And far away betake me,
To seek my native shore;
So long I've dwelt in sadness
I wish not now for gladness,
Earth's joys for me are o'er.

Sore is my grief and lonely,
And I can tell it only
To Thee, my Friend most sure
God, let Thy hand uphold me,
Thy pitying heart enfold me,
For else I am most poor.

My Refuge where I hide me,
From Thee shall nought divide me,
No pain, no poverty:
Nought is too bad to bear it,
If Thou art there to share it;
My heart asks only Thee.

But it was not till the year 1467, when the followers of John Huss formed themselves into a separate Church, that hymns came into common use in the mother tongue. Huss himself laid stress on the people taking part in the song of the Church, and, with a view to this, composed a number of excellent hymns in the Bohemian. These, together with many that had previously existed, were collected by Lucas, a Senior or Bishop of the "Brethren," and formed the "first hymn-book of original compositions in the vernacular to be found in any Western nation which had once owned the supremacy of Rome. Before this, there were two or three collections of German versions of the Latin Hymns and Sequences."*

* Winkworth's "Christian Singers of Germany," p. 95.

But, after all, we must wait till the Reformation for the great outburst of German Hymnody. Before this, the whole influence of the Roman Church, then dominant in the land, was against hymn singing in the vernacular, which could only flourish among the sects, more or less, under its ban. It was only the resolute who had courage enough to defy the dominant Church. In Germany, as in England, the Dissenters were the first hymn-singers, and in both countries this fact restricted the sphere of hymnody. It could not take on national forms. It always, more or less, bore the mark of reproach. In Germany, the Reformation altered all this; indeed, hymn-singing was one great means by which the Reformation movement was fostered. All before were but as the fore-gleams of the coming glory. One of the first things Luther set himself to do, after he had given the German people a translation of the Bible, was to furnish them with a German Liturgy; and, to render this complete, he felt that he must give them German hymns in the place of the Latin Hymns and Sequences which had formerly been sung in the Roman Church. He saw clearly the large part which hymns might fill in the religion of so musical a people as his countrymen. He says:—"For I would fain see all arts, especially music, in the service of Him who has given and created them." On this point, he differed widely from the men who led the Calvinistic Churches. He was of a more human type than Calvin—had a larger heart, and a more gracious idea of religion. He reached a point which it took some generations for the Calvinists to reach, if, indeed, they ever quite reached it. The Puritans, indeed, had in their midst a finer poet than

Luther, but they never introduced even Milton's superb renderings of certain of the Psalms into their worship. What a use Luther would have put Milton to, if he had been a member of his Church! What songs he would have written! Aye, and what music, too! To his friend Spalatin, Luther writes:—"It is my intention, after the example of the prophets and the ancient fathers, to make German psalms for the people; that is, spiritual songs, whereby the Word of God may be kept alive among them by singing. We seek, therefore, everywhere for poets. Now, as you are such a master of the German tongue, and are so mighty and eloquent therein, I entreat you to join hands with us in this work, and to turn one of the psalms into a hymn, according to the pattern (*i.e.*, an attempt of my own) that I here send you. But I desire that all new-fangled words from the Court should be left out; that the words may be all quite plain and common, such as the common people may understand, yet pure, and skilfully handled; and next, that the meaning should be given clearly and graciously, according to the sense of the psalm itself."

"The miner's son, who, in his school-days, had carolled for bread before the doors of the burghers of Eisenach, remembered the old melodies when the hearts of the people were looking to him for the 'bread which satisfieth,' and gave forth out of his treasure-house things new and old. The great Reformer of the German Church was also her first great singer. Luther gave the German people their hymn-book as well as their Bible. He brought over some of the best old hymns into the new worship; not word by word, in the ferry-boat of a literal translation, but entire and living, like Israel through the

Jordan, when the priests' feet, bearing the ark, swept back the waters."*

Thirty-seven hymns he *certainly* wrote. Some have said more, but probably they are in error. Of these, twelve were translations from the Latin, four new versions of the German *Leisen*, and twenty-one original compositions. These came at once into use, and had not to encounter the long-continued opposition which hymns in England had, where they only gradually became incorporated into the common song of the Church. Luther's hymns were at once printed and carried all over the country by wandering students and pedlars; some of them even found their way into Roman Catholic churches, so that a Romanist declared: "The whole people is singing itself into the Lutheran doctrine." Many hymn-books now appeared, four of which contained most of his hymns, and for them he wrote prefaces. After four or five years, Luther taught the people in his own church at Wittenberg to sing in worship, and then the custom spread very swiftly. "Of these, the earliest, the Enchiridion published at Erfurt in 1524 was first placed in the people's hands for reading while the choir was singing, for the congregation was so unused to joining in the public service, that they could not, at once, adopt the new practice."†

By far the best known of Luther's hymns is that on the forty-sixth psalm, which Frederick the Great called "God Almighty's Grenadier March," and which is usually supposed to have been written on his way to the Diet of Worms, on account of the likeness of the

* "Voice of Christian Life in Song," p. 256.

† Winkworth's "Christian Singers of Germany," p. 109.

third verse to Luther's celebrated and oft-quoted reply to Spalatin, who would have dissuaded him from the journey, "If there were as many devils in Worms as there are tiles on the roofs, I would go and not be afraid." Others think that it was composed at the close of the Second Diet of Spires in 1529, which revoked the religious liberty granted in the previous one of 1526, when four Protestant provinces and fifteen free cities *protested*, out of which sprang the name *Protestant*—a name seldom used in Germany, where the word Evangelical is used, but constantly in England.

It is impossible to fix, with certainty, the occasion which gave birth to this hymn. All the efforts to do so have sprung out of conjecture and internal probability. Perhaps the most nervous translation is that by Thomas Carlyle, which I append, but that already quoted in Chapter xvi, by Godfrey Thring, is more suitable for use in public worship:—

A safe stronghold our God is still,
  A trusty shield and weapon:
He'll help us clear from all the ill
  That hath us now o'ertaken.
    The ancient prince of hell
    Hath risen with purpose fell;
    Strong mail of craft and power
    He weareth in this hour:
  On earth is not his fellow.

With force of arms we nothing can;
  Full soon were we down-ridden;
But for us fights the proper Man,
  Whom God Himself hath bidden.
    Ask ye, Who is this same?
    Christ Jesus is His name,
    The Lord Sabaoth's Son:
    He, and no other one,
  Shall conquer in the battle.

And were this world all devils o'er,
And watching to devour us,
We lay it not to heart so sore;
Not they can overpower us.
And let the prince of ill
Look grim as e'er he will,
He harms us not a whit:
For why? his doom is writ;
A word shall quickly slay him.

God's word! for all their craft and force,
One moment will not linger;
But, spite of hell, shall have its course:
'Tis written by His finger.
And though they take our life,
Goods, honour, children, wife;
Yet is their profit small:
These things shall vanish all;
The city of God remaineth.

This is *now* the most popular of Luther's hymns, but one which he called "A thanksgiving for the highest benefits which God has shown in Christ," a kind of doctrinal confession, was at the time, as is not to be wondered at, more popular. "A curious use was made of it in the year 1557, when a number of princes belonging to the reformed religion being assembled at Frankfort, they wished to have an evangelical service in the church of St. Bartholomew. A large congregation assembled, but the pulpit was occupied by a Roman Catholic priest, who proceeded to preach according to his own views. After listening for some time in indignant silence, the whole congregation rose and began to sing this hymn, till they fairly sang the priest out of church. Its tune is that known in England as Luther's Hymn, and tradition says that Luther noted it down from the singing of a travelling artisan." "'Out of the depths I cry to Thee' he sang when recovering from a fainting fit, brought on by the intensity of spiritual conflict; and when, at last, his dead body was borne through Halle, on its way to its last resting place at Wittenberg, his countrymen thronged into the Church where it was laid, and, amidst their tears and sobs, sang this hymn beside it" :—

Out of the depths I cry to Thee,
  Lord God, O hear my wailing!
Thy gracious ear incline to me,
  And make my prayer availing:
On my misdeeds in mercy look,
O deign to blot them from Thy book,
  Or who can stand before Thee?

Thy sovereign grace and boundless love
  Make Thee, O Lord, forgiving;
My purest thoughts and deeds but prove
  Sin in my heart is living:
None guiltless in Thy sight appear.
All who approach Thy throne must fear,
  And humbly trust Thy mercy.

Thou canst be merciful while just,
  This is my hope's foundation;
On Thy redeeming grace I trust.
  Grant me, then, Thy salvation:
Shielded by Thee I stand secure,
Thy word is firm, Thy promise sure,
  And I rely upon Thee.

Like those who watch for midnight's hour
  To hail the dawning morrow
I wait for Thee, I trust Thy power,
  Unmoved by doubt or sorrow.
So thus let Israel hope in Thee,
And he shall find Thy mercy free,
  And Thy redemption plenteous.

Where'er the greatest sins abound,
  By grace they are exceeded;
Thy helping hand is always found
  With aid, where aid is needed;
Thy hand, the only hand to save.
Will rescue Israel from the grave,
  And pardon his transgression.

His sweet Christmas Hymn, "Von Himmel hoch da komm ich her," was written in 1531, for his little son Hans, who was then four years old. It was described in the first editions of his hymn book as "A children's song from the second chapter of St. Luke, drawn up by Dr. M. L."

Oh! let us all be glad to-day,
And with the shepherds homage pay:
Come, see what God to us hath given,
His only Son, sent down from heaven.

Awake, my soul! from sadness rise,
Come, see what in the manger lies:
Who is this smiling infant child?—
'Tis little Jesus, sweet and mild.

Twice welcome, O thou heavenly Guest,
To save a world with sin distressed:
Com'st Thou in lowly guise for me?
What homage shall I give to Thee?

Ah! Lord eternal, heavenly King,
Hast Thou become so mean a thing;
And hast Thou left Thy blissful seat,
To rest where colts and oxen eat?

Were this wide world much wider made,
With gold and costly gems arrayed:
E'en then, by far too mean 'twould be,
To make a little crib for Thee.

No silken robes surround Thy head,
A bunch of hay is all Thy bed!
Where Thou, a King so rich and great,
Art bright as in Thy heavenly state.

Jesus, my Saviour, come to me—
Make here a little crib for Thee:
A bed make in this heart of mine,
That I may aye remember Thine.

Then from my soul glad songs shall ring—
Of Thee each day I'll gaily sing:
The glad hosannas will I raise
From heart that loves to sing Thy praise.

"From the old Latin Psalmody, he gave a free rhymed translation of the *Te Deum*, and several of the Ambrosian hymns. The Funeral Hymn, 'Media in vita in morte sumus' (see Chapter V), composed by Notker, a monk of St. Gall, A.D. 900 (the first lines of which appear in our

Burial Service), he poured forth anew in three verses, and infused into it a tone of confidence and hope very faintly audible in the original."*

I have lingered over Luther's work in hymnody, not because he is largely represented in our English collections —this is not the case: partly because many of his hymns were written for a condition of religious thought so different from that which now prevails, and partly because, in the main, they are in a style and metre which suit the German, but do not suit the English style of music; the former is more massive and solid, the latter lighter and quicker in movement. This accounts for the fact that, from the great stores of German hymnody, comparatively few have become naturalised and popular in England, and even those that have, owe much of their popularity to the fact that, passing through the mind of English translators, they have caught much of the English spirit; in the most popular translations, though the ideas are German, the style is English. Slavishly literal translations have always been failures. Only when a really poetic mind has done the work of translation, have they caught the ear, and moved the heart, of English folk. But I have tarried over Luther rather because he is the real founder in Germany—as was Dr. Watts in England—of a really popular hymnody in the common speech of the people. Concerning the hymnists who followed, I can only speak, and give illustrations, of those whose hymns have come, through translations, into English use. This will be clear when I say that the "Liederschatz" of Albrecht Knapp includes a list of no less than four hundred writers.

*"Voice of Christian Life in Song," p. 257.

Luther's principal co-workers in hymnody were Justus Jonas, his colleague in the department of theology at Wittenberg (who assisted Luther in preparing metrical versions of the Psalms), and Paul Eber, who held a similar relationship to Melancthon.

Nicholas Decius, (died 1529) a converted monk, is well-known by his German version of the "Gloria in Excelsis," which, when wedded to its fine chorale, became popular, and was sung by all classes of the people, and on the most stirring occasions, all over Germany. Mendelssohn introduced it into his Oratorio, *St. Paul.* The following translation of it is by W. Bartholomew:—

To God on high be thanks and praise,
Who deigns our bonds to sever:
His cares our drooping souls upraise,
And harm shall reach us never:
On Him we rest, with faith assured,
Of all that live, the mighty Lord,
For ever and for ever.

"The general character of Lutheran hymnology in the sixteenth century is its true churchliness and popular style. It is doctrinal, devotional, and bears the impress of objectiveness. The poet does not give vent to his own frame of mind, his individual feelings, but the Church itself, through his lips, confesses, believes, comforts, praises, and adores.

"At the same time, it is truly popular, truthful, natural, cordial, bold, and fearless in expression; moving with rapid steps; no pausing, no retrospect, no minute delineations, or extended descriptions, no didactic demonstrations. In its outward form, it followed the old German epos, and popular narrative poetry, and aimed, above all, at being not only read but sung, and sung by the congregation."*

So popular had hymns become, that even royal and noble personages, like the Elector John of Saxony, and the Margrave George of Brandenburg, became contributors to this department. Southern Germany now began to take its share in this work. Hans Sachs, of Nuremburg, the shoemaker (born 1494), wrote and published more than 6,000 poems of every kind, amongst which there were many hymns. One of these, "Why art thou thus cast down, my heart?" is included in "The Chorale Book for England." He had great fears that now his countrymen had become freed from the yoke of Rome they would quarrel among themselves, and he therefore exhorts them to "Love God above all, and thy neighbour as thyself; against that doctrine ban and edict, clergy and laity, school and preaching, monks and old women, will alike be powerless."

Among the Bohemian Brethren arose several writers of great excellence; notably Michael Weiss, (died 1540) pastor of the German-speaking congregations of Landskron and Fulnek, who translated the best of the Bohemian hymns into German for their use, and contributed some of his own. One of the finest is the following Evening Hymn, which has been included in a few English collections:—

Now God be with us, for the night is closing,
The light and darkness are of his disposing;
And 'neath His shadow here to rest we yield us,
For He will shield us.

Let evil thoughts and spirits flee before us;
Till morning cometh, watch, O Master, o'er us;
In soul and body Thou from harm defend us,
Thine angels send us.

* Kurtz's "Church History," vol. ii, p. 123.

Let holy thoughts be ours when sleep o'ertakes us,
Our earliest thoughts be Thine when morning wakes us;
All day serve Thee, in all that we are doing,
Thy praise pursuing.

As Thy beloved, soothe the sick and weeping,
And bid the prisoner lose his griefs in sleeping;
Widows and orphans we to Thee commend them,
Do Thou befriend them.

We have no refuge, none on earth to aid us,
Save Thee, O Father, who Thine own hast made us;
But Thy dear presence will not leave them lonely
Who seek Thee only.

Father, Thy name be praised, Thy kingdom given,
Thy will be done on earth as 'tis in heaven;
Keep us in life, forgive our sins, deliver
Us now and ever. Amen.

"The two friends and fellow-helpers, the pastor and precentor of Joachimsthal — Johann Matthesius and Nicolas Hermann," did excellent work, but of a simpler and freer kind than most of their predecessors. From the former we have "My inmost heart now raises" ("Chorale Book," No. 164), which was used as a daily morning hymn by Gustavus Adolphus, and often sung by his army as their morning prayer. From the latter, we have "The happy sunshine all is gone" ("Chorale Book," No. 166), and "Now hush your cries, and shed no tear" (*Lyra Germanica*, II, p. 251).

In the latter part of the sixteenth century, a different spirit appears in German Hymnody—it is like the age which followed Watts and Wesley—a kind of after-glow. Hymn-writing had become fashionable and common, with the usual results, that its spontaneity and freshness departed. Still, even in this age, striking hymns appeared. To it we owe Ringwaldt's hymn, "Great God, what do I see and hear," which has undergone so many changes in our English collections; and Philip Nicolai's grand hymn, which owes its solemn tone to the remarkable circumstances under which it was written:— "In 1597, during a fearful pestilence in Westphalia, where he was pastor of the little town of Unna, more than 1,400 persons died in a very short time, and from his window he saw all the funerals pass to the graveyard close at hand. From these scenes of death, he turned to the study of St. Augustine's 'City of God,' and the contemplation of the eternal life, and so absorbed himself in them, that he remained cheerful and well amid the surrounding distress." Here is the hymn:—

Wake, awake, for night is flying:
The watchmen on the heights are crying
Awake, Jerusalem, arise!
Midnight's solemn hour is tolling,
His chariot-wheels are nearer rolling,
He comes; prepare, ye Virgins wise;
Rise up; with willing feet
Go forth, the Bridegroom meet:
Alleluia!
Bear through the night your well-trimmed light,
Speed forth to join the marriage rite.

Sion hears the watchmen singing,
Her heart with deep delight is springing,
At once she wakes, she hastes away:
Forth her Bridegroom hastens glorious,
In grace arrayed, by truth victorious;
Her grief is joy, her night is day:
Hail, Worthy Champion,
Christ, God Almighty's Son:
Alleluia!
We haste along, in pomp of song,
And gladsome join the marriage throng.

Hear Thy praise, O Lord, ascending
From tongues of men and angels, blending,
With harp and lute and psaltery.
By Thy pearly gates in wonder
We stand and swell the voice of thunder,
In bursts of choral melody:
No vision ever brought,
No ear hath ever caught,
Such bliss and joy:
We raise the song, we swell the throng,
To praise Thee ages all along.

Which is still better known by its use, in the following form, in Mendelssohn's *St. Paul* :—

Sleepers, wake ! a voice is calling ;
It is the Watchman on the walls,
Thou city of Jerusalem !
For lo ! the Bridegroom comes.
Arise, and take your lamps.
Hallelujah !
Awake ! His kingdom is at hand !
Go forth, go forth to meet your Lord !

Equally striking is the following from his pen :—

Behold how glorious is yon sky !
Lo ! there the righteous never die,
But dwell in peace for ever :
Then who would wear this earthly clay,
When bid to cast life's chains away,
And win Thy gracious favour ?
Holy, holy, O forgive us ;
And receive us, heavenly Father,
When around Thy throne we gather.

Confiding in Thy sacred word,
Our Saviour is our hope, O Lord,
The guiding star before us ;
Our Shepherd, leading us the way,
If from Thy paths our footsteps stray,
To Thee He will restore us :
Holy, Holy, ever hear us,
And receive us, while we gather
Round Thy throne, Almighty Father.

To these hymns he composed chorales, which added largely to their popularity.

"The first period of hymn development in the 17th century, embraces that of the Thirty Years' War (1618-48). David's Psalms become the model and type of the poets ; and the most earnest hymns of comfort in trouble, of imperishable value, spring from the trials of the times. This, of course, caused prominence to be given to personal matters. The influence of Opitz is also seen in church hymns, inasmuch as more care is given to precision and purity of language, as well as to a fluent and pleasing measure. Instead of the expressive brevity and vigorous terseness of earlier times, we meet with a certain cordial expansion and enlargement of the thought."*

In 1644, Martin Rinkart composed what is certainly the most popular, and also one of the most beautiful hymns, the "Te Deum" of Germany, used on all great occasions of national thanksgiving, and which Mendelssohn introduced into his *Hymn of Praise.*

Now thank we all our God,
With heart, and hands, and voices,
Who wondrous things hath done,
In whom His world rejoices;
Who, from our mothers' arms,
Hath blessed us on our way
With countless gifts of love,
And still is ours to-day.

O may this bounteous God
Through all our life be near us,
With ever joyful hearts
And blessèd peace to cheer us:
And keep us in His grace,
And guide us when perplexed,
And free us from all ills
In this world and the next.

All praise and thanks to God
The Father, now be given,
The Son, and Him who reigns
With Them in highest heaven—
The One Eternal God,
Whom earth and heaven adore,—
For thus it was, is now,
And shall be evermore.

It was written on the prospect of peace after the Thirty Years' War. The first two verses are a metrical version of a passage in the apocryphal Book of Ecclesiasticus, which reads as follows:—"Now, therefore, bless ye the God of all, who only doeth wondrous things everywhere,

* Kurtz's "Church History," vol. ii, p. 190.

who exalteth our days from the womb, and dealeth with us according to His mercy. He grants us joyfulness of heart, and that peace may be in our days in Israel for ever; that He would confirm His mercy with us, and deliver us at His time." The following rendering is by William Bartholomew:—

Let all men praise the Lord,
In worship lowly bending;
On His most holy word,
Redeemed from woe, depending.
He gracious is, and just.
From childhood us doth lead;
On Him we place our trust
And hope, in time of need.

Glory and praise to God,—
To Father, Son, be given,
And to the Holy Ghost,—
On high, enthroned in heaven.
Praise to the Triune God:
With powerful arm and strong,
He changeth night to day;
Praise Him with grateful song.

Miss Winkworth's account of Rinkart is so interesting, and shows how much hymns owe, not merely to innate faculty, but to the circumstances of the writer, that I append it:—"This simple but noble expression of trust and praise, with its fine chorale, was composed by Martin Rinkart, in 1644, when the hope of a general peace was dawning on the country. He was one of those provincial clergymen to whom Germany had so much reason to be grateful. The son of a poor coppersmith, he made his way at the University of Leipsic by dint of industry and his musical gifts, took orders, and was precentor of the church at Eisleben, and at the age of thirty-one was offered the place of Archdeacon at his native town of Eilenburg, in Saxony. He went there as the war broke out, and died just after the peace, and throughout these thirty-one years he stood by his flock, and helped them to the utmost, under every kind of distress. Of course, he had to endure the quartering of soldiers in his house, and frequent plunderings of his little stock of grain and household goods. But these were small things. The plague of 1637 visited Eilenburg with extraordinary severity; the town was overcrowded with fugitives from the country districts, where the Swedes had been spreading devastation, and in this one year eight thousand persons died in it. The whole of the town council except three persons, a terrible number of school children, and the clergymen of the neighbouring parish, were all carried off; and Rinkart had to do the work of three men, and did it manfully at the beds of the sick and dying. He buried more than four thousand persons, but through all his labours he himself remained perfectly well. The pestilence was followed by a famine so extreme that thirty or forty persons might be seen fighting in the streets for a dead cat or crow. Rinkart, with the burgomaster and one other citizen, did what could be done to organise assistance, and gave away everything but the barest rations for his own family, so that his door was surrounded by a crowd of poor starving wretches, who found it their only refuge. After all this suffering came the Swedes once more, and imposed upon the unhappy town a tribute of thirty thousand florins. Rinkart ventured to the camp to intreat the general for mercy, and when it was refused, turned to the citizens who followed him, saying, 'Come, my children, we can find no hearing, no mercy with men, let us take refuge with God.' He fell on his knees, and prayed with such touching earnestness that the Swedish general relented, and lowered his demand at last to two thousand florins. So great were Rinkart's own losses and charities that he had the utmost difficulty in finding bread and clothes for his children, and was forced to mortgage his future income for several years. Yet how little his spirit was broken by all these calamities is shown by this hymn, and others that he wrote; some, indeed, speaking of his country's sorrows, but all breathing the same spirit of unbounded trust and readiness to give thanks."

To a period a little later belongs Paul Gerhardt, (1606-1676) perhaps the sweetest of the German hymnists. Miss Winkworth gives the following graphic account of his life:—"He was born in 1606, in a little town, Gräfinhainichen, in Saxony, where his father was burgomaster. The whole of his youth and early manhood fell in the time of war. That it must have been a period full of disappointment and hope deferred for him, is clear enough when we find a man of his powers at the age of forty-five still only a private tutor, and candidate for holy orders. In 1651 he was living in this capacity in the family of an advocate named Berthold, in Berlin. He had already written many hymns, but was as yet unable to publish them; and he was in love with Berthold's daughter, but had no living to marry upon. About the close of that year, however, the living of a country place called Mittenwalde was offered him; he was ordained, and in 1655 he at last married Anna Maria Berthold. At Mittenwalde he passed six quiet years, during which he began to publish his hymns, which immediately attracted great attention, and were quickly adopted into the hymn-books of Brandenburg and Saxony. His name thus became known, and in 1657 he was invited to the great church of St. Nicholas, in Berlin, where his life was soon both a busy and an honourable one. He worked most assiduously and successfully in his pastoral duties; he brought out many hymns, which were caught up by the people much as Luther's had been of old; and he was the favourite preacher of the city, whom crowds flocked to hear. He is described to us as a man of middle height, of quiet but firm and cheerful bearing; while his preaching is said to have been very earnest and persuasive, and full of Christian love and charity, which he practised as well as preached by never turning a beggar from his doors, and receiving widows and orphans who needed help and shelter into his own house. His religion and his temperament alike made him cheerful, and not all the many disappointments of his life seem ever to have embittered his mood; but he had a very tender and scrupulous conscience, and wherever a question of conscience seemed to him to be involved, he was liable to great mental conflict, and an exaggerated estimate of trifles. In theology he was an ardent Lutheran." His portrait in the church at Lübben bears the inscription: "Theologus in cribro Satanæ versatus," a divine sifted in Satan's sieve.

For spontaneity, simplicity, purity, he stands pre-eminent among the German writers, and is perhaps the greatest favourite in England, so much so that I need only mention his hymns. The following are the finest: "Jesus, Thy boundless love to me," translated by John Wesley; "O Sacred Head, once wounded," a hymn by Bernard of Clairvaux, which owes much to Gerhardt's handling, translated by Dr. J. W. Alexander; "Commit thou all thy griefs," translated by John Wesley; and "Evening and Morning," translated by Richard Massie.

The Electress Louisa of Brandenburg deserves mention as a hymnist of no mean order.

George Neumarck (1621-1681) deserves very high rank, and is indeed one of the most famous of German hymnists. Of him, the following touching story is told:—"About two years after the close of the Thirty Years' War in Germany, George Neumarck lived in a poor street in Hamburg. Obtaining a precarious livelihood by playing on the violoncello, after a while he fell sick, and was unable to go his usual rounds. As this was his only means of support, he was soon reduced to great straits, and was compelled to part with his instrument to a Jew, who, with characteristic sharpness, lent him on it a sum much below its value for two weeks, after which, if it were not redeemed, it was to be forfeited. As he gave it up, he looked lovingly at it, and tearfully asked the Jew if he might play one more tune upon it. 'You don't know,' he said, 'how hard it is to part with it. For ten years it has been my companion; if I had nothing else, I had it; and it spoke to me, and sung back to me. Of all the sad hearts that have left your door, there has been none so sad as mine.' His voice grew thick; then pausing for a moment, he seized the instrument and commenced a tune so exquisitely soft that even the Jew listened, in spite of himself. A few more strains, and he sung to his own melody, two stanzas of his own hymn, 'Life is weary; Saviour take me.' Suddenly the key changed; a few bars, and the melody poured forth itself anew, and his face lighted up with a smile as he sung 'Yet who knows the cross is precious.' Then laying down the instrument, he said: 'As God will, I am still,' and rushed from the shop. Going out into the darkness, he stumbled against a stranger, who seemed to have been listening at the door, and who said to him: 'Could you tell me where I could obtain a copy of that song? I would willingly give a florin for it.' 'My good friend,' said Neumarck, 'I will give it you without the florin.' The stranger was valet to the Swedish ambassador, and to him the poet told the story of his trials. He, in his turn, told his master, who, being in want of a private secretary, engaged Neumarck at once, and so his troubles ended. But with his first money he redeemed his instrument, and, on obtaining it, he called his landlady, and his friends and neighbours, to hear him play on it again. Soon his room was filled, and he sung, to his own accompaniment, his own sweet hymn, of which this is one stanza:—

Leave God to order all thy ways,
  And hope in Him whate'er betide;
Thou'lt find Him, in the evil days,
  Thine all sufficient strength and guide,
Who trusts in God's unchanging love,
Builds on the rock that naught can move.

The following hymns from his pen are growing in favour in our country. The first has been translated by Catherine Winkworth:—

If thou but suffer God to guide thee,
  And hope in Him through all thy ways,
He'll give thee strength, whate'er betide thee,
  And bear thee through the evil days;
  Who trust in God's unchanging love,
  Build on the Rock that nought can move.

Only be still, and wait His leisure
  In cheerful hope, with heart content
To take whate'er thy Father's pleasure
  And all-discerning love hath sent:
  Nor doubt our inmost wants are known
  To Him who chose us for His own.

Nor think, amid the heat of trial,
  That God hath cast thee off unheard,
That he whose hopes meet no denial
  Must surely be of God preferred;

Time passes and much change doth bring,
And sets a bound to everything.

All are alike before the Highest;
'Tis easy to our God, we know,
To raise thee up, though low thou liest,
To make the rich man poor and low;
True wonders still by Him are wrought,
Who setteth up and brings to nought.

Sing, pray, and keep His ways unswerving,
So do thine own part faithfully,
And trust His word, though undeserving,
Thou yet shalt find it true for thee;
God never yet forsook at need
The soul that trusted Him indeed.

The second has been translated by W. Bartholomew and introduced by Mendelssohn into his oratorio of *St. Paul.*

To Thee, O Lord, I yield my spirit,
Who break'st in love this mortal chain;
My life I but from Thee inherit,
And death becomes my chiefest gain.
In Thee I live, in Thee I die,
Content—for Thou art ever nigh.

Angelus Silesius, whose real name was Johann Scheffler, (1624-1677) but who adopted the name Angelus after a Spanish Mystic, John of Angelus, of the 16th century, adding Silesius to it because of his birth at Breslau, in Silesia, a physician, so deeply influenced by the Mystic writers, that he found no congenial atmosphere in the somewhat dogmatic and doctrinal Lutheranism of his time—a man of wide charity—is a hymnist of great excellence, as may be seen from the following translation by Catherine Winkworth :—

O Love, who formedst me to wear
The image of Thy Godhead here;
Who soughtest me with tender care
Through all my wanderings wild and drear;
O Love, I give myself to Thee,
Thine ever, only Thine to be.

O Love, who once in time wast slain,
Pierced through and through with bitter woe;

O Love, who wrestling thus didst gain
That we eternal joy might know;
O Love, I give myself to Thee,
Thine ever, only Thine to be.

O Love, of whom is truth and light,
The Word and Spirit, life and power,
Whose heart was bared to them that smite,
To shield us in our trial hour;
O Love, I give myself to Thee,
Thine ever, only Thine to be

O Love, who thus hast bound me fast,
Beneath that gentle yoke of Thine;
Love who hast conquered me at last,
And rapt away this heart of mine;
O Love, I give myself to Thee,
Thine ever, only Thine to be.

O Love, who soon shalt bid me rise
From out this dying life of ours;
O Love, who once above yon skies
Shall set me in the fadeless bowers;
O Love, I give myself to Thee,
Thine ever, only Thine to be.

Equally beautiful is the following, translated by John Wesley:—

Thee will I love, my strength, my tower
Thee will I love, my joy, my crown;
Thee will I love with all my power,
In all Thy works, and Thee alone.
Thee will I love, till the pure fire
Fills my whole soul with strong desire.

I thank Thee, uncreated Sun,
That Thy bright beams on me have shined;
I thank Thee, who has overthrown
My foes, and healed my wounded mind;
I thank Thee, Lord, whose quickening voice
Bids my freed heart in Thee rejoice.

Uphold me in the doubtful race,
Nor suffer me again to stray;
Strengthen my feet with steady pace
Still to press forward in Thy way;
My soul and flesh, O Lord of might,
Transfigure with Thy heavenly light.

Thee will I love, my joy, my crown;
Thee will I love, my Lord, my God;

Thee will I love, beneath Thy frown
Or smile—Thy sceptre or Thy rod;
What though my flesh and heart decay
Thee shall I love in endless day!

Some of his spiritual aphorisms, too, are very suggestive:

" Th' Unspeakable, that men use God to call,
Utters and shows itself in the One Word to all.

God is all virtue's aim, its impulse and its prize,
In Him its sole reward, its only 'wherefore' lies.

The nobler aught, the commoner 'twill be,
God and His sunshine to the world are free.

My God, how oft do I Thy gifts implore,
Yet know I crave Thyself, oh, how much more!
Give what Thou wilt, eternal life or aught,
If Thou withhold Thyself, Thou giv'st me nought.

All goodness flows from God, therefore 'tis His alone;
Evil springs up in thee, that may'st thou call thy own.
Is aught of good in thee? Give God the praise of all;
To claim it for thine own, is ever man's true Fall.

The noblest prayer is, when one evermore
Grows inly liker that he kneels before.

Faith by itself is dead, it cannot live and move
Till into it is breathed the living soul of Love.

The rose demands no reasons, she blooms and scents the air,
Nor asks if any see her, nor knows that she is fair.

How fairly shines the snow, whene'er the sun's bright beams
Illume and colour it with heavenly gleams;
So shines thy soul, white, dazzling as the snow,
When o'er it plays the Day-spring's radiant glow."

Belonging to the same school as Scheffler is Knorr von Rosenroth, (1636-1689) a pious baron and diplomatist, whose "Dayspring of Eternity" (Chorale Book, No. 159) is a lovely hymn, probably composed during a walk at the time of sunrise.

The Pietists (1660—1750) produced many good hymnists, among whom I may mention as known by translations in English, Frederick Rudolph Louis, Baron von Canitz, (1654-1699) Chamberlain to Prince Elector Frederick William, whose morning hymn is very fine.

Come, my soul, thou must be waking,
Now is breaking
O'er the earth another day:
Come to Him who made this splendour,
See thou render
All thy feeble strength can pay.

Gladly hail the sun returning;
Ready burning
Be the incense of thy powers:
For the night is safely ended,
God hath tended
With His care thy helpless hours.

Pray that He may prosper ever
Each endeavour,
When thine aim is good and true;
But that He may ever thwart thee,
And convert thee,
When thou evil wouldst pursue.

Think that He thy ways beholdeth,
He unfoldeth
Every fault that lurks within;
He the hidden shame glossed over
Can discover,
And discern each deed of sin.

Our God's bounteous gifts abuse not,
Light refuse not,
But His Spirit's voice obey;
Thou with Him shalt dwell beholding,
Light unfolding
All things in unclouded day.

Mayst thou on life's morrow,
Free from sorrow,
Pass away in slumber sweet;
And, released from death's dark sadness,
Rise in gladness,
That far brighter sun to greet.

When dying he asked to be lifted to the open window, and his eyes beaming with joy exclaimed: "Oh! if the sight of this created sun is so charming and beautiful, what will be the sight of the unspeakable glory of the Creator Himself?"

Laurentius Laurentii, (1660-1722) is well known by his hymn, "Rejoice, all ye believers."

Charles Henry von Bogatzsky (1690-1774) is known in England rather by his "Golden Treasury," which used to be one of the most favourite books of devotion, than by his hymns, some of which, however, are of great merit.

Joachim Neander (1640-1680), a Bishop of the Church of the United Brethren, who must not be confounded with the great Church Historian of the same name, was one of the most poetic of the German hymnists, as may be seen from the following translation by J. D. Burns:—

Heaven and earth, and sea and air,
Still their Maker's praise declare;
Thou, my soul, as loudly sing,
To thy God thy praises bring.

See the sun his power awakes,
As through clouds his glory breaks;
See the moon and stars of light,
Praising God in stillest night.

See how God this rolling globe
Swathes with beauty like a robe;
Forests, fields, and living things,
Each its Maker's glory sings.

Through the air Thy praises meet,
Birds are singing clear and sweet;
Fire, and storm, and wind, Thy will
As Thy ministers fulfil.

The ocean waves Thy glory tell,
At Thy touch they sink and swell;
From the well-spring to the sea,
Rivers murmur, Lord, of Thee.

Ah! my God, what wonders lie
Hid in Thine infinity!
Stamp upon my inmost heart
What I am, and what Thou art.

"The Pietistic School" were distinguished as hymn-writers by a scriptural-practical and devotional tendency, the spiritual life of believers, the breaking through of grace in conversion, growth in holiness, the changing conditions, experiences, and feelings in the life of the soul, were made the objects of contemplation and description. Their hymns are for the most part no longer for the congregation, for the people, for common worship, but more for individual edification, and for the closet. There are only, relatively speaking, a few hymns of this school that form an exception, and still deserve the name of church-hymns. When pietism declined, the spiritual-poetical inspiration awakened by it declined also gradually; it lost its original truth, power and depth, and degenerated into sentimentality and spiritless trifling with figures, allegories, and phrases." *

To the period between 1690 and 1760 belongs Gerhard Tersteegen (1697-1769) "a mystic of the purest type," and one of the most notable of German hymnists. He is known and loved in England through John Wesley's fine translations of his hymns, "Lo! God is here, let us adore," and "Thou hidden love of God," and probably will be by the hymn which Mrs. Sarah Findlater has rendered so magnificently, "Lord, our God, in reverence lowly," quoted in Chap. XV.

Nicholas Lewis, Count and Lord of Zinzendorf and Pottendorf (1700-1760), was remarkable for his early piety. When quite a child he wrote little notes to Jesus, and threw them out of the window, in the hope that He would find them. His youthful piety was deepened by the sight of an *Ecce Homo* in the picture gallery at Dusseldorf bearing the inscription: "All this I have done for thee; what doest thou for Me?" His earlier years were spent as a layman in philanthropic and missionary work, but later he was ordained, and became a Bishop of the Church of the United Brethren, an office he afterwards—on account of false accusation—resigned.

* Kurtz's "Church History," Vol. ii, p. 235.

His latter days were spent at Herrnhut, where he died May 5th, 1760. His last words to his son-in-law were: "Now, my dear son, I am going to the Saviour. I am ready; I am quite resigned to the will of my Lord. If He is no longer willing to make use of me here, I am quite ready to go to Him; for there is nothing more in my way." He was the real founder of the Moravian Church as it is known to us, the previous form of which, known as the Bohemian Brethren, was of an altogether different type. He was a most prolific hymn-writer—more than 2,000 are said to be from his pen—but a large number are very inferior productions. The best known are "Jesus, Thy blood and righteousness," and "Jesus, still lead on," which is "the first taught to the children in almost every German household." One of his great faults was the exaggerated way in which he spoke of the physical sufferings of Christ. Miss Winkworth says: "Many of his hymns speak of the blood and wounds of Jesus, making a bed in his wounded side, &c., in a way of which it is impossible to give instances." This is a fault common to writers widely severed, as Romanist and Ultra-Evangelical. To the same Moravian company belongs Luise H. von Haym (1724-1782), Superintendent of the Unmarried Sisters' House at Herrnhut, whose child's hymn, translated by Catherine Winkworth, is very beautiful—

Seeing I am Jesus' lamb,
Ever glad at heart I am
O'er my Shepherd kind and good,
Who provides me daily food,
And His lamb by name doth call
For He knows and loves us all.

Guided by His gentle staff,
Where the sunny pastures laugh,

I go in and out and feed,
Lacking nothing that I need;
When I thirst my feet He brings
To the fresh and living springs.

Must I not rejoice for this?
He is mine and I am His.
And when these bright days are past
Safely in His arms at last,
He will bear me home to heaven,
Ah, what joy hath Jesus given!

This is the most favourite children's hymn in Germany. It is learnt and loved by nearly all Protestant children, and is the common prayer which daily they repeat.

Still later we meet with Christian Fürchtegott Gellert (1715-1769), Professor of Poetry and Moral Philosophy in Leipsic University (Lessing and Goethe were among his pupils), the author of "Spiritual Odes and Songs," which Miss Winkworth says "were greeted with an enthusiasm almost like that which greeted Luther's hymns on their first appearance." "'The reverence and affection which Gellert received from all the young men was extraordinary. His lecture-room was always crowded to the utmost; and Gellert's beautiful soul, purity of will, his admonitions, warnings and entreaties, delivered in a somewhat hollow and sad voice, produced a deep impression. A figure not tall, but slender without being thin, soft rather mournful eyes, a very beautiful brow, all rendered his presence agreeable.' Nor was his influence confined to his class-room: a peasant one day laid a load of firewood at his door as a thank-offering for the pleasure derived from his fables; a young Prussian officer sent him a sum of money, entreating him to accept the gift from one whose heart had been raised by his writings; and these were but instances of innumerable similar presents which Gellert used generally to bestow on the poor.

Princes and great people of all kinds made pilgrimages to see him; even Frederick the Great had an interview with him, and pronounced him the most reasonable German professor he had ever come across." "A rumour having spread in Coburg that Gellert had hanged himself, he replied to a friend on hearing it: 'Write to the Coburgers

I have and shall be hanging
For ever on my Lord.'"

The hymn by which he is known in England is "Jesus lives, no longer now," translated by Frances Elizabeth Cox, to whom we owe many fine translations from the German.

To the same period belong Johann Andreas Cramer, and Friedrich Gottlieb Klopstock (1724-1803,—whose poem, "The Messiah," was once so popular); whilst still later there is Novalis (1772-1801—many of their poems were translated by George MacDonald, in a little volume called "Exotics"), and Spitta, Knapp, Gerok, Louise Hensel, and Meta Haussar; some of whose hymns have been translated by Richard Massie, but few have passed from their writings into Church use, save in the case of Spitta (1801-1859), from whom many have been taken, through the renderings of Mr. Massie, in his *Lyra Domestica*. These deserve to be more widely known, as my readers may see by the following specimens. Very full of quiet confidence is the following:—

We are the Lord's, whether we live or die;
We are the Lord's, who for us all hath died;
We are the Lord's, and heirs of the Most High,
We are the Lord's, and shall the Lord's abide.

We are the Lord's—to Him, then, let us live,
With soul and body, both with deeds and words,
While heart, and tongue, and life assurance give,
Of the most precious truth: we are the Lord's.

We are the Lord's,—so shall our hearts ne'er fail,
For one bright star its steady light affords,
To cheer and guide us through the gloomy vale,
It is this blessèd word: we are the Lord's!

We are the Lord's, who will preserve us still,
When none beside Him help to us accords;
In death's last conflict we will fear no ill,
Thy word abideth true: we are the Lord's!

The following is as true in sentiment as it is beautiful in expression:—

We praise and bless Thee, gracious Lord,
  Our Saviour, kind and true,
For all the old things passed away,
  For all Thou hast made new.

New hopes, new purposes, desires,
  And joys, Thy grace has given;
Old ties are broken from the earth,
  New ties attach to heaven.

But yet, how much must be destroyed,
  How much renewed must be,
Ere we can fully stand complete
  In likeness, Lord, to Thee!

Thou, only Thou must carry on
  The work Thou hast begun;
Of Thine own strength Thou must impart
  In Thine own ways to run.

Ah! leave us not; from day to day
  Revive, restore again;
Our feeble steps do Thou direct,
  Our enemies restrain.

So shall we faultless stand at last,
  Before Thy Father's throne;
The blessedness for ever ours,
  The glory all Thine own.

Here is his exquisite hymn calling us by the thought of what we have received, to impart to others:—

O Thou whose grace first found us,
  Whose love our hearts first won,
Thou hast with mercies crowned us,
  As none beside hath done.

Thy mercies bid us bless Thee.
  Thy mercies bid us pray,
That others too may praise Thee,
  And understand Thy way.

Thy mercies bid us witness
  The truth of Thy dear word,
That all may taste its sweetness,
  And bow before the Lord.

And since Thou wert not stricken
  For us alone, but all,
Lord, many save and quicken,—
  We are too few and small!

Here is his lovely Evening Hymn :—

O Lord, who by Thy presence hast made light
The heat and burden of the toilsome day,
Be with me also in the silent night,
Be with me when the daylight fades away.

As Thou hast given me strength upon the way,
So deign at evening to become my Guest;
As Thou hast shared the labours of the day,
So also deign to share and bless my rest.

How sad and cold, if Thou be absent, Lord,
The evening leaves me, and my heart how dead!
But, if Thy presence grace my humble board,
I seem with heavenly manna to be fed.

Fraught with rich blessing, breathing sweet repose,
The calm of evening settles on my breast;
If Thou be with me when my labours close,
No more is needed to complete my rest.

Come, then, O Lord, and deign to be my Guest,
After the day's confusion, toil, and din;
O come to bring me peace, and joy, and rest,
To give salvation, and to pardon sin!

Bind up the wounds, assuage the aching smart,
Left in my bosom from the day just past,
And let me, on a Father's loving heart,
Forget my griefs, and find sweet rest at last!

"In Thy service will I ever," is almost, if not quite, equal to the foregoing.

England has drawn little from German hymnody of a later time than this—chiefly because her own writers have furnished ample material, but partly because the more recent productions of Germany lack the force and distinctiveness of earlier times. Doubtless more would have been drawn from the earlier writers, but that their hymns are so lengthy, and cast in rather a ponderous style, lacking the conciseness and crispness of the finest English hymns. They may be suitable to the land of their birth, but they certainly are not to the English taste. It is best that the staple hymns of each country should be redolent of the soil, or of a soil akin to its own. The hymns that have been drawn from this source are very precious, and we could ill spare them, but it would be a mistake to increase the present proportion of German, or, indeed, of any foreign hymns, in our collections. All hymnals which have started with the idea of increasing that proportion, have been a failure in regard to popular use, and are only valuable as illustrative of German hymnody. Our churches, however, owe a great debt to Catherine Winkworth, Frances Elizabeth Cox, Richard Massie, Jane Borthwick, and her sister—Mrs. Findlater, James Drummond Burns, for their admirable renderings of German hymns, and, in an earlier age, to John Wesley, whose translations have probably never been surpassed.

I will conclude this chapter by the following extract from Alexander Smith, on German hymns in general :—

"In glancing over these German hymns one is struck by their adaptation to the seasons and occurrences of ordinary life. Obviously, too, the writers' religion was not a Sunday matter only; it had its place in the week-days as well. In these hymns there is little gloom; a healthy, human cheerfulness pervades many of them—and this is surely as it ought to be. These hymns, as I have said, are adapted to the occasion of ordinary life, and this speaks favourably of the piety which produced them. I do not suppose that we English are less religious than other nations, but we are undemonstrative in this, as in most things. We have the sincerest horror of over-dressing ourselves in fine sentiments. We are a little shy of religion. We give it a day entirely to itself, and make it a stranger to the other six. We confine it in churches, or in the closet at home, and never think of taking it with us to the street, or into our business, or with us to the festival, or the gathering of friends. Dr. Arnold used to complain that he could get religious subjects treated in a masterly way, but could not get common subjects treated in a religious spirit. The Germans have done better; they have melted down the Sunday into the week. They have hymns embodying confessions of sin; hymns on the near prospect of death; and they have—what is more important—spiritual songs that may be sung by soldiers on the march, by artisans at the loom, by the peasant following his team, by the mother among her children, and by the maiden sitting at her wheel listening for the steps of her lover. Religion is thus brought in to refine and hallow the sweet necessities and emotions of life, to cheer its weariness, and to exalt its sordidness. The German life revolves like the village festival with the pastor in the midst—joy and laughter and merry games do not fear the holy man, for he wears no unkindness in his eye; but his presence checks everything boisterous or unseemly!—the rude word, the petulant act—and when it has run its course, he uplifts his hands and leaves his benediction on his children.

"The *Lyra Germanica* contains the utterances of pious German souls in all conditions of life during many centuries. In it hymns are to be found written not only by poor clergymen, and still poorer precentors, by riband-manufacturers and shoemakers, who, amid rude environments, had a touch of celestial melody in their hearts; but by noble ladies and gentlemen and crowned kings. The oldest in the collection is one written by King Robert of France about the year 1000. It is beautifully simple and pathetic. State is laid aside with the crown, pride with the royal robe, and Lazarus at Dives' gate could not have written out of a lowlier heart. The kingly brow may bear itself high enough before men, the voice may be commanding and imperious enough, cutting through contradiction as with a sword; but before the Highest all is humbleness and bended knees. Other compositions there are, scattered through the volume, by great personages: several by Louisa Henrietta, Electress of Brandenburg, and Anton Ulrick, Duke of Brunswick—all written two hundred years ago. These are genuine poems, full of faith and charity, and calm trust in God. They are all dead now, these noble gentlemen and gentlewomen; their warfare, successful or adverse, has been long closed; but they gleam yet in my fancy, like the white effigies in tombs in dim cathedrals, the marble palms pressed together on the marble breast, the sword by the side of the knight, the psalter by the side of the lady, and flowing around them the scrolls on which are inscribed the texts of resurrection."*

* "Dreamthorpe," by Alexander Smith.

CHAPTER XIX.

FRENCH AND OTHER HYMNS.

Our English Hymnals owe comparatively little to any of the continental nations except the German. This is probably due in part to the fact, that all the Latin races are under the sway of the Roman See, whose doctrine differs largely from ours, whilst in their church worship little space is left for the use of hymns. Had France been Protestant, and therefore psalm-singing, as her lyric gift is quite as strong, if not stronger than that of Germany, she would probably have furnished us with as large, if not a larger, proportion than we have drawn from Germany, especially if her Protestantism had been of the Lutheran rather than the Calvinistic type.* Even the hymns we have taken from France were chiefly written in the Latin tongue for use in French Breviaries. Of some of these I have spoken in earlier chapters of this book in my account of the hymns of Adam of St. Victor, the Bernards, and King

* "In Switzerland, in the Protestant Church of France, and to some extent in Holland, the spread of the German hymns has been checked by the influenee of the Calvinistic churches, which have always feared to give a prominent place to Art of any kind in the worship of God—rather, indeed, have allowed it to creep in on sufferance, than delighted to introduce it as a freewill offering of beauty."—Winkworth's "Christian Singers of Germany,' p. 4.

Robert of France; but to later times belong the following, from whose Latin hymns, translations have passed into some of our English Hymnals :—

From Claude de Santeüil, otherwise known as *Santolius Maglorianus* (1628-1684) we have "Thrice Holy God, of wondrous might" (*Ter sancte, ter potens Deus*); whilst from his brother, J. B. de Santeüil (*Santolius Victorinus*), (1630-1697), we have "In stature grows the Heavenly Child" (*Divine, crescebas, Puer*), "O Christ, who hast prepared a place" (*Nobis, Olympo redditus*), "Long time the fallen human race" (*Pulsum supernis sedibus*), translated by J. Chandler; and "Not by the Martyr's death alone" (*Non parta solo sanguine*), translated by Isaac Williams.

To Charles Coffin (1676-1749), we owe "God from on high hath heard" (*Jam desinant suspiria*), translated by Bishop Woodford; "Great Mover of all hearts, whose hand" (*Supreme Motor cordium*), translated by Isaac Williams; and "As now the sun's declining rays" (*Labente jam solis rota*), "On Jordan's bank the Baptist's cry" (*Jordanis oras prævia*), "What star is this, more glorious far" (*Quae stella sole pulchrior*), "O Lord, how joyful 'tis to see" (*O quam juvat fratres, Deus*), translated by John Chandler.

From Nicolas le Tourneaux, of the latter part of the 17th century, we have "Morn's roseate hues have decked the sky" (*Aurora lucis dum novae*), translated by W. Cooke.

William Cowper translated certain of the *Cantiques Spirituels* of Madame Guyon, which contained about 900 pieces, mostly written to popular ballad tunes. The finest of these is the following, touched with the peculiar and beautiful mysticism of that devoted woman:—

O Thou by long experience tried.
Near whom no grief can long abide,
My Lord! how full of sweet content
My years of pilgrimage are spent.

All scenes alike engaging prove
To souls impressed with sacred love;
Where'er they dwell, they dwell with Thee,
In heaven, in earth, or on the sea.

To me remains nor place nor time;
My country is in every clime;
I can be calm and free from care
On any shore, since God is there.

While place we seek or place we shun,
The soul finds happiness in none;
But with my God to guide my way,
'Tis equal joy to go or stay.

Could I be cast where Thou art not,
That were indeed a dreadful lot:
But regions none remote I call,
Secure of finding God in all.

Then let me to His throne repair,
And never be a stranger there:
Then love divine shall be my guard,
And peace and safety my reward.

Most of the hymns drawn from and written in the French language come to us, as was to be expected, from Protestant sources in Switzerland. Cæsar Malan (1787-1864) was a voluminous hymnist, exceeding Dr. Watts in the *number* of his compositions, but being more akin to Charles Wesley in their character. He is said by his biographer to have written at least a thousand hymns! They were translated into English in 1825 by Ingram Cobbin ("*Hymns by the Rev. Cæsar Malan translated into English verse*"); and in 1866 by Miss Arnold (*Lyra Evangelica*). The best known is the following, translated by G. W. Bethune:—

It is not death to die—
To leave this weary road,
And 'midst the brotherhood on high
To be at home with God.

It is not death to close
The eye long dimmed by tears,
And wake in glorious repose
To spend eternal years.

It is not death to bear
The wrench that sets us free
From dungeon-chain to breathe the air
Of boundless liberty.

It is not death to fling
Aside this mortal dust,
And rise on strong exulting wing,
To live among the just.

Jesus, Thou Prince of Life,
Thy chosen cannot die:
Like Thee they conquer in the strife,
To reign with Thee on high.

Malan was also a musician, and set his hymns to music.

To Jean Frederic Oberlin (1740-1826) is usually ascribed the fine hymn (translated by Lucy Wilson) "O Lord, Thy heavenly grace impart"; but there is reason to believe that it was neither Oberlin's composition nor translation.

The religious movement started by Robert Haldane in the earliest years of the present century gave rise to a School of Swiss Hymnody, to which Dr. Merle D'Aubigne, Felix Neff, and others contributed. At a somewhat later period (1834) the "Chants Chretiens" were published in Paris by Henri Lutteroth, in which were included extracts from Racine, Corneille, and Pictét, and hymns by Adolphe Monod, Alexander Vinet, and others. This is still the most popular Hymnal in the Reformed Church.

To Adolphe Monod (1812-1856), the saintly and accomplished Pastor of Paris, we owe the striking hymn, "Oh, the bitter shame and sorrow," which has found its way into certain English Hymnals. The following translation of his "Que ne puis-je, ô mon Dieu," by Mr. Downton, deserves notice :—

God of my health! I would Thy praise proclaim
And tell to earth and heaven Thy wondrous Name,
Declare the transports of my thankful breast,
And say to all the world that I am blest!

Blest—when I hear Thee speak, and when that word
Which said, "Let there be light," within me heard,
Stoops to instruct me, calms my spirit's strife,
And guides my footsteps in the path of life.

Blest—when I speak to Thee, and though but dust,
Lift to Thy throne my worship and my trust,
With freedom to my Father, as a child;
With trembling to my God, as sin defiled.

Blest, when Thy day, which saw from Chaos' mount
Thy work come forth, Thy First-born from the fount,
Gathers within Thy courts th' adoring throng,
Our zeal's weak flame re-kindling, bright and strong!

Blest—when, beneath Thy strokes, my faithful God,
Smitten in love, in love I kiss the rod:
Weeping, but waiting Thy returning smile,
And near the Cross, and for a little while.

Blest—when, assaulted by the tempter's power,
The Cross my armour, and the Lamb my tower,
Kneeling I triumph—issuing from the fray
A bleeding conqueror—my life a prey!

Blest—ever blest! my Brother, He who died;
His Father mine; His Spirit still my Guide:
What can earth give? what can hell take away,
When God and heaven are mine, are mine for aye?

Alexander Vinet (1797-1867), the devout and thoughtful Professor of Theology at Lausanne, wrote many hymns, most of which appeared first in the "Semeur," a paper to which he often contributed. They are marked by the devout thoughtfulness and delicate phrasing which are characteristic of his discourses. Seven of these have been translated by the Rev. Henry Downton, M.A., for many years the English Chaplain at Geneva, and included in his "Hymns and Verses: Original and Translated," 1873. The following is a specimen. It is a translation of his "Roi des Anges":—

King Divine!
Song of mine
Can it reach Thy heaven and Thee?
And wilt Thou
Stoop so low
That Thy love shall visit me?
Deeps profound
Who shall sound
Without faith, their mystery?

Could my prayer,
Father! dare
All so weak, to rise to Thee,
But that Thou
Deign'st to bow
In Thy tender love to me?
Love untold
Humbly told,
Faith adores the mystery.

From the abyss
Up to bliss,
High to God's eternal throne,
Mounts my prayer,—
Waiting there,
Waiting on His grace alone,
Saviour dear!
Bend Thine ear,
Of my faith the tribute own.

Lord of all!
Hear my call,
For Thyself, Thyself I cry:
Art Thou near?
Nought I fear;
Art Thou absent? then I die.
Helper mine,
King divine,
In me reign eternally!

Few finer hymns are to be found in French than the following—which is a translation by Mr. Downton—of "Je suis à toi," by M. Edmond Scherer, Editor of *Le Temps*:—

Lord, I am Thine, all glory to Thy Name;
I to Thy law my life, myself resign:
Of right Thou dost my love, my worship claim,
And I am Thine!

In paths of doubt I wandered lost of yore,
When lo! upon my path Thou deigndst to shine:
Once was my heart a void, and death in store
Now I am Thine!

The world erewhile enchained my captive soul,
But now I dwell beneath Thy rule divine:
Sweet is Thy yoke; on Thee my cares I roll,
For I am Thine!

Me to receive with welcome to Thy heart
Thine arms outstretched and looks of love combine:
O Lord I come: I choose that better part,
Thine, wholly Thine!

Possessing Thee, I am of all possest,
And 'tis by faith this happy lot is mine:
Upon Thy bosom, Lord, in peace and rest,
Thine, only Thine!

None from Thy book of life shall blot my name,
No tempter from Thy paths my steps incline;
'Tis death, 'tis life, Thy piercing glance of flame,
But I am Thine!

While on this earth I sojourn by Thy will,
My Saviour and my God, that will be mine,
Till safe in Heaven I bless Thy mercy still,
For ever Thine!

French Hymnody as a whole is marked by so great a delicacy of expression that it is almost impossible to reproduce it in our English tongue, and by a subjective tone which renders its hymns more suitable for private than public worship.

From the Italian, we have "Glory be to Jesus" *(Viva, viva Gesu!)*, translated by Edward Caswall. It is taken from the *Aspirazione Divote* of the 17th or 18th century. And "Praised be the Lord our God," a translation of the "Cantico delle Creature," sometimes called "Cantico delle Sole" by St. Francis of Assissi. It was written about the year 1224, and sung daily in the little Convent of Portiuncala. It has been included, with some modifications to adapt it for present day use, in "Worship Song."

Many of the hymns of Denmark have been translated by Gilbert Tait, but none of these have passed into common use. One, however, by Elias Elkildsen Naur, Professor in the Gymnasium at Odense, in Funen, who died in 1728, seems to me very beautiful, and though not quite suitable for public worship, deserves a place among hymns for private use:—

When my tongue can sing no more,
When my lips have ceased to pray,
Silent, may I still adore,—
Eager, Saviour, seek Thy way!
Hear, O Christ, my latest sigh;
Open wide the gates on high,
For my soul, which angels bear
Home to glory, deathless, rare;—

Home to heaven's kingdom sweet;
Home to join the chosen band,
Seraph, seraphim to meet:
Home to courts where reigneth grand
Mercy's Monarch; home to dwell
With the God who loves me well;
Home to all my fathers dear;
Home my Christ to serve and fear.

The one Danish hymn-writer that has become well-known in this country is Bernhardt Severin Ingemann (1789-1862), who was born in Denmark the 28th May, 1789. His father was a clergyman, and he was also intended for the Church. At a comparatively early age he published his poems, mostly of a romantic character, concerning which there was much division of opinion.

He afterwards published a series of romantic-patriotic descriptions of the hero kings of the middle ages, undoubtedly greatly influenced by the writings of Sir Walter Scott. These books are still, and will probably continue to be, the most popular reading amongst the Danish people. Whilst he thus roused the patriotic spirit of his countrymen, his early religious training manifested itself in his hymns, which form a conspicuous part in the Danish Church and School Service. Manly vigour, and almost childlike tenderness, together with true faith and a firm belief that there will be light after the darkness, form the most prominent features in his hymns. Scarcely was any poet more appreciated by his country than Ingemann. On his 70th birthday the Danish children presented him with a splendid golden horn. The subscriptions were limited to a halfpenny, and every child throughout the land gave its mite toward the man, who perhaps even in the same degree as Hans Christian Andersen, had cheered their childhood. He died a few years after greatly lamented.

Few, who ever saw the old poet and his amiable wife—Philemon and Baucis they were called—in their quiet cottage in the beautiful Sorö' surrounded by roses, are likely to forget them.

Through Mr. Baring-Gould's fine rendering, one of his hymns—a singularly inspiring one—" Through the night of doubt and sorrow " *(Igjennem Nat og Traengsel)*, has established itself in English favour.

In her "Voice of Christian Life in Song," Mrs. Charles has given translations of a few Swedish hymns, but, so far as I know, none from this source have passed into English use. The battle-song of Gustavus Adolphus, of Sweden, is probably unique in this respect, that the thoughts were his, and their versification by another. Here is the story:— "The brave king was no man of letters. The fire of faith which burned in his heart was more wont to fuse the iron of heroic deeds than the gold of beautiful words But the thoughts were in his heart; had they not inspired him in march and battlefield? So he told his chaplain,

Dr. Jacob Fabricius what his thoughts were, and the chaplain moulded them into three verses of a hymn, and the simple-hearted hero took them ever afterwards as his battle-song."

Be not dismay'd, thou little flock,
Although the foe's fierce battle shock
Loud on all sides assail thee.
Though o'er thy fall they laugh secure,
Their triumph cannot long endure;
Let not thy courage fail thee.

Thy cause is God's: go at His call,
And to His hand commit Thy all;
Fear thou no ill impending:
His Gideon shall arise for thee,
God's Word and people manfully,
In God's own time defending.

Our hope is sure in Jesus' might;
Against themselves the godless fight,
Themselves, not us, distressing;
Shame and contempt their lot shall be:
God is with us, with Him are we,
To us belongs His blessing.

Wales is rich in hymns—so say those who are acquainted with its hymnody; but, probably on account of the difficulty of rendering them into the English language, only two have come into our hymnals: "Guide me, O Thou great Jehovah," and "O'er the gloomy hills of darkness," by William Williams. The Rev. H. Elvet Lewis has published a volume of translations of Welsh hymns.

CHAPTER XX.

AMERICAN HYMNS.

Great as is the past of English literature, its future is likely to be still greater, both on account of the increase of the English-speaking race, and the variety of lands in which its lot is now cast, for there will be not only a greater number of contributors to the stores of English literature, but the peoples, climate, condition, and scenery will probably give rise to new types both of thought and expression. At present America is the only English-speaking offshoot from the mother country which has existed long enough to develop a literature of its own. Australia is budding into letters, especially of the poetic kind, but, although the promise is great, the time of *fruit* is not yet. In the case of America, however, there has been sufficient time for the bud, the blossom, the slowly-forming fruit, and now we near the harvest, if not the full one, yet the first ingatherings of one which bids fair to rival that of the old country.

My concern in the present chapter is only with one small part of this literary harvest, one which some would exclude as altogether unworthy of a place therein, and not altogether without good reason, since a very large number of the hymns of the past have been so destitute of literary grace or poetic inspiration as to be quite unworthy of a place in literature. Dr. Johnson said of

Dr. Watts, "that he had succeeded in doing better than others, what no one had succeeded in doing well." There was, at that time, a measure of truth in that saying. But before Dr. Watts there had been writers who had written fine hymns, even judged from a literary standpoint, so that even then materials existed for a *good*, if not a *large*, collection of English hymns, which, from a variety of causes, had been strangely overlooked and neglected; whilst among Dr. Watts' six hundred hymns, many of which are very inferior, there are a few grand hymns; and since his time many writers have produced hymns which an unprejudiced judgment would include among the *literary* treasures of the English-speaking race. Amongst such, the hymns of our friends across the Atlantic hold no small or undistinguished place. Indeed, some of the finest work of this kind of recent times has had to travel across the ocean which separates us from that great country.

The excellence of much American hymn-work is due to certain causes which do not prevail in England. One of these is the absence of an Established Church, with its venerable and greatly-loved Liturgy, which allows less space for hymn-singing than do the churches which rely on extemporaneous utterance in their devotional services. Of course there is an Episcopal Church in America, which, like its elder sister in this country, retains—though in an altered form—the Book of Common Prayer in its worship, but that Church is neither the dominant, nor the most influential, nor the most numerous Church of that land. The great majority of the American Churches rely, either altogether or in part, on extemporaneous utterance in their devotional services, and so leave a larger place open for the singing of hymns, than Churches whose services are wholly liturgical.

Another reason for the excellence of much American hymn-writing is to be found in the custom which prevails of inviting those with poetic power to contribute verses for the great anniversaries in their history—social, national, ecclesiastical. This has drawn into the ranks of the hymnists some of the most notable writers. Scarcely an American poet of any eminence could be named who has not been led to consecrate his genius to hymn-production. Some of the finest hymns by American authors have had this origin. In England, the names of our greater poets are conspicuous by their absence from the roll of the hymnists. They have either not thought of hymns as a form for the expression of their genius, or have deemed them unworthy of their powers. And our national customs have done nothing to call out their genius in that direction, save occasionally by asking for an ode, or poem, or song, for some great celebration. What glorious additions to our hymnals might have been made if Lord Tennyson, or Robert Browning, or Lewis Morris had been asked to compose hymns for great occasions, as Oliver Wendell Holmes, John Greenleaf Whittier, and others, have been in America!

It should also be noted that the American poets have been more deeply touched by religious feeling than their brothers in England, so that their poetry is more devotional in its tone. This has made it possible to extract verses from their poems, which, though not written as hymns, have been eminently suited for use in worship.

All these causes combined have conspired to produce a mass of verses which are very remarkable.

Hymn-writing in America began with the present century. Before that time only metrical versions of the Psalms were in use; the first collection having been the celebrated Bay Psalm Book, or New England version, published in 1640, of which it is said that no less than 70 editions were printed in Boston, London, and Edinburgh. This was revised in 1757 by Thomas Prince, but was soon superseded by Tate and Brady's version. Rather later (1750-1780) editions of Tate and Brady were issued with a supplement of hymns, chiefly from Dr. Watts. At the end of the 18th century many editions of Dr. Watts' Psalms and Hymns were published, in some of which the Psalms were amended, by Joel Barlow in 1785, and by Timothy Dwight in 1800. After this time the Metrical Psalms were issued, with hymns appended; in the Episcopal Church, the version of Tate and Brady, and in the Presbyterian and Congregational, Watts' version being used. But as time went on, the Psalms fell more and more into the background, and hymns became prominent.

The hymns used in America have been chiefly drawn from English sources, hardly a tenth part being of native origin. In many collections the proportion of American hymns is much smaller—in the "Methodist Episcopal Hymn Book" of 1849, only 50 out of a total of 1,148 are American; in the "Baptist Service of Song" there are 100 out of a total of 1,129; so that though the store of American hymns is by no means small, and is constantly increasing, yet, as was to be expected from a new community, it is insignificant compared with that of England, which, through many centuries, has been gradually accumulating. But in the future America is destined, I believe, to contribute a larger proportion of hymns, and to exert an immense influence on our English Hymnody.

A great number of American hymnists are quite unknown and entirely unrepresented in our English collections. My concern in the present chapter is chiefly with those whose hymns have found a place in our own hymnals, and these represent the freshest and most vigorous writers of the new country. I will group them under the various Churches to which they belong.

From the Protestant Episcopal Church, hymns by about ten writers have been included in English collections.

Henry Ustic Onderdonk, D.D. (1789-1858), second Bishop of Pennsylvania, who is best known by the hymn of Invitation, which begins, "The Spirit in our hearts."

William Augustus Muhlenberg, D.D. (1796-1879), the great-grandson of Henry Melchior Muhlenberg, the founder of the German Lutheran Church in America, whose Baptismal hymn, "Saviour, who Thy flock art feeding," has deservedly become popular.

George Washington Doane, D.D. (1799-1859), Bishop of New Jersey, was the author of the well-known hymn, "Thou art the way: to Thee alone;" and the Missionary hymn quoted below, a very striking and poetic utterance.

Fling out the banner! let it float
Skyward and seaward, high and wide;
The sun shall light its shining folds,
The Cross on which the Saviour died.

Fling out the banner! angels bend
In anxious silence o'er the sign;
And vainly seek to comprehend
The wonder of the Love Divine.

Fling out the banner! heathen lands
  Shall see from far the glorious sight,
And nations crowding to be born,
  Baptise their spirits in its light.

Fling out the banner! sin-sick souls
  That sink and perish in the strife,
Shall touch in faith its radiant hem,
  And spring immortal into life.

Fling out the banner! let it float
  Skyward and seaward, high and wide,
Our glory, only in the Cross;
  Our only hope, the Crucified!

Fling out the banner! wide and high,
  Seaward and skyward, let it shine:
Nor skill, nor might, nor merit ours;
  We conquer only in that Sign.

Charles William Everest, M.A. (1814-1877), for thirty-one years Rector of Hampden, near New-Haven, Conn., to whom we owe a fine hymn which has been so wretchedly mangled, especially in the third verse, in nearly every English collection, that I quote it in its proper form.

Take up thy cross, the Saviour said,
  If thou wouldst My disciple be;
Take up thy cross with willing heart,
  And humbly follow after Me.

Take up thy cross; let not its weight
  Fill thy weak soul with vain alarm;
His strength shall bear thy spirit up,
  And brace thy heart, and nerve thine arm

Take up thy cross, nor heed the shame,
  And let thy foolish pride be still;
Thy Lord refused not e'en to die
  Upon a cross, on Calvary's hill.

Take up thy cross, then, in His strength,
  And calmly sin's wild deluge brave;
'Twill guide thee to a better home,
  And point to glory o'er the grave.

Take up thy cross, and follow on,
  Nor think till death to lay it down;
For only he who bears the cross
  May hope to wear the glorious crown.

In nearly every English hymnal, save my own, the third verse is made to read thus—

Take up thy cross, nor heed the shame;
Nor let thy foolish pride rebel;
Thy Lord for thee the cross endured,
To save thy soul from death and hell.

A more shameless attempt to force dogma into a hymn, singularly free from it, I do not remember.

Harriet Beecher Stowe (1812-1896), known all over the world as the authoress of "Uncle Tom's Cabin," and the sister of Henry Ward Beecher, of whom, after hearing in London most of the chief preachers, she exclaimed, "Oh, for half-an-hour of my brother Henry," is the authoress of hymns that are greatly prized in churches which do not regard poetry in hymns as a fatal disqualification for their use in public worship. The best known, and they are very beautiful, are the following:—"When winds are raging o'er the upper ocean;" "Still, still with Thee, when purple morning breaketh;" and the hymn on "Abide with Me."

That mystic word of Thine, O sovereign Lord,
Is all too pure, too high, too deep for me;
Weary of striving, and with longing faint,
I breathe it back again in prayer to Thee!

Abide in me, I pray, and I in Thee!
From this good hour, O leave me never more!
Then shall the discord cease, the wound be healed,
The life-long bleeding of the soul be o'er.

Abide in me; o'ershadow by Thy love
Each half-formed purpose, and dark thought of sin;
Quench, ere it rise, each selfish, low desire,
And keep my soul, as Thine, calm and divine.

As some rare perfume in a vase of clay
Pervades it with a fragrance not its own,
So, when Thou dwellest in a mortal soul,
All heaven's own sweetness seems around it thrown.

Abide in me; there have been moments blest
When I have heard Thy voice and felt Thy power,
Then evil lost its grasp, and passion hushed,
Owned the divine enchantment of the hour.

These were but seasons, beautiful and rare;
Abide in me, and they shall ever be;
Fulfil at once Thy precept and my prayer—
Come, and abide in me, and I in Thee.

Arthur Cleveland Coxe, D.D. (1818-1896), Bishop of Western New York, is known by three hymns, all of which are of great merit. "How beauteous were the marks divine!" "Saviour, sprinkle many nations!"—one of the finest of our Missionary hymns—and the very fine verse usually set to a part-song: "Now pray we for our country," but originally written: "Now pray we for our Mother."

He is also the author of another hymn of no little merit, but lacking the unity of thought and compactness of expression of those we have named—"Breath of the Lord, O Spirit blest."

Eliza Scudder (1821-1896) possessed a poetic gift equal to that of Mrs. Beecher Stowe, with a greater mastery of hymn forms, which renders her productions more available for public worship. Her tiny little volume of only fifty pages, "Hymns and Sonnets," by E.S., is more worthy of retention than many a portly volume. In my judgment, two of her hymns, especially, are amongst the very finest of modern times—there is strength, tenderness, melody—every quality needful to a good hymn to be found in them. This is high praise, but my readers shall judge for themselves by the following. The first she calls "Truth"—

Thou long disowned, reviled, oppressed,
Strange Friend of human kind,
Seeking through weary years a rest
Within our hearts to find;—

How late Thy bright and awful brow
  Breaks through these clouds of sin :
Hail, Truth Divine ! we know Thee *now*,
  Angel of God, come in !

Come, though with purifying fire
  And swift-dividing sword,
Thou of all nations the Desire,
  Earth waits Thy cleansing word.

Struck by the lightning of Thy glance,
  Let old oppressions die ;
Before Thy cloudless countenance
  Let fear and falsehood fly.

Anoint our eyes with healing grace,
  To see, as not before,
Our Father in our brother's face,
  Our Maker in His poor.

Flood our dark life with golden day :
  Convince, subdue, enthral ;
Then to a mightier yield Thy sway,
  And Love be all in all.

The second is on "The Love of God"—

Thou Grace Divine, encircling all,
  A shoreless, boundless sea,
Wherein at last our souls must fall ;
  O Love of God most free.

When over dizzy heights we go,
  A soft hand blinds our eyes,
And we are guided safe and slow ;
  O Love of God most wise.

And though we turn us from Thy face,
  And wander wide and long,
Thou hold'st us still in kind embrace ;
  O Love of God most strong.

The saddened heart, the restless soul,
  The toil-worn frame and mind,
Alike confess Thy sweet control,
  O Love of God most kind.

But not alone Thy care we claim,
  Our wayward steps to win ;
We know Thee by a dearer name ;
  O Love of God within.

And filled and quickened by Thy breath,
  Our souls are strong and free,
To rise o'er sin and fear and death ;
  O Love of God ! to Thee.

Her hymn on "Whither shall I go from Thy Spirit, or whither shall I flee from Thy presence?" which she calls "The Quest," is lovely, but a little too subtle for public worship. Her "Vesper Hymn" and "Collect for Ascension Day" are both admirable.

When the Church frees herself from a blind clinging to old hymns, simply because they are old, and becomes free to receive whatever is worthy, for her worship-song, Miss Scudder will be more largely represented in our hymnals. I shall be glad if my reference to her should direct any future editors to a consideration of her exquisite hymns.

Turning to the Presbyterian section of the Church in America, there is little to detain us. She has no Bonar in her ranks. All her writers are more or less echoes.

Samuel Davies (1723-1761), the successor of Jonathan Edwards as President of Princeton College, is remembered as the author of the striking hymn, "Great God of wonders, all Thy ways," which used to be popular, but is somewhat fading in popularity on account of its very strong expressions concerning sinners.

James Waddell Alexander, D.D. (1804-1859), is remembered as the translator of the best version of Paul Gerhardt's noble hymn, "O Haupt voll Blut und Wunden," which begins, "O Sacred Head, now wounded," and of a version of the "Stabat Mater" by Jacopone da Tode.

Thomas Mackellar (born 1812) is the author of many hymns, which have a certain popularity in America, but I have not been able, though I have examined them carefully, to discern a single one distinctive enough to be worthy of importation into England.

George Duffield, M.A. (1818-1888), successively pastor of Presbyterian churches in Brooklyn, Bloomfield, Philadelphia, and the West, is the author of one of the best known and most popular of American hymns. As no other hymn from his pen has the force of "Stand up! stand up for Jesus!" it is natural to conclude that this hymn owes much to the affecting circumstances under which it was written. In 1858 the Rev. Dudley A. Tyng had been engaged in a remarkable mission in Philadelphia, and on the Sunday before his death had preached in Jaynes Hall one of the most stirring sermons of modern times, so that out of the 5,000 present at the delivery, at least a thousand are believed to have been converted. On the following Wednesday he left his study for a moment, and went to a barn where a mule was at work on a horse-power, shelling corn. Patting him on the neck, the sleeve of his silk study-gown caught in the cogs of the wheel, and his arm was torn out by the roots, and in a few hours he died. Just before his death he sent the message, "Stand up for Jesus!" to those assembled at the Young Men's Christian Association prayer-meeting —a message which suggested this hymn, and formed the concluding exhortation of the funeral sermon for Mr. Tyng, which was preached from Eph. vi. 14 by its author. It was printed as a fly-leaf for the Sunday-school scholars by the superintendent; thence it found its way into a Baptist newspaper, and afterwards passed, either in its English or in translated forms, all over the world. It was the favourite song of the Christian soldiers in the army of the James in the American war. The original contains two more verses than are usually now printed in most hymnals.

To Thomas Hastings, Mus. Doc. (1784-1872), we owe three hymns, "Now be the gospel banner!" "Hail to the brightness of Zion's glad morning!" and "Return, O wanderer, to thy home!" which is an appeal rather than, in the truest sense, a hymn. It was suggested by the closing words of a sermon to which Dr. Hastings listened in 1830—"Sinner, come home! come home! come home!"

Of the other hymn-writers of this section of the Church, about twenty in number, there is no need to speak, as their hymns are little known in this country.

The Congregational Church in America has produced a considerable number of hymnists, very few of whom are represented in English Hymnals.

Timothy Dwight, D.D. (1752-1817). President of Yale College, whose "Theology" used to be much in favour, published, by request, a revised version of Watts' Psalms, and such hymns as he thought suitable. He did his work as Professor in spite of failure of sight consequent on small pox, which rendered it impossible for him, during forty years, to read consecutively for fifteen minutes out of the twenty-four hours; whilst the pain behind the eyeballs and in the frontal region of the brain was agonising. The hymn by which he is known in England is, "I love Thy Kingdom, Lord," which is marked by great simplicity and pathos.

Ray Palmer, D.D. (1808-1888), pastor of churches at Bath, Albany, Bellevue Avenue, and also Corresponding Secretary of the American Congregational Union, is by far the most notable hymnist and translator of the American Congregational Church. His hymn, "My faith looks up to Thee," is known all over the world. The story of its origin is thus given in Duffield's "English Hymns":—

"The hymn was written in 1830, but not published (as a hymn) until 1832. The author was in New York City, 'between his college and theological studies,' and was in poor health, and a teacher in a ladies' school. Dr. Palmer says: 'I gave form to what I felt by writing, with little effort, the stanzas. I recollect I wrote them with very tender emotion, and ended the last line with tears.' The manuscript was then placed in a pocket-book, where it remained for some time. Its true discoverer was Lowell Mason, the musician, who asked young Palmer if he had not some hymn or hymns to contribute to his new book. The pocket-book was produced, and the little hymn (then between two and three years old, and never previously utilised, though it had been in print as a poem) was brought to light. Dr. Mason was attracted by it, and desired a copy. They stepped together into a store (it was in Boston), and the copy was made and taken away without further comment. On carefully reading the hymn at home, Dr. Mason was so interested that he wrote for it the tune 'Olivet,' to which it is usually sung. Two or three days later, he again met the author in the street, and scarcely waiting to salute him, he said, 'Mr. Palmer, you may live many years, and do many good things, but I think you will be best known to posterity as the author of "My faith looks up to Thee."'"

The full publication of this hymn occurred in 1832, but it received no particular notice in America. It had, however, obtained a reprint in some religious papers, from one of which the Rev. Andrew Reed, D.D., of

London, secured it while he was in that country. Dr. Reed took it away for his prospective hymn-book, and published it anonymously. "It had," said Dr. J. G. Rankin, "several years of transatlantic life before it was much known in America, and possibly was indebted to its foreign and uncertain origin for its first recognition here, as many another native production has been." "As originally written" (says Mr. Frederick Saunders, in "Evenings with the Sacred Poets"), "the hymn consisted of six stanzas; the first two are omitted, four only being given in the Church collections. It has been translated into Arabic, and much used at missionary stations in Turkey. It has not only been translated into Tamil, but into Tahitian and the Mahratta, and will doubtless find its way wherever the Bible has penetrated." We have ourselves seen it in Chinese, and, in fact, it is to be found wherever American missionaries have rendered into native tongues the hymns familiar to their home churches. Its first appearance in America was in "Spiritual Songs for Social Worship" (by Dr. Thomas Hastings and Dr. Lowell Mason), in 1832. In this book, the tune is entitled "My faith looks up to Thee," but is the same as "Olivet."

Equally good, but in quite a different strain, being richer in thought but less pathetic in expression, is the following, which should be more widely known than it is:—

Lord, my weak thought in vain would climb
  To search the starry vault profound;
In vain would wing her flight sublime,
  To find creation's utmost bound.

But weaker yet that thought must prove
  To search thy great eternal plan,
Thy sovereign counsels, born of love
  Long ages ere the world began.

When my dim reason would demand
  Why that, or this, Thou dost ordain,
By some vast deep I seem to stand
  Whose secrets I must ask in vain.

When doubts disturb my troubled breast,
  And all is dark as night to me,
Here, as on solid rock, I rest,—
  That so it seemeth good to Thee.

Be this my joy, that evermore
  Thou rulest all things at Thy will;
Thy sovereign wisdom I adore,
  And calmly, sweetly, trust Thee still.

In a strain betwixt the two is the following:—

Jesus, these eyes have never seen
  That radiant form of Thine;
The veil of sense hangs dark between
  Thy blessed face and mine.

I see Thee not, I hear Thee not,
  Yet art Thou oft with me;
And earth has ne'er so dear a spot
  As where I meet with Thee.

Like some bright dream, that comes unsought,
  When slumbers o'er me roll,
Thine image ever fills my thought,
  And charms my ravished soul.

Yea, though I have not seen, and still
  Must rest in faith alone,
I love Thee, dearest Lord, and will,
  Unseen but not unknown.

When death these mortal eyes shall seal,
  And still this throbbing heart;
The rending veil shall Thee reveal
  All glorious as Thou art.

Quite equal to these are some of his translations--from Robert II. of France, "Come, Holy Ghost, in love"; from St. Bernard of Clairvaux, "Jesus, Thou joy of loving hearts," one of the finest Communion hymns we possess; and from anonymous Latin authors, "I give my heart to Thee," and "O bread to pilgrims given."

During the last three or four days of his life, Dr. Ray Palmer lay most of the time apparently unconscious.

When told by his son at the beginning of this time that the end was near, he answered "Thank God," in a louder tone of voice than he had employed for some time. Occasionally he would be heard to repeat to himself a hymn of faith and praise, now one of Wesley's and now one of his own. The last words he was heard to utter were spoken not many hours before his death. His lips were seen to move, and listening ears caught a few syllables, inarticulately spoken, of the last verse of his hymn entitled, "Jesus, these eyes have never seen"—

> When death these mortal eyes shall seal,
> And still this throbbing heart,
> The rending veil shall Thee reveal
> All glorious as Thou art."

Dr. Ray Palmer is the most widely-known and deeply-loved hymnist of America.

The Baptist body, like the Congregationalist, has had a large number of hymnists, but there is no one amongst them at all to be compared with Ray Palmer. If we except Philip Bliss (1838-1876), who has become popular by hymns from his pen included in "Sacred Songs and Solos," edited by Ira D. Sankey, and Samuel Francis Smith, D.D., born 1808, who wrote what is practically the American national hymn, "My country! 'tis of thee," and who wrote four verses to complete Alaric A. Watts' hymn, "When shall we meet again," there is no writer of this Church who has secured sufficient notice in England to deserve mention.

The Methodist Church has been so dominated by the hymns of Charles Wesley that practically she has done nothing to enrich the stores of American song. Beyond three writers of children's hymns—Dr. William Hunter (1811-1877), Dr. Thomas O. Summers (1812-1882), and

Fanny J. Van Alstyne (born 1823), I do not discover a single hymnist represented in English collections. A great hymn writer like Charles Wesley—perhaps the greatest the Church has ever had—naturally so fills the worship of the Church he did so much to found, as to discourage others from entering the field, or putting their work into comparison with his.

The Unitarian Church never had a Watts or Wesley to express its conceptions of religion, and so there was a more open field for those in its midst who possessed the poetic gifts. To quote the words of a great authority on American Hymnody, belonging to the Episcopal Church: "It possessed a large share of the best blood and brain in the most cultivated section of America." It has probably contributed the most finished hymns to the treasury of American song. This is not to be wondered at, when it is remembered that the great majority of the more noteworthy poets of America belong to this Church—William Cullen Bryant, Ralph Waldo Emerson, Henry Wadsworth Longfellow, Oliver Wendell Holmes, Jones Very, James Russell Lowell.

It must be remembered that, in the main, the Unitarian Church in America has been far nearer to orthodoxy, both in doctrine and spirit, than that which goes under the same name in England. Many of its hymns are sufficient evidence of this; so much so that when, many years ago, the Religious Tract Society published a volume called *Lyra Americana*, the Editor, in his preface, said: "It would be difficult, or even impossible, to determine the ecclesiastical or doctrinal status of each writer from the internal evidence afforded by his poetry. The great object of their adoration and their grateful love is Christ crucified. All are one in Him. Differences are merged in a common unity when He is the theme. With 'diversity of gifts' there is but 'one spirit.' 'They know but one Saviour, and one God and Father of all, who is above all, and through all, and in us all.'" In a book thus prefaced, I found, out of a total of one hundred and twenty-four hymns, at the very lowest computation, forty-three by writers who belong to the Unitarian Church. But the Editor, judging them only by their productions, declares that they all are one in Christ. And the unprejudiced mind which goes over the chief hymns of this school will agree with this dictum. The *spirit* is eminently and deeply Christian, far more so than in a large number which might be named by orthodox writers. Readers may judge for themselves by the specimens which I append.

Taking them in chronological order, we have—

John Pierpont (1785-1866), whose life was varied and remarkable. After graduating at Yale College, he taught for a time both in an academy and in a private family, then he studied law, and became a barrister—a profession which conscientious scruples led him to give up, and he gave himself to literary and commercial pursuits. At last he entered the Cambridge Divinity School, where he graduated in 1818, and up till 1859 was engaged in the regular ministry over various Unitarian Churches. When the war broke out in 1861, he became chaplain to the Massachusetts regiment, but his increasing infirmities compelled him to retire, and the rest of his life was employed in the Treasury Department at Washington in arranging its Decisions. His hymns combine terseness and tenderness in an unusual degree, as may be seen in the one by which he is best known in England :—

O Thou, to whom in ancient time
The lyre of Hebrew bards was strung;
Whom kings adored in songs sublime,
And prophets praised with glowing tongue:

Not now on Zion's height alone,
Thy favoured worshippers may dwell,
Nor where at sultry noon Thy Son
Sat weary, by the patriarch's well:

From every place below the skies,
The grateful song, the fervent prayer,
The incense of the heart, may rise
To heaven, and find acceptance there.

To Thee shall age with snowy hair,
And strength and beauty, bend the knee;
And childhood lisp with reverent air,
Its praises and its prayers to Thee.

O Thou, to whom, in ancient time,
The lyre of prophet bards was strung,—
To Thee, at last, in every clime,
Shall temples rise and praise be sung.

This hymn was written for the opening of the Independent Congregational Church in Bartin Square, Salem, Massachusetts, December 7th, 1824, to which reference is made in the following verse, which is usually omitted :—

In this, Thy house, whose doors we now
For social worship, first unfold,
To thee the suppliant throng shall bow,
While circling years on years are rolled.

His Morning and Evening Hymns for a child are marked by the characters to which I have already referred, and are very beautiful.

Henry Ware, junior (1794-1843), eldest son of the Hollis Professor of Divinity at Cambridge, was pastor of the Second Church at Boston, in which charge, on account of illness, he had for a time as colleague Ralph Waldo Emerson. Mr. Ware afterwards became Professor of

Pulpit Eloquence and the Pastoral Care in the Cambridge Theological School, a post he held from 1829 to 1842, and, exhausted by his arduous work, retired to Framingham, where he died. Dr. Ware was a hymnist of a very high order. Some of his hymns are full of lyric fire. Perhaps the finest is the following:—

Lift your glad voices in triumph on high,
For Jesus has risen, and man cannot die;
Vain were the terrors that gathered around Him,
  And short the dominion of death and the grave;
He burst from the fetters of darkness that bound Him,
  Resplendent in glory to live and to save,
Loud was the chorus of angels on high,
The Saviour hath risen, and man shall not die.

Glory to God, in full anthems of joy;
The being He gave us death cannot destroy;
  Sad were the life we must part with to-morrow,
If tears were our birthright, and death were our end;
  But Jesus hath cheered the dark valley of sorrow,
And bade us, immortal, to heaven ascend.
Lift, then, your voices in triumph on high,
For Jesus hath risen, and man shall not die!

Probably the best hymn we possess for the opening of an organ we owe to him.

All nature's works His praise declare,
  To whom they all belong;
There is a voice in every star,
  In every breeze a song.
Sweet music fills the world abroad
  With strains of love and power;
The stormy sea sings praise to God,
  The thunder and the shower.

To God the tribes of ocean cry,
  And birds upon the wing;
To God the powers that dwell on high
  Their tuneful tribute bring.
Like them, let man the throne surround,
  With them, loud chorus raise,
While instruments of loftier sound
  Assist his feeble praise.

Great God, to Thee we consecrate
  Our voices and our skill:
We bid the pealing organ wait
  To speak alone Thy will.

O teach its rich and swelling notes
  To lift our souls on high,
And while the music round us floats,
  Let earth-born passion die.

The following, suitable for family gatherings, is exquisitely tender:—

In this glad hour, when children meet,
  And home with them their children bring,
Our hearts with one affection beat,
  One song of praise our voices sing.

For all the faithful, loved and dear,
  Whom Thou so kindly, Lord, hast given,
For those who still are with us here,
  And those who wait for us in heaven;—

For every past and present joy,
  For, honour, competence, and health,
For hopes which time may not destroy,
  Our soul's imperishable wealth;

For all, accept our humble praise;
  Still bless us, Father, by Thy love;
And when are closed our mortal days,
  Unite us in one home above.

William Cullen Bryant (1794-1881), by some regarded as the finest poet of America, has contributed hymns of great delicacy and beauty. These were included in a little book published in 1864, which contained nineteen hymns; another illustration of the fact that the nobler the poet the more reticent he is in the composition of hymns. The best known of his hymns in England, was written for the dedication of a church in Prince Square, New York, afterwards destroyed by fire.

Thou, whose unmeasured temple stands
  Built over earth and sea,
Accept the walls that human hands
  Have raised, O God, to Thee.

And let the Comforter and Friend,
  Thy Holy Spirit, meet
With those who here in worship bend
  Before Thy mercy-seat.

May they who err be guided here
To find the better way;
And they who mourn, and they who fear,
Be strengthened as they pray.

May faith grow firm, and love grow warm,
And hallowed wishes rise,
While round these peaceful walls the storm
Of earth-born passion dies.

The following hymn for Home Missions is the finest we possess for such a purpose :—

Look from Thy sphere of endless day,
O God of mercy and of might;
In pity look on those who stray
Benighted, in this land of light.

In peopled vale, in lonely glen,
In crowded mart, by stream or sea,
How many of the sons of men
Hear not the message sent from Thee.

Send forth Thy heralds, Lord, to call
The thoughtless young, the hardened old,
A scattered homeless flock, till all
Be gathered to Thy peaceful fold.

Send them Thy mighty word to speak,
Till faith shall dawn, and doubt depart,
To awe the bold, to stay the weak,
And bind and heal the broken heart.

Then all these wastes, a dreary scene,
That make us sadden as we gaze,
Shall grow, with living waters green,
And lift to heaven the voice of praise.

The following beautiful hymn of Intercession for Children has usually been ascribed to W. C. Bryant; but is by the Rev. William Bryant, born in 1850 at Folkestone, England, and now Editor of the *Michigan Presbyterian.* It was written at Elizabeth, New Jersey, and appeared in the *New York Witness*, June, 1875.

Standing forth on life's rough way,
Father, guide them;
Oh! we know not what of harm
May betide them!
'Neath the shadow of Thy wing,
Father, hide them;
Walking, sleeping, Lord, we pray,
Go beside them.

When in prayer they cry to Thee,
    Thou wilt hear them:
From the stains of sin and shame
    Thou wilt clear them:
'Mid the quicksands and the rocks,
    Thou wilt steer them;
In temptation, trial, grief,
    Be Thou near them.

Unto Thee we give them up,
    Lord, receive them;
In the world we know must be
    Much to grieve them—
Many striving oft and strong
    To deceive them:
Trustful, in Thy hands of love
    We must leave them.

William Henry Furness (1802-1896) was for more than half a century minister of the Congregational Unitarian Church of Philadelphia. He has been a voluminous and able writer on many subjects, and an eloquent advocate of freedom and peace. To a volume of prayers, called "Domestic Worship," he appended six hymns, one of which for Evening is in my judgment the most suggestive we possess. It embodies the exquisite idea of Blanco White's sonnet—probably the finest in the language, beginning, "Mysterious night, when our first parents knew."

Slowly, by Thy hand unfurled,
Down around the weary world
Falls the darkness; O how still
Is the working of Thy will!

Mighty Maker, here am I,
Work in me as silently;
Veil the day's distracting sights;
Show me heaven's eternal lights.

From the darkened sky come forth
Countless stars—a wondrous birth!
So may gleams of glory start
From this dim abyss, my heart.

Living worlds to view be brought
In the boundless realms of thought.
High and infinite desires,
Flaming like those upper fires!

Holy Truth, Eternal Right—
Let them break upon my sight;
Let them shine serenely still,
And with light my being fill.

Thou who dwellest there, I know
Dwellest here within me too;
May the perfect love of God
Here, as there, be shed abroad.

Let my soul attunèd be
To the heavenly harmony
Which, beyond the power of sound,
Fills the universe around.

Ralph Waldo Emerson (1803-1882), who fills so large a place in American literature, and exercised so deep an influence on religious thought both in that country and in England, is represented in many English Hymnals by the following hymn, which is very distinctive and beautiful:—

We love the venerable house
  Our fathers built to God:—
In heaven are kept their grateful vows,
  Their dust endears the sod.

Here holy thoughts a light have shed
  From many a radiant face,
And prayers of tender hope have spread
  A perfume through the place.

And anxious hearts have pondered here
  The mystery of life,
And prayed the eternal Light to clear
  Their doubts and aid their strife.

From humble tenements around
  Came up the pensive train,
And in the Church a blessing found,
  That filled their homes again;

For faith, and peace, and mighty love,
  That from the Godhead flow,
Showed them the life of heaven above
  Springs from the life below.

They live with God, their homes are dust;
  Yet here their children pray,
And in this fleeting life-time trust
  To find the narrow way.

On him who by the altar stands,
  On him Thy blessing fall!
Speak through his lips Thy pure commands
  Thou Heart, that lovest all.

"All before us lies the way" has often been ascribed to Emerson, but it is by Eliza Thayer Clapp, and first appeared in "The Dial," edited by Margaret Fuller, and to which Emerson contributed.

Frederick Henry Hedge (1805-1890) was one of the most accomplished scholars of America, and occupied the post of Professor of German Literature at Harvard College. In conjunction with Bishop Huntington he edited "Hymns for the Church," where most of his own hymns are to be found. Perhaps the most striking of his original hymns is the following, which is finding its way into many English Hymnals.

It is finished! Man of Sorrows!
From Thy cross our frailty borrows
    Strength to bear and conquer thus!

While extended there we view Thee,
Mighty Sufferer! draw us to Thee,
    Sufferer victorious!

Not in vain for us uplifted,
Man of Sorrows, wonder gifted,
    May that sacred emblem be;

Lifted high amid the ages,
Guide of heroes, saints, and sages,
    May it guide us still to Thee!

Still to Thee! whose love unbounded,
Sorrow's depths for us hath sounded,
    Perfected by conflicts sore.

Honoured be Thy cross for ever;
Star that points our high endeavour
    Whither Thou hast gone before!

His work as a translator is very fine. His rendering of Luther's famous "Ein feste burg ist unser Gott," is of very high merit. The same may be said of his translation of the "Veni Sancte Spiritus."

Henry Wadsworth Longfellow (1807-1883), the most popular, though, in my judgment, not the greatest poet of America, has written much sacred poetry of a very tender kind; but although some editors have included his "Psalm of Life," and his "Hymn for his Brother's Ordination," in their Hymnals, I cannot say that these can rightly be accounted hymns, or that he should be included among the hymnists.

Sarah Elizabeth Miles (born 1807) wrote in her early days three hymns which her father (Nathaniel W. Appleton) recognised as worthy, and sent to be printed. One of these is of great merit, and is known all over the English-speaking world. It first appeared in 1827 in the "Christian Examiner." The following is the full and correct text; it has often been altered, but not improved:

Thou who didst stoop below
To drain the cup of woe,
Wearing the form of frail mortality;
Thy blessèd labours done,
Thy crown of victory won,
Hast passed from earth, passed to Thy throne on high.

Our eyes behold Thee not,
Yet hast Thou not forgot
Those who have placed their hope, their trust in Thee
Before Thy Father's face
Thou hast prepared a place,
That where Thou art, there they may also be.

It was no path of flowers,
Which, through this world of ours,
Belovèd of the Father, Thou didst tread;
And shall we, in dismay
Shrink from the narrow way,
When clouds and darkness are around it spread?

O Thou, who art our life,
Be with us through the strife;
Thy holy head by earth's fierce storms was bowed:
Raise Thou our eyes above,
To see a Father's love
Beam, like a bow of promise, through the cloud.

And O, if thoughts of gloom
Should hover o'er the tomb,
That light of love our guiding star shall be:
Our spirit shall not dread
The shadowy path to tread,
Friend, Guardian, Saviour, which doth lead to Thee.

Stephen Greenleaf Bulfinch (1809-1870), who ministered to various churches in the body to which he belonged, was a man of beautiful spirit, a good classical scholar, and possessed considerable poetic power. Many of his hymns appeared in "Lays of the Gospel." Three of these are becoming increasingly popular. One of the most poetic of our hymns for "The Sabbath-day" is from his pen.

Hail to the Sabbath-day,
The day divinely given,
When men to God their homage pay,
And earth draws near to heaven.

Lord. in Thy sacred hour,
Within Thy courts we bend;
And bless Thy love, and own Thy power,
Our Father and our Friend.

But Thou art not alone
In courts by mortals trod;
Nor only is the day Thine own
When crowds adore their God.

Thy temple is the arch
Of yon unmeasured sky;
Thy Sabbath the stupendous march
Of vast Eternity.

Lord, may that holier day
Dawn on Thy servants' sight:
And grant us in Thy courts to pray
Of pure, unclouded light.

Singularly tender and sympathetic is the following:—

Most gracious Saviour! 'twas not Thine
To spurn the erring from Thy sight;
Nor did Thy smile of love divine
Turn from the penitent its light.

Shall we who own the Christian name,
A brother's fault too sternly view,
Or think Thy holy name can blame,
The tear to human frailty due?

May we, while human guilt awakes
Upon our cheek the generous glow,
Spare the offender's heart that breaks
Beneath its load of shame and woe.

Conscious of frailty, may we yield
Forgiveness of the wrongs we bear;
And strive the penitent to shield
From further sin or dark despair.

And when our own offences weigh
Upon our hearts with anguish sore,
May we remember Thou didst say,
"In peace depart, but sin no more."

His hymn for the Communion strikes a new note, and is full of a large-hearted charity.

We gather to the sacred board,
Perchance a scanty band;
But with us in sublime accord
What mighty armies stand!

In creed and rite howe'er apart,
One Saviour still we own,
And pour the worship of the heart
Before our Father's throne.

A thousand spires o'er hill and vale
Point to the same blue heaven;
A thousand voices tell the tale
Of grace through Jesus given.

High choirs, in Europe's ancient fanes,
Praise Him for man who died;
And o'er the boundless Western plains
His name is glorified.

Around His tomb, on Salem's height,
Greek and Armenian bend;
And through all Lapland's months of night
The peasants' hymns ascend.

Are we not brethren? Saviour dear!
Then may we walk in love,
Joint subjects of Thy kingdom here,
Joint heirs of bliss above!

Whilst the following moves along a line very rare in hymns:—

Hath not thy heart within thee burned
At evening's calm and holy hour,
As if its inmost depths discerned
The presence of a loftier Power?

Hast thou not heard 'mid forest glades,
While ancient rivers murmured by,
A voice from forth the eternal shades,
That spake a present Deity?

And as upon the sacred page,
 Thine eye in rapt attention turned
O'er records of a holier age,
 Hath not thy heart within thee burned?

It was the voice of God, that spake
 In silence to thy silent heart;
And bade each holier thought awake,
 And every dream of earth depart.

Voice of our God, O yet be near!
 In low, sweet accents, whisper peace;
Direct us on our pathway here;
 Then bid in heaven our wanderings cease.

Oliver Wendell Holmes, M.D. (1809-1894), whose delightful books, "The Autocrat of the Breakfast Table," and the "Poet" and the "Professor" in the same series, are known and prized by all lovers of suggestive thought and beautiful English, fills a small place among American hymnists, but fills it as no one else could do. Every reader of the "Professor at the Breakfast Table" will have been struck with the following Sunday hymn, with which one of its chapters closes:—

Lord of all being! throned afar,
Thy glory flames from sun and star,
Centre and sun of every sphere,
Yet to each loving heart how near!

Sun of our life! Thy quickening ray
Sheds on our path the glow of day:
Star of our hope! Thy softened light
Cheers the long watches of the night.

Our midnight is Thy smile withdrawn,
Our noontide is Thy gracious dawn,
Our rainbow arch Thy mercy's sign,
All save the clouds of sin are Thine!

Lord of all life, below, above,
Whose light is truth, whose warmth is love;
Before Thy ever blazing throne
We ask no lustre of our own.

Grant us Thy truth to make us free,
And kindling hearts that burn for Thee;
Till all Thy living altars claim
One holy light, one heavenly flame.

Equally beautiful, but even more tender, is the following hymn of Trust:—

O Love Divine, that stooped to share
Our sharpest pang, our bitterest tear,
On Thee we cast each earth-born care:
We smile at pain while Thou art near!

Though long the weary way we tread,
And sorrow crown each lingering year;
No path we shun, no darkness dread,
Our hearts still whispering, Thou art near.

When drooping pleasure turns to grief,
And trembling faith is changed to fear:
The murmuring wind, the quivering leaf,
Shall softly tell us, Thou art near!

On Thee we fling our burdening woe,
O Love Divine, for ever dear:
Content to suffer, while we know,
Living and dying, Thou art near!

Less known, but very beautiful, is his latest written hymn—"Our Father, while our hearts unlearn."

There are three hymnists born in the same year (1810) who deserve notice. The first is—

Edmund Henry Sears, D.D. (1810-1876), one of the most spiritual teachers of the American Unitarian Church, to whom we owe the volume, "The Heart of Christianity," has given us two Christmas hymns. The first of these, which begins, "Calm on the listening ear of night," is probably the more popular in America, and is described by Dr. Wendell Holmes as "one of the finest and most beautiful hymns ever written." The second, beginning, "It came upon the midnight clear," is the more popular in England, and is, I think, the finer of the two. Dr. Morison of Milton says of this hymn: "I always feel that however poor my Christmas sermon may be, the reading and singing of this hymn are enough to make up for all deficiencies." It is happily too well known to need quotation here.

The second is—

Chandler Robbins, D.D. (1810-1882), the successor of Ralph Waldo Emerson in the charge of the Second Church in Boston, did much good work in improving American hymnody. If for no other, he deserves remembrance as the author of the following hymn for the close of worship:

Lo! the day of rest declineth,
   Gather fast the shades of night;
May the Sun that ever shineth
   Fill our souls with heavenly light.

Softly now the dew is falling:
   Peace o'er all the scene is spread;
On His children, meekly calling,
   Purer influence God will shed.

While Thine ear of love addressing,
   Thus our parting hymn we sing—
Father, give Thine evening blessing;
   Fold us safe beneath Thy wing.

Of this hymn the following story is told:—A company of Bostonians, among whom was Mrs. Hill, a daughter of Dr. Robbins, were returning from England in a Cunard steamer. An aged Scotch Presbyterian minister and his wife were among the passengers. The party were singing hymns on deck at the close of a lovely Sabbath day, when the clergyman went to his state-room and brought a book of hymns and tunes to show them what he said was the sweetest hymn he knew, set to the sweetest tune. What was the Boston lady's surprise to hear him repeat the lines which her own father had written: "Lo! the day of rest declineth," and begin to sing "Bedford Street"—a tune composed for the words by Mr. L. B. Barnes, President of the Handel and Haydn Society, and named after the author's own church, which was in Bedford Street, Boston.*

---

* *Cf.* Putnam's "Singers of Songs of the Liberal Faith," p. 309.

The third is—

James Freeman Clarke, D.D. (1810-1888), was one of the most erudite and popular authors of America. For many years he was minister of the Church of the Disciples in Boston, and for a part of the time held the Professorship of Natural Theology and Christian Doctrine in the Theological School at Cambridge. Many of his hymns are worthy of a place in our English collections. At present, however, only one, perhaps the most distinctive and beautiful of them all, is known at all widely on this side of the Atlantic.

Dear Friend, whose presence in the house,
Whose gracious word benign,
Could once, at Cana's wedding-feast,
Change water into wine—

Come, visit us, and when dull work
Grows weary, line on line,
Revive our souls, and make us see
Life's water glow as wine.

Gay mirth shall deepen into joy,
Earth's hope shall grow divine,
When Jesus visits us, to turn
Life's water into wine.

The social talk, the evening fire,
The homely household shrine,
Shall glow with angel-visits when
The Lord pours out the wine.

For when self-seeking turns to love,
Which knows not mine and thine,
The miracle again is wrought,
And water changed to wine.

William Henry Burleigh (1812-1871), on his mother's side a descendant of Governor William Bradford of the *Mayflower*, was the harbourmaster of New York, and an earnest advocate of temperance and freedom. He wrote many hymns, through which there runs a mingled strain of tenderness and confidence which is very beautiful.

They are becoming better known and more largely used in this country. The most popular are the following:—

Father! beneath Thy sheltering wing
  In sweet security we rest,
And fear no evil earth can bring,
  In life, in death, supremely blest.

For life is good, whose tidal flow
  The motions of Thy will obeys:
And death is good, that makes us know
  The life divine that all things sways.

And good it is to bear the cross,
  And so Thy perfect peace to win;
And naught is ill, nor brings us loss,
  Nor works us harm, save only sin.

Redeemed from this, we ask no more,
  But trust the love that saves to guide—
The grace that yields so rich a store,
  Will grant us all we need beside.

This, too, is of great merit—

Still will we trust, though earth seems dark and dreary,
  And the heart faint beneath His chastening rod,
Though rough and steep our pathway, worn and weary,
    Still will we trust in God!

Our eyes see dimly till by faith anointed,
  And our blind choosing brings us grief and pain;
Through Him alone, who hath our way appointed,
    We find our peace again.

Choose for us, God, nor let our weak preferring
  Cheat our poor souls of good Thou hast designed:
Choose for us, God; Thy wisdom is unerring,
    And we are fools and blind.

So from our sky the night shall furl her shadows,
  And day pour gladness through her golden gates;
Our rough path leads to flower-enamelled meadows,
    Where joy our coming waits.

Let us press on: in patient self-denial,
  Accept the hardship, shrink not from the loss:
Our guerdon lies beyond the hour of trial,
    Our crown beyond the cross.

In a similar vein are the following:—"We ask not that our path be always bright;" "When gladness gilds our prosperous day;" "Lead us, O Father, in the paths of peace;" whilst his Morning Hymn is one of the finest we possess for that season.

For the dear love that kept us through the night,
And gave our senses to sleep's gentle sway—
For the new miracle of dawning light
Flushing the east with prophecies of day,
We thank Thee, O our God!

For the fresh life that through our being flows
With its full tide to strengthen and to bless—
For calm sweet thoughts, upspringing from repose
To bear to Thee their song of thankfulness,
We praise Thee, O our God!

Day uttereth speech to day, and night to night
Tells of Thy power and glory. So would we,
Thy children, duly, with the morning light,
Or at still eve, upon the bended knee
Adore Thee, O our God!

Thou know'st our needs, Thy fulness will supply,
Our blindness—let Thy hand still lead us on,
Till, visited by the dayspring from on high
Our prayer, one only, "Let Thy will be done!"
We breathe to Thee, O God!

Samuel Longfellow (1819-1892), brother of the poet H. W. Longfellow, gave a large amount of attention to Hymnody, and, with Samuel Johnson, compiled one of the best of American hymnals, "Hymns of the Spirit." For the "Book of Vespers" he wrote the two evening hymns now so well known in this country, "Now on land and sea descending," and "Again as evening's shadow falls;" very fine they are. But beyond these the following are finding their way into English hymnals:—

"Prayer for inspiration:"

Holy Spirit, Truth Divine!
Dawn upon this soul of mine;
Word of God, and inward Light,
Wake my spirit, clear my sight.

Holy Spirit, Love Divine!
Glow within this heart of mine;
Kindle every high desire;
Perish self in Thy pure fire!

Holy Spirit, Power Divine!
Fill and nerve this will of mine;
By Thee may I strongly live,
Bravely bear, and nobly strive!

Holy Spirit, Right Divine!
King, within my conscience reign:
Be my Lord, and I shall be
Firmly bound, for ever free.

Holy Spirit, Peace Divine!
Still this restless heart of mine:
Speak to calm this tossing sea,
Stayed in Thy tranquillity.

Holy Spirit, Joy Divine!
Gladden Thou this heart of mine;
In the desert ways I'll sing,
Spring, O Well, for ever spring!

"A New Commandment:"

Beneath the shadow of the cross,
As earthly hopes remove:
His new commandment Jesus gives,
His blessed word of love.

O bond of union, strong and deep!
O bond of perfect peace!
Not e'en the lifted cross can harm,
If we but hold to this.

Then, Jesus, be Thy spirit ours,
And swift our feet shall move
To deeds of pure self-sacrifice,
And the sweet tasks of love.

And "The Church Universal:"

One holy church of God appears
Through every age and race,
Unwasted by the lapse of years,
Unchanged by changing place.

From oldest time, on farthest shores,
Beneath the pine or palm,
One unseen presence she adores,
With silence or with psalm.

Her priests are all God's faithful sons,
To serve the world raised up;
The pure in heart her baptised ones,
Love her communion-cup.

The truth is her prophetic gift,
The soul her sacred page;
And feet on mercy's errand swift,
Do make her pilgrimage.

O living Church, thine errand speed,
Fulfil thy task sublime;
With bread of life earth's hunger feed;
Redeem the evil time!

Jones Very (1813-1880), was a preacher without pastoral charge, who devoted his time chiefly to literary pursuits. There are those who regard him as one of the foremost poets of America. His hymns are very beautiful, but more suited for private reading and family worship than for public worship. The best known are the following:—"Father! Thy wonders do not singly stand;" "Father! there is no change to live with Thee;" "Wilt Thou not visit me?"

James Russell Lowell (1819-1891), the delightful literary critic, the versatile poet, the successful diplomatist, deserves a place among the hymnists for his beautiful Christmas Carol—"What means this glory round our feet?" but his lines on "Freedom" are well suited for singing.

Thomas Wentworth Higginson (born 1823), a descendant of the Rev. Francis Higginson, one of the Puritan settlers of America—originally a pastor of a Free Church at Worcester, and afterwards a colonel of black troops in the American War, in which he was wounded, is one of the literati of America, but he is at the same time one of its most remarkable hymnists. In his recently published book—"Cheerful Yesterdays," he has given a fascinating account of his earlier life. In his hymns there is a warmth and vigour and tenderness which are all too rare. They grow more dear the better they are known. Take the following as examples:—

"The Mystery of God:"

No human eyes Thy face may see;
  No human thought Thy form may know;
But all creation dwells in Thee,
  And Thy great life through all doth flow;

And yet, O strange and wondrous thought!
  Thou art a God who hearest prayer,
And every heart with sorrow fraught
  To seek Thy present aid may dare.

And though most weak our efforts seem
  Into one creed these thoughts to bind,
And vain the intellectual dream,
  To see and know th' Eternal Mind;

Yet Thou wilt turn them not aside,
  Who cannot solve Thy life divine,
But would give up all reason's pride
  To know their hearts approved by Thine.

And Thine unceasing love gave birth
  To our dear Lord, Thy holy Son,
Who left a perfect proof on earth,
  That Duty, Love, and Trust are one,

So though we faint on life's dark hill,
  And thought grow weak and knowledge flee,
Yet faith shall teach us courage still,
  And love shall guide us on to Thee.

"I will arise and go to my Father;"

To Thine eternal arms, O God,
  Take us, Thine erring children, in;
From dangerous paths too boldly trod,
  From wandering thoughts and dreams of sin.

Those arms were round our childhood's ways,
  A guard through helpless years to be;
O leave not our maturer days,
  We still are helpless without Thee!

We trusted hope and pride and strength;
  Our strength proved false, our pride was vain,
Our dreams have faded all at length—
  We come to Thee, O Lord, again!

A guide to trembling steps yet be!
  Give us of Thine eternal power!
So shall our paths all lead to Thee,
  And life still smile, like childhood's hour.

Mr. Higginson's volume of poems—"The Afternoon Landscape"—includes all his hymns.

Alice Cary (1820-1871) and her sister Phœbe Cary (1824-1871) wrote much verse of a suggestive kind from which striking hymns have been culled. "One sweetly solemn thought," by Phœbe, is well known, but the following hymns by Alice are of high merit—"Our days are few and full of strife," "Earth with its dark and dreadful ills," "O day to sweet religious thought," and "To Him who is the life of life."

Lucy Larcom (1826-1893) is fairly well known by her hymn "When for me the silent oar," but others from her pen richly deserve to be known, especially the one beginning—"In Christ I feel the heart of God."

To Mary Artemisia Lathbury (born 1841) we owe the hymn "Break Thou the bread of life," which is perfect in its simplicity, and "Day is dying in the west," which deserves a place in the front rank of Evening hymns.

John Greenleaf Whittier (1807-1892) belonged to the Society of Friends. His writings, pathetically beautiful beyond those of any poet of America, are becoming increasingly prized, and are exerting an immense influence on the religious thought and feeling of England.

It is strange to find among the Quakers, whose assemblies are never enlivened or inspired by song, one contributing so many verses to the worship song of the Church at large. Few of these were written for use in public worship, but many of his verses are so beautiful, so pathetic, so charged with the tenderest Christian feeling, that they have again and again been arranged and inserted in recent Hymnals. His greatest hymn is one extending to thirty-nine verses, called "Our Master," from which many contributions have been taken. At first only a very few verses were taken, but these have gradually been increased until now nearly the whole hymn has found its way into public worship. I give one part as a specimen.

Our Friend, our Brother, and our Lord,
  What may Thy service be?
Nor name, nor form, nor ritual word,
  But simply following Thee.

Thou judgest us; Thy purity
  Doth all our lusts condemn;
The love that draws us nearer Thee
  Is hot with wrath to them.

Our thoughts lie open to Thy sight,
  And naked to Thy glance:
Our secret sins are in the light
  Of Thy pure countenance.

Yet weak and blinded though we be,
  Thou dost our service own;
We bring our varying gifts to Thee,
  And Thou rejectest none.

To Thee our full humanity,
  Its joys and pains, belong;
The wrong of man to man on Thee
  Inflicts a deeper wrong.

Deep strike Thy roots, O heavenly Vine,
  Within our earthly sod,
Most human and yet most divine,
  The flower of man and God!

Apart from Thee all gain is loss,
  All labour vainly done;
The solemn shadow of Thy Cross
  Is better than the sun.

Alone, O love ineffable!
  Thy saving name is given;
To turn aside from Thee is hell,
  To walk with Thee is heaven.

We faintly hear, we dimly see,
  In differing phrase we pray;
But dim or clear, we own in Thee
  The Light, the Truth, the Way!

Other examples of adaptations from Mr. Whittier may be found in the following:—"To weary hearts, to mourning homes," from "The Angel of Patience," a free paraphrase from the German. "Another hand is beckoning us," from "Gone." "All as God wills who wisely heeds," from "My Psalm." "With silence only as their benediction," from "To my Friend on the death of his Sister." "Shall we grow weary in our watch," from "The Cypress-Tree of Ceylon," beneath which venerable Jogees or saints sit, silent and motionless, patiently awaiting the falling of a leaf.

What can be finer than such hymns as the following:—

Dear Lord and Father of mankind,
  Forgive our feverish ways!
Reclothe us in our rightful mind;
In purer lives, Thy service find,
  In deeper reverence, praise.

O Sabbath rest by Galilee!
  O calm of hills above!
Where Jesus knelt to share with Thee
The silence of eternity
  Interpreted by love!

With that deep hush subduing all
  Our words and works that drown
The tender whisper of Thy call,
As noiseless let Thy blessing fall,
  As fell Thy manna down.

Drop Thy still dews of quietness,
  Till all our strivings cease:
Take from our souls the strain and stress;
And let our ordered lives confess
  The beauty of Thy peace.

Breathe through the pulses of desire
  Thy coolness and Thy balm;
Let sense be dumb,—its heats expire:
Speak through the earthquake, wind, and fire,
  O still small voice of calm!

Or the hymn written for the Anniversary of the Children's Mission, Boston, 1878:—

Thine are all the gifts, O God!
  Thine the broken bread;
Let the naked feet be shod,
  And the starving fed.

Let Thy children, by Thy grace,
  Give as they abound,
Till the poor have breathing-space,
  And the lost are found.

Wiser than the miser's hoards
  Is the giver's choice;
Sweeter than the song of birds
  Is the thankful voice.

Welcome smiles on faces sad
  As the flowers of spring;
Let the tender hearts be glad
  With the joy they bring.

Or that for the American Horticultural Society, 1882:—

O Painter of the fruits and flowers,
  We own Thy wise design,
Whereby these human hands of ours
  May share the works of Thine!

Apart from Thee, we plant in vain
  The root, and sow the seed;
Thy early and Thy latter rain,
  Thy sun and dew we need.

Our toil is sweet with thankfulness,
  Our burden is our boon;
The curse of earth's grey morning is
  The blessing of its noon.

Why search the wide world everywhere,
  For Eden's unknown ground?—
That garden of the primal pair
  May never more be found.

But, blest by Thee, our patient toil
  May right the ancient wrong,
And give to every clime and soil
  The beauty lost so long.

Our homestead, flowers, and fruited trees,
  May Eden's orchard shame;
We taste the tempting sweets of these,
  Like Eve, without her blame.

And North and South, and East and West,
  The pride of every zone;
The fairest, rarest, and the best,
  May all be made our own.

Its earliest shrines the young world sought,
  In hill-groves, and in bowers;
The fittest offerings thither brought
  Were Thy own fruits and flowers.

And still with reverent hands we cull
  Thy gifts each year renewed;
The good is always beautiful,
  The beautiful is good.

Or that for the opening of Plymouth Church, St. Paul, Minnesota:—

All things are Thine: no gifts have we,
Lord of all gifts! to offer Thee;
And hence with grateful hearts to-day,
Thy own before Thy feet we lay.

Thy will was in the builders' thought;
Thy hand unseen amidst us wrought;
Through mortal motive, scheme, and plan,
Thy wise eternal purpose ran.

No lack Thy perfect fulness knew;
From human needs and longings grew
This house of prayer, this home of rest
In the fair garden of the West.

In weakness and in want we call
On Thee for whom the heavens are small;
Thy glory is Thy children's good,
Their joy Thy tender Fatherhood.

O Father! deign these walls to bless;
Fill with Thy love their emptiness;
And let their door a gateway be
To lead us from ourselves to Thee!

Where can a hymn for the aged be found, so real, so tender, so truly humble in its tone, as the following, included in one of his last volumes, "The Bay of the Seven Islands and other Poems, 1883."

When on my day of life the night is falling,
And, in the winds from unsunned spaces blown,
I hear far voices out of darkness calling
My feet to paths unknown.

Thou who hast made my home of life so pleasant,
Leave not its tenant when its walls decay;
O Love Divine, O Helper ever present,
Be Thou my strength and stay!

Be near me when all else is from me drifting—
Earth, sky, home's pictures, days of shade and shine,
And kindly faces to my own uplifting
The love which answers mine.

I have but Thee, my Father! let Thy Spirit
Be with me then to comfort and uphold;
No gate of pearl, no branch of palm I merit,
Nor street of shining gold.

Suffice it if—my good and ill unreckoned,
And both forgiven through Thy abounding grace—
I find myself by hands familiar beckoned
Unto my fitting place.

Some humble door among Thy many mansions,
Some sheltering shade where sin and striving cease,
And flows for ever through heaven's green expansions
The river of Thy peace.

There, from the music round about me stealing,
I fain would learn the new and holy song,
And find at last, beneath Thy trees of healing,
The life for which I long.

Such hymns are endearing their author to an ever-increasing number, and wherever sung speedily become favourites.

The examples I have given, and they are only a few flowers out of the great garden of American song, are sufficient to show not only what our friends across the Atlantic have done, but what may be expected from them in the future. It is not too much to say, that any hymnal which does not draw, and that largely, on the stores of American hymnody, must fall very far short of being an ideal one. And editors of the hymnals of the future will be more richly repaid for their search in this quarter than for one devoted to the ancient treasury of the Church—the best of which have been already utilised, and many of which represented a less pure and Christ-like Gospel than those of modern times. Of this department it may be truly said, "Thou hast kept the good wine until now."

CHAPTER XXI.

CHILDREN'S HYMNS.

It was late in the history of the Church before any special provision was deemed necessary for the worship of children. It was probably thought sufficient to admit them to the Church by the rites of Baptism and Confirmation, and if they sang at all, they had to be content with the provision made for their elders. The only ancient hymn for children existing is that of Clemens Alexandrinus, which I quote below in Dr. Dexter's translation. It will be seen that this is a hymn *on behalf* of children, rather than one to be sung by them :—

Shepherd of tender youth,
Guiding, in love and truth,
    Through devious ways:
Christ, our triumphant King,
We come Thy name to sing,
And here our children bring,
    To shout Thy praise.

Thou art our Holy Lord,
The all-subduing Word,
    Healer of strife;
Thou didst Thyself abase,
That from sin's deep disgrace
Thou mightest save our race,
    And give us life.

O wisdom's Great High Priest,
Thou hast prepared the feast
    Of holy love;
And in our mortal pain,
None calls on Thee in vain;
Help Thou dost not refrain,—
    Help from above.

Be ever near our side,
Our Shepherd and our Guide,
Our staff and song:
Jesus, Thou Christ of God,
By Thy perennial word,
Lead us where Thou hast trod;
Make our faith strong.

So now, and till we die,
Sound we Thy praises high,
And joyful sing.
Infants, and the glad throng
Who to Thy Church belong,
Unite, and swell the song
To Christ our King.

That children sang hymns is clear from the story of the seven boys who sang "Gloria, laus, et honor" (see p. 51) before the Emperor Louis, and so obtained St. Theodulph's liberation from prison, but it may be doubted whether any beyond the smallest provision was made of verses suited to their young minds. Even of the early carols, none seem to have been composed for the young. The ancient hymns which were used in some of the great public schools of England, and which have been preserved to our own day, have no special adaptation to this purpose. Indeed, it is pretty clear from the title to the 1560 edition of Sternhold and Hopkins, that, at that time, ordinary hymns were considered suitable enough for children. The following extract shows this—of that version, it says:—"Very much to be used of all sorts of people privately, for their godly solace and comfort; laiying aparte all ungodly songs and ballades, which tend only to the nourishing of vice and corrupting of youth." Here and there a hymn may be found for children in the 17th century in the writings of Wither, Herrick, and Jeremy Taylor, but even these do not seem to have been intended for use in *public* worship. Good Bishop Ken's three hymns, now so well known, were written for use in

Winchester College, and are almost equally suited for adults and for the young. In the beginning of the 18th century, Bishop George Hickes gives in "The Little Office for two or more Young Ladies under the same Governess," a translation of Bernard's "Jesu dulcis Memoria," for use at any time. This shows pretty clearly what the ideas of those times were on this matter. To all intents and purposes, no special provision was made for children until Dr. Watts published his "Divine and Moral Songs," so that he is the first founder of the choir of the children as well as that of their elders. The dedication seems to show that he was led to write such hymns for the use of the children of Sir Thomas Abney, to whose house he went for a short visit, and remained for the rest of his life, never wearing out his welcome; but the preface speaks of the book as having been written at the request of a friend engaged in catechising, who had doubtless felt the need for hymns more suitable to children than then existed. The work gained, as it deserved, a great success, and edition after edition of it appeared, both in London and the provinces. These "Divine and Moral Songs" must not be judged, as they too often have been, from the standpoint of our own time, which has attained to a more gracious theology, and possesses so fine a store of children's hymns. This would be as unfair as to judge Copernicus or Galileo from the standpoint of the age of the Herschels. The first worker in any field is of necessity a pioneer, and only roughly tills the land he occupies; it remains for his successors to reach a higher style of culture. Dr. Watts's hymns enshrine the theology and taste of his age; it could not be otherwise. They have been thrown into the shade by the finer work of his successors; but we must give him his due as opening and first cultivating the field of children's hymnody. Moreover, as he never married, the instinct and knowledge of fatherhood were hidden from him, and his hymns for children, as a consequence, suffer. Without doubt, the finest from his pen is his Cradle Hymn, which, it must be confessed, like too many so-called children's hymns, is suited for singing, not by, but on behalf of, children. It has of late somewhat dropped out of sight, and I therefore quote it:—

Hush, dear child, lie still and slumber,
Holy angels guard thy bed,
Heavenly blessings without number
Gently falling on thy head.

Sleep, my babe; thy food and raiment,
House and home, thy friends provide,
All without thy care and payment;
All thy wants are well supplied

How much better thou'rt attended
Than the Son of God could be,
When from heaven He descended,
And became a child like thee.

Soft and easy is thy cradle;
Coarse and hard thy Saviour lay,
When His birthplace was a stable,
And His softest bed was hay.

Was there nothing but a manger
Wretched sinners could afford,
To receive the heavenly Stranger?
Did they thus affront their Lord?

See the joyful shepherds round Him,
Telling wonders from the sky;
Where they sought Him, there they found Him,
With His virgin-mother by.

'Twas to save thee, child, from dying,
That thy blest Redeemer came;
He by groans and bitter crying
Saved thee from burning flame.

Mayst thou live to know and fear Him,
Trust and love Him all thy days;
Then go dwell for ever near Him,
See His face, and sing His praise.

Many of his hymns are still remembered, though little sung:—"How doth the little busy bee," "'Tis the voice of the sluggard," "Let dogs delight to bark and bite," while others, such as "I sing the almighty power of God," are as frequently sung by adults as children, for whom they are equally suited. For a considerable time, Dr. Watts's hymns for children practically held undisputed possession of the field. In 1754, Cennick published at Dublin "Hymns for Children," in 2 vols.; only one copy of this, (in the Fulneck Library), is known to exist, but later Moravian collections drew many hymns from this source, and one or two in altered, but not improved, forms may be found in children's hymn books of our own time. The following is probably the best:—

O Thou, before whose Father's face
 The children's angels stand,
Grant me, a helpless child, the grace,
 That Thy angelic band

May watch my ways and guard my bed,
 And minister to me,
Till I in death shall bow my head,
 And go to live with Thee.

Happy the children who are gone,
 To Jesus Christ in peace,
Who stand around His glorious throne,
 Clad in His righteousness.

The Saviour whom they loved while here
 Hath wiped their tears away;
They never more can grieve, or fear,
 Or sin, or go astray.

In ceaseless happiness they view
 Our Saviour's smiling face;
That face once marred, in which below
 Men saw no comeliness.

Methinks I hear them joyful sing
 (Ten thousands do the same),
"Salvation to the immortal King,
 To God and to the Lamb!"

O that I may so favoured be,
With them above to join;
O that, like them, I Christ may see,
And He be ever mine.

Grant me but this, Thou great High priest
And when I'm here no more,
Convey me home to endless rest,
Where Thou art gone before.

Charles Wesley attempted, in 1763, to make provision for children's song, by the publication of his "Hymns for Children," but with little success, since he started with the wrong idea, attempting to lift children up to the level of adults, merely adapting his compositions to them by simplicity of diction. Only one hymn from this source ever gained any popularity:—

Gentle Jesus, meek and mild,
Look upon a little child:
Pity my simplicity,
Suffer me to come to Thee.

Fain I would to Thee be brought;
Dearest God, forbid it not:
Give me, dearest God, a place
In the kingdom of Thy grace.

Put Thy hands upon my head,
Let me in Thine arms be stayed;
Let me lean upon Thy breast,
Lull me, lull me, Lord, to rest.

Hold me fast in Thy embrace,
Let me see Thy smiling face.
Give me, Lord, Thy blessing give;
Pray for me, and I shall live.

I shall live the simple life,
Free from sin's uneasy strife,
Sweetly ignorant of ill,
Innocent and happy still.

Oh that I may never know
What the wicked people do!
Sin is contrary to Thee,
Sin is the forbidden tree.

Keep me from the great offence,
Guard my helpless innocence;
Hide me, from all evil hide,
Self and stubbornness and pride,

Lamb of God, I look to Thee;
Thou shalt my Example be;
Thou art gentle, meek, and mild,
Thou wast once a little child.

Fain I would be as Thou art;
Give me Thy obedient heart.
Thou art pitiful and kind;
Let me have Thy loving mind.

Meek and lowly may I be;
Thou art all humility.
Let me to my betters bow;
Subject to Thy parents Thou.

Let me above all fulfil
God my heavenly Father's will;
Never His good Spirit grieve,
Only to His glory live.

Thou didst live to God alone,
Thou didst never seek Thine own;
Thou Thyself didst never please,
God was all Thy happiness.

Loving Jesu, gentle Lamb,
In Thy gracious hands I am,
Make me, Saviour, what Thou art,
Live Thyself within my heart.

I shall then show forth Thy praise,
Serve Thee all my happy days:
Then the world shall always see
Christ, the Holy Child, in me.

Up to this time the idea prevailed that the same author could provide a collection of hymns for children as well as for adults, and that if he could do the one he could also do the other. But now the idea began to dawn that a hymn book, like the Prayer Book and the Bible, required variety in its authorship. One of the earliest *collections* contained one hundred and four hymns, made up of forty-four by Dr. Watts, thirty-five of the Olney hymns, two by Dr. Hawker, the Editor, and a few by other writers. This may serve as a sample of the sort of thing that was then done. But it was not till Women, with their deeper insight into, and tenderer sympathy with child life, entered on this field, that anything like adequate or suitable provision was made for children's song. Indeed, it may be that the way in which the church repressed woman, and kept her from bearing a part in its work, accounts, to some extent, for the lateness of the development of children's hymnody. With the entrance of woman on this sphere there arises a new era. Henceforward she becomes the chief contributor. It will be noticed that a very large proportion of the writers mentioned in this chapter belong to that sex. This was to be expected. The new era dawned in 1810, when Ann and Jane Taylor issued their "Hymns for Infant Minds." These threw into the shade all previous ones for children save the best by Dr. Watts, and for many years were the chief favourites. Like Dr. Watts's, many of them look rather poor by the side of the still finer work of our day, but they mark a distinct step in advance of all that preceded, and the following still hold, and are likely to hold their ground. By Ann Taylor, afterwards Mrs. Gilbert (1782-1866):—"Great God, and wilt Thou condescend," "God is in heaven, can He hear," "Jesus who lived above the sky," "The God of heaven is pleased to see," and "A Captain forth to battle went," perhaps rather more of a poem than a hymn, but which should be better known; whilst by Jane Taylor (1783-1824) there are "When daily I kneel down to pray," "Jesus Christ, my Lord and Saviour," "Love and kindness we must measure." Perhaps most popular of all is "Good David, whose psalms have so often been sung;" to which of the sisters this is due is not known with certainty. Jane Taylor gives the following account of her method of writing her children's hymns:—

"I think I have some idea of what a child's hymn ought to be; and when I commenced the task, it was with the presumptuous determination that nothing should fall short of the standard I had formed in my mind. In order to do this, my method was to shut my eyes, and imagine the presence of some pretty little mortal, and then endeavour to catch, as it were, the very language it would use on the subject before me. If in any instances I have succeeded, to this little imaginary being I should attribute my success, and I have failed so frequently, because so frequently I was compelled to say, 'Now you may go, my dear; I shall finish this hymn myself.'" It is rather a curious thing, that the hymns written by Helen, daughter of Martin Taylor, and niece of Ann and Jane Taylor, which were published under the title of "The Sabbath Bell," and "Missionary Hymns," though in some senses equal to, and perhaps finer, than her better-known aunts', should have almost escaped notice. Until I drew forth some of their treasures and included them in "The Book of Praise for Children," they had almost entirely been lost sight of. I have an impression that whilst the "Hymns for Infant Minds" are likely to wane in popularity, some of those by Helen Taylor are likely to become more widely known and used. They seem to me to reach a higher literary standard, to be more picturesque, and to be more filled with the wider thoughts of religion that now prevail. I anticipate for them a great future. My readers shall judge for themselves. Here is one of the finest missionary hymns ever written for children:—

There is joy above the skies
  If a sinner, only one,
Lifts to Thee, O Lord, his eyes;
  And Thy holy will is done.
    Earth and heaven will happy be
    When all nations worship Thee!

If we live to see those days,
Live to hear the holy songs,
How will better hymns of praise
Pass in music from our tongues!
Happier children we shall be
When Thy glory we shall see.

Now like waters gushing up,
Are the thankful thoughts we think
For the good and pleasant cup
We have every day to drink.
Happy Christian children, we
Every day Thy mercy see!

But the glory will be bright,
Brighter than our words can show;
When all kingdoms see the light
When all lands Thy goodness know!
Earth and heaven will happy be
When the heathen worship Thee!

This is almost equal :--

O, let us all be glad and sing,
Like angels in the sky,
With all our hearts to God our King—
Hosanna let us cry!

He placed us in this happy land,
Like blossoms in the sun—
Like open blossoms we should stand,
Rejoicing every one.

But while we praise Him, let us pray
For countries dark and sad,
That they may hear the word one day,
Which makes our land so glad.

That heathen men may bend their knees
To one great Name alone,
And idols hewed from forest trees
To moles and bats be thrown.

These are from her tiny volume "Missionary Hymns for the use of Children," published in 1846. The following from her "Sabbath Bells" (both vols. are very rare) seems to me very true and beautiful, and far more likely to do a child good than most of the hymns about heaven that have been written for them :—

I love that holy scripture,
  Where I am truly told
About the heavenly city,
  With wall of precious gold;

About the shining river,
  That goeth thro' the street,—
The boughs of life above it,
  With fruit and blossoms sweet.

About the good and perfect,
  With crowns like yonder sun,
Who won those shining garlands
  Where children's feet may run.

This world is sometimes happy,
  With pleasant things I love;
But it must be far better,
  To dwell in heaven above.

Not that the walls are golden,
  The gates are always bright;
Not that the river poureth
  Through every street its light.

Not that a pleasant music
  From golden harps is stirred,
And every sound is sweeter
  Than ear hath ever heard.

But there shall never enter,
  The dark rude thoughts of sin,
That here, are always watching,
  To come the heart within.

And there we shall not find it
  So very hard to be
Gentle and true and patient
  For we the Lord shall see.

And so we shall grow like Him
  All holy things to love;
Oh! it must be far better
  To dwell in heaven above!

The number of hymn-writers for children now begins to be large, and the ideal still higher. Writers begin to recognise the fact that a hymn to be really loved by children must above all things be quick in movement, and picturesque in treatment of its subject. These are the great essentials. Montgomery wrote many for the Sheffield Whitsuntide gatherings of Sunday schools, but these, though marked by his high qualities, have never become popular. The writer of this period who showed that he knew exactly what is required in a children's hymn, but who unfortunately died too early to leave more than one or two, was Thomas Rawson Taylor (1807-1835). The following from his pen has never been excelled:—

There was a time when children sang
  The Saviour's praise with sacred glee,
And all the hills of Judah rang
  With their exulting Jubilee.

O to have joined their rapturous songs,
  And swelled their sweet hosannas high,
And blessed Him with our feeble tongues
  As He—the Man of grief—went by!

But Christ is now a glorious King,
  And angels in His presence bow;
The humble songs that we can sing—
  O! will He—can He—hear them now?

He can—He will—He loves to hear
  The notes which babes and sucklings raise:
Jesus, we come with trembling fear,
  O teach our hearts and tongues to praise!

We join the hosts around Thy throne,
  Who once, like us, the desert trod:
And thus we make their song our own—
  'Hosanna to the Son of God!'

A far finer and healthier hymn than his better-known one for adults "I'm but a stranger here," with its depreciation of earth.

Elizabeth Parson, *née* Rooker (born 1812), wrote two hymns which have been exceedingly popular, and are full of melody and movement—"Jesus, we love to meet," and "O happy land! O happy land!"

Mrs. Shelly, *née* Jackson, wrote "Lord, a little band and lowly," a hymn set in a very tender key, under the following circumstances, which may show that the most effective hymns are usually not laboured compositions, but thrown off in a moment of inspiration. "At a Sunday School meeting in Manchester, the Rev. John Curwen one evening gave a lecture on singing. He sang a very pretty and simple tune, to which he said he had no suitable words, and wished that some one would write a hymn to it. I wrote these verses, and gave them to him after the close of the meeting."*

Many writers now essayed the task of providing children with hymns, but none with very great success. John Burton, Dorothy Ann Thrupp, J. Cawood, and others who belonged to the Evangelical school. The leaders of the Tractarian movement felt the need of hymns embodying their doctrine, and an attempt was made in "The Child's Christian Year" (1841) to meet the want, but this, though a pleasant book for reading, was utterly unsuitable for use in schools. Its chief contributors, John Keble, Joseph Anstice, Isaac Williams, and John Henry Newman, did not possess the gifts for such a work. In my judgment, though some will differ from me on this point, the same may be said of Dr. Neale's "Hymns for Children"; they do not catch the ear of children. Indeed, Dr. Neale owes his distinguished place, not to his original hymns, but to his versions from ancient writers. I do not think a really popular hymn for children can be named from any member of the High Church party until 1848, when Mrs. Cecil Frances Alexander put forth her "Hymns for Children," which at once created a new school, and became its model. She saw that hymns for children should not only be in plain language, but that they should be picturesque,

* "Biographical Notes on the New Child's Own Hymn Book," by J. S. Curwen.

pathetic, and not confined to the severe metres which had so long held possession of the field. Before her there is no writer, save Thomas Rawson Taylor, who fully realised this. In some of her hymns, High Church doctrine is prominent, and robs them of their beauty, but in the majority, she writes so largely as a poetess, that formal doctrine is not apparent. Her hymns are too well-known to need quotation. The best are "Once in royal David's City;" "Every morning the red sun"—to which Mr. Moss's tune, "St. Silas," is one of the most exquisite settings for a children's hymn ever produced; "We are but little children weak;" "All things bright and beautiful." One little known, and not included in her published books, is the following, written for a clergyman in Liverpool, which seems to me specially picturesque:—

Once in the town of Bethlehem,
  Far away across the sea,
There was laid a little Baby,
  On a Virgin mother's knee.
    O Saviour! gentle Saviour!
      Hear Thy little children sing,
    The God of our Salvation,
      The Child that is our King.

It was not a stately palace
  Where that little Baby lay,
With tall servants to attend Him,
  And red guards to keep the way,
    O Saviour! gentle Saviour! &c.

But the oxen stood around Him,
  In a stable, low and dim—
In the world He had created,
  There was not a room for Him!
    O Saviour! gentle Saviour! &c.

For He left His Father's glory,
  And the golden halls above,
And He took our human nature,
  In the greatness of His love.
    O Saviour! gentle Saviour! &c.

Of His infinite compassion,
He can feel our want and woe,
For He suffered, He was tempted
When He lived our life below.
O Saviour! gentle Saviour! &c.

Still His childhood's bright example
Gives a light to our poor homes:
From the blood of His atoning
Still our hope of pardon comes.
O Saviour! gentle Saviour! &c.

Still He stands and pleads in heaven
For us weak and sin-defiled,
God who is a man for ever,
Jesus who was once a child.
O Saviour! gentle Saviour! &c.

Esther Wiglesworth, who belongs to the same school of religious thought, has produced some fine hymns for children, which deserve to be more widely known. The following may be taken as an illustration:—

God sets a still small voice
Deep every soul within;
It guideth to the right,
And warneth us of sin.

If we that voice obey,
Clearer its tones will be,
Till all God's will for us
Clear as noonday we see.

If we that voice neglect,
Fainter will be its tone;
If still unheeded, it
Will leave us quite alone.

O grief! to be allowed
To go our own wild way;
Lord, hold Thy children back,
Lest we so sadly stray.

And help us to attend
To Thy sweet voice divine;
Then, in the judgment day,
Own us, good Lord, as Thine.

The Rev. John Curwen only wrote two hymns, one of which had a curious origin. "A hymn with a similar first line had been inserted in a new edition of the "Child's Own Hymn Book," without the knowledge that it was copyright. At the last moment, when the index was stereotyped, and the book was at press, Mr. Curwen discovered the authorship, and permission to insert it was refused, either for love or money, by the owner of the copyright. As a way out of the difficulty, he wrote this hymn, which now appears in almost every children's collection. Its more extended popularity dates from the time when it came back, with a tune and a chorus, from America"*:—

I'm a little pilgrim,
And a stranger here;
Though this world is pleasant,
Sin is always near.

[Jesus loves our pilgrim band,
He will lead us by the hand;
Lead us to the better land—
To our home on high.]

Mine's a better country,
Where there is no sin,
Where the tones of sorrow
Never enter in.

But a little pilgrim
Must have garments clean,
If he'd wear the white robes,
And with Christ be seen.

Jesus, cleanse and save me,
Teach me to obey;
Holy Spirit, guide me
On my heavenly way.

I'm a little pilgrim,
And a stranger here,
But my home in heaven
Cometh ever near.

Mr. Curwen did much, however, to stimulate children's hymnody by the publication of "The Child's Own Hymn Book," which, at the time it was issued, was far the most suitable collection in existence. Indeed, I am not sure

* "Biographical Notes on the New Child's Own Hymn Book," by J. S. Curwen.

that it is not the first *collection* which really deserved such a title. Beyond many, even of our own day, it kept in view the characteristics which should mark a hymnal for children.

The most noteworthy of modern hymnists for children are the following.

Among women hymnists, we have Mary Lundie Duncan (1814-1840), the authoress of one of the best known of children's hymns, "Jesus, tender Shepherd, hear me," which was included in her tiny book, "Rhymes for my Children." This is probably more frequently used as a little child's evening prayer than any other hymn.

Dorothy Ann Thrupp (1779-1847) is remembered by one hymn, which used to be a great favourite with little children, "A little ship was on the sea."

Anne Shepherd, *née* Houlditch (1809-1857), wrote a little book, "Hymns adapted for the comprehension of Infant Minds," in which was included "Around the throne of God in heaven," which, when children sung more about heaven, was a great favourite. It is very lyric and effective.

Elizabeth Strafford's hymns are well adapted, in their sentiment, for children, but they lack picturesqueness and melody, and so have never become popular. Perhaps the best is:—

Once to our world there came
A little holy child;
Gentle and good and mild,
And Jesus was His name.

He suffered want and pain
Was slighted, scorned, and poor;
All this He did endure,
That we in heaven might reign.

He never disobeyed
His Father's sacred laws;
We only were the cause
Why grief on Him was laid.

And yet He loves us still:
Nor grudges aught we cost;
No sinner would be lost
According to His will.

Oh! that indeed we could
Our naughty ways forsake,
And for our pattern take
This Saviour kind and good.

The path that Jesus trod
Oh may we also tread,
Jesus, our living head,
Lead Thou us up to God.

Jane E. Leeson, who, after a period of retirement from the world, passed away in 1883, wrote many verses for children, which were included in "Hymns and Scenes of Childhood" (1842). They are more remarkable for the suitability of their ideas, than their form and style, to the young. The following, which is her best may serve as a specimen:—

Sweet the lessons Jesus taught,
When to Him fond parents brought
Babes for whom they blessing sought—
Little ones, like me.

Jesus did not answer nay,
Bid them come another day;
Jesus did not turn away
Little ones, like me.

No, my Saviour's hand was laid
Softly on each infant head;
Jesus, when He blessed them, said
Let them come to Me.

Babes may still His blessing share·
Lambs are His peculiar care;
He will in His bosom bear
Little ones, like me.

Saviour, on my infant head
Let Thy gracious hand be laid,
While I do as Thou hast said,
Coming unto Thee.

Frances Ridley Havergal (1836-1879), of whom I have already spoken, has written, as was to be expected, very good hymns for children. Her version of the Lord's Prayer is both tender and concise:—

God in heaven, hear our singing,
  Only little ones are we,
Yet, a great petition bringing,
  Father, now we come to Thee.

Let Thy kingdom come, we pray Thee,
  Let the world in Thee find rest;
Let all know Thee, and obey Thee,
  Loving, praising, blessing, blest.

Let the sweet and joyful story
  Of the Saviour's wondrous love
Make on earth a song of glory,
  Like the angels' song above.

Send Thy Spirit's mighty shower,
  Bring the heathen to Thy Throne,
For the kingdom, and the power,
  And the glory, are Thine own.

The following is rather an address to a child than a hymn, but if that be overlooked, it is of great merit:—

God will take care of you. All through the day
Jesus is near you, to keep you from ill;
Waking or resting, at work or at play,
Jesus is with you, and watching you still.

He will take care of you. All through the night
Jesus, the Shepherd, His little one keeps;
Darkness to Him is the same as the light,
He never slumbers, and He never sleeps.

He will take care of you. All through the year.
Crowning each day with His kindness and love:
Sending you blessings, and shielding from fear.
Leading you on to the bright home above.

He will take care of you. Yes. to the end
Nothing can alter His love for His own;
Children, be glad that you have such a Friend;
He will not leave you one moment alone.

Among male authors we have—

John Henley (1800-1842), a minister of the Wesleyan Church, wrote "Children of Jerusalem," a hymn singularly crisp and effective, and greatly liked by children.

James Edmeston (1791-1867), already mentioned in a previous chapter, wrote many hymns for children, of which the best known is "Little travellers Zionwards," which is now made to commence with the second verse, "Who are they whose little feet," which used to be frequently sung in Sunday Schools.

Andrew Young (born 1807), formerly Head-master of Madras College, in the University of St. Andrews', is the author of the very bright, and, on the whole, healthy hymn on heaven, "There is a happy land." "The story of the origin of this hymn, kindly supplied by Mr. Colin Brown, of Glasgow, is interesting. One of the songs which the Indian palanquin bearers sing as they go, was set to English words about thirty years ago. It became very popular, its burden being 'There is a happy land, where care's unknown.' This song was sung one evening by a lady in Edinburgh, and heard by Mr. Young, then teacher of Niddry School. Being much touched by the beauty of the music, and of the opening idea of the words, Mr. Young was led to write the exquisite hymn, 'There is a happy land, far, far away,' to suit the music."*

John Burton's (1803-1877) hymn, "Saviour, while my heart is tender," is one of the most tender and graceful

* "Biographical Notes on the New Child's Own Hymn Book," by J. S. Curwen.

hymns of consecration for the young we possess; whilst to another author of precisely the same name (1773-1822) we owe the most popular children's hymn on the Bible, beginning "Holy Bible, Book Divine."

Henry Bateman (1802-1872) published a little volume of hymns for children, called "Sunday Sunshine," remarkable for simplicity and naturalness of tone. It is a pity that they are all in one metre, and of the same number of verses, since this renders them somewhat monotonous; but some of them are very good. The use made of Scripture events is often very happy. The following are amongst the best:—

In my soft bed, when quite alone,
 God watches me with care:
Sees me at rising, kneeling down,
 And listens to my prayer.

He follows me through all the day,
 Knows everything I do:
Remembers every word I say,
 My thoughts, and temper too.

If I am kind, God knows it well:
 If I am cross, He hears:
A falsehood, from the truth, can tell:
 He sees my smiles, and tears.

Great God, my footsteps guide, and bless,
 That this to me may be
A thankfulness and happiness,
 That, "Thou God seest me."

The thought of the last verse is very fine. The following, on the Bible, too, is good:—

The good old Book! with histories
 Of many a bygone age;
And promises and prophecies
 On almost every page.

The glorious Psalms, so full of thought
 And teaching good and wise!
And everywhere examples fraught
 With human sympathies.

The holy life of Christ, our Lord.
  His love so pure and free,
And every kind and gentle word
  That helps and teaches me.

Wonderful Book! oh, fill my heart,
  Great God, with Thy true fear:
And, as I read, Thy grace impart
  To make it plain and clear.

Mr. Bateman also wrote a hymn for adults that is worthy of a place in our collections:—

Light of the world! whose kind and gentle care
    Is joy and rest,
Whose counsels and commands so gracious are,
    Wisest and best,
Shine on my path, dear Lord, and guard the way,
Lest my poor heart, forgetting, go astray.

Lord of my life, my soul's most pure desire,
    Its hope and peace!
Let not the faith Thy loving words inspire
    Falter, or cease;
But be to me, true Friend, my chief delight,
And safely guide, that every step be right.

My blessèd Lord, what bliss to feel Thee near,
    Faithful and true:
To trust in Thee, without one doubt or fear.
    Thy will to do;
And all the while to know that Thou, our Friend,
Art blessing, and wilt bless us to the end.

And then, oh then! when sorrow's night is o'er,
    Life's daylight come,
And we are safe within heaven's golden door,
    At home, at home!
How full of glad rejoicing will we raise,
Saviour, to Thee, our everlasting praise.

Richard Henry Smith, the founder and minister of several Congregational churches, whose books on Art were appreciative and suggestive, wrote a few hymns for children. The one quoted below, for a *little* child, is remarkable for its simplicity:—

I am a little child,
And Jesus cares for me,
For even me He wants
His little child to be.

Jesus would take me up,
And keep me on His knee,
And fold me in His arms,
His little child to be.

And I will go to Him,
And I will let Him see
How glad I am to come,
His little child to be.

And I will stay with Him,
For Jesus wishes me,
Though I grow big and old,
His little child to be.

Of the hymns by Mrs. Shepcote, whose "Hymns for Infant Children" are well suited to those for whom they were written, the following is probably the best:—

Jesus, holy, undefiled,
Listen to a little child,
Thou hast sent the glorious light,
Chasing far the silent night.

Thou hast sent the sun to shine
O'er this glorious world of Thine,
Warmth to give. and pleasant glow
On each tender flower below.

Now the little birds arise,
Chirping gaily in the skies;
Thee their tiny voices praise
In the early songs they raise.

Thou, by whom the birds are fed,
Give to me my daily bread;
And Thy Holy Spirit give.
Without Whom I cannot live.

Make me, Lord, obedient, mild,
As becomes a little child;
All day long, in every way,
Teach me what to do and say

Help me never to forget
That in Thy great book is set
All that children think and say,
For the awful Judgment Day.

Let me never say a word
That will make Thee angry, Lord;
Help me so to live in love
As Thine angels do above

Make me, Lord, in work and play,
Thine more truly every day,
And when Thou at last shall come,
Take me to Thy heavenly home.

Emily E. S. Elliot is the authoress of two hymns which are poetic and original in form. Both of them are on the birth of Christ, and are deservedly popular. They should be in every collection for children's use. To render them still more widely known, I quote them :—

There came a little Child to earth
Long ago!
And the angels of God proclaimed His birth,
High and low.

Out in the night, so calm and still,
Their song was heard;
For they knew that the Child on Bethlehem's hill
Was Christ the Lord.

Far away in a goodly land,
Fair and bright,
Children with crowns of glory stand
Robed in white;

In white more pure than the spotless snow,
And their tongues unite
In the psalm which the angels sang long ago
On Christmas night.

They sing how the Lord of that world so fair
A Child was born;
And that they might a crown of glory wear,
Wore a crown of thorn;

And in mortal weakness, in want and pain,
Came forth to die;
That the children of earth might for ever reign
With Him on high.

He hath put on His kingly apparel now,
In that goodly land,
And He leads to where fountains of water flow
That chosen band.

And for evermore, in their robes so fair
And undefiled,
Those ransomed children His praise declare
Who was once a child.

The second is equally suitable for those of riper age :—

Thou didst leave Thy throne and Thy kingly crown
When Thou camest to earth for me:
But in Bethlehem's home was there found no room
For Thy holy nativity.
O come to my heart, Lord Jesus.
There is room in my heart for Thee.

Heaven's arches rang when the angels sang,
Proclaiming Thy royal degree;
But in lowly birth Thou didst come to earth,
And in great humility:
O come to my heart, Lord Jesus,
There is room in my heart for Thee.

The foxes found rest, and the birds had their nest
In the shade of the cedar tree;
But Thy couch was the sod, O Thou Son of God,
In the deserts of Galilee.
O come to my heart, Lord Jesus,
There is room in my heart for Thee.

Thou camest, O Lord, with the living word
That should set Thy people free;
But with mocking scorn, and with crown of thorn,
They bore Thee to Calvary:
O come to my heart, Lord Jesus,
There is room in my heart for Thee.

When heaven's arches shall ring and her choir shall sing
At Thy coming to victory,
Let Thy voice call me home, saying, "Yet there is room,
There is room at My side for Thee":
And my heart shall rejoice, Lord Jesus,
When Thou comest and callest for me.

Jemima Luke (born 1813) is the authoress of the well-known hymn, which deserves to be reckoned classic, "I think when I read that sweet story of old," and which makes us wonder that she never followed it up by the production of others. It was written in a stage coach, for a village school near Poundsford Park, Bath, where the writer's father resided.

Mrs. H. P. Hawkins, one of the Editors of "The Home Hymn Book," which, both for its words and their musical setting, deserves very high praise, has written several hymns for children, all of which are tender and beautiful in a very high degree. Perhaps the finest are the following. The first is for Evening:—

Kind Shepherd, see, Thy little lamb
Comes very tired to Thee;
O fold me in Thy loving arms,
And smile on me.

I've wandered from Thy fold to-day,
And could not hear Thee call,
And oh, I was not happy then,
Nor glad at all.

I want, dear Saviour, to be good,
And follow close to Thee,
Through flowery meads and pastures green,
And happy be.

Thou kind, good Shepherd, in Thy fold
I evermore would keep,
In morning's light or evening's shade,
And while I sleep.

But now, dear Jesus, let me lay
My head upon Thy breast;
I am too tired to tell Thee more,
Thou know'st the rest.

The second is for Morning:—

Thy little one, O Saviour dear,
Has just awoke from sleep,
And through the coming day I know
Thou wilt in safety keep.

Thou hast been watching over me,
Through all the long, dark night:
The darkness is not dark to Thee,
Because Thou art the Light.

I felt so safe and happy, Lord,
Although I could not see,
And softly whispered, ere I slept,
"O God, Thou seest *me*."

I think Thou'rt smiling on me now,
For all seems bright and glad,
But when I'm naughty, Saviour dear,
My heart is always sad.

I want Thy kind and loving smile
To light me all the way;
O, keep me, then, from doing wrong,
Or grieving Thee to-day.

E. C. W., who prefers to keep her anonymity, deserves mention for the simplicity and tenderness of her hymns for children. They were first included in my "Book of Praise for Children." This, for Evening, is very beautiful:—

My Father, hear my prayer
  Before I go to rest;
It is Thy little child
  That cometh to be blest.

Forgive me all my sin,
  And let me sleep this night
In safety and in peace
  Until the morning light.

Lord, help me every day
  To love Thee more and more,
And try to do Thy will
  Much better than before.

Now look upon me, Lord,
  Ere I lie down to rest;
It is Thy little child
  That cometh to be blest.

As is the following:—

Lord, Who hast made me Thy dear child,
  And loved me tenderly,
Oh, hear me when I come to own
  My many faults to Thee!

How often I have thought that I
  A better child would be,
More gentle, loving, kind, and true,
  And pleasing unto Thee.

And yet I have not conquered sin,
  Nor striven as I should:
I have not always looked to Thee
  When trying to be good.

Yet turn not from me, dearest Lord,
  But all my faults forgive:
And grant that I may love Thee more
  Each day on earth I live.

To Jeannette Threlfall (1821-1880) we owe one of the finest of our hymns for children, which has every characteristic needful for such a composition:—

Hosanna! loud hosanna!
  The little children sang:
Through pillared court and temple
  The lovely anthem rang;
To Jesus, who had blessed them,
  Close folded to His breast,
The children sang their praises,
  The simplest and the best.

From Olivet they followed,
  'Midst an exultant crowd,
Waving the victor palm branch,
  And shouting clear and loud:
Bright angels joined the chorus,
  Beyond the cloudless sky—
" Hosanna in the highest:
  Glory to God on high!"

Fair leaves of silvery olive
  They strewed upon the ground,
Whilst Salem's circling mountains
  Echoed the joyful sound:
The Lord of men and angels
  Rode on in lowly state,
Nor scorned that little children
  Should on his bidding wait.

" Hosanna in the highest!"
  That ancient song *we* sing;
For Christ is our Redeemer,
  The Lord of heaven our King:
Oh! may we ever praise Him
  With heart, and life, and voice,
And in His blissful presence
  Eternally rejoice!

Sarah Doudney (born 1842) is better known by her stories than her hymns, but the latter deserve, and will probably secure, a larger place in collections for children than they have, as yet, received, as may be judged from the following (published in 1871):—

For all Thy care we bless Thee,
  O Father, God of might!
For golden hours of morning,
  And quiet hours of night;
Thine is the arm that shields us
  When danger threatens nigh.
And Thine the hand that yields us
  Rich gifts of earth and sky.

For all Thy love we bless Thee;
No mortal lips can speak
Thy comfort to the weary,
Thy pity for the weak:
By Thee life's path is brightened
With sunshine and with song;
The heavy loads are lightened,
The feeble hearts made strong.

For all Thy truth we bless Thee;
Our human vows are frail,
But through the strife of ages
Thy word can never fail;
The kingdoms shall be broken,
The mighty ones will fall,
The promise Thou hast spoken
Shall triumph over all.

O teach us how to praise Thee,
And touch our lips with fire!
Yea, let Thy Dove descending,
Our hearts and minds inspire;
Thus toiling, watching, singing,
We tread our desert way,
And every hour is bringing
Nearer the dawn of day.

To turn to the other sex:—

John Ellerton (1826-1893), has done excellent work in this department. The following hymn is as remarkable for its lyric as its practical tone:—

Day by day we magnify Thee,—
When our hymns in school we raise,
Daily work begun and ended,
With the daily voice of praise.

Day by day we magnify Thee,—
When, as each new day is born,
On our knees, at home, we bless Thee
For the mercies of the morn.

Day by day we magnify Thee,—
In our hymns before we sleep;
Angels hear them, watching by us,
Christ's dear lambs all night to keep.

Day by day we magnify Thee,—
Not in words of praise alone;
Truthful lips, and meek obedience,
Show Thy glory in Thine own.

Day by day we magnify Thee,—
When, for Jesu's sake, we try
Every wrong to bear with patience,
Every sin to mortify.

Day by day we magnify Thee,—
Till our days on earth shall cease,
Till we rest from these our labours,
Waiting for Thy day in peace.

Then on that eternal morning,
With Thy great redeemèd host,
May we fully magnify Thee—
Father, Son, and Holy Ghost.

William Walsham How, of whose hymns for Church use I have spoken in a previous chapter, has also written some admirable ones for children. The following, which appeared, I believe, for the first time in my "Book of Praise for Children," is equal to those of Ann and Jane Taylor, but touched with an altogether tenderer spirit, which is so characteristic of the theology of our day:—

It is a thing most wonderful,
Almost too wonderful to be,
That God's own Son should come from heaven,
And die to save a child like me.

And yet I know that it is true:
He came to this poor world below,
And wept, and toiled, and mourned, and died,
Only because He loved us so.

I cannot tell how He could love
A child so weak and full of sin;
His love must be most wonderful,
If He could die my love to win.

I sometimes think about the cross,
And shut my eyes, and try to see
The cruel nails and crown of thorns,
And Jesus crucified for me.

But even could I see Him die,
I could but see a little part
Of that great Love, which, like a fire,
Is always burning in His heart.

It is most wonderful to know
His love for me so free and sure;
But 'tis more wonderful to see
My love for Him so faint and poor.

And yet I want to love Thee, Lord,
O light the flame within my heart,
And I will love Thee more and more,
Until I see Thee as Thou art.

In an altogether bolder and more jubilant strain is the following, with separate verses for boys and girls:—

Come, praise your Lord and Saviour
  In strains of holy mirth;
Give thanks to Him, O children,
  Who lived a child on earth.
He loved the little children,
  And called them to His side,
His loving arms embraced them
  And for their sake He died.

(*Boys only*).

O Jesu, we would praise Thee,
  With songs of holy joy,
For Thou on earth didst sojourn
  A pure and spotless boy.
Make us, like Thee, obedient,
  Like Thee, from sin-stains free,
Like Thee, in God's own temple,
  In lowly home, like Thee

(*Girls only*).

O Jesu, we too praise Thee,
  The lowly maiden's Son:
In Thee all gentlest graces
  Are gathered into one;
Oh! give that best adornment
  That Christian maid can wear,
The meek and quiet spirit
  Which shone in Thee so fair.

([illegible])

O Lord, with voices blended,
  We sing our songs of praise:
Be Thou the light and pattern
  Of all our childhood's days;
And lead us ever onward,
  That, while we stay below,
We may, like Thee, O Jesu,
  In grace and wisdom grow.

Both Bishop How and Mr. Ellerton have also done good service by the taste and judgment they have brought to bear on the Children's Hymnals which they have borne a part in editing.

Thomas Benson Pollock, of Birmingham (1836-1896), deserves mention as the author of a number of Metrical Litanies, some of which are admirably suited for children's use, as may be seen from the following Litany, of which I quote the first part:—

Jesu, from Thy throne on high,
Far above the bright blue sky,
Look on us with loving eye,
    Hear us, Holy Jesu.

Little children need not fear
When they know that Thou art near,
Thou dost love us, Saviour dear,
    Hear us, Holy Jesu.

Little lambs may come to Thee;
Thou wilt fold us tenderly,
And our careful Shepherd be,
    Hear us, Holy Jesu.

Little lives may be divine,
Little deeds of love may shine,
Little ones be wholly Thine,
    Hear us, Holy Jesu.

Little hearts may love Thee well,
Little lips Thy love may tell:
Little hymns Thy praises swell,
    Hear us, Holy Jesu.

Jesu, once an infant small,
Cradled in the oxen's stall,
Though the God and Lord of all,
    Hear us, Holy Jesu.

Once a child so good and fair,
Feeling want and toil and care,
All that we may have to bear,
    Hear us, Holy Jesu.

Jesu, Thou dost love us still,
And it is Thy holy will
That we should be safe from ill:
    Hear us, Holy Jesu.

Fold us to Thy loving breast,
There may we, in happy rest,
Feel that we indeed are blest
    Hear us, Holy Jesu.

Benjamin Waugh (born 1839), whose "Sunday Evenings with my Children" are so well known, and whose untiring labours on behalf of children, in connection with the London Society for their protection, deserve grateful record, has written many hymns for children, which have not, as yet, come into use so largely as their merit deserves. The following enforces, with great tenderness, a much needed idea:—

Where is Jesus, little children?
  Is He up in heaven?
Has God taken back the present
  Which of old was given?

Where is Jesus, little children?
  Is He in a book?
Has He ceased to talk to people,
  And on them to look?

Where is Jesus, little children?
  With us evermore
He is here, and we may find him
  Shut within this door.

Jesus is a lovely spirit,
  Lowly, pure, and kind;
Feeling in the hearts of people,
  Thinking in their mind.

Self-forgetting, gentle mercy,
  Love that will not die,
These betray the heart of Jesus,
  Tell us He is nigh.

Shut within the souls of children,
  Jesus makes His home;
Where the heart has heard Him knocking,
  And has bid Him come.

Jesus, make in us Thy dwelling;
  Come with us to live;
And to each and all our doings
  Thy dear beauty give.

This, too, is equally good:—

I'll come to Thee, O Jesus Christ!
  I'll Thy disciple be;
Not tears, not deeds, but self I'll bring,
  Because Thou callest me.

I'll follow Thee to watch Thy ways,
  From manger on to grave;
For, step by step, 'tis thus I learn
  Thy sovereign power to save.

I'll strive to do Thy blessèd will,
  Renounce my foolish ways,
And live a life, though stained by sin,
  More worthy of Thy grace.

I'll hope through all my mortal days
  Thee by my side to find;
To feast my eyes, to fire my heart,
  To beautify my mind.

I'll sing Thee here, my spirit's Prince,
  And follow in Thy train,
Until Thy will my place shall change,
  And death shall be my gain;

Then, brighter far than summer's sun,
  More glad than marriage joy,
In serving, praising, crowning Thee,
  Eternal life employ.

This, though rather a tender appeal from the child to the teacher, is yet very natural:—

O, who will show me Jesus Christ?
  O, who will take my hand?
And lead to Him whose words they say
  A child can understand!

Will some one let me see the face
  Which made the children smile,
And lead me through the crowd and throng
  And stop with me awhile?

Will some one let me feel the touch
  Which made the children well,
Cast out the evil things within,
  And made the good ones dwell?

They say that He is somewhere now;
  Will some one show me where?
Will those who know just take my hand,
  And kindly lead me there?

It seems as if I heard a call:
  "Come, little child, to me."
O, Jesus, put it in some heart
  To bring me unto Thee.

Newman Hall (born 1816), who has written many hymns for adults, which do not seem to me very distinctive or original, has, however, struck a really beautiful note in the following hymn for children; which, he tells me, came into his mind as he was walking down Hampstead Hill:—

Day again is dawning,
  Darkness flies away,
Now from sleep awaking
  Let me rise and pray.
Jesus, tender Shepherd,
  Watching while I slept,
Bless the little lambkin
  Thou hast safely kept.

Help me, Lord, to praise Thee,
  For my cosy bed;
For my clothes and playthings,
  For my daily bread;
For my darling mother,
  For my father dear;
For the friends who love me,
  Far away and near.

Robin blithe is chirping,
  Glad the night is o'er;
Larks the light are greeting,
  Singing as they soar:
I'm Thy little birdie,
  May I ever sing,
Goodness making music
  Unto Christ my King.

Daisies now are turning
  Bright eyes to the sun;
And the light is shining
  On them every one:
I'm Thy little flower,
  Jesus, shine on me,
Turning all my lifetime
  Grateful eyes to Thee.

I omit the doxology, as experience has shown that it is not suitable for children, and somewhat mars the simplicity of the previous verses.

Sabine Baring Gould (born 1834), vicar of Lew Trenchard, to whom we owe the fine rendering from the Danish of Ingemann's hymn, "Through the night of doubt and sorrow," and who is the author of "Onward, Christian soldiers, marching as to war," also wrote an Evening Hymn for children, remarkable for its simplicity and picturesqueness, "Now the day is over." It is one of the finest children's hymns for that season in the language.

Albert Midlane (born 1825) has written many hymns, most of which do not rise above mediocrity; but one for children, "There's a friend for little children," has attained to great popularity, and is included in most children's hymnals. It has the picturesqueness and melody which are so vital to a good hymn for children.

Some of William Chatterton Dix's hymns, to which I have already referred (see page 299), are suitable, and, indeed, prized by children, but the following one, written specially for them, seems to me singularly healthy and beautiful:—

In our work, and in our play,
Jesu, be Thou ever near,
Guarding, guiding, all the day,
Keeping in Thy holy fear.

Thou didst toil, a lowly Child
In the far-off Holy land,
Blessing labour undefiled,
Pure, and honest of the hand.

Thou wilt bless our playhour too,
If we ask Thy succour strong;
Watch o'er all we say or do,
Hold us back from guilt and wrong.

Oh! how happy thus to spend
Work and playtime in His sight,
Till the Rest which shall not end,
Till the Day which knows no night.

Francis Turner Palgrave, of whom I have spoken in a previous chapter, has written some of the best hymns for children in the language, among which may be named

"Thou that once on mother's knee," and the following Morning Hymn, which should be better known than it is:

O God, who, when the night was deep,
Hast kept me safe, and lent me sleep,
Now with Thy sun Thou bid'st me rise,
And look around with older eyes.

Each blessèd morning Thou dost give,
I have one morning less to live;
O help me so this day to spend,
To make me fitter for the end.

O bid all evil wishes fly,
The fretful word, and idle eye;
Help me to think, in all I do,
"God sees me: would He have it so?"

Make my first wish and thought to be
For others sooner than for me;
And let me pardon them, as I
Hope for God's pardon when I die.

Be with me when I work and play,
Be with me now and every day,
Be near me, when I pray Thee hear;
And when I pray not, Lord, be near.

His Evening Hymn, beginning "O Lord, who, when Thy cross was nigh," is not quite equal to that for Morning.

Among hymns by anonymous writers, mention should be made of the following:—"Little children, wake and listen," "The fields are all white," and "O, what can little hands do?"

Perhaps the only hymn (if that word be used in its proper sense) for children by one of the great English poets, is the following, by Samuel Taylor Coleridge, which is very simple and beautiful:—

Ere on my bed my limbs I lay,
God grant me grace my prayers to say;
O God, preserve my mother dear
In strength and health for many a year.

And O preserve my father too,
And may I pay him reverence due;
And may I my best thoughts employ
To be my parents' hope and joy.

And now, O Lord, to me impart
An innocent and grateful heart,
That after my last sleep I may
Awake to Thy eternal day.

It is to be regretted that the greater poets did not consecrate their powers to such a work. What noble verses we might have had, if a man like Charles Kingsley had written verses for children, suffused with the spirit of his lovely poem addressed to a child, which I cannot forbear quoting:—

My fairest child, I have no song to give you:
No lark could pipe to skies so dull and gray;
Yet, ere we part, one lesson I can leave you
For every day.

Be good, sweet maid, and let who will be clever:
Do noble things, not dream them all day long;
And so make life, death, and that vast forever
One grand, sweet song.

The only hymnal of any merit for children of the Roman Catholic Church, is that issued by the Rev. Henry Formby, under the title of "School Songs." Concerning the authorship of the hymns included in this book, the Editor gives no hint; some are probably from his own pen. This is one of the best:—

When Jesus halted on his way,
And many throng'd to see,
Though some forbade, yet would He say,
"Come, little ones, to me."

O, happy then that infant band
That gathered round His knee,
And happy they who kiss'd the hand
That bled to set them free.

Had I been near Him on that day,
His gracious smile to see;
Had I been near to hear Him say,
"Come, little ones, to me"—

O, what were then a throne above,
Or seraph's seat on high,
Compared with one sweet glance of love
From that all-pitying eye!

Yet hast Thou not, my Lord and God,
Though on Thy throne above,
Still here on earth Thy own abode,
The altar of Thy love.

O, thither, then, let me repair,
Thy gracious smile to see,
And hear Thee say, in stillness there,
"Come, little one, to Me."

Though no hymnal for children of any great value has been issued by the Roman Catholic Church, yet many in that communion have written good hymns for children; among whom may be named Father Stansfeld, and the Sister Mary Clare of Kenmare, who has, however, since left the Roman for a Protestant Church, whose Easter Hymn I append:—

Hark, the angels bright are singing
In the glorious Easter sky:
Jesus from the grave has risen,
Jesus now no more may die.
Alleluia. alleluia, this is what the angels say,
Alleluia, alleluia, we will sing with them to-day.

Pilate's soldiers tried to keep
Jesus fast within the grave;
And they put a seal and stone
Upon the entrance to the cave.
Alleluia, alleluia, &c.

But when three days passed away,
At the awful midnight hour,
Jesus rose all gloriously
By His own almighty power.
Alleluia, alleluia, &c.

We must die as Jesus died,
But we, too, from death shall rise,
Then with Him, if we are good,
We shall reign beyond the skies.
Alleluia, alleluia, &c.

No greater success has been reached in hymn writing for children than by Matilda Barbara Betham-Edwards (born 1836)—widely known by her works of fiction—especially in the following verses:—

God make my life a little light
 Within the world to glow;
A little flame that burneth bright,
 Wherever I may go.

God make my life a little flower,
 That giveth joy to all,
Content to bloom in native bower,
 Although the place be small.

God make my life a little song
 That comforteth the sad;
That helpeth others to be strong,
 And makes the singer glad.

God make my life a little staff,
 Whereon the weak may rest,
That so what health and strength I have
 May serve my neighbours best.

God make my life a little hymn
 Of tenderness and praise;
Of faith—that never waxeth dim,
 In all His wondrous ways.

Less known, but equally beautiful, is this Evening Hymn from her pen :—

The little birds now seek their nest;
The baby sleeps on mother's breast;
Thou givest all Thy children rest,
 God of the weary.

The sailor prayeth on the sea;
The little ones at mother's knee:
Now comes the penitent to Thee,
 God of the weary.

The orphan puts away his fears;
The troubled hopes for happier years;
Thou driest all the mourner's tears,
 God of the weary.

Thou sendest rest to tirèd feet,
To little toilers slumber sweet,
To aching hearts repose complete,
 God of the weary.

In grief, perplexity, or pain,
None ever come to Thee in vain,
Thou makest life a joy again,
 God of the weary.

We sleep that we may wake renewed,
To serve Thee as Thy children should,
With love, and zeal, and gratitude,
 God of the weary.

Even the Jews have, of late, felt the need of hymns for the use of the children in their schools. A few years ago, a selection from "The Book of Praise for Children," edited by myself, was prepared and published by a Jewish lady, and, strange to say, its origin frankly acknowledged on the title page, and the name of the Editor of the original book given. Not a single hymn by any Jewish writer was added, probably because they have never entered on this field.

It is pleasant to note that the sickly sentimentalism which once prevailed in not a few children's hymns, in which they were made to express disgust at earth, and longing for heaven, such as in "Here we suffer grief and pain," and "I want to be an angel," is, save in quarters least spiritually enlightened, dying out, and before long will probably be regarded as a folly of the past. To help on such a result, I edited and published, many years ago, "The Book of Praise for Children," which, I have been glad to know, was the beginning of a more healthy style of children's hymnal; but, in spite of all that has since been done, and all the improvement that has been made, the ideal children's hymnal is yet a thing of the future. The existing materials are now ample, and all that is wanted is an Editor with sufficient critical discrimination to discern the really good, and sufficient courage rigorously to exclude the unworthy.

CHAPTER XXII.

MISSION HYMNS.

In most great revivals of religion, alike in ancient and modern times, song has played a very important part. This was the case in early times both in the Eastern and Western Churches, and later—in the days of the Reformation—both in Germany and England. But in such times there does not seem to have sprung up, as in later ones, a distinct type of hymns, but the ordinary ones of the Church were deemed suitable. The great Methodist revival of the last century would seem to have been the first which gave birth to a class of hymns specially written for revival services. That movement, however, was fortunate in having for one of its leaders a really great hymnist, perhaps the greatest the Church has yet produced. The hymns of Charles Wesley, however, though suffused with religious feeling, full of emotional expression, and cast in forms eminently adapted to fit them for popular use, were nevertheless so touched with the essentially poetic nature of their author that they were adopted not only in the gatherings of the rude and unlettered, but also in the ordinary worship of the Churches. Doubtless hundreds, if not thousands, of his hymns were used during the first Methodist revival which have since been neglected, and are now only to be found in the collected edition of his works, now used merely as a work of reference.

More recent revivals of religion have not been so fortunate as to possess hymnists with the exceptional ability of Charles Wesley. Dr. Bonar is probably the only example of a really great hymnist in modern times who has consecrated his gifts to the production of verses specially adapted for times of religious revival. The leaders, therefore, of such movements have been compelled to fall back on hymns which had established themselves already in the favour of the Church, and for the novelties which they deemed essential to their collections they have been driven to writers of a very inferior type. And we find, as a consequence, singularly few hymns of permanent value have been produced. Here and there we meet with a hymn of merit, such as "Hark! 'tis the watchman's cry," by an anonymous writer (which though published in "The Revival," has not been included in the well-known Mission Hymnals), and "There were ninety-and-nine which safely lay," by Elizabeth C. Clephane; but modern revival movements have been strikingly deficient in the production of hymns of any great value. A large number of hymns have indeed been *written* for mission services, but they are either so devoid of poetic inspiration or literary merit, or are so marred by objectionable elements or crude theology, that they have not passed into the general worship of the Church. To many of them the remark of Lord Lindsay applies: "The metaphors, it should be observed, derived from love and marriage, as typical of union with God, have given sanction to very reprehensible language and imagery, not only among the Mystic poets of the East, but among the hymn-writers of Christendom."* Such popularity as they have attained is to be ascribed to the lively tunes to which they have been wedded, and the catching, easy choruses by which they are accompanied. The great success of "Sacred Songs and Solos," by Ira D. Sankey, has chiefly arisen from these causes, for most of the new hymns included are exceedingly dull and altogether lacking in the elements which would catch the popular ear, but the bright melodious music, and the chorus in which the common people can readily join, is an excuse for all shortcomings. Indeed, in many cases the words seem to have been written for the music, and are destitute of all that goes to make up a worthy hymn. Illustrations of this will occur to all thoughtful readers of "Songs and Solos." It is a great misfortune that a collection which has attained such a phenomenal popularity was not compiled with greater care and taste, since its music might have given currency to hymns of a far higher and more helpful type. Mr. Sankey himself seems to have felt this, for he once said, "I find it much more difficult to get good words than good music. Our best words come from England; the music which best suits our purpose comes from America."† The common people would sing the nobler hymns of the Church just as readily were they set to easy and melodious tunes if suitable choruses were added. This remark applies in a still stronger degree to many of the hymns used by the Salvation Army. "Songs and Solos" are classic compared with "The Salvation Soldier's Song Book," in which such verses as the following occur.

* "Lectures on Christian Art," page 77.

† "Studies in Worship Music," vol. ii, p. 39.

The Devil and me, we can't agree,
I hate him, and he hates me;
He had me once, but he let me go,
He wants me again, but I will not go.

The publicans are crying out,
Because the Army is going about;
But still about we mean to go,
And rout the Devil and every foe.

We'll sing and pray, and we'll believe,
And sinners shall the truth receive;
We'll preach the truth in every town,
And pull the Devil's kingdom down.

My old companions, fare you well,
I will not go with you to hell;
My happy comrades are so kind,
I've left the world and the Devil behind.

This is not to be wondered at when the method of their production is remembered. It is said that "there are four men at headquarters whose business it is to keep a look-out for new tunes, write 'Army' words to them, arrange them for brass bands, and see them through the press."*

It will of course be said that by means of such movements hymns have been made popular, and are sung on week-days as well as Sundays, in the shop as well as in the Church, in the street as well as in the midst of worship. This seems a gain, and it is such, if devout feeling be in the heart when they are sung. But it is quite as possible to render sacred things common as to render common things sacred. People may almost as well sing the Devil's songs as sing the Lord's songs in an utterly careless spirit. There is a good deal of truth in the following words of Montaigne :—"It is not without very good reason, in my opinion, that the Church interdicts the promiscuous, rash, and indiscreet use of the sacred and divine songs with which the Holy Ghost inspired King David. We ought not to mix God in our actions

* "Studies in Worship Music," vol. ii, pp. 24-25.

but with the highest reverence and honour. That poesy is too divine to be employed only to exercise the lungs and to delight our ears. It ought to come from the soul and not from the tongue. It is not fit that a boy in a shop, amongst his vain and frivolous thoughts should be permitted to entertain and divert himself with psalmody."

Indeed, even Marot's translations of the Psalms, whose superior quality and sacredness should have preserved them from such a use, were sung all over France, and especially in Paris, by the courtiers and courtesans of that corrupt court and city, and for a time it was the fashion to sing them—a fashion which had little influence on the spiritual or even ethical life of the singers.

Aubrey de Vere well says:—

Ye who would build the churches of the Lord,
See that ye make the western portals low:
Let no one enter who disdains to bow.
High truths profanely gazed at, unadored,
Will be abused at first, at last abhorred.

Doggerel tends to such irreverence, whilst hymns of the nobler sort usually, though not alway, tend to uplift and solemnise the minds even of the careless.

There is another danger in relation to hymns of a revival kind. They are naturally and properly occupied with the initial stage of the Christian life—faith in our Lord Jesus Christ—but in too many cases they are retained as the permanent and only collection for worship. For this they are certainly not suited, since they leave untouched many of the great truths which should afterwards occupy the mind, whilst they are not only singularly deficient in those ethical elements by which faith should be directed into right channels, but in some cases they even cast contempt on what Christ laid so much stress—the doing of the will of God—as in the following verses, which are an exaggerated and one-sided delineation of faith :—

> Nothing either great or small—nothing, sinner, no;
> Jesus did it, did it all, long, long ago.
>
> "It is finish'd!" Yes, indeed, finish'd every jot,
> Sinner, this is all you need; tell me, is it not?
>
> When He from His lofty throne stooped to do and die,
> Everything was fully done. Hearken to His cry—
>
> "Weary, working, burden'd one, wherefore toil you so?"
> Cease your doing: all was done long, long ago.
>
> Till to Jesus' work you cling by a simple faith,
> "Doing" is a deadly thing—"doing" ends in death.
>
> Cast your deadly "doing" down—down at Jesus' feet;
> Stand "in Him," in Him alone, gloriously "complete."

And the result is often seen in a religion more erotic than spiritual; more sentimental than practical. Their theology, indeed, is sadly one-sided, and wanting in some of the elements most conspicuous in the teaching of our Lord and His Apostles. It is a great misfortune for any Christian community to be restricted to hymns suitable enough for the *origination* of the Christian life, but not full or varied enough for its after culture. This is like making the lesson books of the Infant class suffice for the whole course of education. The piety of the Church is thus emasculated, and fails in that robustness which should be one of its chief characteristics. And men and women love rather to sing about religion than to practise it—they easily acquire a habit of singing words to sweet music with but very little regard to the meaning of the words themselves. The precept addressed in the ancient Church to the Choregus needs to be borne in mind by all who sing holy songs :—"See that what thou singest with thy lip, thou believest also in thine heart, and what thou believest in thine heart, thou practisest also in thy life."

CHAPTER XXIII.

OF ALTERATIONS IN HYMNS.

The special cross most hymn-writers have had to complain of, and yet to bear, is the alteration of their verses by Editors of Hymnals. In many cases, however, these very writers have themselves done a considerable amount of alteration to hymns by other authors. John Wesley, in the preface to his hymn-book, complains bitterly of the way in which his brother Charles's hymns had been altered. James Montgomery, in the preface to the collected edition of his hymns, makes a similar complaint. But with a strange inconsistency, both of them had been guilty of the very thing they blame in others. John Wesley, in his "Hymn Book for Methodists," altered the hymns of Herbert, Sandys, Austin, and Watts; and in his "Christian Psalmist," James Montgomery did the same in the case of other writers. It would be difficult, indeed, to find a *hymn-book for actual use in public worship* in which a like course has not been adopted. Collections of hymns could be named in which the original texts of hymns, as written by their authors, have been duly preserved; but these were edited on purely *literary principles*, and without any view to being used by worshippers. Adaptation to worship makes a vast difference, and renders necessary a totally distinct method on the part of the compiler, who is compelled to consider the needs, not of a literary class only, but of many classes, to make sure that the verses are *metrically* correct, and so capable of being wedded to music; and that the terms used should be in good taste. He must, moreover, see to it that the verses are in general agreement with the religious views of the congregations for whose use his hymnal is intended. Such considerations render alterations in the case of *certain* hymns, if they are to be included, imperatively necessary. Moreover, some hymns are the result of gradual growth, and represent the work, not only of the original author, but of succeeding hymnists. Examples of this are to be found in such hymns as "O God of Bethel, by whose hand," and "Lo, He comes, with clouds descending." To present these in their original forms would be well in a Thesaurus of Hymns, for purposes of reference or private reading, but would render them distasteful to the great bulk of worshippers. Moreover, some alterations have so established themselves in public favour, that they are accepted as the acknowledged forms in which the hymns should appear. It would show pedantry, and not skilful editing, to give Charles Wesley's hymn, "Hark! how all the welkin rings," in its original form, and not in that in which it is known all over the world, as "Hark! the herald angels sing." In some cases hymn-writers have welcomed certain alterations as being improvements, and afterwards published them in their acknowledged texts. If my readers will pardon the personal reference—I once said of a certain hymn by a living writer, "That is a fine hymn," to which he at once replied, "It owes much to your revision." In the case of hymns by writers still amongst us, permission should undoubtedly be sought and obtained for any desired alteration, and without such permission they should not be adopted. In most cases, where the alterations are based on intelligent criticism, and render the hymn more perfect, they are gladly welcomed. Every one who has set his hand to the task of editing a hymnal knows full well that it is impossible to adhere in every case to the form in which hymns first appeared, or even where altered by their authors, to the text finally adopted by them.

But when all this has been said, it must be acknowledged that, beyond every other form of composition, hymns have suffered at the hands of incompetent or bungling editors, whose alterations, in the vast majority of cases, have been unmistakably for the worse, and very rarely for the better. In many cases, the men who have undertaken the task of editing hymnals have not had a spark of poetic insight or literary ability. The canon that should guide an editor in the matter of alteration is, that he should first of all *know* the original form in which the hymns appeared (which, unhappily, many do not), and that he should not make the slightest alteration without a distinct and intelligible reason—a reason which should commend itself to any critic of taste and judgment. This would preserve our hymnals from the senseless and silly mutilations for which so many of them are at present conspicuous. I will give a few examples of this from a book which offends more frequently and flagrantly against this canon than any with which I am acquainted. Here are a few instances:—John Morrison wrote "Long hath the night of sorrow reigned," his mind full of the *length* of the night of which he was thinking; the whole force of which was taken out by the compilers rendering it "The night of sorrow long hath reigned." The keynote of J. D. Burns' lovely hymn is struck in the first line, "Still with Thee, O my God," which is developed in the after verses of the hymn, where the different portions of the life are enumerated. The compilers struck out the key word *still*, and gave us this feeble line, with its senseless reduplication of the name of God, "With Thee, my Lord, my God." Dr. Faber's grand hymn, "I worship Thee, sweet will of God," is so mangled as to be unrecognisable, and in most of the verses the theme—the will of God—is conspicuous by its absence. Charles Wesley's lovely lyric on "Wrestling Jacob," the loveliest he ever wrote, too perfect to be touched even by the greatest hand, is reduced to the veriest commonplace in many of its parts. One verse of Kelly's fine hymn on "The Cross" is rendered absolute nonsense. Dr. Bonar's fine litany, "*When* the weary, seeking rest," is arranged so that the refrain of each verse answers to the lines which go before—

Hear *then*, in love, O Lord. the cry,
In heaven, Thy dwelling-place on high.

By the substitution of *Thou* for *then*, the whole symmetry of the hymn is destroyed. Such treatment of hymns, unjustified either by theological or literary considerations, deserves to be pilloried, so as to serve as a warning to future compilers. It is an offence not only against the writers whose hymns have been thus mangled, but against the religious body for whose use it was compiled.

When alterations are made for *theological* reasons they should be based on sound principles, and not made to pander to some silly popular prejudice, as in the case of Dean Milman's hymn "When our heads are bowed with woe," which is clearly an appeal to the Christ on His human side, and therefore addresses Him as "Gracious Son of Mary, hear." To alter this line to "Jesu, Son of David, hear," is not only to miss the point of the whole hymn, but to yield to a silly and ultra-Protestant prejudice. When an objection was raised to the original line by a member of the Committee for preparing "The Scottish Hymnal," that it would tend to Mariolatry, Dr. Robertson, of the Greyfriars Church, rose with flushed face and cried aloud, "That line can only lead to Mariolatry if our congregations consist exclusively of born idiots," which happily ended the debate. Many a theological alteration in hymns has had no better justification.

When alterations are made on *literary* grounds it should be quite clear that the change is in that sense an improvement. It *is* such when words which once had a particular meaning, which has since become obsolete, are altered for their present equivalents, or when words permitted by the less fastidious taste of an earlier time are made to give way to those more in harmony with present ideas. Thus an editor is justified in substituting for the word frequently used by the older hymnists, "bowels," the more acceptable word "heart."

Alterations are justifiable when verses not originally written with a view to being sung, and not *metrically* accurate, are rendered so by revision, as in the case of Sir Thomas Browne's grand hymn, "The night is come, like to the day,"* or Bishop Jeremy Taylor's on Christ entering into Jerusalem, or some of Miss Waring's delightful compositions. If hymns like these are to be used in public

* I append an admirable rendering of this hymn for use in worship, kindly prepared for me by Dr. George MacDonald, which shows how exceedingly slight are the alterations which often need to be made. I regret that this version did not come into my hands before the publication of my "Congregational Hymns." If it had, I should certainly have inserted it instead of the version there adopted. My readers should compare this rendering with the original as printed on p. 77.

The night is come: like to the day
Depart not Thou, great God, away.
Let not my sins, black as the night,
Eclipse the lustre of Thy light.
*Keep my horizon, for to me,
The sun makes not the day, but Thee

O Thou, whose nature cannot sleep,
*Up*on my temples sentry keep;
Guard me *a*gainst those watchful foes
Whose eyes are open while mine close;
And let no dreams my head infest
But such as Jacob's temples blest.

While I do rest, my soul advance,
And make my sleep a holy trance,
†That I may, when my rest is wrought,
Awake into some holy thought;
And with as active vigour run
My course as doth the nimble sun.

Sleep is a death, Oh make me try
By sleeping what it is to die;
And down as gently lay my head
*Up*on my grave as now my bed.
Howe'er I rest, great God, let me
Awake again at least with Thee.

And thus assured, behold I lie
Securely, or to wake or die.
These are my drowsy days—in vain
I do now wake to sleep again.
‡O come that hour when *sleep is o'er,*
And I shall wake for ever*more.*

* Keep still in my horizon, for to me
The sun makes not the day, but Thee.
But is a preposition for *without.*

† Changed for the accent.

‡ O come that hour when I shall never
Sleep again, but wake for ever.
The rhyme, being a feminine one, is awkward for singers.

worship such revision must be undertaken. Even then, however, the alterations should be the least that are necessary.

Beyond these, however, there are verses where the *thoughts* are beautiful, and eminently adapted to quicken devotional feeling, but cast in a form unsuited for use in worship. It is a perfectly justifiable thing to recast such, and if it be done skilfully, as in the case of Francis Quarles's hymn, by that eminent hymnist, Henry Francis Lyte, "Long did I toil, and knew no earthly rest," the result may be gratefully accepted. Such a work, however, needs both poetic feeling and skilful manipulation.

Akin to the question of alteration is the justifiableness of the omission of verses. This must be conceded on three grounds: first, that many hymns are far too long for use in public worship; second, that in most long hymns there are inferior verses, which mar rather than improve their effect; third, that some of the finest hymns in the language, such as Father Faber's, contain verses whose sentiment would exclude them from all Protestant worship. But whilst this exclusion be allowed, care must be taken (which, alas! has often been wanting), to preserve the symmetry and course of thought of the hymn. Too many editors have only cared to reduce hymns to the required length, careless altogether whether they preserved their structural unity or not. In many a case, the very verse on which the whole meaning of the hymn turned has been carelessly omitted, as in Montgomery's fine hymn, "Songs of praise the angels sang," the two parts of which are brought into unity by the verse which asks:—

And shall man alone be dumb
Till that glorious kingdom come?

And then answers:—

No! the Church delights to raise
Psalms and hymns and songs of praise.

or in Keble's "There is a book who runs may read," where the visible Book of Nature is made to suggest the invisible one of Grace, and the reason why the soul does not at once pass from the one to the other is indicated in the following verse, too often omitted by editors:—

Two worlds are ours: 'tis only sin
Forbids us to descry
The mystic heaven and earth within,
Plain as the sea and sky.

To omit such verses is like building a house and leaving out the passage which connects the various rooms.

As to the question whether additions to already existing hymns are justifiable, I will not pronounce a definite opinion. I will only say this, that if a hymn be worth retaining, it is very improbable that the writer can be found who will add to it without something like a patch-work effect. In the case of hymns by writers of an earlier time, it is almost impossible to avoid this, since every age has its own undefinable manner, which can scarcely be caught by writers of a later day. "Hymns Ancient and Modern" furnish many illustrations of the futility of such attempts. The critical ear is offended by passing from verses by Dr. Watts to additions in the same metre, but in a more modern style, from the pen of the compilers of that popular work; whilst Bishop Bickersteth, in attempting to add to Cardinal Newman's incomparable hymn, "Lead, kindly light," and perhaps render it a little more *definitely* orthodox, has, by the comparison of styles, only revealed more fully the glory of the original verses and the poverty of the added one. An editor might as well attempt to add a book to the "Iliad," or a scene to "Hamlet!"

A man should not enter on the work of editing a Hymnal unless he is prepared to touch with reverent hand the treasures of thought and feeling with which he has to deal; only absolute necessity should lead him to alter, omit from, or add to hymns—in many cases, the offspring of the holiest moments of saintly lives.

CHAPTER XXIV.

THE NEW ERA IN HYMNODY.

The late Dean Stanley, in a brief estimate of the poetry of John and Charles Wesley, relates the following significant incident: "A distinguished critic of our times, in his professorial chair at Oxford, is reported to have held out in one hand 'The Golden Treasury of English Lyrics,' collected by Francis Turner Palgrave, and in the other 'The Book of Praise,' collected from all English hymnody by Lord Selborne, and to have asked 'Why is it that "The Golden Treasury" contains almost nothing that is bad, and why is it that the "Book of Praise" contains almost nothing that is good?'" And the Dean then proceeded to give this three-fold answer to the question:—(1) that the moment poetry is made a vehicle of theological argument it becomes essentially prosaic, as much or almost as much as if it were employed for arguments on political or philosophical problems; (2) that the very greatness of the words which, either from Biblical or ecclesiastical usage, have been consecrated to the sublime thoughts of religion, misleads the writer into the belief that they are of themselves sufficient to carry on the poetical afflatus; and (3) the temptation which Biblical metaphors have afforded of pursuing into detail, and especially into anatomical detail, expressions derived from the physical structure of the human frame.

A careful examination of the books of Mr. Palgrave and Lord Selborne, however, brings to light other reasons for the vast superiority of the lyrical over the hymnal collection, amongst which these may be mentioned. (1) Both by nature and training Mr. Palgrave was fitted for the work of editing a collection of lyrics, but as much cannot be said of Lord Selborne, whilst it may even be affirmed that his legal training rather unfitted him for editing such a work as "The Book of Praise." And so it has come to pass that whilst Mr. Palgrave recognised the real lyric note wherever he heard it, Lord Selborne, hearing did not hear, so that some of the finest sacred lyrics of earlier days are sought for in vain in his pages. The reader cannot find there such noble examples of *poetic* hymnody as Herrick's lovely litany, "In the dark and cloudy day," or John Mason's "Thou wast, O God, and Thou wast blest," Sir Thomas Browne's "The night is come, like to the day;" Madame Guion's nobly mystical hymn, known to English-speaking folk through Cowper's translation, "O Thou by long experience tried;" John Milton's version of the 84th Psalm, "How lovely are Thy dwellings, Lord," and many others belonging to earlier days, which might be named; whilst, if we come to our own time, some of the greatest names are conspicuous by their absence. It seems scarcely possible, but it is true, nevertheless, that not a single hymn by Father Faber (in some senses, the finest hymnist of the century), Adelaide Ann Procter, Thomas Hornblower Gill, George Rawson, and many others, can be found in a book which professes to represent "the best English hymn-writers." If my memory serves me aright, I have seen somewhere a remark of Lord Selborne's that Mr. Dix's hymn, "As with gladness men of old," shows that the power of hymn-writing has not departed. Departed! Who but a lawyer, held in the iron chain of precedent, would ever think of the power of hymn-writing as likely to depart? Rather has it in the present century flourished in a way to which no previous one can lay claim. Dean Stanley seems to have felt this, since, in the article from which I have already quoted, speaking of the uniform pedestrian style which is unfortunately familiar to English Churchmen in the vast mass of the verses contained in "Hymns Ancient and Modern," says: "It is the English poet of the nineteenth century, not the Latin hymnodists of the fourteenth or fifteenth that have furnished whatever there is of poetical in the collection." It is very greatly to be regretted that a recent editor should have put in a plea for the retention of such inferior hymns, supporting it, as he does, by a reference to the popularity of national ballads.* No illustration could have been more unfortunate, since the ballads that still hold their ground are full of lyric fire—a quality in which the hymns of inferior writers are singularly deficient. It is the absence of such lyric fire from a multitude of hymns still printed which prevents their being sung, and only renders them an incumbrance to the hymnals in which they are retained, hindering them from being valued as a hymnal should be. This is one of the lessons that the Church at large sorely needs to lay to heart. Up to the present time she has

* Dr. Allon in the preface to the "Congregational Psalmist Hymnal."

given, or rather hymn-book editors have forced upon her hymns of the past which once had a place because none better were obtainable, hymns which satisfied the cruder taste of those less cultured days, but which are no longer acceptable to intelligent worshippers. In the Episcopal church this remark applies to the hymns of early and mediæval times, of which but a very small number deserve, on their merits, to be retained, and in the Nonconformist churches to the great mass of the hymns by Watts and Wesley, both of whom wrote far too much for it to be possible that *all* should be of a high quality. Watts wrote between five and six hundred hymns, whilst C. Wesley wrote as many thousands. All Nonconformist hymnals with anything like official sanction have too large an infusion of hymns from these and similar sources. The "Wesleyan Methodist Hymn-Book" is chiefly from the pen of the Wesleys—the hymns of other writers are only supplemental thereto. The "Congregational Hymn Book," consisting of 1,000 hymns, contains 393 by Dr. Watts. The "Baptist Hymnal," containing 920, has 59 of Watts's; whilst the recently-issued and unofficial hymnal edited by Dr. Allon has 65, a fourteenth of the whole. The result is that the remark of the Oxford professor with regard to "The Book of Praise" applies to the great majority of hymnals. The insertion of a large number of mediocre and even inferior hymns on the ground that they were written by authors whose compositions, on account of the paucity of good hymnists, were once highly valued, gives a tone of dulness and insipidity to the collections in which they form so large a part. It renders them like a wilderness in which the oases are few and far apart. And one result is that to most persons of cultivated taste, they seldom, if ever, become, as they should, manuals of devotion for private and family use. In this respect the great majority of hymnal editors have not kept pace either with the tastes or the wishes of the people for whom they cater. This is capable of proof from the actual usage of the Church. The hymns *actually used* in the Established Church are chiefly the more poetic of the older times and those by recent or still living writers; whilst in churches of the Baptist and Independent order, hymns by Watts and those of his school are rapidly passing out of use, only the finest retaining their hold on the affections of the worshippers. It would seem, therefore, that the day of rhymed prose of which Dr. Watts's hymns, save in some twenty-five or thirty examples, consists, is over, and that the church in both its Episcopal and Nonconformist branches is longing to be free from all but the noblest hymns, whether ancient or mediæval, or those of Watts and his followers. Indeed, the reason that once existed for the former bondage no longer holds. Our forefathers in the Established Church were obliged to be content with Sternhold and Hopkins, or Tate and Brady, because no sweeter singers were available. Our forefathers in Independency were content with Watts because he held the field, with scarcely a competitor. But this is no longer the case. The hymnists whose works are now available are legion. The "Dictionary of Hymnology," published by Mr. Murray, under the editorship of the Rev John Julian, includes accounts of no less than 3,000 hymn-writers and 30,000 hymns, so that there is an almost boundless treasury on which the church may draw for her worship-song. And this will render it possible for the church to have hymnals of which it may be said that in them "there is almost nothing that is bad." There is, indeed, no reason why collections for the purpose of *worship* as good as the "Golden Treasury of Lyrics," by Mr. Palgrave, is for *reading*, should not be at the command of our churches. By means of such they might be lifted to a nobler and more spiritual worship, which would ere long produce corresponding results both in heart and life.

James Montgomery, in the preface to his "Christian Psalmist," published in 1825, says, "Hymns, looking at the multitude and mass of them, appear to have been written by all kinds of persons except poets." This remark to a certain extent still holds good, but in a less degree than when he penned it. It may still be said that in hymnody the poets *of the first order* are conspicuous by their absence; but poets, who, if they do not stand in the *first* rank, are yet *really* poets, are more and more conspicuous by their presence. Some little very real poetry may be found among the older treasures of hymnody, though such *poetic* hymns were not incorporated with the earlier hymnals. I refer to hymns by Herrick, Francis Quarles, Sir Thomas Browne, George Herbert, and others; but in recent years there may be numbered among the hymnists of our own country, such poets as William Cowper, Felicia Dorothea Hemans, Henry Francis Lyte, Frederick William Faber, John Keble, John Henry Newman, Francis Turner Palgrave, Walter Chalmers Smith, and others; whilst if we pass across the sea to our kinsmen in the New World, scarcely a poet can be named who has not produced hymns. R. W. Emerson, W. C. Bryant, J. G. Whittier, and O. W. Holmes, are all represented in hymnals. The reason for this union of the poet and hymnist in America is to be found in two facts—one being that all, or nearly all, the American poets were deeply religious men, definitely associated at some time in their history with particular churches; the other being that where, in England, a speech would be asked for some great occasion, in America it is the custom to ask for an ode to be recited, or a hymn to be sung. No one who has considered the subject can doubt that, in our age, poetry in the form of hymns is being furnished for the use of the Church in a degree unknown, or known but rarely, in earlier days. Even those hymnists who can scarcely be classed as poets, and who have not produced poems, are more filled with the poetic spirit than was the case in earlier days.

It is not too much to say, therefore, that we have of late entered on a new era in relation to hymnody, and that the hymnals of the future will be more poetic than those of the past. A hymn should be a lyric poem. Rhymed prose dealing with theological doctrine is not a hymn. There must be that indescribable element we call poetic, proceeding from "the vision and the faculty divine," to render verses, though metrically faultless, a hymn. Wanting this, they want the very life blood of a true hymn. This is the great point of difference between earlier and modern hymns taken as a whole. There are exceptions. Hymns could be mentioned belonging to every age in which the true poetic note can be heard. In Gregory the Great's "Now, when the dusky shades of night retreating." In Godescalcus's "The strain upraise of joy and praise." In Bernard of Clairvaux's "O Jesus, King most wonderful," and "Jesus, the very thought of Thee," from his "Jesu dulcis memoria." In Bernard of Clugny's "To thee, O dear, dear country," and other centos from his "Hora Novissima." In the "Dies Iræ," theologically terrible as it is. Even Dr. Watts, prosaic as most of his hymns are, now and then catches the poetic fire, as in "I'll praise my Maker with my breath," "When I survey the wondrous cross," "Hear what the voice from heaven proclaims," and others which might be named. From Charles Wesley's thousands, many grand poetic hymns may be culled, notably "Come, O thou Traveller unknown" (which Dr. Watts said was worth all the hymns he had ever written), "O Love divine, how sweet thou art," "Jesus, Lover of my soul," and others; but still, speaking broadly, it may be said that the poetic element is more conspicuous in the hymns of the later than of the earlier time. And the reasons for this are not far to seek. One may be found in the fact that, amid the paucity of hymns in earlier times, the writers too often strove to provide hymns in sufficient numbers wholly to supply the needs of the churches to which they belonged. This was probably the case with Ambrose, at Milan; it certainly was so with Dr. Watts, who in his own person provided for the worship-song of the Independents: for a century, at least, no other hymns than his were commonly sung in their assemblies; and with Charles Wesley, who, with his brother John, may be said to have met all the needs of the great Methodist body for a like period.

But now no man feels charged with the duty of providing the entire hymnody of his particular church. Thomas Kelly was probably the last hymnist who attempted to rival Watts in the *number* of the hymns he wrote; in fact, he excelled him, since he wrote 700, where Watts only wrote about 500. No church now draws its hymnody from a single author. Even the Methodists have added hymns by other writers to those by the founders of their great Church. No man, therefore, attempts to produce hymns by the hundred. Quality rather than quantity is the end now sought. Where formerly, hymnals were the product of one or two writers, they are now composed of the writings of hundreds. My own hymnal represents the work of nearly 450 writers and translators. The *all* of one writer has given way to the *best* of many. Thus quality and variety are increasingly the characteristics of our modern hymnals. Every collection at all worthy of use is compiled on an eclectic principle, and draws its materials from all the Christian ages, lands, and churches.

Another reason may be found in the fact that in earlier times the educated who could appreciate that which is poetic were few compared with those too illiterate for such appreciation. The spread of culture has changed, or is rapidly changing all this. The scheme of national education now at work includes the teaching of English literature, so that the scholars grow familiar with some of its noblest works both in prose and verse. This renders the mind capable of appreciating what in former times would have been quite beyond such appreciation. Literature, once the possession of the few, is fast becoming the privilege of the many. It will not be long before it will be impossible to present a hymnal too poetic for common use.

Closely connected with this is the freer theological spirit of our day. In earlier times a Churchman would have looked askance at hymns by a Nonconformist, a

Trinitarian at hymns by a Unitarian; but this is no longer the case. The Presbyterian Bonar, the Independent Watts, the Roman Catholic Newman, are all represented in "Hymns Ancient and Modern," whilst Churchmen of every shade of opinion, Quakers, and even Unitarians, are represented in recent hymnals of the Free Churches. This shows how, in spite of all our ecclesiastical and theological strife, there is growing up a real *religious* unity. Hymns are regarded less and less as the media for the expression of *theological* opinion, and more and more as the expression of *religious* feelings—feelings common to believers in every church. The noblest hymns of our day may be sung by men of widely differing views. They move more in the realm of poetry, which deals with the essentials rather than the accidents of the faith. Their writers dwell in a more distinctively *religious* atmosphere—a larger realm in which their feelings and thoughts can move more freely. Dogmatic theology strikes at the very life of poetry. Even the dogmatist ceases to be a dogmatist when he becomes a poet. And so the decay of dogmatism is synchronous with the growth of poetry in hymns. Even Father Faber sinks from poetry into prose when he makes his hymns the vehicle for Roman teaching. Dr. Newman ceases to be the theological disputant whilst dealing with the essentials of Christianity in his verses. There is scarcely a trace of Calvinism in the hymns of Dr. Bonar. No one would know that Sir John Bowring was a Unitarian from his hymns, certainly not from his best-known one, "In the cross of Christ I glory." As some one has said: "there is little heresy in hymns," for poetry, dealing as it does with the essentials of things, leaves behind points of difference, which, after all, are not of the essence of the matter. Whilst it may still further be noted that the poetic spirit so characteristic of our age has not only prepared men to *appreciate* poetry in hymns, but has also quickened a larger number to attempt their production. In earlier days the Nonconformists were the chief contributors to hymnody; but in recent days Churchmen have more than rivalled them in this respect. This has brought a new element into our hymnody. Culture is more evident in recent than in early hymns. In this the Universities have exercised a deep and widespread influence. Our modern hymnody owes not a little to the classical training, especially the verse-making of Cambridge and Oxford, particularly the latter. The versifying in the classical languages—much-ridiculed, and often justly so—has had much to do with the change. In this respect, if in no other, it has had its uses. University culture is a very marked feature in the hymn-writing, not only of Dean Milman, John Keble, J. H. Newman, F. T. Palgrave, John Ellerton, Bishop How, Dean Plumptre, and others who might be named belonging to the English Church, but also in that of the finest American hymnists. Their hymns often combine the fervour of less cultured hymnists with greater purity of taste. The poetic feeling is both quickened and refined by the atmosphere and pursuits of the places in which the formative years of their life were passed. It is only bare justice to acknowledge how valuable are the contributions which many of the cultured sons of the Established Church have made to the hymnals of our age. The hymns most frequently sung, even in our Nonconformist churches, have been drawn from this source, in many cases almost displacing hymns on the same subjects by earlier writers. Dr. Newman's hymn, written whilst he was in the English Church, "Lead, kindly light," has almost taken the place of the Welsh hymn, "Guide me, O Thou great Jehovah," a fine hymn, but disfigured by the unpoetic line, "Death of death, and hell's destruction," whilst Bishop Ken's great hymn, "All praise to Thee, my God, this night," is not sung half so frequently at evening services as Lyte's "Abide with me, fast falls the eventide," or Keble's "Sun of my soul, thou Saviour dear," or Ellerton's "Saviour, again to Thy dear name we raise." This is to be accounted for by the greater tenderness of these more recent hymnists. Hymns of what may be called a harder type are fast being displaced by those in which the pathetic note is more clearly heard—

Such songs have power to quiet
The restless pulse of care.
And come, like the benediction
Which follows after prayer.

The hymns of earlier days were chiefly written by men whose religious ideas were so saturated by theology that their hymns became of necessity theology in verse—their prayers, their hopes, their joys, expressed themselves naturally in theologic language. Their starting-point was doctrinal, they were students of theology even more than of Scripture, and so the hymn-book became a modified manual of theology.

In nothing was the theological prepossession of the older hymnists more manifest than in their versions of the Psalms; here the Jewish singer becomes often a Calvinist of the purest type, all "the five points" are brought in, the struggles, needs, yearnings, fears, proper to the life of that day, and even of this are rejected, to be replaced by others of quite a different kind, proper only to men living in an atmosphere poisoned by the fume of creeds —sovereignty, satisfaction, purchase, perseverance, and perdition usurping and utterly transforming the words and thoughts of the sweet singer of Israel. (See Psalms 69, 51, and many others in Watts's version.) Of course every Psalm was not thus treated, but about as many as would allow of it were so treated. It should be noted, however, that the Scotch version does not offend in this way, but is an actual version of the Biblical Psalms.

In that age dogmatic theology was supreme, and hence it will be found that very rarely did its hymns grow out of Scripture scenes or events, save those on which theology has too often exclusively fixed its gaze, such as the Birth, the Crucifixion, the Resurrection, and Ascension of our Lord. Few, indeed, are the hymns by writers of the older time which grew out of the other scenes and works of our Lord's ministry. It seems to me that the writers of later times, and of our own age, have drawn their inspiration rather from the Gospels than book divinity, and are, therefore, less theological and more biblical. Nearly every great scene in our Lord's career has given birth to some hymn, not merely, as formerly, the opening and closing scenes of that ministry, but the visit to the Temple, the Baptism in the Jordan, the Temptation, the Miracles of healing or power, the Entry into Jerusalem. The representation of Christ is thus much fuller. It is no longer an outline sketch, but more like a finished picture. This has rendered our modern hymns more picturesque, more vivid, and so more helpful to the worshipper. One of our modern hymn-books is called "The Hymnal Companion to the Book of Common Prayer." A really good hymn-book ought to be a companion to the New Testament—a veritable "Christ in Song."

The theological standpoint of many of the earlier hymn-writers had this further effect on their hymns, that there was not sufficient thought of the needs and times of worship. How few of their hymns are suitable for the opening and close of public worship!—how few those for morning and evening! Hymns of this kind have to be drawn almost exclusively from the writers of the present century. This remark does not apply to the hymns of the Latin Breviaries, which are rich in verses for the various times of the day, but then these have only of late found their way, by means of English translations, into our hymnals. Nearly all our much-loved and often-sung evening hymns are by writers either living or recently departed. And the same remark may be made as to hymns for the various seasons of the year. To all such sublunary matters the elder writers, immersed in theological questions, were quite oblivious. So regardful were they of the future world that the present one seemed beneath their notice. The spirit of their time is well set forth in the words of Mr. Cecil—"I want to see no more sea, hills, valleys, fields, abbeys, or castles. I feel vanity pervading everything but eternity and its concerns, and perceive these things to be suited to children."

There was indeed a subtle kind of Manichæism abroad, which regarded this as the devil's world rather than God's, and interest in it, or love for its beauty, was reckoned a sign of worldliness. Men might gather for worship amid the freshness of spring, or the glory of summer, or the mellowness of autumn, or the frost of winter, but no hymns rose from their lips in harmony with the season. Praise for the visible world, for its beauty, its variety, its loveliness, was a thing almost unheard of, in the worship of former times. A new feeling has grown up in relation to the world, thanks to the influence of poets like Wordsworth, or prose-writers like Charles Kingsley, or scientists whose name is legion. It is felt that thankfulness for the present world is as much a duty as anticipation of the world to come. It is considered no mark of piety to grumble at our earth or call it a waste howling wilderness, but the sign that the piety is either absent, or of an unhealthy kind. And with the growth of this feeling, hymns of a new order—full of discernment for the beauty of the world, full of thankfulness on its account—have come into existence. Do we gather for worship on a lovely morning of spring, we can sing,

"The glory of the spring how sweet."

Amid the richer foliage and beauty of the summer we can sing,

"Summer suns are glowing."

As the leaves grow to a golden tint we can sing, with a regretful feeling for the passing of the summer,

"The year is swiftly waning."

As winter strides with iron tread over the earth, we can comfort ourselves with the touching words—

And yet God's love is not withdrawn,
  His life within the keen air breathes,
His beauty paints the crimson dawn,
  And clothes the boughs with glittering wreaths.

. . . . . .

O God! who giv'st the winter's cold
As well as summer's joyous rays,
Us warmly in Thy love enfold,
And keep us through life's wintry days.

So intent were the older writers on the *unseen* world, that scarcely a hymn is to be found in their writings expressive of harvest joys; indeed, for the most part they so intensely regarded the soul of man, that in view of it all the other parts and faculties of his nature seemed nothing worth. Without any diminution of regard for man's soul, but rather with a clearer discernment of its spiritual nature, our modern hymnists include in their thought his whole humanity as belonging to God. And so a more human feeling runs through their hymns. They express real sorrows and joys, not imaginary ones. Their hymns spring out of the human heart, and not out of theological thoughts concerning man. Many of the older hymns are far off from men, pitched in too high a key to be sung quite truthfully by ordinary men and women. They are not suited for "human nature's daily food." They delight in generalities, and so their words are vague, whether they utter the note of contrition or of praise. For the most part we discern the theologian rhyming about sin, rather than the penitent confessing his wrong-doing; theologic thought of the world, not discernment and thankfulness for its beauty; the ecclesiastic zealous for church relationships rather than one filled with the enthusiasm of humanity, and keenly alive to the brotherhood of man. The *actual* feelings and aspirations of men rarely find expression in the ordinary hymnody of the older time. Its producers turn rather to the doctrinal than the practical parts of Scripture, and embody the arguments rather than express the spirit they should waken in the hearts of men. In seeking expression for many of the feelings of the Christian life, especially such as sympathy, calmness, humility, generosity, we are obliged to turn to the works of hymnists of our own age. The Gospel heard in our pulpits has grown more sympathetic, and our song must be in harmony with our teaching. Sermon and song must keep touch with, and be supplemental of, each other. Those who come to our churches do not want to give utterance to theological platitudes, but to speak out of their hearts to their Father. Conscious of manifold failure, they long to confess the *actual* sins they have committed. Burdened with life's many trials, they would lay down their burden at their Father's feet. Often filled with sorrow as are their hearts, they would be assured of a Divine sympathy, whilst amid their seasons of prosperity they would discern the hand, and give thanks to the Giver of all good. Who are the men able to give voice to their feelings so fully as those whose lot has been cast amid like surroundings, troubled by the same doubts, harrassed by the same temptations, burdened with the same anxieties, filled with the same joys?

I will undertake to say that the hymns by far the most frequently sung in our day are those produced during the present century. The extraordinary popularity of Mr. Sankey's "Songs and Solos" is due to the hymns by recent writers, in its pages; those by earlier ones are rarely used. Of course, among the older hymns there are some so instinct with life, so really songs of the heart, that they live, and are likely to live. Only a living hymnody has much chance of surviving. "The deadest of all dead things," says a recent author, "is a dead theology," and it may be added that the deadest of all dead things is a hymn which has sprung out of a dead theology. Being dead, they will soon be buried out of the sight of all, save antiquarian hymnologists. Their removal from the pages of our hymn-books would be an unmixed blessing, and would render such books more valued, not only as helps to public worship, but as companions for a quiet hour within the home.

In his introduction to "The English Poets," edited by T. H. Ward, Mr. Matthew Arnold says: "The future of poetry is immense, because in poetry where it is worthy of its high destinies, our race, as time goes on, will find an ever surer and surer stay. There is not a creed which is not shaken, not an accredited dogma which is not shown to be questionable, not a received tradition which does not threaten to dissolve. Our religion has materialised itself in the fact, in the supposed fact, or has attached its emotion to the fact, and now the fact is failing it. But for poetry the idea is everything; the rest is a world of illusion, of divine illusion. Poetry attaches its emotion to the idea; the idea *is* the fact. The strongest part of our religion to-day is its unconscious poetry."

Now, in this, as in most of Mr. Arnold's utterances, there is much that is valuable, and much that is the reverse. I do *not* agree with him when he says that the fact is failing us. We are getting ever nearer to the fact, and relying more and more upon it. Christ, the eternal fact, is appearing ever more near and distinct to the eyes of men, and just in proportion to the degree in which many of the dogmas and creeds of the past are fading from our sight does His peerless Personality shine out the more clearly. With this proviso, I do agree with him when he speaks of poetry reaching the idea, or, as I should prefer to say, the essence of everything. Theologians and commentators, who, with a few noble exceptions, never get beneath the surface, will have to give way to the poets—the seers who really see—see into the heart of things. It is so to a large extent even now. Where commentaries used to occupy the shelves of ministers, their place is largely taken by the works of the best poets. Tennyson and Browning are exerting a deeper influence on the theological thought of the age than the professed theologians. The most revealing portions of the Old Testament scriptures have come to us through Prophet and Psalmist, who were the Hebrew analogues of the modern poet. The portions of the Old Testament, most potent in *our* religious thinking, are its poetical books, and the most inspiring preachers of Christianity in recent times have been men of poetic insight. To say nothing of men happily still spared to us, and to confine ourselves, to those known to the elders of the present generation, I may name Frederick William Robertson, of Brighton, Thomas Toke Lynch, Thomas Jones, Alexander Raleigh, James Baldwin Brown, John Ker, Horace Bushnell, and Henry Ward Beecher. The only sermons that live and are read are those with the poetic insight. In his remarkable essay on "Our Gospel a Gift to the Imagination," in the volume entitled, "The Moral Uses of Dark Things," Dr. Bushnell institutes a comparison between Turretin and Bunyan, in which the following striking passage occurs: "The venerable dogmatiser (Turretin) is already far gone by . . . but the glorious Bunyan fire still burns, because it is fire, kindles the world's imagination, more and more, and claims a right to live till the sun dies out in the sky. His Pilgrim still holds on his way, still fresh and strong as ever—nay, fresher and stronger than ever—never to be put off the road till the last traveller is conducted in." All theological books which do not possess the poetic insight soon cease to be read, and, as a theological bookseller once told me, find their way to the mill to furnish paper for the inscription of fresher thought. And the same principle holds good of hymns; only those alive with poetry, which is another way of saying, instinct with life, keep their hold over the hearts of men. But those which are thus alive, since to be so they must touch the reality of the gospel, live on amid all the changes of theological thought. The mere drapery of truth may be removed; she herself remains, and only the men who have gazed thereon and embodied their vision in their verse, keep their place in the worship of the church. Changes of theological thought do not touch such hymns because they enshrine not the vanishing, but the permanent in Christianity. Even the uncultured recognise the presence of life in a hymn; and though editors may include the dead, which ought to have been buried, in their hymnals, the people will consign them to the oblivion they deserve. As Dr. Bushnell well says—and his remarks have a close bearing on the subject before us—"This endeavour to get the truths of religion away from the imagination into propositions of the speculative understanding, makes a most dreary and sad history. . . . . They were plants alive and in flower, but now the flowers are gone, the juices are dried, and the skeleton parts packed away and classified in the dry herbarium called theology." The mass of the older hymns were written in times when "theology" was dominant, and their writers busied themselves with the herbarium rather than walked amid the living gardens of truth, and so their writings smack of the theological museum, instead of being beautiful and fragrant as freshly-plucked flowers. A writer may be found here and there who walked in the living garden, whilst some, occupied chiefly with the herbarium, strayed now and again into the garden of life. Every now and then Dr. Watts finds his way to the fresher air, and when he does, his hymns are living ones, and rightly hold their place in the Church's worship-song. Happily, the herbarium time is nearly over, and now the theologian has to give way to the poet. I once handed a copy of my own Hymnal to a distinguished Roman ecclesiastic, who has himself produced some living hymns, and as he turned its pages he exclaimed, "But this is poetry." I replied, "What right has it to be there unless it be poetry?" In so far as this living spirit pervades our song will our hymnals be in touch with the age, and if they are not, they are unsuited to it. You may as well try to clothe men of to-day with the armour of the barons, as expect them to sing hymns charged with the thoughts of an age that has departed. In so far as the poetic *afflatus* is in the older hymns, they are not for an age, but for all time; but in so far as this is wanting, their day is over. They are no more fitted for our time than the Homilies of the English Church are for the congregations which gather in that Church to-day. The sermons of Jeremy Taylor might be used with profit because they are alive, but the Homilies would empty any church! Our plea is for *living* hymns, to whatever age they may belong, or from whosoever's pen they may come. Such hymns will, for the most part, be found as really in touch with our present thought as with that of the age in which they first saw the light. We can rejoice in the "Pilgrim's Progress," though most of the sermons of that period would send us quickly to sleep. And we can sing the *Te Deum* with as much fervour as the devoted followers of Ambrose did in his church at Milan centuries ago. Dr. Neale, with a poet's instinct, drew from the storehouses of the Ancient Church some of her living hymns, and they are among the greatest favourites of this nineteenth century, whilst a mass of hymns of later times, which lack the poetic life, remain in our hymnals unsung, and even unread. We must let the dead bury their dead, for we cannot galvanise them into life, no matter how powerful be the battery we may employ. And when they are buried, our hymn-books will be among our most highly-prized treasures, and best aids to devotion. Editors and editorial committees want more courage. A very competent editor of a well-known Hymnal once told me, when I criticised his work, "My committee *would* include many hymns I wanted left out, and would not put in many I greatly desired to include." The result is that the book is not nearly so good as it would have been if the editor had been allowed to have his way. Congregations are often in advance of their leaders, and show far greater readiness to appreciate really good hymns than those leaders suppose. Worshippers are tired of the didactic hymns they are often called upon to sing, whilst many of them stand with closed lips when hymns expressive of long-since discarded conceptions of the Gospel are announced in the church. Their quickened consciences revolt against doctrines which cast a darkening shadow over the fair face of truth, and they stand with closed lips when they should be singing the praise of the Great Father. They have learnt that He is better than the best they can conceive of, and they demand hymns which will enable them, like the Psalmist of the olden time, to cry, "So will I go unto the altar of God, unto God my exceeding joy; yea, upon the harp will I praise Thee, O God, my God." And when within the pages of our hymnals none but such hymns are included, the worship of the church will, more than in the past, lead us up to "those shining table-lands to which our God is Sun and Moon."

WORKS OF REFERENCE.

ARTICLES ON HYMNS IN
Dictionary of Christian Antiquities, edited by Dr. W. Smith and Professor Cheetham.
Encyclopædia Britannica (9th edition).
Maclintock's and Strong's Cyclopædia.

DANIEL. Thesaurus Hymnologicus. 5 vols. Leipsic, 1855-6.

MONE. Hymni Latini Medii Aevi. Freiburg, 1853.

KOCH. Geschichte des Kirchenlieds und Kirchengesangs der Christlichen. 4 vols. Stuttgart, 1856.

AUGUSTI. De Hymnis Syrorum Sacris. Wratislaw, 1841.

BIRAGHI. Inni Sinceri e Carmi di Sant' Ambrogio. Milan, 1862.

EBERT. Geschichte der Christlich-Lateinischen Literatur. Leipsic, 1874.

KEHREIN, J. Lateinische Sequenges des Mittelalters. Mainz, 1873.

NEWMAN, J. H. Hymni Ecclesiæ e Breviariis Sarisburiense Romano, &c. 1838.

——— Hymni Ecclesiæ e Breviario Parisiense. 1839.

NEALE, J. M. Hymni Ecclesiæ. 1851.

——— Sequentiæ ex Missalibus. 1852.

——— Hymns of the Eastern Church. London, 1862.

——— Mediæval Hymns and Sequences (3rd edition). 1866.

MILLER, Josiah. Singers and Songs of the Church. 1869.

CHARLES, Elizabeth. The Voice of Christian Life in Song (3rd edition). 1872.

CREAMER, D. Methodist Hymnology. 1848.

PUTNAM, A. P. Singers and Songs of the Liberal Faith. Boston, 1875.

DUFFIELD, S. W. English Hymns: Their Authors and History (3rd edition). New York, 1888.

WINKWORTH, C. Christian Singers of Germany. London, 1869.

KÜBLER, Theodore. Historical Notes to the Lyra Germanica. London, 1865.

MACDONALD, George. England's Antiphon. London, N. D.

CHRISTOPHERS, S. W. Hymn-Writers and their Hymns.
——— The New Methodist Hymn-Book, and its Writers.
BIGG, L. C. English Hymnology. 1873.
PRESCOTT, J. E. Christian Hymns and Hymn-Writers. Cambridge, 1886.
KING, JAMES. Anglican Hymnology. London, 1885.
SCHAFF, PHILIP. Christ in Song. London, 1870.
ROGERS, CHARLES. Lyra Britannica (2nd edition). London, 1868.
ODENHEIMER, W. H. and BIRD, F. W. Songs of the Spirit. New York, 1874.
HOOD, E. P. Isaac Watts: His Life and Writings.
GLASS, H. A. The Story of the Psalters. London, 1888.
KER, JOHN. The Psalms in History and Biography. Edinburgh, 1886.
WRANGHAM, D. S. The Liturgical Poetry of Adam of St. Victor. London, 1881.
CURWEN, J. S. Biographical Notes to The Child's Own Hymn Book.
JULIAN, JOHN. A Dictionary of Hymnology. London, 1892.
TRENCH, R. C. Sacred Latin Poetry. London, 1864.
THE NOTES IN
The Irish Church Hymn Book.
The Book of Praise, edited by Lord Selborne (5th edition). London, 1865.
The Free Church Hymn Book. Edinburgh, 1882.
Hymns for Church and Home, edited by W. F. Stevenson.
Church Hymns, annotated by J. Ellerton.
The Presbyterian Hymnal, edited by James Thin. 1888.
Hymnale Ecclesiæ Sarisburiensis, edited by W. Stubbs, C. Marriott, and A. C. Wilson. Littlemore, 1850.
The Treasury of American Sacred Song, edited by W. Garrett Horder. London, 1896.
THE INDEX OF AUTHORS IN
W. T. Brooke's edition of Giles Fletcher's "Christ's Victory and Triumph." London. 1888.
The Church of England Hymn Book, edited by Godfrey Thring. London, 1882.
Worship-Song, edited by W. Garrett Horder. London. 1894.
Primitive Methodist Hymnal. London, 1887.
The Treasury of Sacred Song, edited by F. T. Palgrave. 1889.

INDEX OF NAMES.

INDEX OF FIRST LINES OF HYMNS.

INDEX OF TITLES OF HYMNS.

HISTORY, BIOGRAPHY, CHURCH MUSIC, &c.

Handbook of Acoustics. By T. F. HARRIS, B.Sc., F.C.S. Fifth edition. Price 3s. 6d.; postage 3d. A handbook for musical students. Contains 18 chapters profusely illustrated; with numerous questions and an Appendix of Examination Papers.

History of English Music. By HENRY DAVEY. A monumental work tracing the history and proving the advanced position, past and present, of English music. Contains many new and important facts. Price 6s.; postage 4½d.

Hymn Lover, The. By Rev. W. GARRETT HORDER. Price 5s.; postage 4d. Second and revised edition. An account of the rise and progress of Hymnody.

Memorials of John Curwen. By his Son, J. SPENCER CURWEN. Price 2s.; postage 3d.

Musical Haunts in London. By F. G. EDWARDS. Chapters on Handel, Haydn, Mendelssohn, Weber, and many other musicians, with stories and pictures of their residences in London. Price 1s.; postage 2d.

Musical Profession, The. By H. FISHER, Mus.Doc. Price 5s.; postage 4d. Contains advice for music teachers in every department of the art.

Musicians of All Times. Compiled by DAVID BAPTIE. Second and cheaper edition, 1s. 6d.; postage 2d. Concise biography of composers, teachers, artists, and all other musical workers, containing 5,000 names.

Student's Musical History. By H. DAVEY. Price 1s.; postage 1½d.; cloth, 1s. 6d.; postage 2½d. The cheapest historical handbook; comprehensive, concise, brought up to date. Third edition.

Studies in Worship Music. First Series. By J. S. CURWEN. Price 5s.; postage 4d. Contains articles and information on various matters relative to Worship Music, arranged in three divisions—Historical, Practical, Descriptive. Second edition, revised and enlarged.

Studies in Worship Music. Second Series. By J. S. CURWEN. Price 2s. 6d.; postage 2½d.; continues above work—articles on the Chapel Royal—Westminster Abbey Choir, &c.

Short Dictionary of Musical Terms, A. By ARNOLD KENNEDY, M.A. Price 1s. (postage 1d.); cloth, 1s. 6d. (postage 1½d.). About 2,700 terms. Gives the phonetic pronunciation of foreign words. German, French, and Italian terms are included.

United Praise. By F. G. EDWARDS. Price 3s. 6d.; postage 3d. Originally advertised as "Common Praise." A practical handbook of Nonconformist Church Music.

LONDON: J. CURWEN & SONS LTD., 24 BERNERS STREET, W.